Television and Radio Announcing

To my wife, Allie
and to my children
Stuart, Jr.
John Christian
Allison Elizabeth Ann

Television and Radio Announcing

Second Edition

Stuart W. Hyde

San Francisco State College

Houghton Mifflin Company · Boston

New York · Atlanta · Geneva, Illinois · Dallas · Palo Alto

Library of Congress Catalog Card Number: 71-132527

ISBN: 0-395-04666-1

Contents

The Second Edition of *Television and Radio Announcing* is a major revision. The field of broadcasting has changed so much in the last decade that a few patches here and there would not do. New data, new emphases, and new specializations had to be included. Broadcast journalism, barely mentioned in the First Edition, required in-depth treatment to match its increased importance in our society. The interview show, so popular on radio and television in recent years, demanded a more detailed discussion of interviewing techniques. And, of course, new equipment, new technical developments, and the latest FCC regulations had to be considered. All material retained from the First Edition was thoroughly reworked and updated, including the "timeless" chapters on voice and diction, the International Phonetic Alphabet, and foreign pronunciation. The result of these changes is a book which presents a realistic picture of the broadcasting industry today, describes the kinds of jobs available to announcers, and discusses the skills and personal characteristics necessary for success in the field.

There is—perhaps fortunately—no formula for automatically producing successful radio and television announcers. No amount of reading, attending lectures, or practicing will insure success. The various human qualities can be combined in limitless ways, and no one can unerringly guide another to the winning combination. Consequently, this text offers no "system" or list of "ten easy steps to becoming an announcer." Instead, it attempts to set down as much material in as many areas of announcing as possible. It offers a wealth of information, but it permits you and your instructor to choose what best suits your needs.

In general, there are two schools of thought on the subject of announcing training. One emphasizes mechanics—developing the student's voice, diction, ability to pronounce, and so on. The other largely ignores mechanics and substitutes a strong emphasis on communicating ideas regardless of skills. Since good announcers have resulted from both approaches, this book advocates neither in particular. Instead, it presents the best of both, allowing you and your instructor to interpret and select as you will.

Some of the material included in this text is extremely basic. The wide range of abilities of the users of the book and the need to forestall common announcing malpractices dictated that it not be omitted. Experience tells us that "knowing" something often differs vastly from practicing it effectively. Take communication through speech, for example. You are undoubtedly aware that announcers are employed for the sole purpose of communicating ideas to an audience. You may not realize, however, that to do this, *announcers must talk to people,* not merely read words *at* them. Hence, the rather extensive treatment of this topic in the text.

In the chapters on pronunciation, the sounds of General American speech, as well as Spanish, Italian, French, and German, have been described and illustrated as completely as possible. The inevitable gap between the spoken word and its printed form may be bridged with a long-playing record available from the publisher. The record has been carefully keyed to the text so that you can check your mastery of all the sounds and illustrative words in Chapters 3 and 5 against the voice on the record.

Part Two consists of drill material obtained from actual broadcast sources. Permission was granted to reprint this material with the understanding that it would be used for practice in the classroom; none of it should be used on a live broadcast. The news copy was chosen for its timelessness; it is impossible to muster enthusiasm for obviously outdated news.

One bit of advice to those of you using this book for a required course. Though you may not intend to become announcers, a thorough study of announcing will stand you in good stead for other reasons. *Everyone* talks, not just announcers. In fact, most of our contact with others involves speech. Consequently, the effort to improve your voice, diction, vocabulary, and ability to express your ideas will not be wasted.

For you who are interested in other phases of broadcasting, it should be noted that announcing is one of the best ways of getting into the industry. Countless directors, writers, stage managers, and executives begin their careers as announcers. Whether you ever announce professionally or not, announcing training will benefit you. As a writer, you will have a better "feel" for copy to be delivered orally; as a director, you will be aware of the problems of the announcers working with you; as an executive, you will be able to guide your announcers' work more effectively. A course in announcing therefore deserves the best efforts of every broadcasting student.

STUART W. HYDE

Acknowledgments

Hundreds of people helped with this book, and I regret that I cannot thank each by name. My students and colleagues at many institutions made numerous suggestions for changing and improving the First Edition. Dozens of individuals at stations, networks, advertising agencies, and equipment manufacturing companies cooperated in supplying photographs, commercials, technical information, and other materials. Several professional announcers gave time relating their experiences and making recommendations. To all who helped and cannot be individually identified, my sincere thanks for your contributions.

Specifically, I would like to thank Professors Paul C. Smith, Charles H. Smith, and John A. Galbraith and Chief Engineer David Wiseman of San Francisco State College for their suggestions and encouragement. Professors from other institutions who gave helpful advice include Gale R. Adkins, University of Kansas; Lawrence C. Blenheim, Temple University; Charles Buzzard, Phoenix College; W. Knox Hagood, University of Alabama; John M. Kittross, Temple University; John McMullen, University of Wyoming; Lee Morrison, New York Institute of Technology; Charles Northrip, University of Alaska; James J. Onder, Eastern Michigan University; Philip G. Prindle, College of San Mateo; B. R. Smith, Marshall University; Raymond W. Stedman, Bucks County Community College; Hollis B. Todd, Mississippi College; James Uszler, Morehead State University.

Specialized help came from Russ Hodges, sportscaster for the San Francisco Giants; Bill Hillman, staff announcer for KPIX–TV, San Francisco; Gil Haar, News Director for KNEW–AM, Oakland, California; Chet Casselman, News and Public Affairs Director, KSFO–AM, San Francisco; Ernie Kreiling, syndicated television columnist; Dr. George P. Wilson, Jr., Iowa State University; Dr. Stanley T. Donner, University of Texas; James Buckner and Joseph Myler, United Press International; Hugh Turner, KTIM–AM and FM, San Rafael, California; Merle Rossman, KSRO–AM, Santa Rosa, California;

Ted Atkins, KFRC–AM, San Francisco; Harold Niven, National Association of Broadcasters; NBC Sports.

Advertising agencies which generously provided commercial copy include Young and Rubicam, Inc.; Post-Keyes-Gardner, Inc.; Edward J. McElroy Advertising; Gross, Pera and Rockey; Kenyon and Eckhardt, Inc.; Wyman/ Anderson-McConnell; Batten, Barton, Durstine and Osborn, Inc.; Clinton E. Frank, Inc.; Campbell-Mithun, Inc.; Ralph P. Coleman and Associates; Bernard B. Schnitzer, Inc.; Falcon Associates; Recht and Company; Albert Frank-Guenther Law, Inc.; Barickman and Selders Advertising, Inc.; Quinn and Johnson, Inc.; Ken Betts Chevron; Sequoia Vacuums; General Time Corporation; John Morrell and Company; General Tire and Rubber Company; Tony Lufrano; The Hoover Company; Smith-Corona Marchant; The Advertising Council; the Office of Economic Opportunity. Walt Kraemer of Wyman/ Anderson-McConnell, Sylvia Simmons of Young and Rubicam, Celeste Meakin of The Advertising Council, James D. Deasy of Post-Keyes-Gardner, and James A. Richardson of Falcon Associates provided suggestions as well as help in obtaining copy.

The National Broadcasting Company, as represented by NBC Sports and NBC News, was most helpful, as were the American Broadcasting Company and Group W Productions. United Press International and the Associated Press extended unlimited use of news copy and news photographs.

The following equipment manufacturers supplied photographs and other materials: Radio Corporation of America; Gates Radio Company; Superscope, Inc.; Vega Electronics Corporation; Electro-Voice, Inc.; Sparta Electronic Corporation; Collins Radio Company; Shure Brothers, Inc.; QRK Electronic Products, Inc. Mr. William A. Raventos of Electro-Voice provided excellent data on microphones.

The drawings on pages 1 and 244 are from *Diary Notebook,* CBS Television Network, William Golden, Designer and Art Director, Feliks Topolski, Artist.

I would also like to thank the College of Marin and its helpful librarians for giving me office space and assistance in developing the bibliographies which appear in the text.

Several contributions to the First Edition reappear in the Second, and their donors should be thanked again: Professors Frederick B. Agard, Cornell University; William G. Moulton, Princeton University; Howard Rhines, KFAC–AM, Los Angeles; the late Stuart Cleveland, Houghton Mifflin Company, whose meticulous attention to the First Edition considerably enhanced its effectiveness and made its revision easier.

Finally, I would like to thank John Poindexter and Penelope Hull of Houghton Mifflin Company for their patient help in editing the Second Edition. Both made excellent suggestions, and if the book does not sound "textbookish," it is largely because they insisted that many of my sentences could be cut 50 per cent without significant loss of meaning.

Part One **Announcing**

Frank McGee reporting from the floor of the 1968 Republican National Convention at Miami Beach. (Courtesy NBC)

One The Role of the Announcer

The radio or television announcer is a unique creation of our times. Though he resembles the town crier, the wandering troubadour, and the newspaper journalist of earlier days, he is essentially a product of the electronic age. Circuses, vaudeville shows, and public ceremonies long used speakers to provide information and maintain continuity, but they were basically unessential: since the audience was gathered in one place and could see and hear the proceedings, voiced introductions were more for building enthusiasm than providing information. But radio, the "blind" medium, was faced with the problem of reaching a scattered audience whose members could not see the event being broadcast. It could not function without direct spoken communication. To cope with this problem a new kind of communicator was invented, called an "announcer," a term that was carried over to television.

The radio or television announcer is, in a sense, a throwback to the preliterate storyteller: he speaks directly to his audience, and this makes his voice and his vocal personality important aspects of his performance. He also resembles the news reporter, for he describes events not personally experienced by the audience. But radio and television possess a power denied to most earlier communication devices: instantaneousness. Radio made it possible for the first time in history to describe directly to millions of people scattered over thousands of miles events happening at that very moment. Television made it possible for them to see the events. And whether the man doing the describing is reporting election returns, introducing musical selections, or conducting a talk show, he is still the "announcer."

We use a variety of terms to describe announcers today, among them "personalities," "jocks," "narrators," "commentators," "analysts," and "reporters." Perhaps the trend away from calling an announcer an announcer is the same one that has seen janitors become "custodians" and garbage men become "sanitary engineers." Or, just as likely, perhaps increased specialization in the field of broadcasting has encouraged more precise nomenclature. Whatever the reason, the term "announcer" will be used throughout this book for the sake of economy whenever the profession is being discussed in general terms. It would be tedious and unnecessary to qualify each statement made about the "announcer" with a catalog of the various specializations included within this generic term. In this book, an announcer is anyone who speaks to his audience through a medium using one of these electronic devices: radio or television transmission over the public airwaves; closed-circuit audio or video distribution; electronic amplification, as in an auditorium or a movie theatre.

Approximately 13,000 Americans are regularly employed as announcers in broadcasting, and an additional 10,000 to 15,000 are free-lance announcers. Since many free-lance announcers work only sporadically, we can assume that not more than 20,000 people earn their full incomes as broadcast announcers. By contrast, more than 115,000 people are employed as radio and television service technicians. The relatively small number of announcing jobs means two things: the field is highly competitive, and the announcer who can offer a station more than announcing abilities has a better chance for initial employment and career advancement. It should also be observed that approximately 85 per cent of all announcers are working for radio stations, and most television announcers begin in radio. Your chances for success will therefore be enhanced if you prepare chiefly for radio announcing, and this means learning time selling, copywriting, running an audio console, weather reporting, news writing, and even station management, as well as announcing.

Only a baker's dozen of major announcing specializations exist in American broadcasting today. They are described briefly below but are not listed in order of importance or employment opportunity. Many announcers perform in two or more of the categories.[1]

1. *Radio staff announcer.* Normally, the staff announcer is not known by name to his listeners. He reads live commercial copy, makes station breaks, introduces program segments, and generally provides an overall structure for the program material of the personalities, newscasters, feature reporters, or disc jockeys.

2. *Television booth announcer.* This announcer is much like the radio staff announcer. He is seldom seen on camera; he reads public-service and commercial announcements while slides or silent films are being screened; he makes the station breaks; he makes the appropriate announcement if the audio or video signal is lost or other technical difficulties arise; he usually makes entries in the program log.

---

[1] No special category has been listed for the announcer on educational radio or television stations. Although presentational technique may be different on educational stations, the announcer still comes under one or more of the general categories.

3. *Radio or television commercial announcer.* Some announcers specialize in delivering commercials. The institutional representative—the announcer who works for one sponsor and personifies the product or company to his audience—is one type of commercial announcer. Another is the announcer engaged "per job" to record any commercial for which he seems suited. Though some announcers enjoy steady employment without ever working for a station, most need a staff position for security and regard taped or filmed commercial assignments as windfalls.

4. *Radio or television newscaster.* News personnel are not normally considered "announcers" since their major attribute, at least theoretically, is news judgment rather than excellence in delivery. In practice, however, the news announcer who is weak in either facet of his work will find little demand for his services. Several specializations within the field of broadcast news that have developed in recent years will be explored in Chapter 9.

5. *Radio or television news analyst or commentator.* This announcer is free to express strong opinions on important topics and is not usually allowed to serve in any other announcing capacity; thus, the analyst or commentator seldom is seen delivering "hard" news or making commercial announcements. The theory behind this is that the commentator, if he is to be accepted as an authority, must be above the mundane. Although he may have arrived at his position through an apprenticeship in newscasting, he is now a specialist. There are few job opportunities for the news analyst or commentator.

6. *Radio disc jockey.* Even though, strictly speaking, any announcer who introduces musical selections can be classified a "d.j.," the term has come to mean a "personality" who sells not only hard rock, chicken rock, middle-of-the-road (MOR), country and Western, rhythm and blues, or soul, but also himself.

Figure 1. Howard K. Smith timing his television news commentary before air time. (Courtesy ABC)

Although practices vary from station to station, most expect the disc jockey to be witty, energetic, and personable in order to attract a following.

7. *Announcer for the "good music" radio station.* Not usually classified as a disc jockey, this announcer has accumulated a large amount of highly specialized training. He introduces musical works, and, since most of them are of foreign origin, he must be able to pronounce names and words in a variety of languages; essential, too, is a knowledge of music and musical terms. In some cases, this announcer is not identified for the audience; in others, like the disc jockey, he is expected to develop a personal following.

8. *Radio or television sportscaster.* A knowledge of *all* sports is requisite for success in this field. The typical sportscaster gives play-by-play descriptions of a few sports—baseball, football, golf, and basketball, let us say—but he very often presents a daily or weekly program *about* sports, as well, covering everything from yacht races to track meets. Thus the sports announcer's knowledge must extend beyond the standard sports. Most play-by-play sportscasters use two kinds of announcers: one to call the game and one to provide color. The latter frequently is a one-sport expert.

9. *Panel or quiz-show moderator.* This specialty is now chiefly confined to television. The moderator usually has earned his reputation in some field other than announcing, and he often owns part of the show. The variety of panel and quiz shows is great, and the kind of announcer appropriate for a game show may be unsuited for "Meet the Press."

10. *Documentary narrator.* Radio documentaries like "March of Time" and "You Are There" are things of the past, as television, of course, is so eminently suited to this kind of program. A television documentary is frequently filmed. After the film has been edited and a script written, the narrator makes his first contact with the project. Local station documentaries, as well as some network productions, use an on-camera narrator even though as much as 90 per cent of the program consists of filmed or videotaped inserts. The current practice is to use news personnel as narrators.

11. *Radio talk-show host.* Radio talk shows take a number of forms, but the duties of the announcer are generally of two related kinds: conversing with a wide range of telephone callers who might want to debate almost anything, and interviewing guests in the studio. Hosts may make their names by being witty, wise, or provoking, but they are not hired unless they are entertaining. The qualities of a successful talk-show host are as elusive as those of a popular disc jockey; specific preparation for such announcing positions is, therefore, impossible to prescribe.

12. *Television talk-show host.* Again, wit, charm, knowledge, resiliency, quickness, and curiosity are attributes of the most popular television talk-show hosts. Many of the currently successful hosts began their careers as announcers,

but obviously they possessed extraordinary talent and ambition. No useful guidelines for success can be offered; the popularity of any television host depends more on his individual background and capabilities than his "announcing" skills.

13. *Sprocket jockey.* This television announcer provides commentary and commercials between segments of cartoons or movies. In many instances, the sprocket jockey is costumed and has a manufactured title, *e.g.,* "Captain Fortune," "Sergeant Savannah," or "Admiral Delta." Women sometimes are employed as "hostesses" for feature-film presentations; they introduce the movie, deliver live commercials, introduce filmed commercials, and occasionally comment on the movie of the day.

Most announcing students are interested in newscasting, sportscasting, or performing as a disc jockey; few seem excited about delivering commercials or making station breaks. This is understandable, but the temptation to concentrate on one kind of announcing should be resisted. In recent years, most large-market radio stations have shifted from multiprogram services to a single-format approach—all news, all top forty, all talk, all classical music, all middle-of-the-road, all telephone talk—making it possible for the announcer, especially the radio announcer, to specialize in the kind of announcing closest to his area of interest and talent. But most announcers still spend at least the first several years of their career working for small-market radio stations, where there is seldom room for the specialist.

Although there really is no such thing as a "typical" radio station, the following outline of announcing duties on a small- or medium-market station is at least realistic:

1. The announcer works a daily three-hour shift on the board. Because no other engineer is on duty, he must have a radiotelephone first-class operator's license. He operates his own audio console and cues up and plays phonograph records and audio tapes. He makes the appropriate entries in the program and operating logs.
2. During the remaining three to five hours of his working day, the announcer may remain in the studio to do the following:
   —prepare and deliver newscasts during another announcer's shift on the board
   —write, announce, and record commercials for local merchants
   —provide preventive maintenance for the broadcasting equipment
   —preview records and make selections for future broadcasts
   —compile a playlist and organize in a binder the commercials, public-service announcements, and station-promotion announcements for his next day's announcing shift
3. The announcer may spend several hours a day away from the station selling commercial time to local businessmen.
4. The announcer may be sent out to make a personal appearance.

The announcer at a medium- or small-market radio station obviously must handle more than announcing duties, and he must be able to do more than one kind of announcing: newscasting, ad-lib "personality" announcing, commercial delivery, and sometimes sportscasting.

Television stations for the most part have retained a multiprogram service, but the number of locally produced television programs has decreased. This, in turn, means fewer opportunities for the local on-camera announcer. With programming hours dominated by network feeds or syndicated film packages, and with more and more commercials coming to the station already videotaped or filmed, the studio television announcer is a member of a vanishing species. In smaller markets, few local merchants can afford the cost of elaborate television productions; for this reason, the television booth announcer who reads commercial copy over a slide has tended to replace the on-the-air commercial announcer. Although job opportunities have actually increased in local news, the general picture of employment at the local station level indicates that the more versatile the announcer is, the greater are his chances for employment and retention.

In studying announcing, then, you are faced with a dilemma: you want to specialize, but in order to obtain, hold, and advance in that important first position, you must be strong in more than one type of announcing and at least competent in most of the other types. This generality naturally has its exceptions, but you should be able to see the risk in specializing too early in your career. First, broadcasting is susceptible to change, and the specialization you prepare for may not exist in ten years. Second, versatility means that at any given moment more job opportunities will be open to you than to the narrow specialist.

Many versatile staff announcers also earn extra money and professional satisfaction from "moonlighting"—taking side jobs. As staff announcer for KPIX–TV, San Francisco, Bill Hillman, for example, makes station breaks, reads copy over slides or silent film, gives "please stand by" announcements in case of program delays, and delivers the newsbreaks read over a "NEWS BULLETIN" slide. This work is regular and demanding, in its way, but it hardly exploits Bill's breadth of knowledge or taps his major interests. So he moonlights. One of his most gratifying side jobs is as a private contractor with the Voice of America for weekly reviews of concerts, plays, and books. In addition, in a typical two-month period he interviewed thirty-four different people for VOA, including:

- —a psychiatrist studying violence in America
- —a physician who had devised a new technique for studying the heart
- —a Nigerian playwright
- —a metallurgist who had developed a new method of rolling steel
- —the new president of a Catholic university
- —the president of a violence-torn college
- —a professor of civil engineering attempting to provide an interface between technology and the liberal arts

—a Nobel laureate in physics on the discovery of complex molecules in interstellar space
—a professor of astronomy on the likelihood of civilizations in other galaxies
—a biochemist on the chemical analysis of lunar soil samples
—a symphonic conductor
—an operatic baritone

Some of these were extensive interviews, recorded for later editing; others were broadcast as recorded. Obviously, only a versatile, inquisitive, and broadly educated announcer could meet such a range of challenges. Yet it must be emphasized that free-lance employment alone seldom is regular or profitable enough to sustain an announcer. A regular announcing position is the base to build on.

Figure 2. Bill Hillman, booth announcer at KPIX–TV, San Francisco. Visible are a line monitor (beneath the clock), an Electro-Voice 635A dynamic microphone, an intercom microphone, a mounted stopwatch, a copy of the program log, and a loose-leaf binder which contains in sequence the commercials, public-service announcements, station promotions, and other scripted materials he will read during his shift. Out of sight to Hillman's left is an air monitor for detecting interruptions in audio or video transmission. The panel in front of his right hand is a switching console allowing him to (1) switch audio and video monitors and the intercom; (2) control the volume of the audio monitor, earphone monitor, and intercom; (3) turn the air microphone on and off. (Courtesy KPIX)

Education and Training

The subject matter of radio is not radio, nor is the content of television television. Both these influential media devote their hours of broadcast to nonbroadcast disciplines like news, weather, music, sports, and drama. Though you should learn performance techniques and the history and theory of mass communication, you should not limit your studies there. The ability to talk knowledgeably about broadcasting, manipulate consoles, turntables, and tape-cartridge units, and interpret skillfully someone else's script is necessary for employment, but you must have more to offer the station and the public. Radio and television have little room today for empty-headed announcers for several reasons. First, the broadcast announcer is being evaluated by increasingly sophisticated listeners. Americans are better informed today than in previous times. Informational media are reaching more people with more messages than ever before. A television generation has grown up which is quick to spot clichés and gimmicks.

Second, as radio stations have moved away from a policy of "something for everyone" to special-appeal formats, they have attracted more homogeneous audiences which know and care a great deal about the program material being offered. Because of this, the majority of listeners to a single-format radio station are quick to detect and resent an announcer's lack of knowledge.

Third, the dramatic explosion of knowledge in the past several years will make inadequate for the 1970's the announcer of the 1950's and 1960's who has not grown with the times. The makers of dictionaries have been adding new words to their new editions at an unprecedented pace; each represents to an announcer not only a new word to pronounce but a new concept, a new technological breakthrough, a newly perceived human condition, or a new phenomenon to know about.

Finally, both radio and television have increased considerably the number of broadcast hours devoted to unscripted presentations. Television-program hosts, radio disc jockeys, interviewers, announcers covering sports and special events, and talk-show personalities use scripted material only occasionally; most of the time they are on their own. With such independence comes the necessity of having much already at hand to share with the audience.

So, what should you study if you intend to become an announcer? This question must be answered in two ways. First, of course, you should pursue studies which will most quickly and obviously prepare you for your first announcing job; second, you should have a general background in the liberal, social, and cultural arts. The following list of courses is arranged under these two headings. It is preposterously large, and you will have to discriminate in choosing the courses you take. But if you are serious about an announcing career, you should understand that not only are both kinds of education important, the breadth of your education is important as well.

You should find courses teaching:

Radio and television announcing concentrating on interpretation, articulation, phonation, use of the microphone, pronunciation, camera presence, ad-libbing, and adapting the individual personality to the broadcast media.

The International Phonetic Alphabet. (If your broadcasting department does not teach this, look to the speech department.)

Skills leading toward a first-class radiotelephone operator's license. (Such a course may have to be pursued in a technical institute; few degree-granting colleges offer it.)

Control-room operations, if previously listed courses do not cover them: theory of control-room operations; extensive practice in manipulating audio consoles, turntables, tape-cartridge machines, and microphones.

Economic aspects of broadcasting or business. (Many small stations hire personnel who function half-time as salesmen and half-time as announcers. Also, the ability to interpret audience-measurement statistics could tip the scales in obtaining a first and second job with a small- or medium-sized radio station.)

Writing for radio and television: commercial copy, news, and station editorials.

Foreign language pronunciation. (Some departments of music offer a course teaching principles of pronunciation for the major languages of the West —French, German, Italian, and occasionally Spanish or Russian.)

Film-making. (Some television stations expect newscasters to be able to film as well as narrate a news story.)

The principles, nomenclature, and strategies of a variety of major sports. (Some physical education departments teach a course in "sports officiating" that offers this information.)

GENERAL EDUCATION

Look for courses in:

Departments of broadcasting viewing broadcast communication from social, intellectual, ethical, aesthetic, psychological, legal, anthropological, and/or historical perspectives.

Departments of journalism stressing the responsibilities of the broadcast journalist in a democratic society. (Few departments of broadcasting are organized to provide in-depth education in journalism.)

One or another of the nonelectronic arts—music, literature, theatre, cinema, art—or in the humanities, which synthesize the arts, emphasizing the ways the arts function in the lives of people.

The social and behavioral sciences—political science, international relations, sociology, economics, psychology.

Linguistics, general semantics, cybernetics, and persuasion.

Anthropology, emphasizing man as a communicating being.

Business and/or economic theory.

Creative writing.

Education, especially child growth and development, educational sociology, educational psychology, and educational technology (especially for the educational-instructional radio or television announcer).

Certainly you must evaluate these suggestions in the light of your own aptitude, interest, and career aspirations. Any college counselor can help you determine their appropriateness and can explore with you other perhaps equally valid disciplines. The important point is that all nonbroadcasting courses will be of lasting benefit and practical value to you only insofar as you use your growing knowledge constantly and increasingly in your daily work.

Attempting to separate "practical" and "theoretical" studies could lead to considerable misunderstanding. The typical degree-granting college requires about 125 semester hours for the B.A. or B.S. degree, of which no more than forty-five would be in broadcasting. And only about one-third of those, or fifteen hours, would be directly related to announcing training; the modern broadcasting department invariably requires courses in broadcast law and regulations, historical, social, and economic aspects of broadcasting, communication theory, writing for radio and television, station management, international and comparative broadcasting, and any of a number of other courses which do not obviously relate to the work of an on-the-air announcer. Such courses, whether taught by a department of broadcasting or a cooperating department, are in the category of liberal education rather than skills training.

Consequently, if you have no aspiration beyond getting your already-developed personality on the air, or if you feel you have enough general educational background, perhaps you should go to the most efficient and economical source for skills training: a good and reputable trade school. This suggestion is not offered in a spirit of condescension or disapproval; for a person who possesses certain abilities and particular aspirations it may be the best one that can be given. But a strong word of caution is warranted: some trade schools are neither reputable nor competent. Beware of broadcasting schools which try to convince you that there are hordes of program directors waiting to vie for your services; that an endorsed "third phone" (radiotelephone third-class operator's permit endorsed for broadcast use) is good enough for most station employment; that "age is no barrier to employment." Competition will be keen, you must have a "first phone" to work combo on most stations, and few stations will hire a novice over thirty. Before enrolling in any trade school, seek the advice of practicing broadcasters or professors of broadcasting. Ethical trade schools will welcome your caution and may even refer you to responsible people for advice.

As you have seen, the field of announcing encompasses an incredible range of activities. Most modern liberal arts colleges and their broadcasting departments are well equipped to help you begin the process of becoming a competent and versatile communicator. For that is what you must be if you expect to be able to face such typical challenges as these:

1. You are a television booth announcer, and you are to read a commercial for a local restaurant featuring international cuisine. You must pronounce correctly *vichyssoise, coq au vin, paella, saltimbocca alla Romana,* and *Hasenpfeffer.*

2. You are a radio staff announcer and must read news headlines including the place names Sault Sainte Marie, Schleswig-Holstein, Santa Rosa de Copán, São Paulo, and Leicester.

3. You are the announcer on a "good music" program and need to know the meanings and correct pronunciation of *scherzo, andante cantabile, Die Götterdämmerung,* and *L'après-midi d'un faune.*

4. You are a commercial announcer, and the copy for a pharmaceutical company demands that you correctly pronounce *hexachlorophene, prophylaxis,* and *epidermic.*

5. You are the "color man" on a sports broadcast and need to obtain extensive historical and statistical information on football in order to fill those inevitable moments of inactivity.

6. You are the play-by-play announcer for a semipro baseball game and must pronounce the following "typical" American names: Martineau, Buchignani, Yturri, Sockolow, Watanabe, Engebrecht, and MacLeod.

7. You have been sent to interview a Nobel prize winner in astrophysics and need to obtain basic information about the subject of this man's research as well as biographical data.

8. You are narrating a documentary and must analyze the intent and content of the program to determine the mood, rhythm, structure, and interrelationship between sound, picture, and script.

9. You are covering a riot and are expected to assess responsibly the human dynamics of the incident.

10. You are a radio disc jockey, and you are on duty when word is received of the unexpected death of a great American (he may be a politician, an entertainer, a scientist); until the news department can take over, you must ad-lib appropriately.

Obviously, no one type of course will completely educate you as an announcer.

The Announcer's Responsibility

Just how important is the announcer? On radio he is the link between the audience and a potential chaos of sounds, noises, or nothingness. On television he is the presenter, the communicator, and the interpreter. Without him both radio and television as we know them would be impossible and meaningless. And, because he usually addresses his listeners directly, he represents economy, as well; no other means of disseminating information is as swift and effective as the word spoken directly from one person to another.

From a different point of view, the announcer is just about as important as the messages he communicates. He can be "good important" or "bad important," with most practicing announcers somewhere in between. If he is trivial, slants the news, misrepresents products, or circulates false rumors, he is negatively important. If he is enlightening, consistently ethical, refuses to endorse shoddy products, and attempts to lay false rumors to rest, he is important in a positive way. To facilitate your education as a "good important" announcer, this book has been organized around the assumption that *you want* to make a responsible and positive contribution through broadcasting.

One broadcast circumstance automatically requires responsible behavior of every on-air announcer: a national emergency. The *Rules and Regulations* of the Federal Communications Commission (FCC) include a section which affects every broadcast licensee—*The Emergency Action Notification System* and *The Emergency Broadcast System,* providing for controlled communications in the event of national emergencies. The document states:

> The objectives of this subpart are to provide an expeditious means for the dissemination of an Emergency Action Notification (with or without an Attack Warning) to licensees and regulated services of the Federal Communications Commission and to the general public during conditions of a grave national crisis or war and to provide for an Emergency Broadcast System (EBS), which would be activated upon release of an Emergency Action Notification by direction of the President of the United States.

These two systems are also available for broadcasting warnings about local "day-to-day emergencies posing a threat to the safety of life and property," including tornadoes, toxic gasses, tidal waves, earthquakes, and civil disorders, and for appeals for medical assistance. Even the most bored announcer giving the most pedestrian day-in, day-out service would become important if the EBS were activated during his on-air time. He might have only to go off the air to keep his broadcast signal from guiding in attacking missiles; or his announcements might help save the lives of hundreds of people.

Most broadcast announcers are also subject to "social" responsibility. Nearly all announcers, like it or not, influence society through their "visibility" and prestige. Years ago, Paul F. Lazarsfeld and Robert K. Merton perceived and described the "status-conferral function" of the mass media. In essence, they told us that the general public attaches prestige to those who appear on the mass media and are more readily influenced by prestigious people than equals. The public's reasoning is circular: "If you really matter, you will be at the focus of attention; and if you *are* at the focus of mass attention, then you must really matter." The newscaster, then, is not simply an efficient conveyor of information; as a radio or television "star" he carries on his shoulders the burden of knowing that he is trusted and believed in as a qualified authority. Even the entertainment-program host or the disc jockey has automatic—though possibly unwarranted—prestige. As an announcer on any broadcast medium, you should be aware of your status and try to measure up to it.

Not all announcers have this sense of social commitment, and not all who do are in a position to accomplish very much. Still, you should be aware of the opportunities you may have to enlighten or confuse the public. As a nation, we have been slow to perceive and attack serious problems: urban deterioration, increasing crime, pollution of land, air, and water, racial inequities, poverty, the rise of antidemocratic action groups, increased use of drugs, and so on. If you are committed to using the mass media to make a better society, you are already responsible and potentially important as the kind of communicator demanded by our times.

Two Principles of Communication

The Announcer as Communicator

The key to successful radio and television announcing is the ability to *communicate as effectively as possible ideas or feelings to other human beings.* Understanding and believing that communicating effectively ought to be the goal is by no means the same thing as doing it. For some the ability to communicate comes easily and is effortlessly adapted to radio or television performance. For most, however, the difficulties in being effective, economical, and accurate even in daily conversation are constant reminders that much work lies ahead. This chapter explains the communicative process and offers specific advice on interpreting written copy. At the end of the chapter, the ad-lib announcer is briefly discussed. Subsequent chapters include exercises in both reading and ad-libbing.

Unfortunately, many announcing students feel they have succeeded when they can *sound like* an announcer. American broadcasting has been served by several generations of announcers, and a distinct "announcerish" sound has evolved. Tune across the radio dial in any part of the country and you will soon hear someone trying very hard to approximate the phonation, articulation, phrasing, and pronunciation of the stereotyped announcer. His effort is misplaced; he is not supposed to be a mimic. Good announcing is not *imitation;* it is *communication.* Most outstanding announcers succeed because they are unique. They retain their individuality as they focus on getting their message across. True communication begins when an announcer *learns who he is, reflects himself in his delivery, cares about the messages he is sending, and knows that he is speaking to individuals, not a crowd.* Developing your vocal apparatus or expanding your vocabulary alone cannot guarantee that you will become an effective communicator. Try always to be aware of two other aspects of effective oral communication: reflecting your personality, and communicating the ideas you are expressing.

The Process of Communication

The chain of events we call the process of communication begins with an idea. This idea may arise in the mind of a newswriter, an agency copywriter, an editorial writer, or a station or network continuity writer. To be more specific, the newswriter may begin with the idea "big explosion in New York City"; the advertising copywriter may conceive the thought "this automobile is safer than all others"; the editorial writer may decide "Senator Johnson will win his election"; and the continuity writer may think the thought "this song was written by Cole Porter."

Now these are as yet only thoughts, the raw material out of which the final copy will be made. The very words used to conceive the ideas may never appear in the final copy. The next step is to symbolize the ideas in words which will best communicate the thoughts. The ability to select the most effective and unhackneyed words and arrange them well is the art of writing; the ability to communicate these words orally to a listener is the art of announcing.

Presenting written ideas to a listener through an oral interpreter has a distinct advantage over presenting ideas directly through the printed word. On a very basic level, the skilled announcer will not misread words; on another level, he will show the relative importance of the various parts of the message, as well as the proper mood and degree of seriousness of the copy. The skilled announcer will, therefore, present the material in its most persuasive and readily understood form.

The potential disadvantage of oral communication is that the radio or television announcer may fail to present the written material effectively and understandably. Too often the announcer merely reads words without communicating ideas. As we have seen, a word is only a symbol of an idea; if the idea is not clear in the mind of the announcer, or if the announcer lacks the ability to transmit it effectively through his spoken word, the idea has a reduced chance of being communicated to and absorbed by the listener. Of course, reading words with no interpretation whatsoever will convey some of the ideas to an attentive listener—if, indeed, such a reader has any listeners. But this is not good announcing, and no amount of rationalization can justify it.

Many radio announcers (the mere fact that he knows he is being seen as he speaks makes this less true of the television announcer) feel that if all the words in a message are read aloud with no mispronunciations and in low, resonant tones, their entire obligation to the material has been discharged. This, of course, is not true. Make it a point to listen to as many news reporters and commercial announcers as you can and study their deliveries. Listen especially to those you have come to avoid. Decide for yourself which among them are mere readers of words and which are true communicators. In all probability you will discover that you have unconsciously formed the habit of tuning in those announcers who communicate best and tuning out those who communicate least. The layman may not, of course, think in terms of the communicative ability of a given announcer, but he is nonetheless affected by it. He finds himself unconsciously listening to those who are best able to help him receive and assimilate ideas. He is, at the same time, being swayed to causes, concepts, and products, however subtly.

Many announcers on television do a consistently better job of communicating than their counterparts on radio because they are virtually forced to give some physical interpretation to their copy. Their eyes, mouth, hands, and arms all convey meaning to the viewer. Though these alone can achieve only a relatively low level of communication, they enhance and extend the shades of meanings when combined with good vocal delivery. Perhaps most important of all, the mere fact that physical interpretation is expected of the television announcer gives him a rather compelling reason for thoroughly analyzing his copy. Having to demonstrate a product, point to visual materials, or cue a film adds to the amount of preparation needed for even an adequate job. Though the radio announcer—especially the overworked disc jockey—may read much of his copy "cold," in television it is not uncommon to spend weeks producing a one-minute filmed commercial. As a matter of fact, some filmed commercials are more expensive and take longer to produce than many half-hour entertainment programs. This extra investment of time and money does not automatically insure a successful commercial; only a good script and a first-rate performance can do that. Failure to be spontaneous and convincing, to use the intimate nature of the medium, or to use his face, hands, and other nonverbal tools of communication can make an announcer seem an uninspired voice working at odds with an unrelated face and body.

As noted above, some radio announcers apparently believe that only their voices are important. They attempt to project energy and conviction as they speak or read into a microphone without using the rest of their bodies. Energy is easy to simulate, but unless genuinely motivated by the content of the message, it usually seems phony; uncalled-for enthusiasm hinders rather than helps communication. To avoid it, you should announce for radio as though your listener were in the booth with you. You should use your face, hands, and body as you speak, as you do in ordinary conversation. Integrating all the tools of communication should help clarify and intensify your message, despite the fact that your listener cannot see you. Good physical gesturing for both radio and television is marked by two considerations: (1) honest motivation and (2) harmony with the size and moods of the ideas being expressed. The oversize grins, frowns, grimaces, and sweeping arm movements taught to generations of declaimers seldom are appropriate to radio or television.

If merely reading words constitutes a low level of oral communication, what is good oral communication? As has already been implied, *good communication occurs when the listener or viewer receives an undistorted and effective impression of the ideas of the writer or of the ad-lib speaker, with proper emphasis on each of the parts which make up the whole.*

Basic to good interpretation is a thorough understanding of the material to be presented. Just as a musician or a conductor must understand the intentions of the composer, so must the announcer understand the intention of the writer. With the exceptions of the ad-lib announcer, the disc jockey, and the news analyst who writes his own copy, the announcer is an *interpretive* rather than a *creative* artist. Like the musician, he may at times create his own copy, but in most instances both serve as a link between creator and audience.

Furthermore, the art of the musician is not just manufacturing beautiful tones or demonstrating great technical skill; it is also faithfully interpreting and executing the intention of the composer. If beautiful tones and technical proficiency are integral to the correct interpretation, then the musician should aim for both. If, on the other hand, the composer has asked for thin, strident, or ugly tones, correct interpretation demands sacrificing "beauty." To relate this again to announcing, however beautiful the voice of a given announcer and however rapidly and unfalteringly he may be able to read copy, he is not truly a good announcer unless he uses his ability to communicate the ideas and the values of the writer as the writer originally conceived them.

Interpreting the Copy

Understanding the intention of the writer is more difficult and demanding than is commonly thought. Many specific considerations are involved and must be discussed at length. An excellent approach to analyzing copy has been prepared by Dr. Stanley T. Donner, Chairman of Radio-Television-Film at the University of Texas:

1. Read the copy twice to get the general meaning.
2. State the specific purpose of the copy in one brief sentence.
3. What is the general mood of the copy?
4. Where does the mood change?
5. What are the parts of the copy?
6. What changes of meaning are involved in each part of the copy?
7. What help is punctuation in reading the copy?
8. Are there any words or allusions you do not fully understand or cannot pronounce?
9. Read the copy aloud.
10. Do you have any genuine interest in the subject matter of the copy? Do you reveal this interest?
11. Who is your listener? Can you visualize him? Are you able to establish rapport with him? Are you actually talking to him?
12. If the copy is "good literature," who is the author? Is it important to know his history and what he was trying to do in his writings?
13. Should you know anything about the origin and background of this copy?
14. Do you need to do any characterization?

This list of considerations suggests much more than might seem obvious at first reading. Let us elaborate on Dr. Donner's points:

1. *Read the copy twice to get the general meaning.* One problem confronting anyone who spends time and effort preparing copy for oral delivery is that overconcentration on pronunciation or timing may obscure the overall meaning and purpose. To avoid this, you should form an impression of the wholeness of the piece by reading through it at least twice before undertaking any of the more detailed work of preparation.

2. *State the specific purpose of the copy in one brief sentence.* This is the most important single decision you will make. You must, at this point, determine the major objectives of the copy. Just as it is pointless to begin a trip to some undetermined destination and then wonder why you did not arrive at a satisfactory place, so it is foolish to begin interpreting copy without first formulating its goal. Your job as an oral interpreter is choosing appropriate means; it is first necessary to determine appropriate ends. The interpretations of two identical sentences will vary if the sentences are used in different contexts or for different purposes; similarly, pieces of broadcast copy which seem superficially to call for the same delivery may actually require quite different interpretations. Raising questions about the purpose of the copy will help determine this.

Read this ten-second commercial:

```
ANNCR:  See the all-new MG, on display tomorrow at the

        Foreign Motorcar Center, 16th and Grand.

        You'll love the MG's new lines.  For a genuine

        thrill, see the new MG tomorrow.
```

Now, state the specific purpose of this copy. If you decided that the purpose is to awaken interest in the new MG automobile, you analyzed the copy correctly. If you decided that the purpose was to promote the name and address of the sponsor, you were incorrect. The phrase, ". . . at the Foreign Motorcar Center, 16th and Grand," is subordinate to the idea of "the all-new MG." Although it is uncommon to subordinate the name and address of the sponsor, the copy clearly indicates that it should be done in this instance. Perhaps the sponsor has the only foreign car agency in the town, or sponsor identification has been built up over a period of months by placing other more conventional commercials in this same time slot and on this same station. The moral here is that it is unsafe to decide automatically that the name and address of the sponsor is, *per se,* the phrase to be stressed in all copy.

Let us look at another piece of copy for the same advertiser:

ANNCR: See the famous MG sportscar at the Foreign

Motorcar Center at 16th and Grand. Serving

you since 1933, it's the Foreign Motorcar

Center, 16th and Grand, for the beautiful MG.

Here the identical phrase, "at the Foreign Motorcar Center, 16th and Grand," has been used but for a different purpose. Despite the double mention of the MG, the name of the automobile is subordinate to the name and address of the sponsor. If you decided in analyzing this copy that the purpose is to impress the sponsor's name, address, reliability, and service, you analyzed it correctly.

3. *What is the general mood of the copy?* Having determined the purpose of the copy, you may now determine its mood. To some extent the number of words in the copy will limit the degree to which you can control the mood, especially in commercial copy. In the commercials for the Foreign Motorcar Center, you must read thirty words in ten seconds, or 180 words a minute—which is just about as rapidly as one can or should read aloud. In most radio or television work, excluding commercial announcements written with inflexible time limits in mind, the copy may be shortened or lengthened to allow for a proper rate of delivery and hence the correct mood. The length of time taken for still other kinds of announcements—the introduction to a musical composition, for example—is not a particularly important consideration, although, as you will note in the chapter on the disc jockey (Chapter 10), split-second timing frequently is. In sportscasting, the determinants of mood are set by the action of the game.

Read the following eight news items and determine the mood of each:

(BLIZZARD)

ONE OF THE WORST BLIZZARDS IN THE MEMORY OF OLD

RESIDENTS HAS STRUCK WESTERN NEBRASKA AND KANSAS AND

THE PANHANDLES OF OKLAHOMA AND TEXAS. AN UNKNOWN

NUMBER OF DRIVERS WERE STRANDED ON HIGHWAYS YESTERDAY,

AND SOME STILL WERE WITHOUT HELP TODAY AS THE SNOW

CONTINUED. WINDS UP TO 74 MILES AN HOUR CREATED

DRIFTS WHICH BLOCKED HIGHWAYS AND AT MANY POINTS

VISIBILITY WAS ZERO.

DRUGS BY HIGH SCHOOL STUDENTS HAS BEEN ANNOUNCED BY
THE OFFICE OF EDUCATION.

THE PROGRAM IN THE MENDOCINO COUNTRY SCHOOL AT
UKIAH, NORTHERN CALIFORNIA, IS ONE OF 19 TRAINING
PROJECTS IN 8 STATES WHICH WILL RECEIVE A TOTAL OF
$740,000 FOR EXPERIMENTAL TRAINING OF EDUCATIONAL
PERSONNEL.

"WE EXPECT THAT SOME OF THESE EXPERIMENTAL
PROJECTS AND A FEW OTHERS TO BE ANNOUNCED LATER WILL
BECOME MODELS FOR OTHER SCHOOLS," SAID DON DAVIES,
SSOCIATE COMMISSIONER FOR EDUCATIONAL PERSONNEL
VELOPMENT.

ONE PURPOSE IS TO PREPARE NEW KINDS OF WORKERS TO
FF THE NATION'S SCHOOLS.

ANOTHER PROJECT WILL BE TO TRAIN POTENTIAL
OUTS AMONG HIGH SCHOOL STUDENTS IN LOS ANGELES
MENTARY SCHOOL TUTORS.

LSON PRISON, CALIFORNIA) -- TOWER GUARDS SHOT
DED TWO CONVICTS TODAY TO BREAK UP A VICIOUS
WEEN THE TWO IN THE PRISON YARD.

ON SPOKESMAN SAID PARTS OF BOTH EARS OF ONE
RE BITTEN OFF DURING THE FIERCE STRUGGLE.

ALL ROADS IN WESTERN KANSAS ARE CLOSED AND A

13-COUNTY AREA IN SOUTHWEST NEBRASKA AROUND MC COOK

IS ISOLATED. ALL ROADS FROM GRAND ISLAND, NEBRASKA

TO THE WEST ARE IMPASSABLE.

HIGHWAYS IN EASTERN COLORADO ARE CLOSED WITH

AND DUST REDUCING VISIBILITY FROM POOR TO ZERO

OKLAHOMA PANHANDLE IS VIRTUALLY CUT OFF FROM

WORLD WITH SNOW DRIFTS IN PLACES AS DEEP AS

AT DODGE CITY, KANSAS, THE DRIFTS WERE REP

FEET HIGH.

ABOUT 300 MEN, WOMEN, AND CHILDREN

FROM SNOWBOUND CARS YESTERDAY IN THE

AND WERE GIVEN SHELTER IN THE SCHOOL

ORDERS WERE ISSUED IN GARDEN CITY

KANSAS, FOR RESIDENTS TO STAY AT

WAS REPORTED WITHOUT ELECTRICAL

THE CITY OF HAYS, KANSAS,

AND A STATE OF EMERGENCY WAS

AND TELEGRAPH LINES WERE OU

WAS OPERATING ON AN EMERG

(ADDICTS)

WASHINGTON -- USE

STUDENT COUNSELORS

THE SPOKESMAN SAID ALBERT JOHNSON, 37, A LOS
ANGELES BURGLAR, AND LEONARD THOMPSON, 34, A SAN
FRANCISCO BURGLAR, REFUSED TO HEED LOUDSPEAKER
COMMANDS TO HALT THEIR MURDEROUS FIGHT.

TOWER GUARDS WERE ORDERED TO OPEN FIRE. SHOOTING
FROM 200 FEET AWAY, THE GUARDS HIT JOHNSON IN THE
UPPER LEG. THOMPSON WAS HIT TWICE IN A LEG AND ONCE
IN THE FOREARM.

THE BULLETS FINALLY STOPPED THE FIGHT. THE TWO
CONVICTS THEN WERE TREATED IN THE PRISON HOSPITAL.

(CRASH)

FOUR PERSONS WERE KILLED NEAR SAUK CITY, WISCONSIN,
LAST NIGHT IN A HIGHWAY CRASH INVOLVING 2 PASSENGER
CARS AND A SEMI-TRAILER TRUCK. THE TRUCK DRIVER WAS
TAKEN TO A HOSPITAL, BUT HIS INJURIES WERE DESCRIBED
AS NOT SERIOUS.

(BOY)

DOCTORS IN SPOKANE, WASHINGTON, FOUND NO APPARENT
INJURIES EXCEPT TIRE BRUISES WHEN THEY EXAMINED
5-YEAR-OLD MICHAEL HOUSTON AFTER HE HAD BEEN RUN OVER
BY THE DUAL WHEELS OF A 12 AND ONE-HALF TON STREET
GRADER. MIKE HAD HITCHED A TRICYCLE TOW BEHIND THE
HUGE VEHICLE, OUT OF SIGHT OF THE DRIVER. SOFT DIRT

PUSHED UP BY THE GRADER APPARENTLY SERVED AS A CUSHION
WHEN IT BACKED OVER THE BOY.

(DOG)

 (GALVESTON, TEXAS) -- THE FRUITS OF POLITICAL
VICTORY WILL FOREVER BE DENIED TO BLACKIE, THE MONGREL
DOG WHOSE CASE ROCKED THE DOG-CATCHING SET-UP OF
GALVESTON, TEXAS. BLACKIE HAS BEEN FOUND DEAD,
EVIDENTLY SHOT BY A PERSON OR PERSONS UNKNOWN.

 BLACKIE WAS THE CENTRAL FIGURE IN A GUNFIGHT, IN
WHICH 2 TEENAGE BOYS BATTLED POLICE AND DOG-CATCHERS
FOR AN HOUR LAST WEEK. THE BOYS, ROBERT GARCIA AND
CHARLES LAYMAN, SAID A DOG-CATCHER TRIED TO SHOOT
THEIR PUP. THE DOG-CATCHER SAID HE ONLY WANTED TO
SCARE BLACKIE. THE CASE CAUSED THE CITY TO END ITS
CAMPAIGN AGAINST STRAY DOGS. BUT BLACKIE IS NO MORE.

(DRUGS)

 (WASHINGTON)--THE GOVERNMENT WANTS RADIO DISC
JOCKEYS TO START TALKING ABOUT THE DANGERS OF DRUG
ABUSE IN HOPES THEY WILL BE ABLE TO INFLUENCE MILLIONS
OF TEENAGERS TUNED IN.

 "THEY WON'T LISTEN TO THEIR PARENTS OR THEIR
TEACHERS," SAYS FORMER FOOTBALL COACH BUD WILKINSON,
NOW A CONSULTANT TO THE PRESIDENT. "MAYBE THEY'LL

LISTEN TO PEOPLE THEY'VE COME TO RESPECT, WHO TALK

THEIR OWN LANGUAGE. THE DISC JOCKEY HAS A UNIQUE

RELATIONSHIP WITH TEENAGERS."

(INDIAN)

    (FORT CARSON, COLORADO)--THERE IS ONE SOLDIER AT

FORT CARSON, COLORADO, WHO NEVER GETS A HAIRCUT AND

N E V E R SHAVES. AND HIS OFFICERS NEVER REPRIMAND

HIM FOR HIS BEARD AND LONG HAIR. HE IS SPECIALIST

FOURTH CLASS GOKUL SINGH, A SIKH (SEEK), BORN IN INDIA.

AND BECAUSE OF HIS RELIGIOUS TENETS HE IS PERMITTED

TO KEEP HIS LONG HAIR AND BEARD, AND WEAR A TURBAN

AND A SWORD.

(END SUMMARY)

Notice in these news items the great range of emotion and mood; no two, in fact, are alike. Ask yourself these questions to determine mood: (a) What is the specific purpose of this story? (b) What word or brief phrase sums up the purpose? (c) What mood is best suited to the purpose? (d) How can it best be communicated? Now let us look at two commercials with a wide difference in mood. Read both and ask the same questions about each.

VIDEO	AUDIO
WS ANNCR; SALE DISPLAY ITEMS AND RED LETTER DAYS SIGNS IN BG. MILLER'S VARIETY SIGNS UNDER TABLE AND ABOVE ANNCR.	ANNCR: It's that time of year again, folks -- RED LETTER DAYS at Miller's Variety Stores! But this year Miller's is celebrating its tenth anniversary, so they've

	gone all out to make it the biggest, the best, the most unbe-lievable sale in history!
DOLLY TO DISPLAY TABLE SHOT OF YARDAGE.	For the homemaker . . . preshrunk cotton yardage in a variety of dazzling new patterns . . . only 29¢ a yard.
CUT TO TS OF TOOLS.	For that handyman around the house . . . a complete 100-piece snap-on tool set at the low, low, lowest price ever . . . $19.95!
CUT TO TS OF HAIR DRYER.	For sister, a famous-make hair dryer that'll guarantee she'll be on time for that heavy date . . . and for only $13.99!
CUT TO TS OF TOYS.	And, for Junior . . . toys, toys, and still more toys! Match-O-Matic, only 88¢ . . . friction cars, 77¢ . . . and a complete electric train set--transformer, track, engine, and eight cars-- for just $6.99!
CUT TO TS OF PET ITEMS.	And Miller's didn't forget Fido and Tabby! Dog and cat collars

	. . . leashes . . . and all kinds
	of toys . . . take them away for
	only 49¢!
DOLLY OUT TO WS.	Yes, folks, RED LETTER DAYS at
	MILLER'S VARIETY STORES are here!
	Sale starts <u>this Friday</u>, so plan
	to get there early. Help us
	celebrate <u>our</u> tenth, while <u>you</u>
	cash in on the spectacular
	bargains.
TAKE SLIDE 1: "MILLER'S VARIETY, 16th AND GRAND, YOUNTVILLE; WAUWATOSA SHOPPING CENTER; ON THE MALL."	MILLER'S VARIETY STORES are located at 16th and Grand in Yountville, in the Wauwatosa Shopping Center, and downtown in the Mall. And RED LETTER DAYS are at all three loca- tions! Remember . . . <u>this Friday</u> . . . MILLER'S VARIETY.

The second commercial was prepared by Young and Rubicam, Inc.

<u>VIDEO</u>	<u>AUDIO</u>
OPEN WITH CAMERA ZOOMING INTO GARDEN.	
EVE APPEARS.	Hello. I'm Eve and I live in the
	Garden of Eden . . . and it's
	really paradise.

EVE HOLDS BOTTLE OF CRANAPPLE JUICE.	Um! A lot of these juicy apples hanging around. Do you know that apples make you wise and an apple a day keeps the doctor away? Anyway, Ocean Spray took a lot of these juicy apples and they stuffed them into this bottle and they threw in a few little red cranberries and they shook the stuff up and they call it Ocean Spray Cranapple Juice. Oh wow! It's great. I know that the cranberries give it a great tang but really, it's largely apple juice. So I don't understand why Ocean Spray calls it Cranapple. Like I think that it should be called apple-cran.
EVE PICKS APPLE.	Right?
EVE BITES APPLE.	Ocean Spray ought to wise up.

What a difference of mood in the two examples! The first, for Miller's Variety Stores, is designed to capture and hold attention through vitality, speed, and the illusion of importance. A maximum amount of copy is used and many different shots of sale products are shown. Every effort is made to encourage direct action on the part of the viewer. The Cranapple Juice commercial, on the other hand, attempts to hold attention in a quieter, more subtle way, with an attractive woman and the mere notion of a new kind of juice drink. No attempt is made to convince the viewer that this product is the miracle of the century or that he should rush out at once to buy a bottle. The actress or announcer who portrays Eve must sense and reflect the satire in the commercial.

4. *Where does the mood change?*   A long piece of copy may contain several moods, though the dominant one may remain constant. In commercial copy, one common construction calls for a change from gloom to joy as the announcer first describes a common problem (halitosis, loose dentures, irregularity, etc.) and then tells you how his product can solve it. Spot such changes as you give your commercial a preliminary reading and indicate them on your script. Unless the script calls for mock-serious delivery, be careful not to overexaggerate the moods.

In narrating an extended television or film documentary or presenting a five-, fifteen-, or thirty-minute newscast, changes of mood are more numerous and more apparent. The next time you watch a documentary on television or listen to a newscast, make it a point to note those changes; note, too, the devices the speaker uses to reflect the shifting moods. In carefully working out such changes in mood, the narrator or announcer contributes to the flow, unity, and overall meaning of the presentation.

In newscasting, as we have seen, changes in mood usually coincide with changes in news items. But many newscasts begin with brief headline summaries which call for many changes within a short span of time. Read these headlines and determine the changes in mood:

HERE IS THE LATEST NEWS FROM THE ASSOCIATED PRESS:

THE SECRETARY OF STATE HAS CAUTIONED THE KREMLIN

THAT TIME IS NOT UNLIMITED TO REACH SOME AGREEMENT

ON DISARMAMENT.

A FIGHTER PLANE HAS CRASHED INTO A RESIDENTIAL

AREA, KILLING THE PILOT AND THREE MEMBERS OF A TEXAS

FAMILY.

THE SEASON'S LONGEST HEAT WAVE APPEARS TO BE

BREAKING AS COOL AIR AND RAIN SPREAD OVER THE EASTERN

HALF OF THE COUNTRY.

A THREE-YEAR OLD GIRL HAS BEEN PULLED ALIVE FROM

A FORTY-FOOT WELL IN MICHIGAN.

AND, THE LATEST WITNESS AT THE HOUSE RACKETS

COMMITTEE HEARING HAS TAKEN THE FIFTH AMENDMENT

ONE-HUNDRED AND FORTY TIMES.

The moods implicit in each of these headlines require great flexibility, a challenge which confronts the newscaster daily.

5. *What are the parts of the copy?* Almost any example of well-written copy will show rather clearly differentiated parts. On the most basic level, copy may be broken down into the Aristotelian beginning, middle, and end. The beginning is the introduction and is customarily used to gain attention. The middle, or body, contains most of the information. In commercials, the middle tells us the advantages of this product over all others; in newscopy, it contains the details of the story; in music copy it gives background information on the piece or the composer. The end is generally used for summing up the most important points. In commercials it frequently urges action or repeats the name, address, and telephone number of the sponsor.

In most copy these three parts may be further subdivided. Commercial copy frequently follows this organization:

(a) Getting the attention of the listener or viewer.

(b) Giving some concrete reason for further interest and attention.

(c) Explaining step by step why this product or service is superior.

(d) Mentioning or implying a price lower than the listener has been led to believe.

(e) Repeating some of the selling points.

(f) Repeating the name and address of the sponsor.

Read the following copy prepared by Young and Rubicam, Inc., for *Time* magazine and divide it into its component parts:

GENERAL #552
r24

TIME MAGAZINE
BB 24393
SPOT: 4014

ED BRYCE

(SOUND: INTRO & UNDER)

Early in this century, German novelist Hermann Hesse

wove mystical novels like <u>Siddhartha</u> and <u>Steppenwolf</u>

about man's search for identity. Worshipped by the

students of his own time, Hesse has now found a de-

voted new audience in today's college youth. Recently

in its Books Section, TIME, The Weekly Newsmagazine,

examined in depth the Hesse phenomenon: his life, the

development of his art, the extent of his influence.

Always TIME's Books Section offers some special in-

sights; for example, a survey of particularly skillful

women writers, a sketch of the legal and literary

struggles of the outrageous J.P. Donleavy, or an

evaluation of rediscovered manuscripts and newly

published journals. Each week, TIME reveals new as-

pects of the fascinating world of books, from witty

discussions of the ephemeral to detailed studies of

men whose thoughts span generations. The world of

books, explored for 24 million readers around the

globe in TIME -- the most important magazine to the

world's most important people.

(SOUND: UP & FADE)

One word of caution: much copy, and in particular the least hackneyed, frequently uses an original and unique arrangement of the parts. For this reason, no formula or rules of structure can be automatically applied in analyzing copy. The principles listed above are by far the most commonly used in copywriting, but they are not rigidly followed.

6. *What changes of meaning are involved in each part of the copy?* It follows that if one segment of an announcement is intended to point out a problem

and another to suggest a solution, two different related meanings are involved. The change in meaning will, therefore, affect the announcer's interpretation; he may change his voice, his pace, his volume, his gestures, or his distance from the microphone. Changes in meaning can occur within a single section or even within a single sentence in copy. Careful analysis of copy will disclose them, and careful interpretation will project them. Read this public-service announcement and note the changes of meaning in it:

KEEP AMERICA BEAUTIFUL   The Advertising Council
CAMPAIGN

60 SECONDS

If you tossed the remains of a box lunch over the brink

of the Grand Canyon, you might set a long distance

record for littering. But nobody in his right mind

wants that kind of record -- nobody WANTS to litter.

It's thoughtlessness that turns otherwise nice and

bright people into litterbugs. So think. Think ...

before you scatter trash all over the landscape.

Remember -- every litter bit hurts YOU. Our parks

and play areas, our roads and streets and beaches and

waterways, belong to all of us. Litter spoils the

view ... can cause automobile and boating accidents

... costs tax dollars to clean up. Wherever there's

rubbish to pick up, the taxpayers pick up the check.

So, carry a litterbag in your car and boat. Hold all

your rubbish for the first trash container -- that's

where it belongs. Remember -- living in litter is not

for people. America is the most beautiful place on

earth. Let's keep it that way. Let's Keep America

Beautiful!

7. *What help is punctuation in reading the copy?* In addition to words, the writer uses punctuation marks to encode his message. They are his way of under-scoring mood, tempo, and rhythm, comparable to the marks indicating volume, tempo, or mood used by composers. No musician or conductor would disregard musical signs; as an oral interpreter, you should use punctuation marks as simi-lar aides in clarifying, emphasizing, contrasting, or dramatizing your copy. You may want to develop your own system of marking copy so that you can spot im-portant punctuation quickly. A few of the more commonly used marks are:

(a) A slanted line (/), called a virgule, between words to approximate the comma.

(b) Two virgules (//) between sentences, or between words, to indicate a longer pause.

(c) Lines under words to be stressed.

(d) Enlarged question marks and exclamation marks.

(e) Crescendo (∧) and decrescendo (∨) marks to indicate that a passage is to receive an increase or decrease in stress.

8. *Are there any words or allusions you do not fully understand or cannot pronounce?* To interpret someone else's copy, you must understand the mean-ings of the words. You should cultivate the habit of looking up in an authorita-tive dictionary all unfamiliar words. This means developing a healthy skepticism about your own vocabulary; through years of silent reading, you have probably learned to settle for approximate meanings of many words. For a quick test, how many of these words can you define and use correctly?

peer	impassible
burlesque	ordnance
fulsome	immerge
mendicant	apposite
catholic	ascetic

Write the meaning you associate with these words opposite each, then check your definitions in any standard dictionary. Some of these words are heard and seen frequently; others only look or sound familiar. If you correctly defined more than four, you have an unusually large vocabulary.

Correct pronunciation of words is equally as important as accurate understanding. You should, therefore, also be skeptical about your ability to pronounce words correctly. Check your familiarity with these words by writing them out phonetically:

drought	accessories
forehead	junta
toward	worsted (yarn or cloth)
diphtheria	pestle
asterisk	primer (textbook)

Compare your transcriptions with those in Kenyon and Knott's *A Pronouncing Dictionary of American English*. You may consider yourself exceptional if you were not guilty of at least five mistakes.

In addition to using and pronouncing words correctly, you must understand any allusions in your copy. Look at a few common ones and again check your knowledge:

"He was hoist by his own petard."
"He found himself between Scylla and Charybdis."
"He was considered a quisling."
"He has a Shavian wit."
"He was given to spoonerisms."
"She was as false as Cressida."
"He had the temper of Hotspur."
"He suffered as mightily as Prometheus."

You cannot expect to be familiar with all allusions in every piece of copy. During your career you may read copy written by hundreds or even thousands of people, each drawing on a separate fund of knowledge. You can, however, cultivate the habit of finding out about allusions initially beyond your ken. Self-discipline is required, since it is exceptionally easy to convince yourself that context will make an allusion clear to an audience even if you do not understand it. The Bible, Shakespeare, and classical works are common sources; dictionaries of word origins, encyclopedias, and guides to mythology are also useful.

9. *Read the copy aloud.* Because you will perform aloud, you should practice aloud. Copy written for radio or television differs from copy written for newspapers, magazines, or books. Good broadcast copy usually makes poor silent reading. Short, incomplete, or ungrammatical sentences are often found in perfectly acceptable radio and television scripts:

ANNCR: Been extra tired lately? You know, sort of logy and dull? Tired and weary—maybe a little cranky, too? Common enough, this time of year. The time of year when colds are going around. And when we have to be especially careful of what we eat. Vitamin deficiency can be the cause of that "down-and-out" feeling. And Supertabs, the multiple vitamin, can be the answer. . . .

This is quite different from the copy an agency would write to advertise the same product in a newspaper. Reading it correctly requires a kind of skill developed most rapidly by practicing aloud.

Reading a long script can be difficult. You cannot afford to make even the minor errors the silent reader may make, like skipping over words or sentences, passing over material he does not understand or is unable to pronounce, and resting his eyes when they become tired. As an announcer, you must read constantly, read everything before you, read it accurately and with appropriate expression, and do all this with little opportunity to rest your eyes. As your eyes tire, you are more and more likely to make reading mistakes. One way of giving your eyes the rest they need is by "reading ahead": when your voice is at about *this* point, your eyes should be about *here*. When your eyes have reached the end of the sentence, you should be able to glance away from your script while you finish speaking the words. Practice this, and you should be able to read even fifteen-minute newscasts without excessive eye strain. But as you practice, make certain you do not fall into an irritating habit of many announcers who read ahead—going into a monotonous, decelerating speech pattern at the end of every sentence. Unless you guard against it, you may be unconsciously relaxing your interpretation as you rest your eyes.

Another way to avoid eye strain is to use oversize type in broadcast copy. Many radio and television stations make typewriters of this kind available to members of the news department. Commercials are reproduced with conventional type, but their brevity makes eye strain unlikely.

10. *Do you have any genuine interest in the subject matter of the copy? Do you reveal this interest?* Whatever the purpose or nature of the copy to be read, you must show an interest in it if you are to interpret it effectively. In many instances you will have a genuine interest in the subject; in others—say in introducing a candidate you dislike or reading commercial copy for a product you have never tried—you may have to work hard to generate interest. But as a professional, you cannot afford to show indifference or disrespect for persons, products, or musical selections, so you must try to put your feelings and biases aside.[1] You are an intermediary between those who supply information and those who receive it. You act as a magnifying glass: to enhance perceptions with the least possible distortion. In introducing *Tannhäuser,* it should not matter that you like Bach and detest Wagner; such prejudice has no place in your work. The admirers of any type of music deserve to have it introduced without antipathy.

In reading commercial announcements, the problem can be more critical. Any sensible announcer will find it difficult to deliver a paean of praise for a product he does not believe in. Even harder is delivering copy which offends listener and

---

[1] Several successful announcers, of course, have made their reputations on their prejudices.

announcer alike. Especially tasteless are certain radio commercials intended for youthful audiences, in which the disc jockey is required to use slang thought by some middle-aged copywriter to reflect the speech in vogue:

> ANNCR: (*to be read in a jivey, groovy, jazzy style, man*) Hey, there, you hip chicks, hearken to the word from THE MAN! Wanta flip the hip of that guy in your life? Well, then, y'all come hitherwards to THE THREAD, that groovy, grooviest den for young hens this side of else-where! Cast a glance at swim suits that y'hafta look at twice to see! (*Etc., etc., ad nauseam*)

Some stations refuse to run such commercials; some ask permission to rewrite or paraphrase the material; some allow the announcer to express his disdain for the copy; but most stations demand that the commercial be delivered effectively and without comment. How do you develop a belief in the product you are sell-ing under such circumstances? If you are smart, you will not try; if you are sensi-tive *and* smart, you will try to persuade management and agency personnel that bad copy results in bad business—for station and advertiser alike.

At least as offensive as the copy reproduced above is the type written for the radio and television "pitchman." The time may come when you will be asked to function as a contemporary counterpart of the old "medicine man." Regardless of the financial rewards, beware and be wary: respectable employers do not hire pitchmen. As far back as 1956, the National Association of Broadcasters spelled out the disservice to broadcasting rendered by the fast-talking "barker":

> The "pitchman" technique of advertising on television is inconsistent with good broadcast practice and generally damages the reputation of the industry and the advertising profession.
>
> Sponsored program-length segments consisting substantially of continuous demonstrations or sales presentations violate not only the time standards estab-lished in the Code but the broad philosophy of improvement implicit in the voluntary Code operation and are not acceptable.[2]

As with other offensive copy, the announcer who receives "pitchman" copy must decide whether he does or does not want to help disseminate it.

Even with good or merely acceptable copy, you may find yourself reading commercials for literally hundreds of different products; you cannot possibly develop a belief in each of them. Perhaps these guidelines will prove helpful: (1) where you must read a great many commercials, including those for compet-ing products, and where it is impossible to generate honest enthusiasm for all of them, the best you can do is read every one with as much effectiveness and interpretive skill as possible; (2) where you are the exclusive spokesman for a product, or have a long-time personal relationship with a sponsor, try to gain first-hand knowledge of the product and communicate your honest belief in it; (3) where you find yourself reading copy which is offensive or which advertises

---

[2] *The Television Code of the National Association of Radio and Television Broadcasters,* 1958 revision.

products you know to be inferior, work to have the copy changed or the account dropped; (4) where your best efforts are unsuccessful in changing or dropping bad copy, look for another job.

In introducing political candidates or news commentators whom you believe to be dangerous or foolish, you face again the problem of conscience: should you refuse to perform? A decision to leave is certainly more honest than remaining in the hope of lessening their effect.

Assuming that your announcing copy deserves genuine interest, how can you reflect it in your interpretation? Certainly not by ranting, raving, table-thumping, or fender-pounding. Honest enthusiasm is seldom noisy or obtrusive. It manifests itself in inner vitality and quiet conviction. If we listen to a politician addressing a huge crowd, we expect him to demonstrate his enthusiasm with vocal and physical histrionics. He usually is speaking on matters of national importance, and he is in a situation where he can exploit crowd psychology to build enthusiasm. As a radio or television announcer, you seldom will be dealing with life-or-death matters—advertisers to the contrary notwithstanding—and you will be speaking to small groups of people who are, in effect, only a few feet away. In a sense, you are a guest in their living rooms. Your conviction is revealed through a steady focus on your listeners, your earnestness, and your personality. Notice that this does not rule out the possibility of a humorous commercial or introduction. Being sincere does not mean being sombre!

11. *Who is your listener? Can you visualize him? Are you able to establish rapport with him? Are you actually talking to him?* Several aspects of this problem of communication have already been mentioned, but one more point needs to be made. Throughout most of this chapter we have referred to the problems of *reading* scripts. It might be better if you considered your job to be *talking* scripts. Even though you work from a script and your listeners know it, they appreciate it when you sound as if you are not merely reading aloud. The best way to achieve a conversational style is to visualize the person to whom you are speaking and talk your material to him.

12. *If the copy is "good literature," who is the author? Is it important to know his history and what he was trying to do in his writings?* As an announcer you may some day be engaged to read the words of a famous author. Aside from the normal considerations of script analysis, timing, phrasing, and mood determination, you should make a brief study of the author and his works. If, for example, you were hired to narrate a filmed documentary on the life of William Faulkner, you would do a better job if you could take to the script some information about his life, his strong ties to Oxford, Mississippi, his feelings about the South, the Snopes and Sartoris families and the forces they symbolically represent, and the criticism of his work. And this means research.

13. *Should you know anything about the origin and background of this copy?* Unlike brief commercials which tend to be self-explanatory, some longer and

more complex pieces will be better interpreted if you know the author and understand his intentions. Consider what you should find out before attempting these announcing assignments:

1. Narrating a series of radio programs on Afro-American history.
2. Narrating a series of television programs on the Soviet educational system.
3. Narrating a program on the American Constitution.
4. Narrating a program on the women's liberation movement.

Each of these jobs requires specialized knowledge and an understanding of the author's motivations. Commercials, quite obviously, are designed to sell products or services, but what are the purposes of the programs used above as examples? One good way to find out is by talking to authors, producers, and directors. On a basic level, you will learn whether the program is intended to be an objective "fact piece" or a position statement. You also may discover the mood the author wants conveyed. You can also question passages which puzzle you, suggest improvements, and ultimately do a better job of interpretation.

14. *Do you need to do any characterization?* You may be asked at times to read copy calling for characterization. Commercials and documentaries are often written for actors, but both free-lance and staff announcers may find themselves with such assignments. Courses in acting and participation in plays—including radio and television plays—will help you learn character interpretation. At times commercials call for no real characterization but do demand a foreign accent or a regional dialect. Most commonly, commercials are written for these dialects: Scandinavian, English, Irish, Scottish, German, Russian, "Transylvanian" (middle European), Southern, New England, and rustic Western. The dialects of most ethnic minorities in America are seldom heard today because they are considered harmful stereotypes. If you practice both characterization and dialects, your job opportunities will expand considerably.

These, then, are some points to be considered in preparing your copy. You cannot, of course, apply every point each time you pick up a piece of copy. In time you should develop a conditioned reflex which will allow you to size up a script and interpret it effectively without relying on a checklist. In the meantime, the suggestions above may help you spot your weaknesses and measure your progress.

Ad-Lib Announcing

At some point, you are sure to find yourself working without a script, when all your acquired skills of phonation, articulation, or interpretation cannot guarantee effective communication. When you are on your own as an ad-lib announcer, only your ability as a compelling conversationalist will earn you listeners. Much of the broadcast day consists of unscripted shows; disc jockeys, telephone-talk hosts ("communicasters"), interviewers, children's show personalities, and panel moderators are among those who seldom see a script and must conduct their programs spontaneously.

Ad-lib announcing can be practiced, but it is doubtful if it can be taught. The formula for success is easy to state but difficult to apply: know what you are talking about, be interested in what you are saying, be eager to communicate with your listener, and try to develop an attractive personality. The cardinal rule for any performer has been well stated by Dr. Hubert Heffner: *never bore your audience*. The ad-lib announcer has a greater opportunity to be boring than the reader of scripts. Scripts usually are tightly written, while ad-lib announcers often suffer from logorrhea. Scripts have specific objectives, while ad-lib announcers frequently ramble on with no apparent purpose in mind. Scripts call for interruptions only when they are motivated, but ad-lib announcers all too often throw in another question just as their guest is about to make an important point in answer to the *last* question. Despite pitfalls, the challenges and opportunities of ad-lib announcing make the endeavor worth the risks. With the criteria listed above as a guide, practice ad-libbing at every opportunity, using a tape recorder for self-evaluation.

A few more words about those criteria:

1. *Knowing your subject.*   Ordinarily we take this for granted. We expect a sportscaster to have a thorough knowledge of sports, and a disc jockey to know the music he plays. The problem arises when an announcer must ad-lib on an unfamiliar topic. As a staff announcer you may at any time be asked to interview a person about whom you know little and about whose special field you know nothing at all. Suppose, for example, you are to interview an astrophysicist about a discovery he has made. How would you prepare for this interview? Most radio and television stations maintain a "futures file"—a collection of press releases, newspaper and magazine clippings, and other factual and biographical material—and you might begin your research there. If time permits, you should extend your research to the kinds of reference works listed in Chapter 9. Having completed your research, you should be able to frame some tentative questions and write an opening and closing for your interview. (See Chapter 12.)

2. *Being interested in what you are saying.*   It seems superfluous even to raise this point, yet one who listens attentively to radio or television ad-lib announcers can detect many who seem to have no interest in what they are saying. Boredom, acquired through years of repetitious activity, is the cause of this malaise. The best cure is to try constantly to grow with your subject. The sports announcer who asks athletes today the same questions he asked twenty years ago deserves to be bored and boring.

3. *Wanting to communicate with your listeners.*   Only if you really want to communicate should you consider radio or television announcing in the first place. If you just want to speak *for* and *to* yourself, buy a tape recorder and have fun "doing your own thing."

4. *Developing an attractive personality.* Very little can be offered on this point. Most people who are attractive to others have found out how to be truly themselves, are able to show their interest in others, and have wide-ranging intellectual curiosity. Wit, wisdom, and charm are easily detected and warmly appreciated but hard to come by.

This chapter opened with the observation that "The key to successful radio and television announcing is the ability *to communicate as effectively as possible ideas or feelings to other human beings."* All of the ensuing suggestions were offered as various means to that end. In the last analysis, though, your success as an announcer will be determined by a factor which cannot be taught, studied, or purchased—talent. With talent, careful attention to the suggestions in this book can help you grow toward true professionalism; without it, hard work may develop your abilities to a level of adequacy, but further growth may be impossible. Before committing yourself to an announcing career, you should make a serious appraisal of your talent. First, assume that you *are* talented (mental outlook is terribly important for any performer; if you think you are untalented, you almost certainly will measure down to that level). Second, set yourself a target date for your evaluation, and establish a work regimen. Allow yourself at least six months of practice before attempting to appraise the results. Third, practice, practice, practice! Finally, evaluate as honestly and objectively as you can. If you have any doubts, ask qualified people to help you. Do not compare yourself with an established professional; he has twenty or thirty years' headstart. Your purpose is to measure your growth and your potential. If you discover that you simply do not have enough ability to satisfy your aspirations, face up to it. If, on the other hand, the evidence indicates a promising future, intensify your practice. If nothing more comes of your hard work, you will benefit from extended practice in oral communication.

Three The International Phonetic Alphabet

As an American announcer, you face unique and challenging problems in pronunciation. In music copy you must constantly read words in French, Spanish, Italian, German, and Russian fluently and correctly. In newscasting you are asked not only to master the correct pronunciation of all words and names in these and other languages, but to know as well when and how to Anglicize many of them. Unlike your British counterpart, you are not allowed to Anglicize categorically and will be thought odd if not incompetent if you say DON KWICKS-OAT for *Don Quixote*. And though you are expected to follow German rules of pronunciation when speaking the name of Richard Wagner, it now has become acceptable to Anglicize the name of George Frederick Handel.

As is well known, the pronunciation of American English is subject to few rules. Foreigners tell us that English is among the most difficult of languages to learn for this reason. Whereas in Spanish the letters *ch* are always pronounced as in the name *Charles,* in American English *ch* may be pronounced in the following different ways:

> *ch* — "sh" as in *Cheyenne.*
> *ch* — "tch" as in *champion.*
> *ch* — "k" as in *chemist.*
> *ch* — two separate sounds as in the name *Macheath.*

Other examples might be cited. The letter *a* is pronounced differently in such words as *cap, father, mate, care, call, boat,* and *about.* Similar variations are seen in all other vowel sounds and in most consonants as well. For example, *th* is pronounced differently in *Thomas, through,* and *then; r* is pronounced differently in *run, fire,* and *boor.* At times letters are silent, as in *mnemonic, Worcester,* and *Wednesday.* At other times and for as little reason, a word is correctly pronounced only when all letters in it receive some value, as *misunderstood* and *plenipotentiary.* The letters *ie* are sometimes pronounced "eye," as in *pie,* and sometimes "ee," as in *piece.* Two words with almost identical spellings, *said* and *maid,* have quite different pronunciations. In short, the only constant is variation and change.

Of course, common words like those above do not cause difficulty. But try to determine the correct pronunciation of the following words according to your knowledge of language and any "rules" of pronunciation you may have learned:

quay	flaccid	dais
mortgage	interstices	gunwale
medieval	forecastle	brooch
egregious	cliché	phthisic

After checking these words in any good dictionary, you certainly must agree that no amount of puzzling over the word and no available "rules" would have helped.

Correct American pronunciation of English is not only inherently illogical, it changes with time and common usage, generally tending toward simpler forms. It is becoming more and more acceptable to pronounce *clothes* KLOZE, for example, to leave the first *r* out of *February,* and to slide over the slight "y" sound in *news* so that it becomes NOOZ.

The whole problem of English pronunciation was reduced to its most obvious absurdity by George Bernard Shaw, who wrote the letters *ghoti* and asked how his manufactured word was to be pronounced. After all attempts had failed, Shaw answered that it was to be pronounced FISH. The *gh* is pronounced F as in *enough,* the *o* is pronounced I as in *women,* and the *ti* is pronounced SH as in *motion.*

If you have difficulty pronouncing words whose spelling offers little help, you may be doubly perplexed by American proper names and place names derived from foreign originals. As a sportscaster, for example, you cannot assume that a player named Braun gives his own name the correct German pronunciation, BROWN. He may pronounce it BRAWN or BRAHN. If you tried to pronounce every foreign-derived name as it would be pronounced in the country of origin, your audience would wince every time you failed to follow established custom. Of course, if the athlete in question *prefers* the original rather than the Anglicized pronunciation, you should follow his wishes.

American place names present the same problem. In Nebraska, Beatrice is pronounced BEE-AT'-RIS. In South Dakota, Pierre is pronounced PEER. In California, Delano is pronounced DUH-LANE'-O. In Kentucky, Versailles is pronounced VER-SALES'. In Georgia, Vienna is pronounced VYE-EN'-UH. Any community, of course, has the right to pronounce its name as it pleases. In the Southwest, Spanish place names are conventionally pronounced neither as the Spanish original nor as they seem to be spelled. The *San* in *San Jose* is pronounced SAN (as in *sand*) rather than the Spanish SAN (as in *sonnet*), and HO-ZAY is used rather than an Americanized JO-ZAY or the Spanish HO-SAY. Because the only standard for pronouncing place names is the common practice of the natives of the region, you must be on guard to avoid error. All American communities have specialized and capricious ways of pronouncing street names and the names of suburbs, nearby towns, and geographical landmarks; radio and television announcers who are new to an area and who consistently offend listeners with mispronunciations may not be around long enough to learn regional preferences. Bostonians may not care if you mispronounce *Pago Pago,* but they will be outraged if you make *Quincy* rhyme with *mince-ee.*

It is not surprising that the problems inherent in American pronunciation have given rise to various systems of phonetic transcription. The Associated Press and the United Press both phoneticize their copy where the pronunciation of a name or city is not commonly known. Their system may be understood from two examples:

(UPI)

    (BAD KREUZNACH / BAHT KROYTS'-NAHK / WEST

GERMANY) -- ARMY SPOKESMEN SAY VETERAN PARATROOPER

FRED JACKSON IS EAGER TO JUMP AGAIN, AS SOON AS

DOCTORS THINK HE'S READY.

(UPI)

    AN EXPRESS TRAIN ROARED OFF THE RAILS AT 70 MILES

AN HOUR NEAR THE TOWN OF BOLLENE (BOHL-LEHN'), WHILE

CARRYING VACATIONERS BACK TO PARIS FROM THE RIVIERA.

This system, about as simple and immediately usable as a system can be, is used widely not only in news copy but in music and sports copy as well. Though it is quite handy, it does have limitations. In the first place, the phonetic spellings are only approximate. In the case of *Bad Kreuznach,* above, the system allowed the transliterater to indicate that the final German "d" is sounded as a "t." The system failed, however, when it came to the German "ch," for no arrangement of English letters can indicate that this sound is to be pronounced like the Scottish "ch" in *loch.* In BOHL-LEHN', is the last syllable "lain," "lean," or "len"?

The limitations of wire service phonetics are well revealed by a notice carried on the UPI radio wire:

Imagine the problem of trying to make the twenty-six letters of the alphabet represent more than forty speech sounds! How would *you* phoneticize *A Shaw* to show that it rhymes with "how"? Clearly, SHOW is not satisfactory, since we immediately pronounce it "sho." What about SHAU? Not too good, since many would pronounce this like the first syllable in the name "Shaughnessy." In truth there simply is no foolproof way of using the English alphabet to indicate accurate pronunciation. The teletype machine is stuck with this limitation—at least for the time being—but the announcer is not. Although the majority of professional announcers have, over the years, preferred to use the crude system of phonetic transcription to which the typewriter is limited, there is no reason why you should settle for that. If you intend to spend the next thirty or forty years of your life as a speaker of words and a reader of scripts, a few hours spent learning a complete and accurate system of phonetic writing is a small investment in your future. If you listen carefully to newscasts in your area, you will detect the lengths to which some announcers go to eliminate from their news copy foreign words and names they cannot pronounce, even with the help of wire-service phonetics.

American dictionaries provide one system of phonetic transcription. Using the regular letters of the English alphabet (often with the addition of the schwa vowel, discussed on p. 51), they add to them marks or symbols indicating pronunciation. Thus, the letter "a," when given a straight line across its top—ā—is always pronounced as in *ale, fate,* or *labor*. These symbols, called diacritical marks, have at least three important limitations. First, they are difficult to learn and remember. After years of almost daily use of dictionaries, most of us still must check the meanings of the symbols at the bottom of each page. A second disadvantage is that diacritical marks were not designed for use by oral readers. The marks are small and vary only slightly in their configurations. When accuracy under pressure is demanded, diacritical markings often fail to meet the test. A final limitation of the dictionary method of transcription is that the key words used to identify symbols vary in pronunciation from area to area. To learn that *fog* is pronounced as *dog* tells a Texan that "fawg" rhymes with "dawg," just as it tells a Rhode Islander that "fahg" rhymes with "dahg." Most modern dictionaries have moved toward more accurate pronunciation guides; they have added symbols for foreign speech sounds, eliminated some ambiguity through the use of more standardized key words, and included a few pronunciation symbols from more sophisticated systems of phonetic transcription. They remain, however, less than satisfactory for serious students of speech.

To overcome the ambiguities of earlier systems of speech transcription, the International Phonetic Alphabet (IPA) was devised. Though it, like any other system which attempts to transcribe sounds into written symbols, is not totally accurate, it comes closer to perfection than any other system in widespread use. The International Phonetic Association has assigned individual written symbols to all the speech sounds of the major languages of the world. Thus, whether the language is French, German, or English, the symbol [e] is always pronounced "ay" as in *bait*. Speech sounds not found in English have distinct symbols—for example, [x] represents the sound *ch* as in the German word *ach* and no other sound, and [y] represents the sound *u* as in the French word *lune*.

Although IPA seems formidable at first, it is actually easier to learn than the system of diacritical markings found in dictionaries. You will find many uses for it and should make every effort to learn and practice it. Few professional announcers are familiar with IPA—and, it must be admitted, manage to get along quite well—but they would benefit from it. Most announcers have learned their craft in an entirely pragmatic way, through on-the-job training and years of trial and error. An organized, academic approach to the study of announcing is not really a substitute for job experience; properly considered, the study of announcing should both lay a foundation for and serve as an ongoing adjunct to professional experience. IPA, then, is a useful tool for accelerating professional growth. John A. Galbraith, now a college teacher of broadcasting but for many years an announcer, newscaster, and news director, has this to say about IPA:

> Only since I began to teach broadcast speech have I come to appreciate the true value of knowing and using the IPA. Would that I had possessed this tool during those frequent periods of my announcing and newscasting career when copy was filled with names and places that were complete strangers. The IPA would have saved me time, disagreements, and several embarrassing experiences.

The International Phonetic Alphabet has these advantages for the announcer: (1) it is an unvarying system of transcription in which one symbol represents only one speech sound; (2) every sound in any language, however subtle it may be, is invested with a separate symbol; (3) once the correct pronunciation of each sound is learned, it allows almost no possibility of error due to regional dialect; (4) it is the most nearly perfect system of describing human speech sounds yet devised.

As time goes by, IPA commands more and more attention. The excellent *NBC Handbook of Pronunciation* (New York: Thomas Y. Crowell, 1964)—virtually a "must" for any announcer—transcribes names and places into IPA. Many foreign-language dictionaries and texts use IPA to indicate correct pronunciation.

Drama departments use IPA to help teach dialects, and music departments use it to teach singers foreign pronunciation. The Kenyon and Knott *A Pronouncing Dictionary of American English* (Springfield, Mass.: G. & C. Merriam, 1953) and the *English Pronouncing Dictionary,* Thirteenth Edition, by Jones and Gimson (New York: E. P. Dutton, 1968) both transcribe exclusively into IPA.

Aside from its obvious value in coping with problems of pronunciation, IPA is useful in other ways. By breaking speech down into its component sounds and by investing each sound with a separate symbol, errors in phonation and articulation can be isolated, identified, and worked on. John Galbraith puts it this way:

> With knowledge of the IPA, it is possible for me to identify and compare various sounds of speech and *know* that what I perceive with ear and eye are valid auditory reference points with which to achieve good speech. They are the same sounds now and for the rest of my life, and will be perceived in nearly an identical manner by any other person in the world who knows the IPA. With this tool I have positive references by which I can learn and use speech appropriate to my time and location.

A further word on the use of IPA. As with any attempt to indicate correctness in speech sounds, IPA defines each sound in terms of its use in a particular word. Thus, in indicating the correct sound of the symbol [i], IPA tells us that it is pronounced as the vowel sound of the word *bee*. Though this poses no problem where the key word is pronounced uniformly throughout the United States and Canada, a distinct problem arises where regional variations in the pronunciation of the key words exist. For example, in southern British, as well as in the speech of eastern New England, the sound [ɑ], as in *father*, is not used in words spelled with *o*, and the sounds [ɒ], as in the eastern New England *wash*, and [ɔ], as in *bought*, are not differentiated; thus *bomb*, *wash*, and *bought* are all pronounced with the same vowel sound, which varies from [ɒ] to [ɔ]. This should be borne in mind when consulting Daniel Jones's *An English Pronouncing Dictionary*, where the phonetic character [ɔ] is used for all three of these vowel sounds. The speech sounds and the key words used in describing them are found in General American speech, unless otherwise indicated. The resident of any region of the United States or Canada where General American is not spoken should bear this in mind, since he will experience some difficulty learning IPA symbols if he gives the key word a regional pronunciation. Since General American is the most widely accepted speech for radio and television in the United States and Canada, you should make every effort to master it.

The International Phonetic Alphabet

IPA symbols represent vowel sounds, diphthongs or glides, and consonants. In this section of the book, only the sounds in American speech will be listed. Symbols for foreign speech sounds will be discussed in Chapter 5.

Vowels

Vowel sounds are classified as front vowels and back vowels, depending on where they are formed in the mouth. The front vowels are produced through the vibration of the vocal folds in the throat and are articulated by the tongue and teeth near the front of the mouth. The back vowels are produced in the same manner but are articulated by the tongue and mouth opening in the rear of the mouth. The front vowels are:

[i] This sound is pronounced "ee" as in *beet*. Phonetically, then, *beet* is spelled [bit].

[ɪ] This sound is pronounced "ih" as in *bit*. Phonetically, *bit* is spelled [bɪt].

[e] This sound is pronounced "ay" as in *bait*. Phonetically, *bait* is spelled [bet].

[ɛ] This sound is pronounced "eh" as in *bet*. Phonetically, *bet* is spelled [bɛt].

[æ] This sound is pronounced "aah" as in *bat*. Phonetically, *bat* is spelled [bæt].

[a] This sound is pronounced "aah," as the word *bath* is pronounced in the eastern United States. This sound is not usually heard in General American speech, but the symbol must be learned since it is a part of two of the diphthongs to be considered later. *Bath*, spelled phonetically as an Easterner would pronounce it, is [baθ].

These, then, are the front vowels:

Vowel	Key Word
[i]	*beet* [bit]
[ɪ]	*bit* [bɪt]
[e]	*bait* [bet]
[ɛ]	*bet* [bɛt]
[æ]	*bat* [bæt]
[a]	(*bath*) [baθ]

If you pronounce each of these sounds in turn, beginning at the top of the list and running to the bottom, you will find your mouth opening wider as you move from one sound to the next. As your mouth opens, your tongue is lowered and becomes increasingly relaxed. These symbols—like all phonetic symbols—should be written with characters of equal size. No capitals are used, even for proper nouns.[1]

Before moving on to the back vowels, it is necessary to discuss the two front vowels [i] and [ɪ]. If you look in an American or English dictionary, you may be surprised to discover that the final sounds of words such as *Friday*, *busy*, and *worry* are given the pronunciation [ɪ], as in *ill*. Now there can be no doubt that

[1] All IPA symbols have been enclosed in brackets throughout this book, and the use of brackets has been restricted to IPA symbols; thus, all letters and words which appear in brackets can be identified immediately as being IPA symbols rather than ordinary Roman letters.

in General American speech, as well as in the speech of most other sections of the country, these words have a distinct [i] sound. Kenyon and Knott, in their *Pronouncing Dictionary of American English*, take note of this fact, but indicate that minor variations in the pronunciation of this sound are too complex to pin down. They, like most other American dictionaries, simply use the [ɪ] symbol for those words in which the sound may actually be either [ɪ] or [i]. Thus they arrive at the pronunciation [sɪtɪ] for *city*. Though it is doubtful that more than an infinitesimal number of Americans actually pronounce the word in this manner, most Americans *do* pronounce the final sound in the word somewhere between a distinct [ɪ] and a distinct [i]. You are advised to make note of this discrepancy in phonetic transcription and to follow whatever practice seems to serve your needs best.

We move now to the six back vowels:

[ɑ] This sound is pronounced "ah" as in *bomb*. Phonetically, the word *bomb* is spelled [bɑm]. (Note: Because the English language makes much use of unsounded letters, like the final *b* in *bomb*, there is frequently an unconscious tendency to include these in phonetic transcriptions. You should remember that you are transcribing sounds, not letters, and should disregard all letters not sounded in the original spelling of the words.)

[ɒ] Except for eastern New England, this sound is heard infrequently in the United States. It is halfway between the [ɑ] sound, above, and the [ɔ] sound, below. It is sometimes heard in the word *wash*, when not given the customary pronunciation of [wɑʃ].

[ɔ] This sound is pronounced "aw" as in *bought*. Phonetically, *bought* is spelled [bɔt].

[o] This sound is pronounced "o" as in *boat*. Phonetically, *boat* is spelled [bot].

[ʊ] This sound is pronounced "ooh," as in *book*. Phonetically, *book* is spelled [bʊk].

[u] This sound is pronounced "oo" as in *boot*. Phonetically, *boot* is spelled [but].

Vowel	Key Word
[ɑ]	*bomb* [bɑm]
[ɒ]	(*wash*) [wɒʃ]
[ɔ]	*bought* [bɔt]
[o]	*boat* [bot]
[ʊ]	*book* [bʊk]
[u]	*boot* [but]

If you pronounce each of these vowel sounds in turn, you will find your mouth closing more and more and the sound being controlled at a progressively forward position in your mouth.

Only two other vowel sounds remain, "er" and "uh," unfortunately the two which cause the most trouble to students of phonetics. Before getting to their symbols, let us look at two words: *further* and *above*. In the word *further*, two "er" sounds appear. Pronounce this word aloud and you will discover that because of a stress on the first syllable, the two "ers" sound slightly different. The same is true of the two "uh" sounds in the word *above*. Because the first syllable of this word is unstressed while the second is stressed, there is a slight but definite difference in the two sounds. The International Phonetic Alphabet makes allowances for these differences by assigning two symbols each to the "er" and "uh" sounds:

[ɝ]   Stressed "er," as in the first syllable of *further*.
[ɚ]   Unstressed "er," as in the second syllable of *further*.
[ʌ]   Stressed "uh," as in the second syllable of *above*.
[ə]   Unstressed "uh," as in the first syllable of *above*.

The word *further*, then, is spelled [fɝðɚ] in IPA, and *above* is spelled [əbʌv]. The unaccented "uh" sound—[ə]—is given a special name—the "schwa" vowel. Naturally, in a one-syllable word with an "uh" or an "er" sound, the sound is stressed. For this reason in all one-syllable words both "er" and "uh" are represented by their stressed symbols:

bird [bɝd]   *sun* [sʌn]

church [tʃɝtʃ]   *come* [kʌm]

One exception to this rule occurs in foreign phrases, where a phrase such as *Voici le chapeau* will be so run together as to make the "uh" in the *le* become a schwa: [vwɑsiləʃɑpo]. ·

Diphthongs

A diphthong actually is a combination of two vowel sounds. If you will say aloud the "ow" of *how*, you will notice that it cannot be completed without moving the lips. There is no way of holding the sound of the entire diphthong; you can hold only the last of the two vowels of which it is formed. The diphthong "ow" as in *how* is actually the rapid movement from the vowel [a] to the vowel [ʊ]. The English diphthongs are:

[aɪ]   This sound is pronounced as a rapid combination of the two vowels [a] and [ɪ]. The key word is *bite*, spelled [baɪt] in IPA.

[aʊ]   This sound is pronounced as a rapid combination of the two vowels [a] and [ʊ]. The key word is *how*, transcribed as [haʊ] in IPA.

[ɔɪ]   This sound is pronounced as a rapid combination of the two vowels [ɔ] and [ɪ]. The key word is *toy*, transcribed [tɔɪ] in IPA.

[ju]   This sound is pronounced as a rapid combination of the two sounds [j] and [u]. The key word is *using*, transcribed as [juziŋ] in IPA.

[ɪu] This sound is pronounced as a rapid combination of the two vowels [ɪ] and [u]. The key word is *fuse*, transcribed as [fɪuz] in IPA. (Notice the subtle difference between the sounds of the last two diphthongs.)

In addition to these diphthongs, the vowel [e], as in *bait*, is actually a diphthong, since its pronunciation in a word such as *say* involves a glide from [e] to [i]. In other instances—the word *fate*, for example—the [e] is cropped off more closely. Because it changes according to context, the [e] sound may be transcribed either as a pure vowel, [e], or as a diphthong, [eɪ]. It will be so found in various dictionaries and other works using IPA.

The diphthongs, then, are:

Diphthong	Key Word
[aɪ]	*bite* [baɪt]
[aʊ]	*how* [haʊ]
[ɔɪ]	*toy* [tɔɪ]
[ju]	*using* [juzɪŋ]
[ɪu]	*fuse* [fɪuz]
[eɪ]	(*say*) [seɪ]

Consonants

With few exceptions, the IPA symbols for consonant sounds are their American-English equivalents. The consonants are therefore the most readily mastered IPA symbols.

In general, consonants may be classified as either voiced or unvoiced. If you say aloud the letters, *b* and *p*, cutting off each without adding a vowel sound, you will notice that each is produced in exactly the same way, except that *b* involves phonation (a vibration of the vocal folds) and *p* is merely exploded air, with no phonation at all. Since most consonants are related this way, they will be listed in their paired relationships rather than alphabetically.

[p] This is exploded air with no phonation, as in *poor* [pʊr].
[b] This is a phonated explosion, as in *boor* [bʊr].

[t] This is exploded air with no phonation, as in *time* [taɪm].
[d] This is a phonated explosion, as in *dime* [daɪm].

[k] This is exploded air with no phonation, as in *kite* [kaɪt].
[g] This is a phonated explosion, as in *guide* [gaɪd].

[f] This is escaping air with no phonation, as in *few* [fɪu].
[v] This is escaping air with phonation, as in *view* [vɪu].

[θ] This is escaping air with no phonation, as in *thigh* [θaɪ]. It is similar to the consonant [f] but has a different placement of the tongue and lips. The Greek letter theta [θ] is its symbol, making it easier to remember.
[ð] This is escaping air but with phonation, as in *thy* [ðaɪ].

[s] This is escaping air without phonation, as in *sing* [sɪŋ].
[z] This is escaping air with phonation, as in *zing* [zɪŋ].

[ʃ] This is escaping air without phonation, as in *shock* [ʃɑk].
[ʒ] This is escaping air with phonation, as in *Jacques* (French) [ʒɑk].

[tʃ] This is an unvoiced, or unphonated, combination of [t] and [ʃ]. It is pronounced as one sound, as in *chest* [tʃɛst].

[dʒ] This is a voiced, or phonated, combination of [d] and [ʒ]. It is pronounced as one sound, as in *jest* [dʒɛst].

These are the paired consonants. The following ones have no direct counterparts.

[h] This is an unvoiced sound, as in *how* [haʊ].
[hw] This is an unvoiced sound, as in *when* [hwɛn].
[m] This is a voiced sound, as in *mom* [mɑm].
[n] This is a voiced sound, as in *noun* [naʊn].
[ŋ] This is a voiced sound, as in *sing* [sɪŋ].
[l] This is a voiced sound, as in *love* [lʌv].
[w] This is a voiced sound, as in *watch* [wɑtʃ].
[j] This is a voiced sound, as in *yellow* [jɛlo].
[r] This is a voiced sound, as in *run* [rʌn].

Most consonants present relatively little difficulty, but a few are potential sources of confusion and deserve special consideration.

The word *fire* is usually pronounced [faɪɚ] in the United States, but it is frequently transcribed as [faɪr] by the authors of dictionaries and phonetics texts. The problem here is that the "r" sound in a word such as *run* is really quite different from the "r" sound in the word *fire*, which is to say that the "r" sound differs depending on its position in a word. Beyond this, there is yet another difference: the *r* in *boor* is different from the *r* in *fire*, even though both are in the same position in the words and both follow vowel sounds. This difference stems from the fact that it is easy to produce an [r] after the vowel [ʊ] but difficult to produce an [r] after the diphthong [aɪ]. If you transcribe *fire* in the conventional manner as a one-syllable word—[faɪr]—you must be careful to avoid having it become [far], as it is often pronounced in the South.

Certain combinations of sounds may be transcribed in two ways, either of which is as accurate as the other. The word *flattery*, for example, may be transcribed either [flætɚi] or [flætəri]. The difference in the way [ɚ] and [ər] are pronounced is imperceptible to most ears.

Another potential source of trouble comes from the plural ending "s." Years of conditioning have taught us that most plurals end in an "s," though in actuality they end in a "z" sound—*brushes, masters, dozens, kittens,* and so on. Make certain, when transcribing into IPA, that you do not confuse the two symbols [s] and [z].

The common construction –*ing* tends to make one think of a combination of [n] and [g] when transcribing a word like *singing*. Many students transcribe this as [sɪngɪng]. In IPA a distinct symbol, [ŋ], is used for the "ng" sound. The correct transcription of *singing* is [sɪŋɪŋ]. Another common error is to add a [g] after the [ŋ]. This is, of course, unnecessary and incorrect.

The symbol [j] is never used to transcribe a word like *jump*. The symbol [dʒ] is used for this sound. The symbol [j] is always pronounced as in *young* [jʌŋ], *yes* [jɛs], and *William* [wɪljəm]. The symbol [y] is used only to represent a sound in the French and German languages.

Note that many of the consonants change their sounds as they change their positions in words or are combined with different vowel sounds. We have already seen how the "r" sound does this. A similar change takes place in the "d" sound. Note it in the first syllable of the word *dazed*. Because the initial *d* is followed by a vowel sound, [e], the *d* is sounded. But where the *d* appears in the final position of the word, it is merely exploded air and is only slightly different from the sound a *t* would make in the same position. The only way the final *d* could be sounded would be if a slight schwa sound were added.

The syllabic consonants. Three of the consonants, [m], [n], and [l], can be sounded as separate syllables without a vowel sound before or after them. Though a word such as *button* may be pronounced [bʌtən], in colloquial speech the [ə] sound often is missing, and the word is represented [bʌtn̩]. In such a transcription, as you can see, the syllabic consonant is represented by a short line under the symbol. A few words using the syllabic consonants follow:

button [bʌtn̩]	*punkin* [pʌŋkn̩]
see 'em [sim̩]	*hokum* [hokm̩]
saddle [sædl̩]	*apple* [æpl̩]

Accent and Length Marks

Accent marks. Thus far most of the words transcribed into IPA have been of one syllable. Polysyllabic words must be transcribed with accent marks to indicate the relative stress to be placed on the various syllables. In the word *familiar* we have three syllables, [fə], [mɪl], and [jɚ]. In General American speech the first of these syllables receives little stress, the second receives the primary emphasis, and the third receives about the same degree of emphasis as the first. To indicate relative stress in a word, IPA uses a mark ['] *before* the syllable being modified. If the line is placed above the syllable, as before the first syllable in the word *facing* ['fesɪŋ], it indicates that the syllable is to receive the primary accent in the word. If the mark is placed below the syllable, as before the first syllable of the word farewell [ˌfɛr'wɛl], it indicates that the syllable is to receive secondary accent. A third degree of stress is possible for which no mark is provided—namely, an unstressed sound. To clarify this, let us take the word *satisfaction*. A continuous line, drawn under the word, indicating the degrees of accent or stress placed on the syllables when uttering them, would look about like this:

sæt ɪs fæk ʃən

⎯⎯⏜⏝⎯⎯⎯⎯

From this line we can see that there are three rather distinct degrees of emphasis in the word. This word would be transcribed [ˌsætisˈfækʃən]. The primary mark is used for the syllable [fæk], the secondary mark for the syllable [sæt], and no mark at all for the two unstressed syllables, [ɪs] and [ʃən]. Because secondary stress varies from slightly less than primary stress to slightly more than the unstressed syllables in a word, the secondary accent mark is used for a wide range of emphasis, although it is used only once per polysyllabic word.

Because the schwa vowel [ə] and the unaccented [ɚ] vowel are by definition unstressed, they need no further mark to indicate stress. Because the [ʌ] vowel and the [ɝ] vowel are by definition stressed, they, too, need no additional mark where they appear in a word. The words *further* [fɝˈðɚ] and *above* [əbʌv] may thus be transcribed without accent marks of any kind.

The length mark.   The colon [ː] appearing after any phonetic symbol indicates that the sound immediately preceding it is to be prolonged. This is most common in foreign words and names, as in the name of the Italian composer Puccini [putʃiːni].

For handy reference, all IPA symbols used to transcribe American-English speech are listed below.

VOWELS

SYMBOL	KEY WORD	SYMBOL	KEY WORD
[i]	*beet* [bit]	[ɔ]	*bought* [bɔt]
[ɪ]	*bit* [bɪt]	[o]	*boat* [bot]
[e]	*bait* [bet]	[ʊ]	*book* [bʊk]
[ɛ]	*bet* [bɛt]	[u]	*boot* [but]
[æ]	*bat* [bæt]	[ɝ]	*bird* [bɝd]
[a]	*bath* [baθ] (Eastern)	[ɚ]	*bitter* [bɪtɚ]
[ɑ]	*bomb* [bɑm]	[ʌ]	*sun* [sʌn]
[ɒ]	*wash* [wɒʃ] (infrequent)	[ə]	*sofa* [ˈsofə]

DIPHTHONGS

[aɪ]	*bite* [baɪt]	[ju]	*using* [ˈjuzɪŋ]
[aʊ]	*how* [haʊ]	[ɪu]	*fuse* [fɪuz]
[ɔɪ]	*toy* [tɔɪ]	[eɪ]	*say* [seɪ]

CONSONANTS

[p]	*poor* [pʊr]	[ʃ]	*shock* [ʃak]
[b]	*boor* [bʊr]	[ʒ]	*Jacques* [ʒak]
[t]	*time* [taɪm]	[tʃ]	*chest* [tʃɛst]
[d]	*dime* [daɪm]	[dʒ]	*jest* [dʒɛst]
[k]	*kite* [kaɪt]	[h]	*how* [haʊ]
[g]	*guide* [gaɪd]	[hw]	*when* [hwɛn]
[f]	*few* [fɪu]	[m]	*mom* [mɑm]
[v]	*view* [vɪu]	[n]	*noun* [naʊn]
[θ]	*thigh* [θaɪ]	[ŋ]	*sing* [sɪŋ]
[ð]	*thy* [ðaɪ]	[l]	*love* [lʌv]
[s]	*sing* [sɪŋ]	[w]	*watch* [wɑtʃ]
[z]	*zing* [zɪŋ]	[j]	*yellow* [jɛlo]
		[r]	*run* [rʌn]

Drill Material

Transcribe the following simple words into IPA:

1. ten   _____

2. goat   _____

3. sat   _____

4. wait   _____

5. which   _____

6. shoot   _____

7. whither   _____

8. murder   _____

9. church   _____

10. mutter   _____

11. caught   _____

12. looking   _____

13. easy   _____

14. awhile   _____

15. louder   _____

16. usable   _____

17. loiter   _____

18. about   _____

19. bombing   _____

20. moisten   _____

(Correct transcriptions of these words, pronounced as in General American speech, will be found on page 243.)

For additional practice, transcribe any of the passages from this book into IPA. Always remember, however, that IPA is used to transcribe *speech*, not written words. Pronounce the word aloud as you write it, preferably breaking it down into its component sounds. In transcribing the word "broken," for instance, say to yourself the very first sound, "b," then add the second, "br," then the third, "bro," and so on. Because one sound in a word may condition the sound which precedes or follows it, it is suggested that an additive process like this be followed rather than an approach which isolates each sound from all others.

Four Voice and Diction

The obvious success of some radio and television announcers who possess barely adequate to downright poor voices and are apparently incapable of good articulation would seem to indicate that a pleasing voice and good diction are unimportant. This assumption, however, fails to consider the following points: (1) Most announcers who have poor voices have already gained fame in some other field, *e.g.*, sports, news reporting, music, or politics. (2) Those who have poor voices and have gained their fame entirely on radio or television generally possess rare and compelling personalities. (3) Although you may not have a good innate speaking voice, you can improve the one you have. There can be no excuse for failing to improve your speaking voice and to acquire good habits of diction.

For these reasons, then, the present chapter will help you isolate, define, and analyze your speech abilities and problems. It will also provide exhaustive drill material for correcting minor speech problems. It is not, however, to be considered a substitute for a qualified speech correctionist in cases where problems are more serious. In discussing the speech sounds of the English language, the symbols of the International Phonetic Alphabet (IPA) will be used for unequivocal accuracy (see Chapter 3). If you have not yet mastered IPA, a more conventional, though crude, system of phonetic transcription is given, as well.

Your "speech personality" is made up of seven variables: (1) pitch, (2) volume, (3) tempo, (4) pronunciation, (5) vitality or enthusiasm, (6) voice quality, and (7) articulation.

Pitch

Unless yours is a special case, you should speak at the lowest comfortable pitch level. Be careful, however, to avoid establishing your pitch so low that you cannot go still lower for selected words; you will sound strained and monotonous.

There are several ways of determining your optimum pitch, including one which involves using a piano. Sit at the piano and sing the scale as high and low as you comfortably can, striking the note which accompanies each sound. You probably will find that your range covers about two octaves. Your optimum speaking pitch should be a note close to the midpoint of the lower of the two octaves. Now, begin reading a prose passage. When you come to a vowel that can be prolonged, strike the note that should be your optimum pitch and see if you are above or below it. Check your own conclusions with a qualified speech teacher.

Volume

Volume level is seldom a problem in broadcast speech. Microphones are so sensitive that they pick up even the weakest voices. You should, therefore, speak at the most comfortable volume which brings out your best vocal quality. If you need to speak up, you may be sure that the audio operator will tell you so. Your volume level for most radio and television work should approximate the level of conversation in a quiet room. Occasionally you may find yourself overprojecting when appearing on a television program using a boom mike which is several feet away and over your head. Because you cannot see the microphone, you may find yourself trying to "throw" your voice to the camera, which may be fifteen feet away. But because your audience is, in effect, only three or four feet away and because boom mikes are extremely sensitive and highly directional, you need not speak above a normal conversational level.

Tempo

As mentioned on page 176, your rate of delivery will often be determined by the number of words to be read in a given period of time. Beyond this, there is no "correct" speed at which you should speak or read. A different rate of delivery is appropriate for slug commercials, relaxed commercials, newscasts, interviews, musical introductions. Where no time limit is imposed, gear your reading speed to the mood of the copy. Keep in mind that most of us speak too rapidly much of the time. Listen carefully to your readings on a tape recorder and decide whether you need to work consciously on slowing down or speeding up. Aside from a good basic rate of delivery, you should also work for variety in speed. Speeding up for "throw-away" lines and slowing down for emphatic statements will help you give more meaning to your copy.

Pronunciation

"Correct" pronunciation for broadcasting, as established by the major networks and most radio and television stations, is based on the speech spoken, with slight regional variations, by the majority of well-educated Americans and English-speaking Canadians. This speech is called "General American." Loose and un-scientific though this name is, it is about as close to one as we can get. There is, of course, really no "correct" American pronunciation; most of us, from whatever region, enjoy the idiosyncrasies of speech of all regions. And today it is the practice of many stations and networks to subordinate their earlier emphasis on General American speech to other criteria: ability to communicate, warmth, poise, expert knowledge of a subject, wit, or an outstanding ability to ad-lib. Despite this, you will have a wider choice of announcing opportunities if you cultivate General American speech. It is especially important to avoid the substandard speech sounds of some regions, for example, the nasalized and prolonged [aʊ], as in the word *cow*, heard in parts of the West and Midwest; the glottal stop of some residents of the East, as in the word *bottle* [bɑʔl]; the thick and whistling "s" sounds heard occasionally in the Southwest; and the hard [æ] sounds and the transformation of [t] into [d] in words such as *cattle* and *battle*, heard in the Far West.

For an example of General American speech, listen to the reading of "William and His Friends" on the LP record made to accompany this text and available from the publisher.

Vitality

Two speakers with nearly identical speech habits and qualities may sound quite different if they vary greatly in vitality or enthusiasm. Though speed and vitality often are directly related, they are not necessarily interdependent. Some speakers are slow, deliberate, but intense, while others are fast-paced but unenthusiastic. Most announcers are able to increase or decrease the vitality of their performances and do so according to the mood or the purpose of the occasion. But beyond normal adjustments for appropriateness, you should avoid forcing yourself to adopt a degree of vitality which is out of phase with your personality and your vocal characteristics. Most speakers are at their best when they are being themselves; you may need years of study and practice to develop your latent speech potential, but you will waste your time and energy if you try to substitute a made-up personality for your own.

Voice Quality and Articulation

The remainder of this chapter is concerned with voice quality and articulation—the two most important and demanding aspects of human speech. Speech is the process of making meaningful sounds. These sounds are created (in the English language) by vibration of the vocal folds or cords, nasal resonance, and exploded air. Speech sounds are controlled and patterned by the degree of closure of the throat, the use or lack of use of the nasal passages, the placement of the tongue, the use of the teeth, and the use of the lips. Problems arising from improper use of vocal folds and resonance cavities are problems of *quality;* those arising from improper placement or use of the articulators are problems of *articulation.*

The following readings were designed to discover minor problems in voice quality and articulation. In each, all speech sounds of the English language appear in initial, medial, and final positions. Each sound is given at least once, with the more common sources of speech difficulty given at least twice. The passages are nonsensical, but you should read them as though they made a great deal of sense. Try to use your regular patterns of inflection and stress and your normal delivery rate so that errors in voice quality or articulation can be detected. After recording the first passage, "William and His Friends," compare your performance with that on the LP record prepared to accompany this text. By doing so, you should be able to spot any variations in voice production and control and then decide whether they are extreme enough to be changed. The same reading can be used to determine whether or not you are using General American speech.

WILLIAM AND HIS FRIENDS

This is the story of a little boy named William.

He lived in a small town called Marshville. Friends

he had galore, if one may judge by the vast numbers

of children who visited his abode. Every day after

school through the pathway leading to his house, the

little boys and girls trudged along, singing as though

in church. Out into the yard they came, a vision of

juvenile happiness. But, joyous though they were,

they served only to work little William up into a

lather. For, although he assuaged his pain with comic

books and the drinking of milk, William abhorred the

daily routine. Even Zero, his dog, was aghast at the

daily appearance of the running, singing, shuffling,

open-mouthed fellows and girls. Beautiful though the

sight may have been, William felt that they used the
avenue leading to his abode as an awesome item of lush
malfeasance. Their little oily voices only added fuel
to the fire, for William hated music. "Oooo," he would
say, "they mew like cats, baa like sheep, and moo like
a cow. My nerves are raw." Then back into his menage
the little gigolo would scamper, fast action earnestly
being his desire.

To the long-suffering instructor of announcing who has had as much of William
as he can take, the following alternate reading is dedicated:

THE BATTLE OF ATTERBURY

The big battle was on! Cannons thundered and
machine guns chattered. The troops, weary after
months of constant struggle, found themselves reju-
venated by a vision of triumph. Atterbury, the junc-
tion of three main roads, was on the horizon. Using
whatever annoying tricks he could, Jacques Deatheridge,
the former millionaire playboy, was much in charge as
he eyed the oil capitol of the feudal republic. Few
men would now say that the Beige Berets had not cashed
in on Jacques' flash of genius. Then the rather uncommon English fellow, a zany half-wit to many who now
would writhe in agony, looked puzzled for a moment;

the mob on top of Manhasset Hill was frantically throw-

ing him a signal. He snatched the message from the

courier. "My gracious," he muttered, "Atterbury is

our own capitol!" Elated, nonetheless, he invited

his overawed band to play in his honor. After a solo

on the drums, Jacques spoke to the multitude: "Re-

joice, my fellow citizens! All is not bad! At least

our troops have won one victory!"

Speech sounds may be classified in a number of ways. First of all, we classify sounds as vowels, diphthongs, and consonants. A vowel is defined (rather loosely) as a pure phonated tone which does not use the articulators and which can be held indefinitely without changing. If you will say aloud the vowel [ɑ] (AH) you will note that you can hold it as long as your breath lasts without substantial change in its sound. Now say aloud [ɔɪ] (OY), a diphthong. You will note that the sound glides from [ɔ] to [ɪ] and that you cannot hold a pure tone. You *can* hold the last part of this sound indefinitely, but that is only because it turns into [ɪ], a pure vowel. Now, try to say aloud the consonant [p]. You will note that, unless you add to this sound some vowel sound, you cannot even say it: the [p] is merely exploded air and cannot be prolonged. Other consonants, such as [n], *can* be prolonged, but note that as soon as you stop using your articulators (in this in-stance the tip of the tongue has been placed on the gum ridge behind the upper front teeth), the sound turns into the vowel [ʌ]. Consonants, then, may or may not use phonation but necessarily use the articulators.

Vowels

The English language contains twelve vowel sounds (phonemes), if we do not consider the three or four sounds which lie between members of these twelve and which occur rarely—and on a regional basis only—in American speech (see Chapter 3). These sounds are usually classified according to the placement in the mouth of the tongue, the only articulator which materially affects their pro-duction.

[i]   The vowel [i] (EE), as in *beet* [bit], is formed by holding the mouth slightly open, placing the tip of the tongue on the back surface of the lower front teeth, and arching the tongue toward the front of the mouth so that the sides of the tongue are in contact with the molars.

[ɪ]   The vowel [ɪ] (ɪʜ), as in *bit* [bɪt], is formed by placing the tip of the tongue on the back surface of the lower front teeth and lowering and relaxing the tongue slightly more than for the [i].

[e]   The [e] (ᴀʏ) sound, as in *bait* [bet], is formed much the same as the [ɪ] sound, but the mouth is in a more open position and the tongue lies almost flat in the mouth.

[ɛ]   The [ɛ] (ᴇʜ) sound, as in *bet* [bɛt], finds the mouth still farther open than for the [e] sound, but with the tongue in just about the same relative position.

[æ]   The [æ] (ᴀᴀʜ) sound, as in *bat* [bæt], finds the mouth quite open and the tongue lying flat on the bottom of the mouth. A certain tenseness in the jaws is noticeable.

[ɝ]   The [ɝ] and [ɚ] (ᴇʀ) sounds, as in *bird* [bɝd] and *bitter* [bɪtɚ], are formed by holding the mouth slightly open and holding the tongue back in the mouth, with the tip poised somewhere about the midpoint between the hard palate and the floor of the mouth.

[ʌ]   The [ʌ] and [ə] (ᴜʜ) sounds, as in *sun* [sʌn] and *sofa* ['sofə], are formed by holding the mouth slightly open with the tongue flat on the bottom of the mouth. The tongue is quite relaxed.

[u]   The [u] (oo) sound, as in *boot* [but], is formed by holding the front of the tongue in approximately the same position as for the [i] sound, but with the rear of the tongue in a raised position. The lips are rounded and extended.

[ʊ]   The [ʊ] sound, as in *book* [bʊk], is formed in much the same way as the [u], except that the lips are more relaxed and slightly more open.

[o]   The [o] (oʜ) sound, as in *boat* [bot], is made by rounding the lips and raising the tongue slightly in the rear of the mouth.

[ɔ]   The [ɔ] (ᴀᴡ) sound, as in *bought* [bɔt], is made by holding the lips open (but not rounded) and raising the tongue slightly in the rear. The tip of the tongue lies low on the gum ridge under the front lower teeth.

[ɑ]   The [ɑ] (ᴀʜ) sound, as in *bomb* [bɑm], is made with the mouth quite open and the tongue lying flat and relaxed in the mouth.

No special exercises for faulty formation of vowel sounds are given, since the drills which accompany the following sections on diphthongs and consonants are as suitable as any for this purpose.

Diphthongs

The diphthong, or glide, as it is sometimes called, is a combination of two vowel sounds spoken in rapid order, with a glide from one sound to the other. The diphthongs are represented in the alphabet of the International Phonetic Association by a combination of the two vowels which form them. Unfortunately for the learner, however, IPA has chosen to use [a] instead of the more common [ɑ], and [ɪ] instead of the more correct [i] in some of these symbols. The diphthongs and their symbols are:

[aɪ]   as in *bite* [baɪt]
[aʊ]   as in *bout* [baʊt]
[ɔɪ]   as in *boy* [bɔɪ]
[ju]   as in *beauty* ['bjuti]

The vowel [e], as may be detected by saying it aloud, is actually a glide, since the sound quite definitely goes from [e] (AY) to [ɪ] (IH). It is, therefore, sometimes considered a diphthong and is given the symbol [eɪ] in IPA.

The diphthongs are sources of trouble to many students. There is a tendency in many parts of the United States to nasalize the [aʊ] diphthong, or to turn it into some other sound. If you have trouble with the diphthongs, practice making each of the vowel sounds which form them and then speak them with increasing rapidity. The following exercises will help only if you are producing the sounds of the diphthongs correctly.

Exercises

[aɪ]   1. I like my bike.
2. Lie in the silo on your side.
3. Fine nights for sighing breezes.
4. Why try to lie in the blinding light?
5. Si tried to fly his kite.
6. My fine wife likes to fly in my glider.
7. Try my pie—I like it fine.
8. Shy guys find they like to cry.
9. My sly friend likes to be wined and dined.
10. Like all fine and right-minded guys, Mr. Wright liked best to try to find the slightest excuse to lie about his life.

[aʊ]   1. Flounce into my mouse's house.
2. Cows allow just about too much proudness about them.
3. Round and round went the loudly shouting lout.
4. A mouse is somewhat louder than a louse in a house.
5. A bounding hound went out on the bounding main.
6. Grouse are lousy bets when abounding results are found.
7. A cow and a mouse lived in a house.
8. The louder they proudly cried, the more the crowd delighted in seeing them trounced.
9. They plowed the drought-stricken cow pasture.
10. Allow the grouse to shout louder and louder, and you just about drown out the proud cows.

[ɔɪ] 1. A toy needs oiling.
    2. The soybeans are joyously coiling.
    3. Floyd oiled the squeaky toy.
    4. Goya painted Troy in oils.
    5. His annoying voice was boiling mad.
    6. The oyster exploited the joyous foil.
    7. Roy and Lloyd soiled the toys.
    8. Joy, like a spoiled boy, exploited his friends.
    9. Hoity-toity men make Lloyd boil.
   10. What kind of noise annoys an oyster?
       A noisy noise annoys an oyster.

[ju] 1. A few beautiful girls are using perfume.
    2. I used to refuse to use abusive news.
    3. The kitten mewed, but I refused to go.
    4. The music was used to enthuse.
    5. The beautiful view used to confuse.
    6. June was beautiful.
    7. The newest pupil was wearing his suit.
    8. The cute kitten mewed.
    9. He eschewed responsibility for the news.
   10. The few new musical numbers were confusing to the beautiful girl.

Consonants

There are twenty-five consonant sounds (phonemes) in the English language. They may be classified in a number of ways, the most basic of which is according to whether they are voiced or not. Thus the letter *b*, spoken with a vibration of the vocal folds, is called a voiced consonant, whereas *p*, formed in exactly the same way but not phonated, is called an unvoiced consonant. A more detailed (and thus more useful) system of classification describes how the sound is formed. On this basis the consonants are classified as:

1. *Plosives.* These sounds begin with the air from the throat blocked off, and with a release of the air the sound is formed. The plosive consonants are [p], [b], [t], [d], [k], and [g].

2. *Fricatives.* These sounds are created by the friction of air through a restricted air passage. The fricative consonants are [f], [v], [θ] (as in *thin*), [ð] (as in *the*), [z], [s], [ʃ] (as in *shoe*), [ʒ] (as in *vision*), [j] (as in *yellow*), [h], and [hw] (as in *when*).

3. *Nasals.* These sounds are resonated in the nasal cavity. The nasal consonants are [n], [m], and [ŋ] (as in *sing*).

4. *Semivowels.* These sounds are similar to the true vowels in their resonance patterns. The consonants [w], [r], and [l] are the semivowels.

5. *Affricates.* These sounds combine a plosive with a fricative. The consonants [tʃ] (as in *choose*), and [dʒ] (as in *jump*) are the affricates.

One final method of classifying speech sounds must be mentioned—the system that describes the consonants according to their place of articulation. In this classification the consonants are described as:

1. *Labial or bilabial.* The lips are primarily responsible for the consonants so described. Labial consonants are [p], [b], [m], [w], and, in a less obvious way, [hw].

2. *Labiodental.* In forming these sounds, the lower lip is in close proximity to the upper teeth. Labiodental consonants are [f] and [v].

3. *Interdental or lingua-dental.* In these sounds the tongue is between the upper and lower teeth. Interdental consonants are [θ] (as in *thin*) and [ð] (as in *then*).

4. *Lingua-alveolar.* In these consonants the tip of the tongue (lingua) is placed against the upper gum ridge (alveolus). The lingua-alveolar consonants are [n], [t], [d], [s], [z],[1] and [l].

5. *Lingua-palatal.* In these sounds, the tip of the tongue touches (or nearly touches) the hard palate, just behind the gum ridge. Lingua-palatal consonants are [j] (as in *yellow*), [r] (as in *rain*), [ʃ] (as in *shoe*), [ʒ] (as in *vision*), [tʃ] (as in *chew*), and [dʒ] (as in *jump*).[2]

6. *Lingua-velar.* In these sounds, the rear of the tongue is raised against the soft palate (velum), and the tip of the tongue is lowered to the bottom of the mouth. Lingua-velar consonants are [k], [g], and [ŋ] (as in *sing*).

7. *Glottal.* The glottal consonant, [h], is formed by a passage of air between the vocal folds, but without vibration of those folds.

These various methods of classification will prove helpful in discussing the consonants since they quite accurately describe their most significant characteristics. In the following discussion, as in Chapter 3, voiced and unvoiced consonants formed in the same way are considered together.

[b]   The consonant [b] is a voiced, labial plosive. It is formed by first stopping the flow of air by closing the lips, then releasing the built-up air as though in an explosion.

Exercises

1. Big Bill bent the bulky box.
2. The Boston Bull was bigger than the boy.

[1] Many people form the [s] and the [z] with the tip of the tongue against the *lower* gum ridge. If no speech difficulty results from this, there is no reason to change it.
[2] Some speech authorities classify [ʃ], [ʒ], [tʃ], and [dʒ] as lingua-alveolar sounds, but the preponderance of modern scholarly opinion places them in the lingua-palatal category.

3. Libby lobbed the sobbing lobster.
4. The ribbing was robbed from the jobber.
5. Bob could rob the mob.
6. The boxer baited the big boy, while the mobster hobbled about the sobbing, crabby boy named Bob.

[p] The consonant [p] is an unvoiced labial plosive. It is formed exactly the same as [b], except that it is unvoiced. It is, therefore, merely exploded air.

Exercises[3]

1. Pretty Paula peeked past the platform.
2. Peter Piper picked a peck of pickled peppers.
3. Happy people appear to approach unhappiness happily.
4. Approximately opposed in position are Dopey and Happy.
5. Stop the cap from hitting the top.
6. Apparently the perfect approach to happiness is practiced by the popular purveyor of apoplexy, Pappy Perkins.

[t] The consonant [t] is an unvoiced, lingua-alveolar plosive. As this description suggests, the [t] is formed by the release of unvoiced air which has been temporarily blocked off by the pressure of the tongue tip against the upper gum ridge. The [t], like the [p], is best softened for radio and television speech.

Exercises

1. Tiny Tim tripped toward the towering Titan.
2. The tall Texan tried to teach the taxi driver twenty tall tales of Texas.
3. Attractive though Patty was, the battling fighters hesitated to attempt to please her.
4. The bottled beetles were getting fatter.
   (For extra work with the medial *tt*, try saying the following with increasing speed: beetle, bittle, bayttle, bettle, battle, bottle, boottle, berttle, buttle.)
5. The fat cat sat in the fast-moving draft.
6. Herbert hit the fat brat with the short bat.

[d] The consonant [d] is a voiced lingua-alveolar plosive. Except that it is voiced, it is the same as the [t]. (Say *tot*, then *dod*, and you will find that

---

[3] In working with these exercises, as with all of those devoted to the plosives, try to keep the "popping" under control. The blast of air which accompanies these sounds is frequently magnified by the microphone.

your articulators repeat the same positions and movements for each. Deaf people who read lips cannot detect any difference in voiced and unvoiced pairs and must therefore rely on context for understanding.)

Exercises

1. Don dragged the dull, drab dumptruck up to the door.
2. The dry, dusty den was dirtier than Denny's delightful diggings.
3. The ladder added to the indeterminate agenda.
4. The sadly padded widow in the middle looked addled.
5. Around the lad the red-colored rope was twined.
6. Glad to lead the band, Fred allowed his sad friend to parade around.

[k]   The [k] is an unvoiced lingua-velar plosive. It is formed by releasing unphonated air which has momentarily been blocked from passage by the pressure of the rear top of the tongue against the hard palate.

Exercises

1. Keep Kim close to the clothes closet.
2. A call came for Karen, but Karen wasn't caring.
3. Accolades were accorded to the picnicking dock-workers.
4. Action-back suits were accepted on occasion by the actors playing stock *commedia* characters.
5. Like it or not, the sick man was picked.
6. Rick kept count of the black sacks.

[g]   The consonant [g] is a voiced lingua-velar plosive, and is formed like the unvoiced [k].

Exercises

1. The good girl with the grand guy glanced at the ground.
2. One glimpse of the good, green earth, and the goose decided to go.
3. Agog with ague, the agonizing laggard stood agape.
4. Slogging along, the haggard, sagging band lagged behind.
5. 'Twas brillig, and the rig did sag.
6. The rag bag was big and full, but the sagging trigger was clogged with glue.

[f]   The consonant [f] is an unvoiced labiodental fricative. It is formed by releasing air through a restricted passage between the front teeth and the lower lip.

1. The fish fry was a fairly fashionable affair.
2. Flying for fun, Freddy found the first fairly fast flying machine.
3. Affairs of affection are affable.
4. The affected *aficionado* was afraid of Africa.
5. The laugh graph showed a half-laugh.
6. The rough toff was off with his calf.

[v] The consonant [v] is a voiced labiodental fricative and is formed exactly the same as the [f], except that it is phonated.

Exercises

1. A vision of vim, vigor, and vitality.
2. Viola was victorious with Vladimir's violin.
3. Avarice, averred the maverick on the avenue, is to be avoided.
4. An aversion to lavender obviously prevents the inveterate invalid from involving himself avidly in mauve.
5. A vivid avarice was obviously invested in the avoidance of the man on the avenue.
6. Live, live, cried the five live jivesters.

[θ] The consonant [θ] (as in *thin*) is an unvoiced interdental fricative. The [θ] is frequently a source of trouble since the microphone tends to amplify any slight whistle which may be present. In making this sound, place the tongue up to, but not into, the space between the upper and lower teeth, which are held about one-eighth inch apart. Air passing over the top of the tongue and between its tip and the upper front teeth makes this sound.

Exercises

1. Think through thirty-three things.
2. Thoughts are thrifty when thinking through problems.
3. Cotton Mather lathed his bath house.
4. The pathway to the wrathful heath.
5. The thought of the myth was cutting as a scythe.
6. Thirty-three thinking mythological monsters, wearing pith helmets, wrathfully thought that Theobald was through.

[ð] The consonant [ð] (as in *them*) is a voiced interdental fricative and is formed the same as the [θ], except that it is phonated.

Exercises

1. This, the man then said, is older than thou.
2. The man therein was thereby less than the man who was theretofore therein.
3. Other people lather their faces further.
4. I'd rather gather heather than feathers.
5. Wreathe my brow with heather.
6. I seethe and breathe the truths of yore.

[s] The consonant [s] is an unvoiced lingua-alveolar fricative. It is one of the more common sources of trouble for the announcer. A slight misplacement of the articulators may cause a whistle, a thick, fuzzy sound, or a lisp. There are two methods of producing the [s], neither of which seems clearly superior to the other. In the first of these, the sides of the tongue are in contact with the upper teeth as far forward as the incisors. The tip of the tongue is held rather high in the mouth, and a fine stream of air is directed at the tips of the upper front teeth. The teeth, meanwhile, are held slightly apart. The second method of making the [s] finds the tongue fairly low in the mouth at the rear and at the tip, with the tongue just behind the tip raised in the mouth to make a near contact with the gum ridge. A fine stream of air is permitted to flow through this passage, down toward the front teeth, which are held slightly apart. Because most microphones tend to exaggerate any slight whistle or excessive sibilance, work for a softened [s].

Exercises

1. Should Samson slink past the sly, singing Delilah?
2. Swimming seems to survive as a sport despite some circumstances.
3. Lessons on wrestling are absurd, asserted Tessie.
4. Assurances concerning some practices of misguided misogynists are extremely hysterical.
5. The glass case sits in the purse of the lass.
6. Past the last sign for Sixth Place the bus lost its best chance to rest.

[z] The consonant [z] (as in *zoom*) is a voiced lingua-alveolar fricative and is formed exactly as the [s], except for phonation.

Exercises

1. The zippy little xylophone had a zany sound.
2. The zoological gardens were zoned by Zola for the zebras.

3. The fuzzy, buzzing bees were nuzzling the trees.
4. He used the music to enthuse the buzzards.
5. Was the buzz that comes from the trees caused by the limbs or the bees?
6. His clothes were rags, his arms were bare; yet his features caused his admirers to gaze as though his misery was a blessing.

[ʃ]   The consonant [ʃ] (as in *shoe*) is an unvoiced lingua-palatal fricative. It is made by allowing unvoiced air to escape with friction from between the tip of the tongue and the gum ridge behind the upper front teeth. Although this sound is not a common source of difficulty, guard against its becoming a thick, unpleasing sound. To form the [ʃ], make certain that air does not escape around the sides of the tongue, and keep the central portion of the tongue fairly low in the mouth.

Exercises

1. Shortly after shearing a sheep, I shot a wolf.
2. The shapely Sharon shared her chateau with Charmaine.
3. Mashed potatoes and hashed cashews are flashy rations.
4. The lashing gale thrashed; lightning flashed; and the Hessian troops gnashed their teeth.
5. A flash flood mashed the cash into trash.
6. Fish wish that fishermen would wash their shoes.

[ʒ]   The consonant [ʒ] (as in *vision*) is a voiced lingua-palatal fricative and is formed the same as [ʃ], but with phonation. It is seldom found in an initial position in English.

Exercises

1. Jeanne d'Arc saw visions in the azure sky.
2. *Measure for Measure* is not the usually pleasurable Shakespearean play.
3. A hidden treasure was pleasurably unearthed from the beige hill with great precision.
4. The seizure was leisurely measured.
5. The edges of his incision had the *noblesse oblige* to form an elision.

[h]   The consonant [h] is an unvoiced glottal fricative. It is seldom a source of difficulty to the speaker, but many announcers tend to drop the "h" in certain combinations. Note that the "h" is definitely present in most words beginning with "wh." Note that the consonant [h] depends entirely on the sound which follows it and cannot, therefore, be articulated at the end of a word.

1. The huge hat was held on Henrietta's head by heaps of string.
2. Halfway home, the happy Herman had to have a hamburger.
3. Manhattan abhors one-half the upheaval of Manhasset.
4. "Ha-ha-ha," said the behemoth, as he unhitched the horse.

[tʃ] The consonant [tʃ] (as in *charm*) is an unvoiced lingua-palatal affricate. It is, by this definition, formed with the tongue against the gum ridge behind the upper teeth, and consists of both the pent-up release of air of the plosive and the friction of the fricative.

Exercises

1. Chew your chilly chop before you choke.
2. Choose your chums as cheerfully as children.
3. An itching action follows alfalfa pitching.
4. The richly endowed Mitchells latched on to much money.

[dʒ] The consonant [dʒ] (as in *justice*) is a voiced lingua-palatal affricate and is formed exactly as the [tʃ], except for phonation.

Exercises

1. The junk man just couldn't joust with justice.
2. Joan jumped back in justifiable panic as Jud jettisoned the jet-black jetty.
3. Adjutant General Edgewater adjusted his midget glasses.
4. The edgy fledgling was judged unjustifiably.
5. The edge of the ledge was where Madge did lodge.
6. Trudge through the sedge and bridge the hedge.

[m] The consonant [m] is a voiced labial nasal. It is articulated with the lips completely closed; the phonated sound does not pass into the mouth, as with most other speech sounds, but into the nasal cavity through the naso-pharyngeal port. In a final position, the mouth remains closed, but in an initial position the mouth must open, not to sound the [m], but to move immediately to the sound which follows. The same sound, printed [m̩], indicates that the sound is to be formed by itself, independent of any vowel sound. It occurs in speech in constructions such as "keep 'em clean," which would be transcribed phonetically as [kip m̩ klin].

Exercises

1. Mother meant more than my miserable money.
2. Merton moved my midget mailbox more to my right.
3. Eminent employers emulate immense amateurs.
4. Among amiable emigrants, Ermgard admitted to mother, him, and me inestimable immaturity.
5. Slim Jim and Sam climbed the trim limb.
6. Rhythm hymns they perform for them.

[n] The consonant [n] is a voiced lingua-alveolar nasal. Unlike [m], it can be sounded with the mouth open or closed, since the tongue, rather than the lips, blocks off the air and forces it through the nasal cavity. The [n], too, can be used as a complete unit of speech, and it appears as [n̩] in the International Phonetic Alphabet. The commonly heard pronunciation of a word like *meeting*, in which the [ŋ] sound is dropped, would thus be transcribed as [mitn̩]. The [n] is responsible for much of the excessive nasality characteristic of many irritating voices. If you detect, or some one detects for you, a tendency to overnasalize sounds, several sessions with a tape recorder learning how it feels to soften and improve these sounds should prove helpful.

Exercises

1. Ned's nice neighbor knew nothing about Neil.
2. Now the new niece needed Nancy's needle.
3. Indigestion invariably incapacitated Manny after dinner.
4. Many wonderful and intricate incidentals indirectly antagonized Fanny.
5. Nine men were seen in the fine mountain cabin.
6. Susan won the clean garden award and soon ran to plan again.

[ŋ] The consonant [ŋ] (as in *sing*) is a voiced lingua-velar nasal. It is formed much as the consonant [g], but lacks the plosive quality of that sound. One of the most common problems involves turning this sound into an [n̩] in words which end with *-ing*. The announcer must, of course, determine whether or not it is appropriate in his particular position to drop this sound. The newscaster will undoubtedly decide that he should not; the disc jockey or sports announcer, depending on his own speech personality, may decide that it is permissible. One additional but not widespread problem involving this sound is the practice in some parts of the eastern United States of adding a [g] in such words as *singing*, and saying [sɪŋgɪŋ].

Exercises

1. The English singer was winning the long contest.
2. He mingled with winged, gaily singing songbirds.
3. The long, strong rope rang the gong.
4. Running and skipping, the ringleader led the gang.
5. Among his long songs, Engel mingled some lilting things.
6. Along the winding stream, the swimming and fishing were finding many fans.

[l] The consonant [l] is a voiced lingua-alveolar semivowel. In forming the [l], the tip of the tongue is placed against the upper gum ridge, and phonated air escapes around the sides of the tongue. The [l] presents little difficulty when in an initial or final position in a word, but it is so frequently a source of trouble when in a medial position that a special discussion of this sound is in order. If you will say aloud the word *William*, you will note that the tip of the tongue is placed low in the mouth for the [wɪ], is raised to the upper gum ridge for the [l], and is returned to the floor of the mouth for the [jəm]. Quite obviously, it is easier to speak this name without moving the tongue at all. When doing so, the name then sounds like [wɪjəm], and the [l] sound is completely lost. Unlike some of the English speech sounds which may, in informal delivery, be softened or dropped without loss in effectiveness, the lost medial [l] is definitely substandard and should never occur in the announcer's speech. Note that the [l], like the [m] and [n], is capable of forming a speech entity by itself, in a word such as *saddle* [sædl̩].

Exercises

1. A million silly swallows filled their bills with squiggling worms.
2. Willy Wallace willingly wiggled William's million-dollar bill.
3. Lilly and Billy met two willing fellows from the hills.
4. A little melon was willingly volunteered by Ellen and William.
5. Bill filled the lily pot with a million gallons of water.
6. The mill filled the foolish little children's order for willow leaves.

[w] The consonant [w] is a voiced labial semivowel. It is formed by a movement of the lips from a rounded, nearly closed position to an open position. The tongue is not in any particular position for the [w], but is positioned according to correct placement for the following vowel sound. A common speech fault is occasioned by insufficient movement of the lips in making the [w].

Exercises

1. Worried Willy wouldn't waste one wonderful word.
2. The wild wind wound round the woody wilderness.
3. The wishing well was once wanted by Wally Williams.
4. Wouldn't it be wonderful if one walrus would wallow in the water?
5. Walter wanted to wash away the worrisome watermark.
6. Always sewing, Eloise wished the wonderful woman would want one more wash dress.

[hw] The consonant [hw] is an unvoiced labial fricative. It is a combination of the two consonants [h] and [w] and is achieved by forming the lips for the [w] sound but releasing the air which makes the [h] sound first. The [w] follows immediately, and the [h] is thus barely heard. Although the [h] sound in words such as *when* is lost by most speakers, the radio or television announcer should include the sound at least until such time as it drops out of our language altogether—which it seems to be doing.

Exercises

1. Mr. Wheeler waited at the wharf.
2. Wherever the whippoorwill whistled, Whitby waited.
3. Why whisper when we don't know whether or not Mr. White's whelp is a whiz?
4. Why not wholesale,[4] whispered the white-bearded Whig?
5. Whitney whittled the white-headed whistle.
6. On Whitsun, Whittier was whipping Whitman on a whim.

[j] The consonant [j] as in *yellow* is a voiced lingua-palatal fricative. Like the [l], the [w], and the [r], a slight glide is necessary during the delivery of this sound. Although it causes little difficulty when in an initial position in a word, the medial [j] frequently follows a double *l* (*ll*) construction and therefore is sometimes involved in the speech problem which arises from dropping the medial [l]. Americans often mispronounce the name *William* [wɪjəm] and the word *million* [mɪjən].

Exercises

1. Young Yancy used yellow utensils.
2. The millionaire abused the useful William.

[4] Where the word begins with a distinct [h] and does not move immediately to a [w], the [w] is dropped.

3. Yesterday the youthful Tillyard yelled "Yes."
4. The Yukon used to yen for yokels.
5. Yorick yielded to the yodeler from Yonkers.
6. The yegg yelled at William.

[r]   The consonant [r] is a voiced lingua-palatal semivowel. In certain areas of the United States and in England, the [r] is frequently softened or completely dropped. In General American speech, however, all the [r]'s are sounded, though they need not and should not be prolonged, or formed too far back in the throat. A voice described as "harsh" quite frequently overstresses the [r] sounds. A word of warning is in order at this point: in attempting to soften your [r]'s, be careful to avoid affectation; a pseudo-British accent is unbecoming to Americans and Canadians. Few speakers can successfully change only one speech sound. The slight softening of the [r] should be only one part of a general softening of all harsh sounds in your speech.

Exercises

1. Rather than run rapidly, Rupert relied on rhythm.
2. Robert rose to revive Reginald's rule of order.
3. Apparently a miracle occurred to Herman.
4. Large and cumbersome, the barge was a dirty hull.
5. Afraid of fire and sure of war, the Rear Admiral was far away.
6. The bore on the lower floor left his chair and went out the door.

Additional drill material can be found in a number of textbooks on voice and diction, including *Voice and Articulation Drillbook*, Second Edition, by Grant Fairbanks (New York: Harper and Row, 1960) and *Improving Voice and Articulation* by Hilda Fisher (Boston: Houghton Mifflin, 1966). Both of these excellent books use IPA symbols.

Five Foreign Pronunciation

One of the more common shortcomings of American announcers is an inability to pronounce foreign words. This is a serious handicap, since news copy and "good" music continuity are often filled with them. Ideally, several years' study of every major language would best prepare you for your work. But because time and human capacities do not usually permit such thoroughness, the next-best solution is learning the rules of pronunciation of the languages you are most likely to need. This chapter provides a detailed discussion of Spanish, Italian, French, and German pronunciation and a brief mention of Oriental and Slavic languages. The drill section includes news and music copy using several languages.[1]

Although correct foreign pronunciation is stressed in this chapter, proper pronunciation for radio and television is *not* always the same as the correct pronunciation. In Chapter 3 you saw that the foreign-derived names of Americans and American cities are usually Americanized. Similarly, conventionalized pronunciations of foreign cities, nations, people, and musical compositions, though not correct, are usually to be preferred on radio and television. For example:

Spelling	*Correct Pronunciation*	*Conventional Pronunciation*
Paris	PAH-REE' [pa'ri]	PAIR'-IS ['pɛrɪs or 'pærɪs]
Copenhagen	KOEBN-HAU'-N [købŋ'haun]	KOPE'-UN-HAIG'-UN ['kopən'hegŋ]
Rossini	ROS-SEE'-NEE [ros'siːni]	RAW-SEE'-NEE [rɔ'siˌni]

You are, then, expected to use correct foreign pronunciation for certain words and to modify it for others. The problem amounts to knowing when it is correct

---

[1] The publisher has issued an LP record on which qualified native speakers pronounce the Spanish, Italian, French, and German words appearing in boldface type in this chapter. Information about the contents and cost of this record may be obtained by writing to Houghton Mifflin Company, 110 Tremont Street, Boston, Massachusetts 02107.

to be incorrect. This dilemma poses at least three possibilities when pronouncing foreign or foreign-derived words: (1) you may pronounce them as do the natives of the country of origin; (2) you may modify them to conform with conventionally accepted American usage; (3) you may completely Anglicize them. There are, regrettably, few rules to guide you. The absolutist position that the "correct" pronunciation is never wrong offers no help. Even the most extreme advocate of "correct" pronunciation would admit that a news bulletin beginning "PAH-REE', FRÃHS" [pa'ri frɑ̃ɪs], is affected and in poor taste.

In the absence of ironclad rules, the following suggestions, which seem in accord with the best practice among topflight announcers in the United States and Canada, are offered. They seek order in a situation which is by definition disorderly, so they cannot guarantee answers to all pronunciation questions which may arise.

1. *Give the names of cities and countries the familiar, conventionalized pronunciation current in the United States.* The citizens of Germany call their country "Deutschland"; the word "Germany" is not even a German word. If it were, its German pronunciation would differ considerably from that used by Americans. There is no point in either applying the German rules of pronunciation to the name "Germany" or calling Germany "Deutschland" in this country.

In most instances, we spell foreign city names as they are spelled in their own country but pronounce them in conventionalized ways true neither to their original pronunciations nor to any rational system of Anglicization. This presents no problem where the name is in more or less constant use, as are Paris, Berlin, or Copenhagen. The problem arises when a relatively unknown city, such as Eleusis [ɛ'lusɪs], São Paulo [ˌsɑ̃ʊ'paʊlʊ], or Rheims [ræ̃ɪs], is suddenly thrust into the news. Here, if pronunciation rules do not solve the problem, you should check a standard pronunciation guide, several of which are to be found in almost every broadcast station, and at least one of which should be in the personal library of every announcer. The Kenyon and Knott *A Pronouncing Dictionary of American English* (Springfield, Mass.: G. & C. Merriam, 1953) and the *NBC Handbook of Pronunciation* (New York: Thomas Y. Crowell, 1964) both give conventionalized pronunciations of foreign place names for broadcast use. To repeat, there is often no virtue in using the correct foreign pronunciation for a foreign place name. The correct Japanese pronunciation of Iwo Jima is EE-WAW'-DJEE-MAH [i'wɔdʒimɑ], but it is customary in this country to say the technically incorrect EE'-WO DJEE'-MUH ['iˌwo'dʒimə].

2. *Pronounce the names of American cities derived from foreign namesakes as the natives of that American city pronounce it.* Vienna, Versailles, Marseilles, and Alhambra are all names of American cities, and not one of them is correctly pronounced as its foreign counterpart. The pronunciation guides listed above will give you the correct local pronunciations of these and other cities and towns.

3. *In pronouncing the names of foreigners, follow one of the following rules:* (a) if the person is alive and his preference known, pronounce his name as he

would like you to pronounce it; (b) if the person is very well known and a conventional pronunciation has been developed, follow that pronunciation; (c) if the person is not well known and his preference has not been expressed, follow the rules for pronouncing his native tongue.

4. *In pronouncing the names of Americans derived from foreign names, follow one of these rules:* (a) if the person's preference is known, pronounce the name as he would like you to pronounce it; (b) if the person's preference is not known, pronounce the name the way other Americans of the same name do. If the name is DuBois and the person is an American, you will be safe pronouncing it DUE-BOYZ rather than DUH-BWAH.

5. *In pronouncing the titles of foreign musical compositions, let these rules guide you:* (a) if the title is in common use and the customary pronunciation is quite close to the original, use this pronunciation. (b) If the title is in common use but the customary pronunciation is not nearly correct, compromise between the conventional and the accurate. Thus, while the conventional pronunciation of *Tann-häuser* (TAN'-HOWZ-ER) is too far from correct standards for broadcast use, the correct German pronunciation may be a little too extreme for American tastes. A slightly softened TAHN'-HOY-ZER is the best solution. (c) If the title is little known and has no conventionalized pronunciation, pronounce it according to the rules of pronunciation in force in its country of origin. Although it may sometimes be desirable to soften some foreign words slightly for American ears, you cannot, in this instance, go wrong by being "correct."

In the present chapter the correct rules of foreign pronunciation will be discussed and illustrated. In each instance the correct pronunciation will be transcribed into IPA symbols, as well as the less precise symbols of the radio-television wire services. Before taking up each language in detail, one word of caution is in order. Because most modern European countries are comprised of many formerly independent states, regional variations in pronunciation abound. The pronunciation given in this chapter follows that established by qualified natives as "standard" pronunciation. Deviations from it are not necessarily substandard.

Spanish Pronunciation

Spanish, unlike English, is a strictly phoneticized language. Once you have mastered the rules of Spanish pronunciation, you will know how to pronounce any Spanish word you see in print. Although a few letters have more than one speech sound, the surrounding letters in the word are an infallible guide to their pronunciation.

Stress

Spanish words have one strong-stressed syllable. All other syllables receive no stress at all. There is no such thing as secondary stress; any syllable in a word is either stressed or not, with no middle ground.

Many Spanish words carry an accent mark over one of the vowels, *e.g.*, **médico,** and this indicates that the syllable the vowel appears in receives a strong stress. Unlike the accent marks in French, it does not affect the pronunciation of the vowel. Two general rules govern words which carry no mark:

1. Words ending in a consonant other than **n** or **s** are stressed on the *last* syllable, as in the following examples: **usted** [u'stɛd], **canal** [kɑ'nɑl], **señor** [se'ɲɔr].

2. Words ending in **n, s,** or a vowel are stressed on the *penultimate* (next-to-last) syllable, as in the following examples: **joven** ['xoven], **señores** [sen'jɔres], **hombre** ['ɔmbre].

Spanish Vowels

Spanish has five vowels—**a, e, i, o,** and **u.** Whether the vowel is stressed or unstressed, it seldom moves from its customary sound. The chief exceptions are **i** and **u** where they form part of a diphthong. No vowel ever becomes the schwa [ə], as, for example, does the letter *a* in the English word *about.*

a The vowel **a** is always pronounced "ah" [ɑ], as in *father.* Examples: **balsa** ['bɑlsɑ] (BAHL'-SAH); **casa** ['kɑsɑ] (KAH'-SAH).

e The vowel **e** is pronounced "ay" [e], as in the English word *bait,* but it sometimes becomes more of an "eh" [ɛ], as in *met,* depending on its context. When it has the "ay" sound, it is never prolonged and allowed to glide into an "ee" sound. Examples: **meses** ['meses] (MAY'-SAYS); **deberes** [de'beres] (DAY-BAY'-RAYS); **gobierno** [go'βjɛrno] (GO-BYEHR'-NOH).

i The vowel **i,** except when part of a diphthong (see below), is always pronounced "ee" [i], as in the English word *machine.* Examples: **definitivo** [defini'tiβo] (DAY-FEE-NEE-TEE'-VO); **pipa** ['pipɑ] (PEE'-PAH).

o The vowel **o** is usually pronounced "oh" [o], as in the English word *hoe,* but depending on its context, it may become more of an "aw" [ɔ] sound. Examples: **contrata** [kon'trɑtɑ] (KOHN-TRAH'-TAH); **pocos** ['pokos] (POH'-KOHS); **hombre** ['ɔmbre] (AWM'-BRAY).

u The vowel **u,** when not a part of a diphthong, is pronounced "oo" [u], as in the English word *rule.* Examples: **luna** ['lunɑ] (LOO'-NAH); **público** ['publiko] (POO'-BLEE-KO).

Spanish Diphthongs

ia, ie, io, and **iu** If you pronounce the sounds "ee" and "ah" together very rapidly, they form a sound very close to "yah." A similar change occurs in rapidly saying aloud the two component vowels in **ie** ("yay"), **io** ("yo"), and **iu** ("you"). These sounds, called diphthongs because they are a combination of two vowels, are represented as follows in IPA: [jɑ], [je], [jo],

[ju]. In pronouncing them, sound both component sounds, but make sure that the **i** becomes a [j]. Examples: **piano** ['pjɑno] (PYAH'-NO); **mientras** ['mjentrɑs] (MYAYN'-TRAS); **naciones** [nɑ-'sjones] (NAH-SYONE'-AYS); **viuda** ['vjudɑ] (VYOO'-DAH).

ei   The Spanish **ei** is pronounced "ay" [e], as in the English word *rein*. Example: **seis** [ses] (SAYSS).

ai   The Spanish **ai** is pronounced "eye" [aɪ]. Example: **bailar** [baɪ'lɑr] (BUY-LAHR'). (Note: At the ends of words, ei and ai are spelled **ey** and **ay.**)

oi   The Spanish **oi** is pronounced "oy" [ɔɪ] as in *loiter*. Example: **heroico** [ɛr'ɔɪko] (EH-ROY'-KO).

ua, ue, ui, and **uo**   The Spanish **u** preceding another vowel is pronounced like the English *w* [w]. Examples: **cuatro** ['kwɑtro] (KWAH'-TRO); **puente** ['pwɛnte] (PWEN'-TAY); **cuidar** [kwi'dɑr] (KWEE-DAR'); **cuota** ['kwotɑ] (KWO'-TAH). (But note the exceptions under **gu** and **qu** below.)

au   The Spanish **au** is pronounced "ow" [aʊ]. Example: **autobus** [aʊto'bus] (OW-TOE-BOOS').

eu   The Spanish **eu** is pronounced by running "eh" [ɛ] and "oo" [u] together rapidly. Example: **deuda** [dɛ'udɑ] (DEH-OO'-DAH).

Spanish Consonants

b   At the beginning of a word or after **m,** like the English *b*: **bueno** ['bweno] (BWAY'-NO); **nombre** ['nombre] (NOHM'-BRAY). In other positions it is more like the English *v*, although it is produced with both lips instead of the upper teeth and lower lip. The IPA symbol for this sound is [β]. Example: **alabar** [ɑlɑ'βɑr] (AH-LAH-BAHR'). (Note: There is no way of indicating this sound with conventional type, and the B is used in the wire-service example to avoid confusion.)

c   The Spanish **c** has two values. (1) Before **e** or **i** it is soft. The Castilian speech—fairly standard in most of Spain—pronounces this as *th* in *thin*. In southern Spain and in Spanish America it is pronounced *s* as in *say*. You should base your choice on the origin of the person or title, unless a large Spanish-speaking audience in your area would consider Castilian pronunciation affected. Examples: **ciudad** [sju'dɑd] (SYOU-DAHD'), or [θju-'dɑd] (THYOU-DAHD'). (2) In all other positions, the **c** is pronounced "k" as in *car*. Examples: **cura** ['kurɑ] (KOO'-RAH); **acto** ['ɑkto] (AHK'-TOH). The sound of "k" preceding an **e** or an **i** is spelled **qu** (see below).

cc   The first **c** is by definition hard, and since **cc** appears only before **e** or **i,** the second **c** is soft. Example: **acceso** [ɑk'seso] (AHK-SAY'-SOH), or in Castilian Spanish [ɑk'θeso] (AHK-THAY'-SO).

ch   The Spanish **ch** is pronounced *ch* [tʃ], as in *church*. Example: **muchacha** [mu'tʃatʃa] (MOO-CHA'-CHA).

d   At the beginning of a word, or after **n** or **l,** the Spanish **d** is much like the English *d*: **dios** [djos] (DYOS); **caldo** ['kɑldo] (KAHL'-DO). In other positions it is more like a weak voiced *th* [ð] as in the English word *weather*. It is made by extending the tongue a short distance beyond the front teeth, and thus weakening the sound. Example: **padre** ['pɑðre] (PAH'-THRAY). (Note: Since this sound is still more of a [d] than a [ð], the [d] will be used in this chapter.)

f   The Spanish **f** is pronounced as the English *f*. Example: **flores** ['flores] (FLO'-RAYS).

g   The **g** has two values. (1) Before **e** or **i,** the **g** is pronounced much like the German *ch* [x], as in *ach,* or the Scottish *ch,* as in *loch*. It is a guttural sound, with tightening and some rasp in the rear of the mouth but no vibration of the vocal folds. Examples: **general** [xene'rɑl] (KHAY-NAY-RAHL'); **gente** ['xente] (KHAYN'-TAY). (2) In all other positions, the **g** is hard, as in *gag*. Examples: **gala** ['gɑlɑ] (GAH'-LAH); **largo** ['lɑrgo] (LAHR'-GO). (Note: Since the sound [x] does not occur in English, the wire services have difficulty transcribing it. Sometimes they use CH and sometimes KH. When CH is used, there is no way of knowing whether [x] or [tʃ] is intended. We shall transcribe it as KH in this chapter, but you should be alert to the frequent inconsistencies in transcribing this sound when you come to the wire-service drill material in Part Two.)

gu   When the sound of a hard **g** occurs before **e** or **i,** it is written **gu.** In this convention the **u** is merely a marker and has no sound of its own. Example: **guía** ['giɑ] (GHEE'-AH).

gü   The two dots over a **ü,** when it is between **g** and **e** or **i** (**güe, güi**), indicate that the **ü** is a part of a diphthong, to be sounded like a "w." Example: **agüero** [ɑ'gwero] (AH-GWAY'-RO).

h   Except in the combination **ch** (see above), **h** is a superfluous letter—the only one in the Spanish language. Examples: **habas** ['aβɑs] (AH'-BAHS); **adhesivo** [ɑde'siβo] (AHD-AY-SEE'-BO).

j   Exactly like the first pronunciation of the Spanish **g** given above. Example: **junta** ['xuntɑ] (KHOON'-TAH); ['dʒuntɑ] (JOON'-TAH) is also acceptable.

l   Very similar to the English *l,* although the Spanish keep the rear of the tongue flat. Example: **labios** ['lɑβjos] (LAH'-BYOS).

ll   In Castilian Spanish, **ll** is pronounced much like the *lli* [lj] in *million*. However, in most parts of Spanish America, **ll** is pronounced like the *y* [j] in *yes*. Example: **calle** ['kɑlje] (KAH'-LYAY) or ['kɑje] (KAH'-YAY).

m   Like the English *m*. Example: **cambio** ['kɑmβjo] (KAHM'-BYO).

n   There are three pronunciations for the letter **n.** (1) Before **ca, co, cu, qui,**

que (that is to say, before any "k" sound) and before **g** or **j**, it is pronounced *ng* [ŋ] as in *sing:* **tango** ['taŋgo] (TAHNG'-GO). (2) Before **f, v, p,** or **b,** it is pronounced like the English *m:* **confiado** [kom'fjɑdo] (KOM-FYAH'-DO). (3) In all other instances it is pronounced like the English *n:* **manojo** [mɑn'oxo] (MAH-NO'-KHO).

nn   Very rare. Both **n**'s are sounded. Example: **perenne** [pe'renːe] (PAY-RAYN'-NAY).

ñ   The Spanish **ñ** is pronounced *ny* [ɲ] as in *canyon.* Example: **señor** [se'ɲor] (SAY-NYOR').

p   Like the English *p.* Example: **padre** ['pɑðre] (PAH'-THRAY).

qu   Like the hard **c**, with the **u** never sounded. This occurs only before **e** or **i**. Examples: **qué** [ke] (KAY); **aquí** [ɑ'ki] (AH-KEE').

r   The Spanish **r** has two values, neither of which is like the English. (1) At the beginning of a word, or after **l, n,** or **s,** the tongue is trilled against the roof of the mouth. Examples: **rico** ['riko] (RREE'-KO); **honrado** [on'rado] (OWN-RRAH'-DO). (2) In other positions it is a single flip of the tongue against the roof of the mouth. Example: **caro** ['kɑro] (KAH'-RO).

rr   The **rr** is used to indicate a full trill where the rule would call for a single flip of the tongue were the single **r** used.

s   There are two pronunciations of this letter: (1) Before **b, d, g, l, m, n, r,** and **v,** it is pronounced like the English *z.* Example: **mismo** ['mizmo] (MEEZ'-MO). (2) In other instances it is pronounced as the English *s* in *sea.* Example: **cosa** ['kosɑ] (KOH'-SAH).

sc   In both Castilian and non-Castilian, **s** plus the hard **c** ([s] plus [k]) are always pronounced separately. Example: **disco** ['disko] (DEES'-KO). In non-Castilian, **s** plus soft **c**, being identical sounds, are merged. Example: **discernir** [disɛr'nir] (DEE-SAIR-NEAR'). In Castilian, **s** plus the soft **c** (which is actually [θ]) are pronounced separately. Example: **discernir** [disθɛr'nir] (DEES-THAIR-NEAR').

t   Much like the English *t.* Example: **trato** ['trɑto] (TRAH'-TOE).

v   The same as the Spanish **b,** with the same positional varieties (see above under **b**).

x   Normally like the English *x* [ks] in the word *vex.* Example: **próximo** ['proksimo] (PROCK'-SEE-MO). Before a consonant, the Castilian pronunciation is like the Spanish **s: expreso** [ɛs'preso] (ESS-PRAY'-SOH). The words for *Mexico* and *Mexican* are pronounced with the **j** [x] sound: **México** ['mexiko] (MEH'-KHEE-KO).

y   Much like the English *y* in *year.* Example: **yerba** ['jɛrbɑ] (YEHR'-BAH). In certain instances, instead of representing a consonant, the letter **y** substitutes for the vowel **i:** (1) as the second element of a diphthong at the end of a word, *e.g.,* **rey** [re] (RAY); (2) initial in a few proper names, *e.g.,*

Ybarra [i'bɑrɑ] (EE-BAH'-RAH); (3) as the word for *and, e.g.,* **pan y vino** [pɑni'vino] (PAHN-EE-VEE'NO).

z   The letter **z** follows the same rules as the soft **c,** above. Examples: (Castilian) **jerez** [xe'reθ] (KHAY-RAYTH'); (Spanish-American) **jerez** [xe'res] (KHAY-RAYSS').

Practice pronouncing the following Spanish words and names:

Toledo	Segovia	Albéniz	Cabezón
Guernica	García	Manuel de Falla	*Danzas españolas*
Falange	Ramírez	Granados	*Pepita Jiménez*
Cuernavaca	San Sebastián	Sarasate y Navascuez	Oviedo

Italian Pronunciation

Italian, like Spanish, has a phonetically strict writing system. Although it is not quite as thoroughgoing as Spanish spelling, which tells you everything about the pronunciation of a word, it is a thoroughly businesslike system. Italian conventional spelling does not consistently mark stress, and in the unmarked words certain vowel qualities are likewise undifferentiated. Aside from this, Italian presents few difficulties to the student.

Stress

Italian words have one strong-stressed syllable, while the other syllables are completely unstressed. Unlike English, there are no half-stresses. The relatively small number of words stressed on the last syllable are always marked with an accent over that vowel, *e.g.,* **sarà** [sɑ'rɑ] (SAH-RAH'). Most Italian words are stressed on the penultimate syllable, *e.g.,* **infinito** [infin'ito] (EEN-FEE-NEE'-TOE). Many words are stressed on the antepenultimate syllable, *e.g.,* **medico** ['mediko] (MAY'-DEE-KOE). A few Italian printing houses mark such words with a grave accent mark over the vowel in the syllable to be stressed, but this is not the general rule. To help in the examples in this chapter, an accent mark will be used to show stress on some syllable other than the penultimate. (The grave accent will also be used to indicate an open e [ɛ] or an open o [ɔ], but this should cause no confusion, since syllables containing open e and open o are always stressed in Italian.)

Italian Vowels

Italian has seven basic vowel sounds but uses only the five letters **a, e, i, o,** and **u** to represent them. Stressed or unstressed, each keeps its distinctive quality, though stressed vowels tend to be lengthened before single consonants, *e.g.,* the first vowel of **casa** is longer than that of **cassa.**

a   The vowel **a** is always pronounced [ɑ], as in *father*. Examples: **là** [lɑ] (LAH); **pasta** ['pɑstɑ] (PAH'-STAH).

e   The Italian **e** varies from the pronunciation "ay" [e] to "eh" [ɛ]. Although there are ways of determining the "correct" pronunciation in each instance, the rules are complex and need be of no concern here. Most Northern and Southern Italians, including the best educated, have just one **e,** which may vary somewhat according to the consonants which precede or follow it. This pronunciation is understood and accepted everywhere. Where accent marks are given, the acutely accented **é** tells you that the pronunciation is [e], while the grave accent, **è,** tells you that the pronunciation is [ɛ]. Examples: **débole** ['debole] (DAY'-BO-LAY); **prèsto** ['prɛsto] (PREH'-STOE).

i   Much like the English *i* in *machine*. Example: **pipa** ['pipɑ] (PEE'-PAH).

o   Speakers who distinguish between two **e** sounds also distinguish two qualities of **o,** namely, a close **o** [o], as in *go,* and an open **o** [ɔ], as in *bought.* Dictionaries sometimes indicate the close **o** with an acute accent, *e.g.,* **pólvere** ['polvere] (POHL'-VAY-RAY), and the open **o** with a grave accent, *e.g.,* **còsta** ['kɔstɑ] (KAW'-STAH). As with the open and close **e,** the difference between the two varieties of **o** is minor, and most speakers who use only one **e** sound likewise use only one **o** sound.

u   Much like the *u* in *rule*. Examples: **luna** ['lunɑ] (LOO'-NAH); **futuro** [fu'turo] (FOO-TOO'-ROH).

Italian Diphthongs

The Italian vowels **a, e, i, o,** and **u** form many different combinations to produce the diphthongs. Although they may seem somewhat complex at first glance, they are quite easily mastered.

ia   The **ia** diphthong, except when it follows **c** or **g,** finds the **i** becoming a "y" [j] sound and the **a** retaining its regular pronunciation. Example: **piano** ['pjɑno] (PYAH'-NOH). When the **ia** follows **c,** the **i** merely serves as a silent marker to indicate that the **c** is soft ([tʃ] like the *ch* in *chair*). Example: **Ciano** ['tʃɑno] (TCHAH'-NOH). When the **ia** follows **g,** the **i** merely serves as a silent marker to indicate that the **g** is soft ([dʒ] like the *g* in *gem*). Example: **Gianinni** [dʒɑ'nini] (DGAH-NEE'-NEE).

ie   The **ie** diphthong, except for the few instances in which it follows **c** or **g,** finds the **i** becoming the "y" [j] sound and the **e** retaining its regular pronunciation. Examples: **pièno** ['pjeno] (PYAY'-NOH); **cielo** ['tʃelo] (TCHEH'-LOH). Like the **ia** diphthong, the **ie** following **c** or **g** serves to indicate that the soft pronunciation is to be used, and the **i** has no other function.

io   The **io** diphthong, except where it follows **c** or **g,** finds the **i** becoming a "y" [j] sound and the **o** retaining its regular pronunciation. After **c** or **g,**

the **i** serves only as a silent marker to indicate that the soft pronunciation is to be used. Examples: **Mario** ['mɑrjo] (MAH'-RYO); **bacio** ['bɑtʃo] (BAH'-TCHOH); **Giorgio** ['dʒɔrdʒo] (DGAWR'-DGOH).

iu   The **iu** diphthong, except where it follows **c** or **g**, finds the **i** becoming a "y" [j] sound and the **u** retaining its regular pronunciation. Following **c** or **g**, the **i** serves as a silent marker to indicate that the preceding sound is soft. Examples: **iuta** ['jutɑ] (YOU'-TAH); **acciuga** [ɑ'tʃugɑ] (AH-CHEW'-GAH); **giù** [dʒu] (DGOO).

ai, oi, and **ui**   These diphthongs are merely the glide from **a, o,** and **u** to the "ee" sound. Examples: **mai** [maɪ] (MY); **pòi** [pɔɪ] (POY); **guida** ['gwidɑ] (GWEE'-DAH).

ua, ue, and **uo**   These diphthongs all find the **u** becoming *w* (as in *will*) and the **a, e,** and **o** each retaining its permanent sound. Examples: **guàio** ['gwɑjo] (GWAH'-YOH); **sàngue** ['sɑŋgwe] (SAHNG'-GWAY); **cuòre** ['kwɔre] (KWAW'-RAY).

au   The **au** diphthong is pronounced like the *ow* [aʊ] in *how*. Example: **Làura** ['laʊrɑ] (LAU'-RAH).

Italian Consonants

An all-important feature of Italian pronunciation is the occurrence of both "single" (or short) and "double" (or long) consonants. In Italian, a written double consonant (**cc, rr, zz,** etc.) always means a spoken double consonant. The nearest thing in English to the Italian double consonant is the effect produced in such two-word expressions as "ought to," "guess so," or "sick cat." These have their counterparts in the Italian words **òtto, messo,** and **seccare.** Note that this is not really a doubling of the sound so much as it is a prolonging of it. Before a double consonant (as in **canne**), a stressed vowel is perceptibly shorter than before a single consonant (as in **cane**). In the following discussion of the Italian consonants, several words will be listed without phonetic spellings for practice.

b   Like the English *b*. **barba, bianco, buòno, bambino, babbo, sàbbia, labbra.**

c   The **c** has two values: (1) before **e** or **i**, it is "soft," like the *ch* [tʃ] in *church*. Examples: **cena, cènto, fàcile, Lècce, spicci, accènto.** When the sound of the soft **c** [tʃ] occurs before **a, o,** or **u,** it is written **ci** (**ciò**), and the **i** is merely a silent marker with no sound of its own. Example: **bacio** ['bɑtʃo] (BAH'-TCHOH). (2) In all other positions, the **c** is "hard," which is like the *c* in *call* [k]. Examples: **caldo, cura, clèro, bocca, sacco, pìccolo.**

ch   The **ch** occurs only before **e** or **i**, where it represents the hard **c** [k]. Examples: **che** [ke] (KAY); **vècchio** ['vɛkːjo] (VEHK'-KYOH).

d   Much like the English *d*. Examples: **dardo, duòmo, càndido, freddo, rèddito, iddìo.**

f Like the English *f*. Examples: **faccia, fiato, fiume, gufo, bèffa, ràffio, soffiare.**

g The g has two values: (1) before **e** or **i**, it is "soft," like the *g* in *gem* [dʒ]. Examples: **gènte, giro, pàgina, legge, viaggi, suggèllo.** When the sound of the soft **g** [dʒ] occurs before **a, o,** or **u**, it is written **gi (già)**, and the **i** serves only as a silent marker with no value of its own. Example: **Giovanni** [dʒo'vanːi] (DGOH-VAHN'-NEE). (2) In all other positions, except as described below, the **g** is "hard," like the *g* in *good* [g]. Examples: **gamba, góndola, guèrra, lèggo, agganciare.**

gh Occurs only before **e** or **i**, where it represents the "hard" *g* [g]. Example: **ghiàccio** ['gjatʃːo] (GYAHTCH'-OH).

gli The Italian **gli** is like the English *lli* in *million*. When another vowel follows, as it usually does—in the next word in the case of the definite article **gli** ("the")—the **i** is a silent marker and represents no sound of its own. Inside a word, the consonant sound is always double. Remember, in pronouncing **gli**, the **g** has no value whatsoever, and when followed by another vowel, the **i** has no value. The entire sound, then, becomes [l] plus [j]. Examples: **figlio** ['filːjo] (FEE'-LYOH); **paglia** ['palːja] (PAH'-LYAH); **pagliacci** [pa'ljatʃːi] (PAH-LYAHCH'-CHEE); **gli altre** ['jaltri] (YAHL'-TREE).

gn Like the English *ny* [ɲ] in *canyon* (Spanish ñ). Inside a word the sound is always double. Examples: **signore** [si'ɲːore] (SEEN-NYO'-RAY); **giugno** ['dʒuɲo] (JOON'-NYOH).

h Except in the combinations **ch** and **gh** (see above), **h** is the only superfluous letter in Italian. In native words it occurs only at the beginning of four related forms of the verb **avere** ("have"). The word **hanno**, then, is pronounced exactly as the word **anno**, *i.e.*, ['anːo] (AHN'-NO).

j The letter **j** is not regularly used in Italian, except as a substitute for the letter **i** in proper names (*e.g.*, **Jàcopo** for **Iàcopo**), or in a final position as a substitute for **ii** in plurals, *e.g.*, **studj** for **studii**.

l Can be pronounced as the English *l*, though the Italians pronounce it with the tongue flat and unraised in the back of the mouth. Examples: **lavoro, lièto, Itàlia, giallo, bèlla, nulla.**

m Like the English *m*. Examples: **mièle, mùsica, fame, mamma, gèmma, fiammìferi.**

n Like the English *n*, including [ŋ] (*ng* as in *thing*) where it precedes hard **c** or hard **g**. Examples: **nòno** ['nɔno] (NAW'-NOH); **bianco** ['bjaŋko] (BYAHNG'-KOH); **inglese** [ɪŋ'gleze] (ING-GLAYZ'-AY).

p Much like the English *p*. Examples: **papa, prète, capo, dóppio, zuppa, appòggio.**

q The same as the hard **c,** and always followed by **u** which is always sounded [w] as part of a diphthong. Examples: **quadro, quindi, dunque, quèrcia.** When doubled, it appears as **cq: acqua, nacque, acquistare.**

r Where single **r** appears, it is manufactured with a single flip of the tongue tip against the roof of the mouth. Where the double **r** appears, it is a trill of the tongue tip, as with the Spanish **rr**. Examples: **Roma, rumore, dramma, carro, burro, orrore.**

s In most positions, the Italian **s** is pronounced like the *s* in *sea*. Examples: **sole** ['sole] (SO'-LAY); **sfida** ['sfidɑ] (SFEE'-DAH); **rosso** ['rosːo] (ROHS'-SOH). Before any of the voiced consonants, **b, d, g, l, m, n, r,** or **v,** the **s** is pronounced like the *z* in *zoo*. Examples: **sbaglio** ['zbɑlːjo] (ZBAH'-LYOH); **disdegno** [di'zdeɲo] (DEE-ZDAY'-NYOH); **slancio** ['zlɑntʃo] (ZLAHN'-CHOH). Single **s** between vowels is pronounced either [s] or [z], with [s] generally preferred in Tuscany and [z] elsewhere. Examples: **casa, francese, còsa.**

sc Before **e** or **i, sc** is pronounced [ʃ] like the *sh* in *shoe*. Inside a word, it is pronounced double. Examples: **scelto** ['ʃelto] (SHAYL'-TOH); **pesce** ['peʃːe] (PAYSH'-SHAY). When this sound occurs before an **a, o,** or **u,** it appears as **sci.** In this convention, the **i** is merely a silent marker and is not pronounced. Examples: **sciame** ['ʃame] (SHAH'-MAY); **asciutto** [ɑ'ʃːutːo] (AHSH-SHOOT'-TOH). The spelling **scie** is the same as **sce.** In all other positions, **sc** is pronounced like the *sk* in *ski*. Examples: **scale** ['skɑle] (SKAH'-LAY); **tasca** ['tɑskɑ] (TAH'-SKAH).

sch The **sch** occurs only before **e** and **i** where it represents *s* as in *say* plus hard *c* as in *come*. Example: **schiavo** ['skjɑvo] (SKYAH'-VOH).

t Much like the English *t*. Examples: **tèsta; tòrto; triste; gatto; sètte; prosciutto.**

v Like the English *v*. Examples: **vivo; Verona; vuòto; bevve; òvvio; avviso.**

z The Italian **z** is ambiguous, representing both [ts] like the *ts* in the word *cats* and [dz] like the *ds* in the word *beds*. In an initial position, there is no firm rule for its pronunciation: *e.g.*, **zèlo** ['dzɛlo] (DZEH'-LOH); **zio** ['tsio] (TSEE'-OH). Internally, [ts] is general after **r** and **l**: **fòrza** ['fɔrtsɑ] (FAWR'-TSAH). A single **z** between vowels is [ts]: **-azione** [ɑ'tsjone] (AH-TSYOH'-NAY).

Practice pronouncing the following Italian words and names:

Arcangelo Corèlli	*Il barbiere di Siviglia*
Giovanni Pierluigi Palestrina	*La cenerentola*
Ottorino Respighi	*L'Italiana in Algeri*
Gioacchino Rossini	*Tosca*
Doménico Scarlatti	*Chi vuole innamorarsi*
Giuseppe Tartini	*Il matrimonio segreto*
Beniamino Gigli	*Le nozze di Figaro*
Dusolina Giannini	*La finta giardiniera*
Franco Ghione	*Così fan tutte*
Giàcomo Puccini	*La gioconda*

French Pronunciation

French, like English, uses complicated spelling conventions including numerous superfluous letters, sequences of letters representing single sounds, several ways of writing one sound, or the use of one letter to represent several sounds. But on the whole, French spelling is more systematic than English, and with practice one can learn to read French with an acceptable pronunciation.

Stress

French words, as well as entire phrases and sentences, have about equal accent on each syllable up to the last one, which is a little more heavily stressed. In the name of the French composer, **Debussy** [dəbysi] (*),[2] the syllable –sy gets a slight extra stress if you pause or stop after it, but not if you don't. In the sentence **Debussy est bien connu** ("Debussy is well known"), only the final sound of the phrase gets that extra bit of stress: [dəbysi ɛ bjɛ̃ kɔˈny] (*).

French Oral Vowels

French has three classes of vowel sounds: twelve oral vowels, four nasal vowels, and three semivowels. Because a single speech sound in French may have as many as six different spellings, the vowels, nasal vowels, and semivowels will be grouped by sound rather than alphabetically.

Many of the sample words include a sound which is somewhere between an [o] (OH) and an [ɔ] (AW). In IPA the symbol for this sound is [ǫ], but since it is not much used in French dictionaries, there is little point in using it here. Authoritative reference works use the symbol [ɔ] to describe the **o** and **au** in **école** and **Paul,** even though the actual sound is probably closer to an [o]. To avoid confusion, sample words will be transcribed as they are in standard reference works. As you become familiar with the French language, you may want to modify conventional transcription practices to suit your own standards of accuracy.

French has a number of speech sounds which do not occur in English, and each has been given an IPA symbol. Most of them are described below, but two need early and special explanation. The French tend to prolong a final **l** or **r** sound in an unvoiced, recessive manner. These sounds are especially noticeable when the words they are in terminate a phrase or are sounded separately. IPA invests each of them with a small circle—[l̥], [r̥]—to distinguish them from other **l** and **r** sounds. Note that these symbols differ from the English syllabic consonant symbols [l̩] and [r̩], and they sound quite unlike anything in the English language.

---

[2] The French **u** and the German **ü** are both represented by the IPA symbol [y]. This sound does not occur in English, and no combination of English letters can approximate it phonetically. An asterisk enclosed in parentheses (*) is used throughout to indicate words and sounds which cannot be approximated with wire-service phonetics.

There is no satisfactory way of approximating these sounds in wire-service phonetics, but you will find them represented in this book in this manner:

Word	IPA	Wire Service
siècle	[sjɛkl̩]	(SYEH-KL(UH))
mettre	[mɛtr̩]	(MET-R(UH))

IPA Symbol	Description of Sound	French Spelling	Examples
[a]	Between *a* in *father* and *a* in *bat*	a	**patte** [pat] (PAHT)
		à	**déjà** [deʒa] (DAYZHAH)
[ɑ]	Like the *a* in *father*	a	**phase** [fɑz] (FAHZ)
		â	**pâte** [pɑt] (PAHT)
[e]	Like the *e* in *they*, but without the final glide	e	**parlez** [parle] (PAR-LAY)
		é	**été** [ete] (AY-TAY)
		ai	**gai** [ge] (GAY)
[ɛ]	Like the *e* in *met*	e	**mettre** [mɛtr̩] (MET-R(UH))
		ê	**bête** [bɛt] (BET)
		è	**frère** [frɛr] (FRAIR)
		ei	**neige** [nɛʒ] (NEHZH)
		ai	**frais** [frɛ] (FREH)
		aî	**maître** [mɛtr̩] (MET-R(UH))
[i]	Like the *i* in *machine*	i	**ici** [isi] (EE-SEE)
		î	**île** [il] (EEL)
		y	**mystère** [mistɛr] (MEES-TAIR)
[o]	Like the *o* in *hoe*, except that the final glide toward an "oo" sound is omitted	o	**chose** [ʃoz] (SHOZE)
		ô	**hôtel** [otɛl] (O-TEL)
		au	**haute** [ot] (OAT)
		eau	**beauté** [bote] (BO-TAY)
[ɔ]	Like the *ou* in *bought*, but shorter	o	**école** [ekɔl] (AY-KAWL) or (AY-KOLE)
		au	**Paul** [pɔl] (PAUL) or (POLE)
[u]	Much like the *u* in *rule*	ou	**vous** [vu] (VOO)
		où	**où** [u] (OO)
		oû	**coûter** [kute] (KOO-TAY)
[y]	Pronounced with the tongue as for [i], but with the lips rounded as for [u]	u	**lune** [lyn] (*)
		û	**flûte** [flyt] (*)

[o]	Pronounced with the tongue as for [e] ("ay"), but with the lips rounded as for [o] ("oh")	eu œu	feu [fø] (*) vœux [vø] (*)
[œ]	Pronounced with the tongue as for [ɛ] ("eh"), but with the lips rounded as for [ɔ] ("aw")	eu œu	seul [sœl] (*) sœur [sœr] (*)
[ə]	This is the schwa vowel, a simple "uh" sound, like the sound of *a* in *about*. It occurs mainly in pre-final syllables.	e	semaine [s(ə)mɛn] [3] (S(UH)-MEN) neveu [nəvø] (*)

The [ə], or "uh" sound, occurs also in nine common little words consisting solely of a consonant plus this vowel, namely **ce, de, je, le, me, ne, que, se,** and **te,** most of which are always prefinal in a phrase, *e.g.,* **je sais** [ʒəse] (ZHUH-SAY); **le roi** [lərwa] (LUH-RWAH). If you listen carefully to a French speaker, you may decide that the vowel sound in each of these short words is closer to [œ] than to [ə]. Despite what your ears tell you, all standard French dictionaries transcribe these words with the schwa. This practice will be followed here to avoid confusion, but you should be careful not to give these words a fully Americanized [ə] (UH) sound.

At the end of many words an extra **e** is written after one or another of the above vowels. This is the so-called "mute e" and has no effect on the pronunciation. Examples: **épée** [epe] (AY-PAY); **craie** [krɛ] (KREH) or (KRAY).

Obviously, certain spellings fail to distinguish between pairs of vowel sounds: **a** represents both [a] and [ɑ]; **e** and **ai** represent both [e] and [ɛ]; **o** and **au** represent both [o] and [ɔ]; **eu** and **œu** represent both [ø] and [œ]. Following consonants often give clues; *e.g.,* before **r** in the same syllable [ɛ, ɔ, œ] always appear and never [e, o, ø], but there are no sure rules. Fortunately it does not matter too much, because the distinctions between two members of a given pair are rarely important in conversation, and many educated speakers of French do not scrupulously observe all of them.

French Nasal Vowels

In producing the nasalized vowels, which have no counterpart in English, the breath passes through the mouth and nose simultaneously, giving a quality sharply and importantly distinct from that of the oral vowels. There is no way of signifying these sounds with wire-service phonetics, and for this reason pro-

---

[3] The schwa vowel [ə], when enclosed in parentheses, indicates that the value given is less than normal. *Semaine* is pronounced almost as a one-syllable word.

nunciation of words using nasalized vowels will be transcribed only into IPA symbols.

The nasalized vowels are, in essence, the sounds which result in certain cases where [ɑ], [ɛ], [ɔ], or [œ] precedes **m** or **n**. In these constructions, the **m** or **n** serves only to indicate that the preceding vowel sound is nasalized and is not pronounced as an entity.

IPA Symbol			Before an M		Before an N
[ɑ̃]	Nasalized [ɑ]	am	chambre [ʃɑ̃br̩]	an	avant [avɑ̃]
			champagne [ʃɑ̃paɲ]		français [frɑ̃se]
		em	temple [tɑ̃pl̩]	en	entente [ɑ̃tɑ̃t]
			semblable [sɑ̃blabl̩]		pensée [pɑ̃se]
[ɛ̃]	Nasalized [ɛ]	im	simple [sɛ̃pl̩]	in	cinq [sɛ̃k]
		ym	symphonie [sɛ̃fɔni]	yn	syntaxe [sɛ̃taks]
		aim	faim [fɛ̃]	ain	bain [bɛ̃]
		eim	Rheims [rɛ̃ɪs]	ein	peintre [pɛ̃tr̩]
[ɔ̃]	Nasalized [ɔ]	om	sombre [sɔ̃br̩]	on	pont [pɔ̃]
			rompu [rɔ̃py]		bonbon [bɔ̃bɔ̃]
[œ̃]	Nasalized [œ]	um	humble [œ̃bl̩]	un	lundi [lœ̃di]

It should be noted that Kenyon and Knott's *A Pronouncing Dictionary of American English* substitutes the symbol [æ̃] for [ɛ̃] and the symbol [õ] for [ɔ̃], above. However, most French dictionaries follow the practice given above, and so it is used here. You should be aware, however, that the nasalized [ɛ] is actually closer in sound to a nasalized [æ] and that the nasalized [ɔ] is actually closer to a nasalized [o].

French Semivowels

Certain combinations of French vowels or of vowels and consonants combine to form new sounds as follows:

IPA Symbol	Description of Sound	French Spelling	Examples
[j]	Before the vowel, like English *y* in *yet*	i	hier [jɛr] (YEHR)
			Pierrot [pjɛro] (PYEH-ROH)
		ï	païen [pajɛ̃] (*)
			aïeux [ajø] (*)
		y	payer [pɛje] (PEH-YAY)
			yeux [jø] (*)

After the vowel, like *y* in *boy*	il	**travail** [travaj] (TRAH-VAH-EE)
		soleil [sɔlɛj] (SAW-LEH-EE) or (SOH-LEH-EE)
		œil [œj] (*)
	ill	**Marseille** [marsɛj] (MAR-SAY-EE)
		faillite [fajit] (FAH-YEET)
		bouillon [bujɔ̃] (*)
	ll	**fille** [fij] (FEE-(YUH))
		sillon [sijɔ̃] (*)

The writing **ill** is ambiguous, since it represents either the diphthong [ij], as in the last two examples, or the sequence **il,** as in **mille** [mil] (MEEL) or **village** [vilaʒ] (VEE-LAZH).

In the diphthong [jɛ̃], the nasal vowel is written **en** by exception: **ancien** [ãsjɛ̃]; **rien** [rjɛ̃].

[w]	Like the English *w* in *win*.	ou	**oui** [wi] (WEE)
		ouest [wɛst] (WEST)
		avouer [avwe] (AH-VWAY)

The diphthong [wa] is written **oi,** as in **loi** [lwa] (LWAH). When it is followed by another diphthong beginning with [j], the letter **y** is used between: **foyer** [fwaje] (FWAH-YAY); **joyeux** [ʒwajø]. The diphthong [wɛ̃] is written **oin,** as in **point** [pwɛ̃], **joindre** [ʒwɛ̃dr̥].

[ɥ]	Pronounced with the tongue as for [j], but with the lips rounded as for [w]; occurs mainly before the letter **i.**	u	**suisse** [sɥis] (*)
		nuit [nɥi] (*)
		cuir [kɥir] (*)

French Consonants

The French consonants, with a few exceptions, do not represent as many different sounds as do the vowels; for this reason, they will be arranged alphabetically.

The French letters **b, d, f, m, n, p, t, v,** and **z** represent one sound each and are pronounced much the same as in English. Except as treated separately below, doubled consonant letters (**nn, rr, tt,** etc.) have the same values as the corresponding singles.

c Before **e, i, y,** or with the cedilla (**ç**) before any vowel, "soft" like the English *c* in *city* [s]. Examples: **cent** [sã] (*); **grâce** [gras] (GRAHSS); **cité** [site] (SEE-TAY); **précis** [presi] (PRAY-SEE); **ça** [sa] (SAH); **reçu** [rəsy] (*). Before **a, o, u,** or a consonant, or in a final position, and when it is without the cedilla, "hard" like the English *c* in *cat* [k]. Examples: **calme** [kalm]

(KAHLM); **encore** [ăkɔr] (*); **cri** [kri] (KREE); **siècle** [sjɛkl̥] (SYEH-KL(UH));
sec [sɛk] (SECK). Double **cc** represents [ks] or simply [k], depending on
the following letter; thus **accident** [aksidã] (*), but **accord** [akɔr] (A-KAWR).

ch   Usually like the English *sh* in *shoe* [ʃ]. Examples: **chapeau** [ʃapo] (SHAH-
POH); **Chopin** [ʃɔpɛ̃] (*); **riche** [riʃ] (REESH); **marché** [marʃe] (MAR-SHAY).
In a few newer words of Greek derivation, the **ch** stands for a hard "c":
psychologie [psikɔlɔʒi] (PSEE-KAW-LAW-ZHEE) or (PSEE-KOH-LOH-ZHEE).

g   Before **e, i,** or **y,** it is "soft," like the English *z* in *azure* [ʒ]. Examples:
geste [ʒɛst] (ZHEST); **mirage** [miraʒ] (MEE-RAZH); **agir** [aʒir] (AH-ZHEER).
The combination **ge,** with the mute **e,** is used to represent soft *g* before
a or **o.** Example: **bourgeois** [burʒwa] (BOOR-ZWAH). Before other vowels
or consonants (other than **n**), the **g** is hard like the English *g* in *gag* [g].
Examples: **garçon** [garsɔ̃] (*); **goût** [gu] (GOO); **règle** [rɛgl̥] (REG-L(UH)).
The combination **gu,** with the mute **u,** is used to represent a hard *g* before
e, i, or **y.** Example: **vogue** [vɔg] (VAWG) or (VOHG).

gn   Much like the English *ny* in *canyon* [ɲ]. Note that this represents a different sound from the similar symbol [ŋ]. Examples: **Mignon** [miɲɔ̃] (*);
Charlemagne [ʃarləmaɲ] (SHAR-L(UH)-MAH-NY(UH)).

h   Except in **ch** and **ph,** this letter represents no sound at all. Examples:
histoire [istwar] (EES-TWAHR); **honnête** [ɔnɛt] (AW-NET) or (OH-NET). Between two vowels, however, the **h** indicates that the vowels form separate
syllables rather than a diphthong. Example: **envahir** [ãvair] (three syllables,
the nasalized "ah," followed by "vah," and completed with "eer.")

j   Like the English *z* in *azure* [ʒ]; the same as the French soft **g.** Examples:
jardin [ʒardɛ̃] (*); **Lejeune** [ləʒœn] (*).

l   Can be pronounced like the English *l,* although the French pronounce it
with the tongue flat and not raised at the back. Examples: **lache** [laʃ]
(LAHSH); **ville** [vil] (VEEL—one syllable). At the end of a word, where
the **l** is pronounced separately, the French make the **l** voiceless. The IPA
symbol for this is [l̥]. Example: **débâcle** [deˈbɑːkl̥] (DAY-BAHK-L(UH)).

ph   The same as **f.** Example: **philosophie** [filɔzɔfi] (FEE-LAW-ZAW-FEE) or (FEE-
LOH-ZOH-FEE).

q   Like the English *k.* It is normally followed by a **u,** which is always mute.
Examples: **quatre** [katr̥] (KAHT-R(UH)); **cinq** [sɛ̃k] (*). The **q** is doubled
by writing **cq,** *e.g.,* **acquitter** [akite] (AH-KEE-TAY).

r   Not like the English *r.* It is pronounced by most speakers as a guttural
sound, with tightening and vibration in the region of the uvula. Examples:
rose [roz] (ROSE); **terre** [tɛr] (TEHR). The French **r,** when final after a
voiceless consonant, is frequently spoken with a voiceless sound which is
scarcely audible. IPA indicates this sound with the symbol [r̥]. The closest
approximation of it in wire-service phonetics would be as "R(UH)," with the

"(UH)" representing a very deemphasized "uh" sound. Example: **Joffre** [ʒɔfṛ] (ZHAW-FR(UH)) or (ZHOF-FR(UH)).

s   Between vowels like the English *z* in *crazy* [z]. Examples: **désir** [dezir] (DAY-ZEER); **raison** [rɛzɔ̃] (*); **Thérèse** [terɛz] (TAY-REZ). Single **s** in other positions and double **s** always, are like the English *s* in *sea* [s]. Examples: **Seine** [sɛn] (SEN); **message** [mɛsaʒ] (MEH-SAZH).

sc   Before **e, i,** and **y**, it is soft, like the English *sc* in *science*. Example: **descendre** [desɑ̃dṛ] (*). Elsewhere, as [s] plus [k]. Example: **escorte** [ɛskɔrt] (ES-KAWRT) or (ES-KORT).

x   Usually like the English *x* in *extra*. Example: **expliquer** [ɛksplike] (EX-PLEE-KAY). An initial **ex-** before a vowel becomes [gz]. Example: **exercice** [ɛgzɛrsis] (EGGZ-AIR-SEES).

Remarks on Final Consonants

Generally speaking, consonants written at the ends of French words are not sounded, *e.g.*, **trop** [tro] (TROH); **part** [par] (PAR); **voix** [vwa] (VWAH); **allez** [ale] (AH-LAY). An almost complete exception is **l**, *e.g.*, **national** [nasjɔnal] (NAH-SYAW-NAHL) or (NAH-SYOH-NAHL). Often **c, f,** and **r** are sounded at the ends of words, *e.g.*, **chic** [ʃik] (SHEEK); **chef** [ʃef] (SHEF); **cher** [ʃer] (SHAIR). Where the final **r** is preceded by an **e (er)**, the **r** usually is silent, and the vowel is like the *e* in *they* [e]. Example: **papier** [papje] (PAH-PYAY).

On the other hand, all the consonant sounds are pronounced at the ends of words when they are followed by a mute **e**. Examples: **place** [plas] (PLAHS); **garage** [garaʒ] (GAH-RAZH); **rive gauche** [riv goʃ] (REEVE-GOASH). This includes **m** and **n,** which before the final mute **e** have their regular values and do not indicate that the preceding vowel is nasal. Examples: **aime** [em] (EM); **pleine** [plɛn] (PLEN). Contrast these with **faim** [fɛ̃] (*f* plus nasalized *eh*), and **plein** [plɛ̃] (*pl* plus nasalized *eh*).

In all the above cases, the addition of an **s** (often the plural sign) after a consonant plus or minus the mute **e** has no effect on the pronunciation. Thus **places** is the same as **place, parts** is the same as **part, temps** is the same as **temp.** Likewise the addition of **nt** (a plural sign in verbs) to a word ending in mute **e** does not change anything, *e.g.*, **chantent** and **chante** both are pronounced [ʃɑ̃t] (*sh*, as in *shoe*, plus the nasalized *ah*, plus a final *t*).

A final word on what the French call liaison, or linking, when the ordinarily silent consonant at the end of a word is sounded before a word beginning with a vowel sound. In liaison, *d* is pronounced [t], *g* is pronounced [k], *s* and *x* are pronounced [z], and nasalized *n*'s are sometimes denasalized. Examples: **grand amour** [grɑ̃tamur] (*); **sang impur** [sɑ̃kɛ̃pyːr] (*); **les autres** [lezotṛ] (LEH-ZOH-TR(UH)) or (LAY-ZOH-TR(UH)); **deux hommes** [døzɔm] (*); **mon ami** [mɔnəmi] (MOH-NAHMEE).

Practice pronouncing the following French names, words, and phrases:

Georges Bizet	Prosper Mérimée
Gabriel Fauré	Marcel Proust
Camille Saint-Saëns	*L'enfant prodigue*
Vincent d'Indy	*Danseuses de Delphes*
Maurice Chevalier	*Jardins sous la pluie*
Benoit Coquelin	*La demoiselle élue*
Rachel	*Le chant des oiseaux*
Guy de Maupassant	*Si mes vers avaient des ailes*

German Pronunciation

The English spelling system contains a great many excess letters. French resembles English in this respect, but German, like Spanish and Italian, is economical in its spelling system, with every letter (or combination of letters, such as **sch**) usually representing one sound in the pronunciation of a word.

German actually is easier to pronounce than it first appears to be. Long German words usually are simply combinations of stem words, plus prefixes and suffixes. When you know how to identify these elements you will know where to break each word into syllables, and from that point on pronunciation is quite simple. The formidable word **Arbeitsgemeinschaft,** for example, is easily divided into **Ar, beits, ge, mein,** and **schaft** by anyone familiar with the way German words are put together. Also, all German nouns are capitalized. This should help you identify parts of speech, which should make for better interpretation of German titles and phrases.

Stress

Most German words are accented on the first syllable: **stehen** ['ʃteɪən] (SHTAY'-N), though not when they begin with a prefix: **verstehen** [fer'ʃteɪən] (FER-SHTAY'-N). Foreign words often are accented on some syllable other than the first, to conform with their native pronunciation: **Philosophie** [fiːloːzoɪ'fi] (FEE-LOH-ZOH-FEE'). In compound words, the first component is usually accented: **Götterdämmerung** ['gœtər,demərʊŋ].[4]

The German syllable **en,** when final in a word or word component, is deempha-

---

[4] This word is impossible to represent with wire-service phonetics because of the unique way Germans sound the syllable **er** at the ends of words or word components. This sound is transcribed [ər] in IPA, but rendering it UHR or UR would be misleading. In German speech, the "r" sound is almost completely lost, and the unaccented "uh" [ə] is nearly all that remains. The sound is quite different from the French [r], so the same wire-service phonetics cannot be used. Throughout this section, the German **er** will be transcribed as (UH(R)). The word **Götterdämmerung** would then be indicated (GUH(R)-TUH(R)-DEM-MER-RUNG).

sized so that it is nearly lost. The syllabic consonant [n̩] would be a fair way of representing this sound in IPA, but all standard German reference works transcribe it as [ən]. Standard practice will be followed for IPA transcriptions, but in wire-service phonetic equivalents, the letter N, without a preceding vowel sound, will be given. Example: **geben** [ˈgeːbən] (GAYB'-N).

At the end of a word and when otherwise unaccented (as, for example, where it appears in an unaccented prefix), the German letter e is pronounced as the "schwa" vowel, *i.e.*, as an unaccented "uh." The IPA symbol for this sound is [ə]. Examples: **sehe** [ˈzeːə] (ZAY'-UH); **gesehen** [gəˈzeːən] (GUH-ZAY'-N).

German Short Vowels

German has four classes of vowel sounds: seven short vowels, seven long vowels, three diphthongs, and one special vowel which occurs only unaccented. As with the French vowels, they will be arranged according to sound rather than by their German spelling.

IPA Symbol	Description of Sound	German Spelling	Examples
[a]	Like the English *a* in *father*, but much shorter	a	**Gast** [gast] (GAHST) **fallen** [ˈfalən] (FAHL'-N)
[ɛ]	Like English *e* in *bet*	e	**Bett** [bɛt] (BET) **essen** [ɛsən] (ESS'-N)
	The spelling ä is used for this sound when the basic form is **a**	ä	**Gäste** [gɛstə] (GUEST'-UH) **fällt** [fɛlt] (FELT)
[ɪ]	Like the English *i* in *hit*	i	**blind** [blɪnt] (BLIHNT) **Winter** [ˈvɪntər] (VIHN'-TUH(R))
[ɔ]	Like the English *au* in *caught*, but much shorter	o	**Kopf** [kɔpf] (KAWPF) **offen** [ˈɔfən] (AWF'-N)
[œ]	Pronounced with the tongue as for "eh" [ɛ], but with the lips rounded as for "aw" [ɔ]	ö	**Köpfe** [ˈkœpfə] (*) **öffnen** [ˈœfnən] (*)
[ʊ]	Like the English *u* in *put*	u	**Busch** [bʊʃ] (BUSH) **Mutter** [mʊtər] (MUH'-TUH(R))
[y]	Pronounced with the tongue as for "ih" [ɪ], but with the lips rounded as for "oo" [u]	ü	**Büsche** [ˈbyʃə] (*) **Mütter** [ˈmytər] (*)

Notice that the German spelling generally shows when an accented vowel is short by the device of writing two consonant letters or a double consonant letter after it.

German Long Vowels

IPA Symbol	Description of Sound	German Spelling	Examples
[ɑ]	Like the English *a* in *father*	a	**ja** [jɑː] (YAH)
			Grab [grɑːp] (GRAHP)
		ah	**Kahn** [kɑːn] (KAHN)
		aa	**Staat** [ʃtɑːt] (SHTAHT)
[e]	Much like the English *e* in *they*, but without the final glide	e	**geben** [geːbən] (GAYB'-N)
		eh	**gehen** [geːən] (GAY'-N)
		ee	**See** [zeː] (ZAY)
	When spelled ä or äh, the pronunciation usually is still "ay" [e].	ä	**Gräber** ['greːbər] (GRAY'-BUH(R))
		äh	**Kähne** ['keːnə] (KAY'-NUH)
[i]	Much like the English *i* in *machine*	i	**Schi** [ʃiː] (SHE)
			Lid [liːt] (LEET)
		ih	**Ihn** [iːn] (EEN)
		ie	**Lieder** ['liːdər] (LEE'-DUH(R))
[o]	Like the English *ow* in *blow*, but without the final glide	o	**so** [zoː] (ZO)
			oben ['oːbən] (OB'-N)
		oh	**Lohn** [loːn] (LOAN)
		oo	**Boot** [boːt] (BOAT)
[ø]	Pronounced with the tongue as for "ay" [e], but with the lips rounded as for "oh" [o]	ö	**Römer** ['røːmər] (*)
		öh	**Löhne** ['løːnə] (*)
[u]	Much like the English *u* in *rule*	u	**du** [duː] (DOO)
			Mut [muːt] (MOOT)
[y]	Pronounced with the tongue as for "ee" [i], but lips rounded as for "oo" [u]	ü	**Brüder** ['bryːdər] (*)
		üh	**rühmen** ['ryːmən] (*)

Notice that German spelling has four ways of showing that an accented vowel is long: (1) the vowel is at the end of a word: **ja, je, schi**, etc.; (2) the vowel is followed by only one consonant: **Grab, haben, wen**, etc.; (3) the vowel is followed by an unpronounced *h*: **Kahn, gehen, ihn**; (4) the vowel is written double: **Staat,**

See, Boot—in which case **ie** counts as the doubled form of **i: Lieder.** There are relatively few words in which long vowels are not indicated in this way. A few sample exceptions: **Papst** [pɑːpst] (PAHPST); Mond [moːnt] (MOANT).

The double dot over **ä, ö,** and **ü** is called an umlaut. The old-fashioned spellings for these umlaut vowels, **ae, oe,** and **ue,** still survive in a few names: **Goebbels, Goethe, Huebner.** You will also encounter these spellings where a type font (as, for example, the wire-service machines) has no special umlaut letters. Typewriters can simulate the umlaut with quotation marks, but wire-service machines cannot return, as a typewriter carriage can, to add the marks after the letter is transmitted.

German Diphthongs

IPA Symbol	Description of Sound	German Spelling	Examples
[aɪ]	Like the English *ai* in *aisle*.	ei	**Leid** [laɪt] (LIGHT)
			Heine ['haɪnə] (HIGH'-NUH)
		ai	**Kaiser** ['kaɪzər] (KY'-ZUH(R))
		ey	**Meyer** ['maɪər] (MY'-UH(R))
		ay	**Bayern** ['baɪərn] (BUY'-URN)
[aʊ]	Like the English *ou* in *house*.	au	**Haus** [haʊs] (HOUSE)
			Glauben ['glaʊbən] (GLOUB'-N)
[ɔɪ]	Like the English *oi* in *oil*.	eu	**Leute** ['lɔɪtə] (LOY'-TUH)
		äu	**Häuser** ['hɔɪzər] (HOY'-ZUH(R))

Notice the difference between **ie,** as in **Lied** [liːt] (LEET), and **ei,** as in **Leid** [laɪt] (LIGHT).

German Consonants

b †[5] As in English, but see below.

  c Like English *k*. Rare in native German words.

 ch In native German words, **ch** stands for two slightly different sounds: (1) After back vowels (**a, o, u,** or **au**), it is a sound like the *ch* in the Scottish word *loch*, in which the breath stream is forced through a narrow opening between the back of the tongue and the soft palate. The IPA symbol for this sound is [x], and wire services transcribe it as either CH or KH. Examples: **Bach** [bɑx] (BAHKH); **Buch** [buːx] (BOOKH). (2) After front sounds, including the front vowels [i], [ɪ], [ɛ], etc., the sound is produced by forcing the breath stream through a narrow channel between the front of the tongue and the hard palate. Many Americans make this same sound

---

[5] A dagger (†) refers to the section below, p. 103, entitled "Voiced and Voiceless Consonants."

(although considerably weaker) in pronouncing the *h* of such words as *hue*, *huge*, or *human*. The IPA symbol for this sound is [ç], but, since the symbol [x] has been accepted by many authorities (including Kenyon and Knott) to represent both sounds, it will be so used here. Examples: **ich** [ɪx] (IHKH); **München** [ˈmynxən] (*): **Bräuche** [ˈbrɔɪxə] (BROY'-KHUH); **Bäche** [ˈbɛxə] (BEKH'-UH). In a few foreign words, **ch** stands for [k]: **Charakter** [kaˈraktər] (KUH-RAHKT'-TUH(R)).

chs Like English *ks:* **wachsen** [ˈvɑksən] (VAHKS'-N).

ck As in English: **Stück** [ʃtyk] (*).

d † As in English, but see below.

dt Like English *t:* **Stadt** [ʃtɑt] (SHTAHT).

f As in English: **fahl** [fɑːl] (FAHL).

g † As in English, except as noted below, and when it appears in a final position as **ig**, where it becomes the "ch" [x] sound, as described above under the **ch** following a front vowel. Example: **hungrig** [ˈhuŋrɪx] (HOONG'-RIHKH).

gn Both letters are sounded, as in the English name *Agnes:* **Gnade** [ˈgnɑːdə] (GNAH'-DUH).

h As in English, when it occurs initially in a word or at the beginning of an element in a compounded word: **Haus** [haʊs] (HOUSE); **Rathaus** [ˈrɑːt,haʊs] (RAHT'-HOUSE). On the use of the unpronounced **h** as a mark of vowel length, see the discussion of the long vowels above.

j Like English *y* in *youth:* **jung** [juŋ] (YOONG).

k As in English.

kn Both letters are sounded, as in the English word *acknowledge:* **Knabe** [ˈknɑːbə] (KNAH'-BUH).

l Can be pronounced like the English *l*, although it is spoken with the tongue flatter in the mouth.

m As in English.

n As in English.

ng Always like the English *ng* [ŋ] of *singer* and never like the English *ng* plus *g* [ŋg] in *finger*. Examples: **singen** [ˈziŋən] (ZING'-N); **Hunger** [ˈhuŋər] (HOONG'-UH(R)).

p As in English.

q Occurs only in the combination **qu**, pronounced [kv]: **Quelle** [ˈkvɛlə] (KVEL'-LUH).

r Pronounced with a slight guttural trill at the back of the tongue (although some northern and western dialects use the front of the tongue). On final –**er**, see above under the discussion of unaccented vowels.

s † Like the English *z:* **so** [zoː] (ZO); **Rose** [ˈroːzə] (ROH'-ZUH); but see below under "Voiced and Voiceless Consonants."

ss As in English.

sch Like the English *sh* in *shoe:* **schon** [ʃon] (SHOWN).

sp At the beginning of a word, or as part of a compound, like English *sh* plus *p:* [6] **springen** [ˈʃprɪŋən] (SHPRING'-N); **Zugspitze** [ˈtsuːkʃpɪtsə] (TSOOK'-SHPITZ-UH). Otherwise, like the English *s* plus *p:* **Wespe** [ˈvɛspə] (VES'-PUH).

st At the beginning of a word, or as part of a compound, like **sh** plus **t:** [6] **Stück** [ʃtyk] (*), **Bleistift** [ˈblaɪˌʃtɪft] (BLY'-SHTIFT). Otherwise like English *st:* **Westen** [ˈvɛstən] (VEST'-N).

t As in English.

th Always like *t:* **Thomas** [ˈtoːmɑs] (TOE'-MAHS).

tz Like *tz* in *Schlitz.*

v † In German words, like the English *f:* **vier** [fɪr] (FEAR); in foreign words, like the English *v:* **November** [noːˈvɛmbər] (NO-VEM'-BER); but see below, "Voiced and Voiceless Consonants."

w Always like the English *v:* **Wein** [vaɪn] (VINE).

x As in English.

z Always like the English *ts:* **zu** [tsu] (TSOO).

German Voiced and Voiceless Consonants

German has five pairs of voiced–voiceless consonants—that is, consonants produced in the same way, except that the first of each pair is pronounced with some vibration of the vocal folds, while the second member of each pair is produced with the vocal folds open and not vibrating. These pairs are: **b–p, d–t, g–k, v–f, z–s.** Voiced **b, d, g, v,** and **z** occur chiefly before vowels. When they stand at the end of a word or part of a compound, or before **s** or **t,** they are automatically replaced by the corresponding voiceless sound, although the spelling is not changed. This means that in these positions—finally, or before **s** or **t**—the letters **b, d, g, v,** and **s** stand for the sounds [p], [t], [k], [f], and [s], respectively. Examples:

Gräber [ˈɡreːbər] (GRAY'-BUH(R))   *but*   **das Grab** [ɡrɑːp] (GRAHP)
Räder [ˈreːdər] (RAY'-DUH(R))   *but*   **das Rad** [rɑːt] (RAHT)
tragen [ˈtrɑːɡən] (TRAHG'-N)   *but*   **du trägst** [treːkst] (TRAYKST)
Motive [moːˈtiːvə] (MO-TEE'-VUH)   *but*   **das Motiv** [moːˈtiːf] (MO-TEEF')
lesen [ˈleːzən] (LAYZ'-N)   *but*   **er las** [lɑːs] (LAHS)

Practice pronouncing the following German names and words:

Wolfgang Amadeus [7] Mozart   Lebensgefährlich
Franz Neubauer   *Dass sie hier gewesen!*

---

[6] Some northern dialects pronounce the **sp** and **st** in these positions [sp] and [st], as in English.
[7] Amadeus, being a Latin name, does not follow German rules of pronunciation.

Die schöne Müllerin	*Die Götterdämmerung*
Dietrich Buxtehude	*O fröhliche Stunden*
Schmücke dich, o liebe Seele	*Ein' feste Burg*
Max Bruch	*Der fliegende Holländer*
Frühling übers Jahr	*Die verklärte Nacht*

Other Languages

Although the languages of the Orient and the Slavic countries (including Russia) are of great importance in the world today, no special pronunciation sections are devoted to them. For this omission two reasons can be given.

First, the Chinese, Japanese, Hindustani, Arabic, and Russian alphabets differ considerably from the Roman alphabet used in Western Europe and America. Since these alphabets are not widely known in Western Europe and America, and since, furthermore, special typewriters or fonts of type are required to set them in print, you will probably never see these languages written in their original alphabets in a news release or a piece of music copy; they are almost always transliterated into the Roman alphabet as phonetically as possible. For example, the Russian name **Хрущев** is a meaningless jumble to a person not familiar with the Russian alphabet. But when it is transliterated into one of the languages we have been discussing in this chapter, it becomes immediately pronounceable. The German spelling of this name, for example, is "Chruschtschow"; Italian newspapers are less consistent, spelling it either "Kruscev" or "Krusciov"; the French transliterate the name as "Khrouchtchev"; the Spanish use either "Krutchev" or "Krushchev"; and in America the spelling seems to have become standardized as "Khrushchev." Each language transliterates the name differently according to its own system of spelling.

Second, we have a tendency to conventionalize the words of these languages to a greater extent than any others. To return to our example, Khrushchev is usually pronounced KROOSH'-CHEV by our newscasters. But the correct Russian pronunciation is [xru'ʃtʃɔf]. (Of the various transliterations of this name in the previous paragraph, only the German version is nearly accurate—and then, of course, only to a German-speaking person!) In a similar way, we tend to conventionalize the names of political figures, writers, composers, and musical compositions. Learning the rules of correct pronunciation for these languages, then, would be gilding the lily.

Bibliographical Note

For the specific rules of pronunciation for languages other than those discussed in this chapter, see Mario A. Pei, *World's Chief Languages* (New York: Devin-Adair, 1949) or Claude Merton Wise, *Applied Phonetics* (Englewood Cliffs, N.J.: Prentice-Hall, 1957). For a rather complete discussion of the International Phonetic

Alphabet and its uses, see John S. Kenyon and Thomas A. Knott, *A Pronouncing Dictionary of American English* (Springfield, Mass.: G. & C. Merriam, 1953). For the phonetic transcriptions of most common foreign words and names, see the *NBC Handbook of Pronunciation*, originally compiled by James F. Bender and revised for the Third Edition by Thomas Lee Crowell, Jr. (New York: Thomas Y. Crowell, 1964).

A test of skill in foreign pronunciation has been contributed by Professor Jerome D. Henderson of the University of Maine. It is heavy reading, but it is exactly the kind of script you will be asked to read if you apply for a position with a "good music" station.

Good evening, and welcome to "Evening Concert,"
three hours of the finest in classical listening
pleasure. This evening's special concert features
excerpts from major works of French, German, Italian,
and Spanish composers.

Included in this evening's presentation are por-
tions of Die Entführung aus dem Serail, by Wolfgang
Amadeus Mozart; L'amore dei tre ré, written by Italo
Montemezzi; and Ariadne auf Naxos, by Richard Strauss.

Other operatic excerpts will be heard from Gaetano
Donizetti's La fille du régiment; Claude Debussy's
Pelléas et Mélisande; Arrigo Boito's Mefistofele; and
Gioacchino Rossini's Il barbiere di Siviglia.

Following this, we will hear El retablo de Maese
Pedro, a short opera by de Falla. This work features
Manuel Ausensi, Julita Bermejo, and Carlos Luque. The
Coros Cantores and the Gran Orquesta Sinfónica are
under the direction of Indalecio Cisneros.

The operatic portion of this evening's concert will end with the famous aria from Giacomo Puccini's Tosca: "Va, Tosca! Nel tuo cuor s'amnida Scarpia."

The second half of "Evening Concert" will feature light symphonic masterpieces. This portion will begin with The Moldau, by Friederich Smetana, after which will be heard the first movement of Symphony No. 1, by Robert Schumann. Other selections will include portions of Symphonie fantastique by Hector Berlioz; Suite No. 1 from L'Arlésienne, by Georges Bizet; and A Midsummer Night's Dream, by Felix Mendelssohn.

The final selections on this evening's concert are two cantatas by Johann Sebastian Bach: Cantata No. 61, "Nun komm, der heiden Heiland," and Cantata No. 130, "Herr Gott, dich loben alle wir."

And now, "Evening Concert" begins with Die Entführung aus dem Serail, by Wolfgang Amadeus Mozart.

Six   The Technical Side

Announcers must master many aspects of broadcasting in addition to good delivery. Some of them—identifying, selecting, and using microphones; cueing and playing records and audio-tape cartridges; operating audio consoles; the use of hand signals—are explored in some detail in this chapter. You should give them special attention if you intend to become a professional announcer. Since television announcers seldom operate broadcast equipment, the emphasis in this chapter will be on radio station equipment and procedures.

The Announcer and Broadcast Equipment

As an announcer you will be surrounded by costly and delicate equipment which, if abused or improperly operated, can defeat your best announcing efforts. Television announcers seldom touch broadcast equipment, but they must know how to relate to cameras and microphones. Radio announcers frequently are expected to operate everything found in a typical small-station control room: microphones, turntables, rack-mounted tape recorders, tape-cartridge units, and audio consoles. This section is an elementary introduction to equipment. You should supplement your reading with practice, for no book can develop your manipulative skills or train your ears to make audio judgments.

Before turning to the equipment itself, a preliminary suggestion seems in order. Because broadcast equipment and station practices vary so much, you should seek help from the studio engineer as soon as you arrive at a new station. Specifically, ask him:

—what kind of equipment is used at the station
—what modifications (if any) have been made which might affect its handling or performance

—what idiosyncrasies the equipment has

—how to report malfunctioning equipment

—to show you the polar patterns of the microphones you will use

—what special procedures you should know about

—what special sensitivities he and other members of the technical staff may have about the use and abuse of equipment

If you establish a friendly working relationship with the studio engineer, and if you are secure enough to admit that you need his help, the chances are very good that he will give you any amount of coaching.

Microphones

When sound waves enter a microphone, they set in motion a chain of events culminating in the apparent recreation of the sound on a radio or television receiver. The microphone, as the first link in the chain, is of primary importance. If a microphone is improperly selected, improperly used, or damaged, the sound will be affected adversely throughout the remainder of its trip to the listener and will appear distorted.

Microphones transform sound waves into electrical impulses and are usually classified in three different ways: by internal structure, by pickup or polar pattern, and by intended use. As an announcer you probably will not select the microphones you use, but you should be able to recognize the types given to you so that you can use each one to your best advantage.

INTERNAL STRUCTURE

Ribbon or velocity microphones. The ribbon microphone (see Figure 3) contains a metallic ribbon, supported at the ends, between the poles of a permanent magnet. The ribbon moves when sound waves strike it, generating voltage which is immediately relayed to the audio console. The straight ribbon or velocity microphone is extremely sensitive to all sounds within a great frequency range, is flattering to the human voice, is unaffected by changes in air pressure, humidity, or temperature, and is not prone to picking up reflected sound. You should consider requesting an RCA 77–DX or BK–5B if you want your voice to sound deeper and more resonant, if you have problems with excessive sibilance, or if you tend to pop your plosive consonants. When using a ribbon mike, it is best to stand or sit approximately two feet from it and speak directly into it.[1] However, most announce booths and control rooms are too small to permit a two-foot distance between announcer and mike without introducing serious acoustical

---

[1] The word "mike" is used in this book as the abbreviation of "microphone." Audio engineers generally prefer "mic" and look down on "mike" as plebeian. However, since "mic" has not yet found its way into textbooks, dictionaries, or popular periodicals, it offends the eye of most readers.

Figure 3. Ribbon or velocity microphones. **A.** RCA 44–BX. **B.** RCA 77–DX. (Courtesy RCA)

A   B

problems. Unless the booth is well treated with sound-damping material, you probably will have to work about a foot from the mike. This range, with a ribbon mike, usually makes voice quality deeper, so if you find you have voice reproduction problems at close range, move to one side of the mike and speak across its front screen.

Although most ribbon microphones are not used in television, the RCA 77–DX is widely used in both radio and television. It is one of the few microphones which can be adjusted to a variety of pickup patterns and sound characteristics, and your work will be affected by the way it is set. For voice work the ribbon mike is significantly more flattering when the set screws are turned to "Voice 1" and "Bidirectional."

Dynamic or pressure microphones. In the dynamic or pressure mike (see Figure 4), a lightweight molded diaphragm attached to a small wire coil is suspended in a magnetic field. Sound waves striking the diaphragm are relayed to the coil, and the movement of the coil within the magnetic field transforms physical energy into electrical impulses. The dynamic microphone has a number of advantages: it is more rugged than other types, it can be used outdoors with less wind blast, it can be made as small as a person's thumb, and it can perform better in a wider range of applications than any other type of mike. Only a well-trained audio man is likely to be bothered by the fact that it does not reproduce the subtle colorations achieved by a high-quality ribbon or condenser mike. In using a dynamic mike, you should stand about a foot away and to one side of the front screen of the instrument. By talking slightly across the screened surface, you should project your voice quality at its best; this is doubly true if you have a tendency to shout or are given to sibilance or popping.

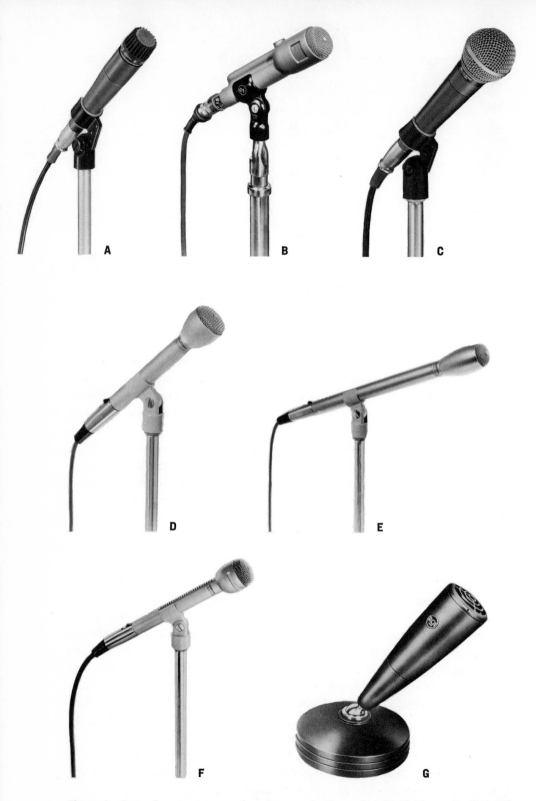

Figure 4. Dynamic or pressure microphones. A. Shure SM 57 Unidyne. **B.** E–V 666. **C.** Shure SM 58. **D.** E–V 635A. **E.** E–V RE55. **F.** E–V RE15. **G.** RCA BK–1A Commentator. (**A, C** courtesy Shure Bros. **B, D, E, F** courtesy Electro-Voice. **G** courtesy RCA)

Despite continual improvement of internal diaphragm suspension systems, lavaliere dynamic mikes must be used with care to avoid picking up unwanted noise. A script being thumbed or rattled three inches away from the lavaliere will be as loud or louder than a voice coming from a foot or more away. Clothing brushing against the surface of the mike will sound like a forest fire. Nervous toying with the microphone cable will transmit scratching and rumbling sounds directly into the microphone.

Condenser microphones. Condenser mikes (see Figures 5 and 6) are most often seen in professional recording studios or at stereo FM stations. The condenser is similar to the pressure mike in that it has a diaphragm, but instead of a coiled wire it has an electrode as a backplate. A capacitance between the diaphragm and the electrode varies with the minute movements of the diaphragm as they reflect the sound waves. If you are asked to work with a high-quality condenser mike, you should treat it as you would a dynamic microphone. If you find that the extreme sensitivity of the condenser is giving you sibilance or popping problems, try working farther away from it, and try speaking across it—one or both of these adjustments should correct the problem.

Figure 5. Sony C–77 FET condenser tele-microphone. (Courtesy Superscope, Inc.)

Figure 6. Sony C–37 FET condenser microphone. (Courtesy Superscope, Inc.)

PICKUP OR POLAR PATTERNS

The pickup pattern of a microphone is the shape of the area around it where it picks up sounds with maximum fidelity and volume. Nearly any microphone can pick up sounds from areas outside the ideal pattern, but their quality will not be as good. For best results, the sound source (*e.g.,* you) should be within the pickup pattern and generating enough volume to allow the engineer to keep his volume control knob at a minimal level. If you are out of the pattern (off mike) or if you speak too softly, the audio man will have to turn up his volume control and the microphone will automatically distort your voice and transmit unwanted sounds from outside the pattern. On television, if you use a lavaliere mike or a boom mike, you need not be concerned about pickup patterns: both types of mike were designed to be invisible or unobtrusive on camera and do not require you to do more than project your voice at an adequate volume level. When you use a desk, stand, hand-held, or control-room mike, you cannot ignore the pickup pattern of the instrument being used. You are expected to position yourself properly and adjust yourself and the mike to improve the sound.

Manufacturers classify microphones according to five pickup patterns: (1) unidirectional—only one side of the mike is live; (2) bidirectional—two sides of the microphone are live; (3) cardioid—the pattern is a predominantly unidirectional heart shape; (4) omnidirectional (nondirectional)—the mike is live in all directions; (5) multidirectional (polydirectional)—two or more patterns can be achieved by adjusting a set screw.

Descriptions and engineering diagrams (see Figure 7) of microphone pickup patterns are inadvertently misleading for two reasons: first, they do not show the three-dimensionality of the pattern; second, they do not indicate that the pattern changes when the relationship between instrument and sound source changes. A unidirectional microphone, for instance, is only unidirectional so long as the screen allowing sound to enter is vertical and at the same height as the sound source. When the instrument is tipped so that the screen is parallel to the floor, or when it is placed a little below or above the sound source, it becomes omnidirectional. In both applications, the actual pickup area is a near-perfect globe abutting on the face of the instrument.

Because cardioid mikes can be positioned in every conceivable relationship between instrument and sound source, the patterns vary in design and are especially difficult to understand from engineering diagrams. The complex cardioid pattern, shown in two dimensions on engineering data sheets, is significantly different when the mike is hand-held and when it is stand-mounted at a thirty-degree angle. The data sheet will show you whether a particular cardioid microphone has a narrow or wide angle of front sound acceptance, as well as the areas of rear acceptance and rejection, but only actual practice with cardioid mikes will teach you how to position them. In studying the typical pickup patterns in Figure 7, remember that (1) the actual pattern is three-dimensional, and (2) the illustrations for unidirectional mikes, including cardioid patterns, show the mike

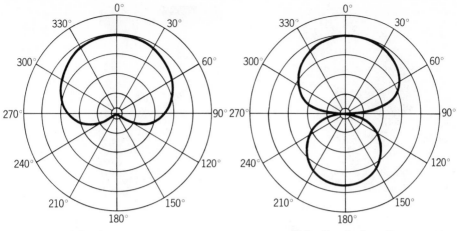

Unidirectional polar pattern

Bidirectional polar pattern

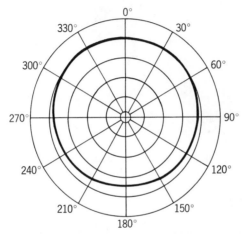

Omnidirectional polar pattern

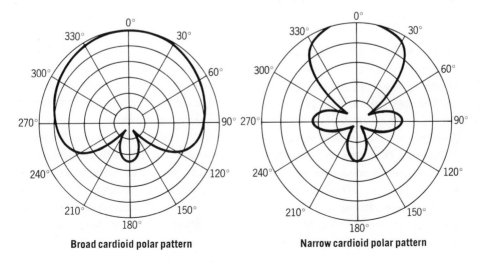

Broad cardioid polar pattern

Narrow cardioid polar pattern

Figure 7. Microphone polar patterns.

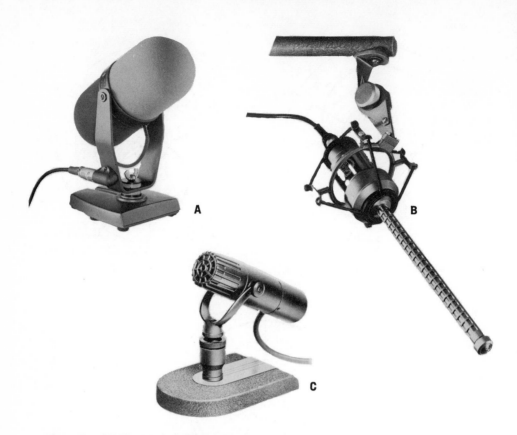

Figure 8. Studio boom microphones. A. Shure SM 5 (dynamic). B. E–V 642 (dynamic). C. RCA BK–5B (ribbon). (A courtesy Shure Bros. B courtesy Electro-Voice. C courtesy RCA)

lying flat with the screen pointed toward "0," while the omnidirectional illustration shows the screen pointing directly toward you.

SELECTING MICROPHONES

Both radio and television have developed diversified production approaches, and, as a result, microphones have become increasingly specialized. A microphone of one design may be ideal for one kind of work and inappropriate for another, even though its pickup pattern and internal structure conform to the requirements of both jobs. One dynamic omnidirectional mike may have been designed to be hand-held while a second may have been miniaturized for use as a lavaliere. A rugged dynamic mike may be best for a high-volume disc jockey and a sensitive condenser for voice work on a stereo FM station. As an announcer you can expect to work with a dozen or more different microphones over the years. In the following list of the mikes you will most likely encounter, a few have been included which are no longer being produced; chances are good that you will begin your announcing career with older equipment.

Make and Model	Internal Structure	Pattern	Function
E–V RE15	dynamic	cardioid	*Announce mikes* in radio control rooms, announce booths (both radio and television), and for off-camera film and television narration. May be mounted on floor or desk stands or on goose necks.
E–V 666	dynamic	cardioid	
E–V 635A	dynamic	omni	
RCA 77–DX	ribbon	multi	
RCA BK–5B	ribbon	cardioid	
Shure SM 57	dynamic	cardioid	
Shure SM 58	dynamic	cardioid	
Sony C–37 FET	condenser		
RCA 44–BX	ribbon	bi	*Stand mikes* for producing radio commercials and off-camera narration
RCA 77–DX	ribbon	multi	
Altec 639	ribbon & dynamic	multi	
Shure SM 57	dynamic	cardioid	
Shure SM 58	dynamic	cardioid	*Hand-held mikes,* indoor or outdoor use. Can be mounted on desk stands for sportscasts.
E–V 635A	dynamic	omni	
E–V RE55	dynamic	omni	
E–V 655C	dynamic	omni	
Shure SM 5	dynamic	cardioid	
RCA BK–5B	ribbon	cardioid	
RCA 77–DX	ribbon	multi	*Studio boom mikes*
E–V 642	dynamic	cardioid	
E–V 666	dynamic	cardioid	
E–V 649 A or B	dynamic	omni	
RCA BK–6B	dynamic	omni	*Lavaliere mikes*
RCA BK–12A	dynamic	omni	
RCA BK–1A	dynamic	uni	*Television desk mikes* (often the same as announce booth mikes)
E–V 666	dynamic	cardioid	
Vega-Mike	dynamic	omni	*Wireless microphone* for remote locations. (Wireless microphones are miniature FM transmitters, and an FCC license is required for their use.)

Condenser mikes are notably absent from this list because you will encounter them less frequently in broadcast work (see page 111).

Advances in microphones are constantly being made, and it is probable that instruments not listed will be in use by the time you enter the industry. But de-

A

B

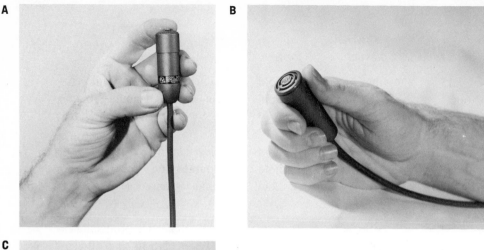

C

Figure 9. Lavaliere microphones. A. E–V 649B (dynamic). B. RCA BK–6B (dynamic). C. RCA BK–12A (dynamic). (A courtesy Electro-Voice. B, C courtesy RCA)

spite improvements in miniaturization, sensitivity, and fidelity, the principles of microphone use will probably remain the same for many years.

Cueing Records

A good portion of your time on the job will probably be spent cueing up and playing records. Tape cartridges are replacing most transcription discs and non-cartridge audio tapes for commercials and station I.D.'s, but you can expect to work with discs, too. In this section little attention is given to audio-tape cartridges, since you can learn to play them in less than five minutes. The cartridge is loaded with a looped, endless audio tape which automatically rewinds as it is played. You insert the cartridge into a slot in the playback machine and press a button to start the tape; after the tape has played, allow it to run until it stops by itself: it has automatically recued and is ready for another playing. If you stop the tape before it recues, you will get the "dead air" after the sound during its next playing, and it will automatically stop when it has reached the cue position. (See Figure 11.)

The essential difference between a disc and a transcription is simply that a transcription is made for broadcast use only, whereas a disc is made both for

Figure 10. Vega Professional 56 wireless microphone and receiver. (Courtesy Vega Electronics Corporation)

home and broadcast use. Discs may be of many sizes: six-and-a-half, seven, ten, or twelve inches in diameter. Transcriptions are usually either twelve or sixteen inches in diameter. Discs may play at 33⅓, 45, or 78.26 (usually called 78) revolutions per minute. Few 78 rpm discs are still in use, and many radio stations no longer maintain equipment for playing them. Transcriptions are almost always played at 33⅓ rpm. The correct playing speed is usually indicated on the label of any disc or transcription.

Most broadcast turntables are made up of the following: (1) a rotating turntable with a drive mechanism concealed underneath; (2) a pickup or tone arm; (3) one or more pickup cartridges; (4) an off-on switch; (5) a variable equalizer; (6) a speed switch; (7) an attachment for playing the large center-hole 45 rpm discs.

Figure 11. Sparta tape-cartridge playback unit. (Courtesy Sparta Electronic Corporation)

1. *Rotating turntable.* The turntable is usually started by bringing a small rubber capstan driven by an electric motor into contact with the inside rim of the turntable. The contact between the capstan and the rim is firm, and the rubber consequently is somewhat flattened against the metal. If you carelessly leave the capstan engaged for long periods of time when the motor is not running, the rubber will take on a permanent flat place, destroying the accuracy of the turntable's speed.

The turntable itself is usually made of metal. A felt or rubber pad covers it, and the disc or transcription is placed on top of this. The pad is not attached to the metal, and many announcers merely hold the pad, turn on the power, and release the pad to start the record.

Many turntables have a large recessed metal hub in the center. By removing the rubber or felt pad and turning the hub slightly, it may be raised to accommodate the large-holed 45 rpm discs.

2. *Pickup or tone arm.* Pickup arms used in broadcasting are both counterbalanced and "damped" to prevent damage to records. In modern practice, a tone arm will be adjusted to put less than one gram of pressure on the grooves of the record, while viscous damping—the use of fluid silicone in a hydraulic application—prevents the arm from making sharp, sudden movements. Studio turntables reserved for transcriptions or 78 rpm discs may be set for five grams pressure, since these records require more weight to prevent groove jumping.

3. *Pickup cartridges and styli.* Two types of pickup cartridges are used with broadcast tone arms: the first is a single-stylus plug-in cartridge which must be changed when going from a standard to a microgroove or a monaural to a stereo disc; the second is a turnaround head, most often equipped with 1-mil and 3-mil styli which are changed by moving a short stem. Stereo cartridges have a .7-mil stylus and, with a tone arm set to track with less than two grams pressure, can be used on any type of record without causing damage.

Record labels should give you all the information you need to select the proper stylus. Use a standard 3-mil monaural stylus on 78 rpm discs and 33⅓ rpm transcriptions unless the record is microgroove; use a 1-mil microgroove monaural stylus on 45 and 33⅓ rpm monaural discs and on microgroove transcriptions; where available, use a stereo stylus on all stereo records; if necessary, use a 1-mil monaural stylus on stereo records that can be played safely with a microgroove stylus.

4. *Off-on switch.* All turntables are equipped with a power switch. Some tables rotate whenever this switch is on; others can be stopped mechanically even while the power is on (see *"Speed switch,"* below).

5. *Variable equalizer.* Some turntable assemblies are equipped with variable equalizers, or filters, which allow you to control the frequencies being transmit-

ted. Old discs and discs poorly recorded or pressed can sometimes be made to sound better by eliminating high frequencies. Most microgroove and stereo records sound best when they are played without filtration.

6. *Speed switch.*   Turntables are provided with speed-selector switches, usually offering a choice of 33⅓, 45 and 78 rpm. Some offer only two speeds—33⅓ and 45—and some include a neutral position. When the switch is put at neutral, the turntable stops. If a turntable has a neutral position, always set the speed switch there when the machine is not in use. Only by switching to neutral can you disengage the rubber wheel from the inner rim of the turntable, whether the power is off or not.

Discs and transcriptions have "dead" grooves before the sound begins. Because you do not want several seconds of dead air between your announcement and the start of the recording, you must "cue up" your records. Cueing involves these steps: (1) While one record is being broadcast, place the next selection on a spare turntable. (2) If necessary, change the stylus to one suited to the record. (3) Using a control on the audio console (see the next section for specifics), activate the cue box or cue speaker. (4) Place the stylus on the outside groove of the record. (5) Disengage the drive mechanism so that the table spins freely. (6) Spin the table in a clockwise direction until you hear the start of the sound on the cue speaker. (7) Stop the table and turn the record counterclockwise. (8) When you hear the sound—now being played backwards—stop, continue spinning the record a short distance into the "dead air" grooves. (9) Engage the drive mechanism at the proper operating speed. To play the disc on the air you need only open the volume control and turn on the power switch.

Some operators prefer other ways of starting a record. One method begins with the power switch on and the speed switch in neutral; to play the record, move the

Figure 12. QRK 12/Custom turntable; can be completed with any standard tone arm. (Courtesy QRK Electronic Products, Inc.)

switch to the appropriate speed. Another method is called "slip starting." With the power switch on and the turntable in motion, hold the felt or rubber pad on which the record rests, thus preventing the record from turning with the table; to start the record, merely release the pad. Some operators slip start by holding the record edge with slight finger pressure while both the turntable and the felt pad turn beneath.

The reason for turning the record back to a point in the dead air is to allow the turntable to reach its operating speed before the sound begins. Any turntable needs a little time to go from 0 rpm to its operating speed, and before it gets there, sound will be distorted. Such "wowing" is as unacceptable as several seconds of dead air; a little practice with a particular turntable should enable you to cue records unerringly. Some turntables—such as the QRK (Figure 12) —are designed to achieve speed in one-eighth of a second (one-sixteenth of a revolution) at $33\frac{1}{3}$ rpm, while others of older vintage require half a revolution. Both types are common, and both have their champions.

Audio Consoles

Even announcers who have no need for an FCC operator's license will, at some time in their careers, have to operate a station audio console. The audio console, or "board," picks up the electrical impulses coming from microphones or turntables, mixes the sound in the proper proportions if more than one signal is coming in, controls the amplitude of the electrical impulse, amplifies the sound, and sends it, via another amplifier, to the transmitter. Microphones usually are positioned on or very near the console, and at least two turntables and two or more audio-tape cartridge machines will also be found in close proximity. The physical arrangement will vary in small details, but it is usually similar to the KTIM–AM and FM, San Rafael, announce booth in Figure 27. Most disc jockeys, especially those on all but the largest stations, and announcers reading station breaks, spot commercial announcements, and news, work from a control room and operate their own audio consoles. Combining announcing and audio engineering is called "working combo."

At first glance, an audio console is a little frightening. Its parts are labeled cryptically. The dials, keys, and switches resemble those on an airplane instrument panel. Actually, with an understanding of the function of an audio board and a little practice with boards of different makes, you should have no difficulty even with types you have never operated before.

In recent years, audio-control equipment has become increasingly complex and versatile. Audio boards now sometimes include built-in equalizers, filters, separate VU meters for each channel, and panoramic potentiometers ("pan pots") which can shift the sound from one channel to another. The vertical fader has almost completely replaced the rotating potentiometer on recording studio boards. If you expect to become an audio engineer, you will have to master equipment of such complexity. As an announcer working combo, however, it is

Figure 13. Sparta A–20 audio console. (Courtesy Sparta Electronic Corporation)

most unlikely that you will be expected to work this kind of console; the typical console operated by a radio announcer probably will remain a simple instrument for the foreseeable future.

STANDARD CONSOLE FEATURES

Most boards used by combo operators, however different they may seem at first glance, are essentially alike. You will find that many boards used in broadcasting are "custom made"—that is, station engineers have modified a standard board in one or several ways. Additionally, each station uses the input potential of its board in a unique way. You should, therefore, not merely learn to operate

Figure 14. RCA BC–8 consolette. (Courtesy RCA)

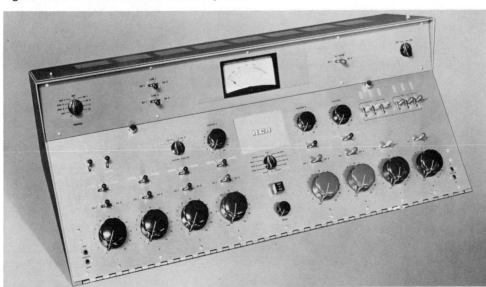

Figure 15. RCA BC–7 stereo consolette. (Courtesy RCA)

one board by rote; if you understand the reasons for doing what you do, you should be able to transfer to other consoles with little additional instruction.

A stereo board is no problem for the radio combo operator. Stereo discs are already balanced so the operator does not have to correct them on the board. Program announcements are usually given over only one of the two broadcast channels, but even when both channels are used, the console's controls will maintain an even balance. If the stereo signal reaching the transmitter is distorted, the combo operator merely notes it and asks the telephone company to check the lines.

A description of even a simple monaural console, however, can be confusing and deceptively formidable if you are not familiar with engineering nomenclature and electronics. Consequently, our investigation of a typical audio console stresses function—how the board relates to your work.

We have seen that the sounds of radio begin with electrical impulses coming from microphones, discs, and tapes. Let us suppose that we are designing our own console, adding elements as we perceive a need for them, to serve a moderate-sized AM radio station. This means it will be monaural rather than stereo, and a compromise between extremes of complexity and simplicity. Our station has four production areas, a *control room* (which houses the console), an *announce booth,* a *broadcast newsroom,* and a small *production studio.* Each area

Figure 16. Gates Yard II audio console, featuring a built-in cue speaker. (Courtesy Gates Radio Company)

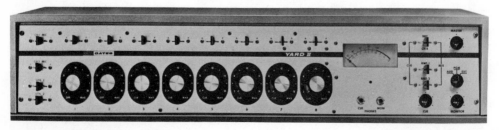

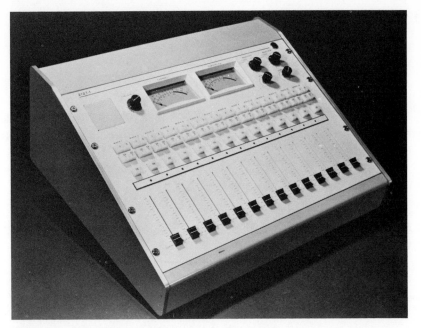

Figure 17. Collins 212T–1 stereo console with vertical faders. (Courtesy Collins Radio Company)

has one microphone, except for the production studio which has two. Our first problem is to feed the outputs of five microphones into our console. Mikes generate weak signals, so the output of each must be boosted—amplified—before we can send its signal out of the board to a recorder or a transmitter. If we were operating only one microphone in our radio station, one amplifier would be adequate for our needs, just as a single amplifier is sufficient for a public address system. But since we have inputs from several sound sources and need, as well, to mix these sounds with one another, we will need more than one amplifier at this stage, plus another to collect and regulate their outputs. The amplifiers which receive and boost signals from our microphones are called *preamplifiers,* and the one which collects, boosts, and sends sounds to the transmitter or tape recorder is called the *program amplifier*.

At this point, we would seem to need five preamplifiers (preamps) to match our five microphones, but we can economize here. We can install *input selector switches* (Figure 20A), which will allow us to feed more than one mike into the same preamp. If we knew that we would never want to mix the inputs from two or more of our mikes, or that we would not need to use more than one mike at a time, we could install a five-input selector switch which would feed selectively into one preamp. But we need more versatility than this, so we reach a compromise between the extremes of five preamps and one. Three preamps and three three-input selector switches will serve us well (see Figure 18).

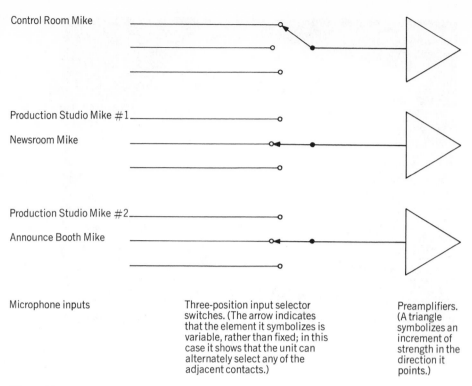

Control Room Mike

Production Studio Mike #1

Newsroom Mike

Production Studio Mike #2

Announce Booth Mike

Microphone inputs

Three-position input selector switches. (The arrow indicates that the element it symbolizes is variable, rather than fixed; in this case it shows that the unit can alternately select any of the adjacent contacts.)

Preamplifiers. (A triangle symbolizes an increment of strength in the direction it points.)

Figure 18

We have freed our control-room mike from conflict with other mikes. This is important because this mike serves as both a broadcast and a talk-back microphone. We now can send our voice into any of our three other production areas without having to move our input selector switch. And we can use our control-room for live announcements while we are recording an announcement—through our board—from any other production area.

We put the two production-studio mikes through two different channels so that we can use both of them at the same time; if we fed both to the same selector switch, we would be unable to mix the sounds coming from both mikes. The unused channels into our selector switches can be connected to microphones any time the need arises.

We now see two problems calling for two more controls: we need to vary the volume of sound going from the preamplifier to the program amplifier, and we need a switch for opening and closing our microphones. We can regulate the volume of sound by adding for each input a simple volume control called a *potentiometer* or *pot* (Figure 20B). The pot—also known as a *fader, mixer, attenuator,* or *gain control*—can be operated by either a rotating knob or a vertical slider. We could settle for a two-position "off-on" switch, but we add, instead, a three-position *channel selector switch* (Figure 20C). This gives us a position for "Off" and two channels for sending signals; if we had only one channel, we could not use our board for two functions at the same time. With two channels, we can broadcast a news roundup from our newsroom at the same time we receive and record UPI Audio news for later broadcast. Each of our two channels gets its own program amplifier, so we now have a total of five amplifiers for our board—three preamps and two program amplifiers. Our board has become a two-channel monaural audio console.

In adding volume controls (pots), we have raised another problem: how can we judge the volume? We cannot listen to ourselves on a conventional radio receiver, since the sound of our broadcast would reenter the open microphone and create an unearthly howl called feedback. So we add a meter which gives us a picture of the sound (Figure 20D). We call this a *VU* meter or *VI,* standing for volume-unit meter or volume indicator. We place it at the top and center of our board where it is easily visible. (Stereo boards require a separate meter for each channel.) Our VU meter has a swinging needle which registers volume on a calibrated scale. A semicircular black line registers volume units from one to one hundred, at which point it becomes a red line. If we are too low on the scale we are said to be "in the mud," and if we are too high we are "bending the needle" or "spilling over." If we peak too high on the scale we can damage our equipment. Even though ours is a monaural board, we install two VU meters, one for each channel. This allows us to see the output of both channels at the same time; if we had only one meter we would need to add a selector switch for choosing which channel we wanted to observe.

We now have everything we need to pick up sounds from four different production areas and send them through the board to a transmitter or tape recorder. We can open and close our mikes, mix the signals from two mikes, boost the signal strength, see our volume level, and regulate the volume; we also have two channels and can broadcast through one of them while using the other for a different purpose.

Now we need to go back and provide for additional sound sources. This means adding pots, but we need not add a separate pot for each potential sound source; input selector switches will allow us to feed three signals selectively through each pot. We already have three microphone pots; by adding five more pots and their attendant input selector and channel selector keys, our board can accommodate all these inputs:

Sound Source	Pot Number
Control-room mike	1
Production studio mike 1 Newsroom mike	2
Production studio mike 2 Announce booth mike	3

Turntable 1
Tape cartridge 1   4
Tape recorder 1

Turntable 2
Tape cartridge 2   5
Tape recorder 2

Network program feed
UPI Audio   6
Remote line 1

Mobile news unit
Remote line 2   7
Line for telephone callers

Spare for emergencies or future needs   8

The network feed provides us with hourly news summaries; UPI Audio sends us dozens of news stories and interviews each day which we tape for later inclusion in our own newscasts; we have our own mobile news unit, and its messages are sent to a receiver in master control before being fed through our board. Remote lines are used for sports events, live coverage of important news events, and the like. The telephone line is used during talk shows; callers are put on the air with a seven-second tape delay. The spare lines could be used for a third turntable, tape-cartridge machine, and tape recorder. In a television station board, several lines would be used for video-tape recorders and film projectors.

To avoid the difficulties in manually balancing the simultaneous inputs from several sound sources, we add a *master pot* (Figure 20E) for each channel which feeds into the program amplifiers and is capable of raising or lowering at the same time the volume of all sounds going through the channel. After balancing our microphone and turntable pots, our VU meter may tell us that the mixed sound is too weak or too strong; all we have to do to control it is adjust the master pot of the appropriate channel.

In order to hear material being broadcast or recorded, we add a *monitor speaker* for each of our two channels. If we have patched Channel 1 to the transmitter, we can listen to our programming on Monitor Speaker 1; Monitor Speaker 2 can be used to audition material not then being broadcast, or to listen to program materials being recorded for later broadcast. The monitor speakers need amplifiers of higher power than the program amplifiers to boost the signal to the level needed to activate the loudspeakers. Each has its own *monitor pot* (Figure 20F) so that we can raise and lower the volume of sound in the control room; we also install a *channel monitor switch* (Figure 20G), so that we can selectively monitor Channels 1 and 2. *Muting relays* are installed to cut off our monitor speakers whenever our control-room mike is opened.

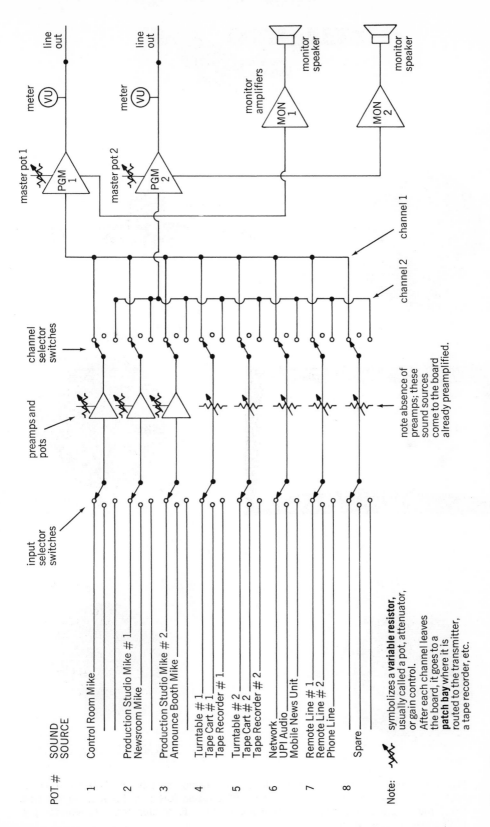

Figure 19

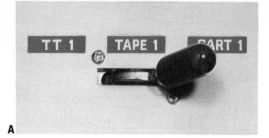

A

B

C

D

E

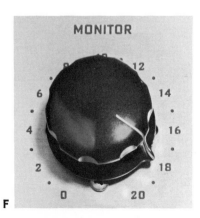

F

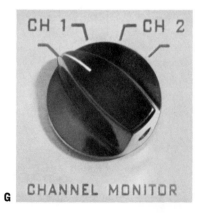

G

Figure 20. Audio console elements. A. Input selector switch. **B.** Potentiometer or "pot." **C.** Channel selector switch in the "off" position (CH 1 is the audition position, CH 2 the program position). **D.** VU meter or VI. **E.** Master pot. **F.** Monitor pot. **G.** Channel monitor switch.

Before airing discs or tapes which are not self-cueing, we must cue them up, and this means we must be able to hear them without broadcasting the sound. So we add a *cue speaker* or cue box with its own cue amplifier fed by all non-microphone pots. When each of these pots is turned to an extreme counterclockwise position, our cue amplifier and speaker are automatically activated. We could use other arrangements but this one seems best; with a turntable or tape pot turned completely off and into cue, there is no possibility of accidentally sending our cueing sounds out over the air—unless, of course, our control-room mike were open at the same time. To make sure that we do not confuse cueing sounds with program sounds, we locate the monitor speakers and the cue speaker in different parts of the control room.

Finally, we add a *headphone jack* for *headphones,* so that we can listen to either channel without having sound emanate from our monitor or cue speakers; both speakers automatically cut off when we plug in. This feature allows us to talk over music on the air. We can listen to the balance between our voice and the music without using the monitor speaker, which, of course, would create feedback. We also use 'phones to cue records when working combo. With the cue speaker dead there is no chance of cueing sounds accidentally being broadcast over our control-room mike.

Now our audio console is complete. We could, of course, add feature after feature, but nothing more is really needed for most modern radio applications. Many radio stations are now installing far simpler consoles than the board we have put together, but you cannot reasonably expect to find one at every station. The majority of consoles in operation today were designed when radio production was more complex than at present. The board we have created is typical of them and is a practical compromise between the extremes of simplicity and complexity marking the special-purpose boards now being manufactured.

To check your understanding of the elements common to most audio consoles, look carefully at Figures 13–17 and 20 in this chapter. You should be able to identify most of the visible features, even though variations in design will probably preclude complete identification.

Radio and Television Hand Signals

Because the operator of a television audio console is separated from the announcer by a soundproof glass partition, and because in both radio and television studios no voices other than those of the performers should be raised, visual signals have been developed for transmitting instructions. Even though most radio programming no longer involves elaborate production set-ups, the hand signals developed in the days of live, complex radio production are still used. The disc jockey who knows only the specific technique of production for his daily work is the despair of those for whom he might *some day* want to work—documentary or instructional film-makers, producers of radio commercials, the

Voice of America, or any other unit which engages in elaborate and professional audio production. And even though most local television productions are simply staged, the television announcer who wants to graduate to more complex and challenging productions simply must know more than the bare minimum of production procedures. For these reasons, you should memorize and practice the standard radio and television hand signals.

Since these signals project so graphically the commands they represent, it is tempting to assume that a general understanding of them is enough. Actually, the hand signals are precise and require more than a superficial awareness of their broader meanings. Wasted time and effort and, in extreme cases, serious mistakes may be avoided by knowing the signals cold.

Although most of the signals are used in both rehearsal and performance, two hand signals are used almost exclusively in rehearsal to avoid having to turn on the "talk-back" or studio address system (which has its microphone in the control room and its speaker in the studio) and to make unnecessary one more voice on the frequently overcrowded studio communications system. Because the television announcer is not in a position to see the director, he receives visual hand signals from the floor manager. During rehearsals, since silence need not be maintained, the floor manager usually passes on the instructions orally *when they are not to be delivered as hand signals during the actual performance.* The signals most used during rehearsals are these:

1. *Take a level.* The hand signal for this instruction is not standardized and varies from station to station. You should recognize at least these two signals for this request: (a) The director holds his arm before him, palm down and hand perfectly flat, and moves the hand back and forth as though he were leveling a pile of sand. (b) He holds his arm at about face level with the tip of the thumb touching the tips of the fingers, then opens and closes the hand rapidly, as though to say, "Go on and gab." The leveling signal is preferred, as announcers tend to respond to the "gab" signal with meaningless prattle, useless to the engineer who is trying to take a level on actual speech.

Because so much time and effort are wasted in taking microphone levels, it seems worthwhile to dwell on them. Before the production begins, the audio engineer must know the volume levels of all its audio inputs—voices, music, and sound effects—for it is his job to blend them in the proper volume proportions and with the best audio quality. It is no exaggeration to state that the proper blending of the various sounds is the most noticeable distinction between amateur and professional productions.

Each voice in a production has different characteristics, and each speaker operates at a different volume level. The audio engineer can help you make the most effective use of your voice, but he needs your cooperation in order to do so. When giving a level, it is imperative that you read from the actual script so that the engineer can hear the vocal characteristics, including volume, which will later mark your on-the-air performance. It is also important that you read for a long enough time to allow the engineer to complete his work. The customary malpractice which goes on in amateur or poorly organized professional productions might best be illustrated by a brief scene:

> (ENGINEER *is waving his hands and arms frantically, trying to attract the attention of the* ANNOUNCER. *In the studio below, the* ANNOUNCER *is doing his favorite imitations—Ed Sullivan, Richard Nixon, W. C. Fields, and Sammy Davis, Jr.)*

ANNCR: Reminds me of a slight peccadillo I once was . . .

ENGINEER: What's the matter with him? Doesn't he see me waving?

ANNCR: (*Now doing his imitation of an airplane dropping bombs.*) Mmm-mmmmmmmmmmmmmmm . . . BOOM!

ENGINEER: (*Finally turning off the studio mikes and opening the talkback.*) Hey, down there—how about giving me a level?

ANNCR: O.K. Yah-tah-tah, yah-tah-tah. Is that enough?

ENGINEER: (*Who has only now managed to turn off his talk-back and open the announcer's mike.*) What was that? What did you say?

ANNCR: I said is that enough?

ENGINEER: Is *what* enough? I haven't heard anything yet.

ANNCR: (*Now deciding to give the engineer a fighting chance, repeats nonsense syllables for a minute or so.*)

This scene is only slightly exaggerated. To make matters worse, the announcer, after giving his "level," will probably completely change his distance from and position on the microphone for the performance.

A better procedure follows: (a) The announcer constantly keeps his eye on the control room while waiting for signals from the director or the audio engineer. (b) On receiving the hand signal to give a level, he carefully moves into the exact position he intends to occupy during the program and reads from his script exactly as he will during the program. (c) The engineer then gives the appropriate hand signals to enable the announcer to find his optimum position on mike and establish his correct volume level. (d) The announcer, even while reading for the audition, keeps in visual contact with the engineer and makes the adjustments the engineer deems necessary. (e) The announcer continues reading until he is given a sign that the level is satisfactory. (f) The announcer and the engineer decide whether changes in volume called for in the script should be accomplished by the announcer or by adjustments of the volume control.

2. *Open my microphone.* The announcer uses this signal to indicate that he wants to establish communication with the control room. The signal is not used during a performance unless the program is, at that moment, emanating from some source other than the announcer's studio. To indicate this request, the announcer points his finger at his microphone and repeats the gesture until the mike is opened.

The remaining hand signals are used both during rehearsal and during actual performances. In rehearsal they should be obeyed with as much speed and seriousness as on the air.

3. *Watch me.* This signal is usually given by the director to the announcer, but in television it may be given by the floor manager on orders from the director. The purpose of the command is to prepare the announcer for some subsequent direction, including, at the outset of the program, the cue indicating that they are on the air. The hand signal is usually pointing the index finger to the eye. Because this is a static signal and thus easy to miss from the floor, it is usually preceded by an *attention* signal, which is waving the arm. The two signals, then, would be given in this order:

> *Attention.* The director (or television floor manager) waves his hand beside his face with the fingers extended.
>
> *Watch me.* After seeing that he has the attention of the announcer, the director points his index finger to his eye. In television, the floor manager must assume that the announcer has seen him, since an on-camera announcer cannot nod his recognition of the signal.

4. *Stand by.* The stand-by signal is given by the director at any time in a program when the announcer cannot judge the specific moment to pick up his cue—at the very outset of the program; when the announcer's performance must be coordinated with title cards, films, persons he cannot see, or music or sound he cannot hear; or when a pause has interrupted his reading. The stand-by signal is made by holding the hand slightly above the head, fingers together, and palm toward the announcer.

5. *Cue.* In almost every instance, the stand-by signal will precede the cue signal and the cue signal will follow the stand-by signal. The director rarely gives either alone. The cue signal consists of rapidly lowering the upraised arm, with hand and index finger extended, so that the finger points directly at the announcer receiving the cue. The cue signal given at the beginning of the program tells the announcer that he is to begin reading or speaking—that he is now on the air. The same signal given during the program tells the announcer that he should now begin to read the next passage in his script.

6. *Cut.* The director makes the cut signal to indicate to the announcer that he is to stop reading at once. It is made by drawing the index finger across the throat. In some studios this signal is used to tell the announcer that he should come to the end of his remarks as swiftly as possible. You should be prepared for this translation of the signal, even though such usage is discouraged; the cut signal should be used only to indicate an immediate halt.

One important matter must now be considered. The most crucial moment of any program is the point at which it goes on the air. Most of the mistakes made in professional productions occur here. The process of getting the show on the air is complicated, and notwithstanding the skill of professional directors and broadcast engineers, so many possibilities for error exist that occasional false starts are inevitable. Utter confusion usually—and unnecessarily—results when, shortly after receiving the cue to begin, the announcer is given the cut signal, then a stand-by immediately followed by a cue signal. Should the announcer begin over again? Should he pick up where he left off? Probably he should begin again. In an on-the-air situation, the director will not stop the production because of some minor error such as a "wowed" record (see page 120) or a bad interpretation from the reader. The only reason for stopping the show and starting again is that a technical error has prevented the program from going out over the air. This could mean that the entire opening has been a false start or merely that the announcer's microphone was not open. In any event, when the announcer receives a cut signal followed by a stand-by and then a cue signal within the first minute or two of the production, he should cut immediately and then read from the very beginning again. If the cut signal comes later in the program, he should return to the beginning of the most recent passage for which he was given a cue.

7. *Louder; softer.*　The director may occasionally ask you to increase or decrease your volume. The signal to increase volume is made by holding the hand before the body, palm up, and then raising the hand. The signal to decrease volume is made by holding the hand before the body, palm down, and then lowering the hand. Any adjustment in volume should be slow and smooth to avoid a noticeable change.

8. *Move left; move right.*　A speaker is said to be "off mike" when he is not directing his voice to the proper spot for the particular microphone, which usually means that he is too far to the left or right or too close to or far away from the microphone. Six signals have been devised to show the announcer that he is off mike. If he is too far left, the director flags his left arm (on the announcer's right, of course) up and down beside his body. If he is too far right, the director makes the same signal with his right arm.

9. *Move closer to the mike; move away from the mike.*　The director may give the signal to move closer to the microphone in one of two ways: (a) by holding his hands before his body, palms up, and then drawing his hands together; (b) by holding his hand before his face, palm toward his mouth, and then slowly moving it toward his mouth. The signals to move away from the microphone are naturally the reverse of these.

10. *On the nose.*　This signal indicates that the program is proceeding at the correct pace. It may be given at any time during the program and is made by pointing the index finger to the nose.

11. *Speed up.*　The director gives the speed-up signal to make the announcer increase the rate of his delivery. It does not tell the announcer how much or for

how long he is to speed up, but subsequent directions will indicate that he has not sped up enough, has sped up too much, or is right on time. The speed-up signal is made by holding the hand before the body, the index finger extended, and then rotating the hand.

12. *Slow down.*   The slow-down signal, also called the stretch signal, tells the announcer that he is going too fast. The director makes it by pulling his hands apart, as though pulling taffy. It may be given to indicate that the announcer's speed is interfering with his delivery or the mood of the program, but it is usually given to indicate that unless the announcer slows down, the program will end before the time is up. When he receives this signal, the announcer should begin reading his copy at a slower rate and watch for subsequent directions. In some instances, a previously cut portion of his script may now be reinserted. Insertions should not be made, however, if there is any possibility that they will harm the production. One instance where an insertion would be appropriate is on a radio news program for which the announcer himself has selected or written the copy. On a television newscast, an insertion would not be advisable if the camera director would be left with his cameras, film chain, or studio cards in the wrong position or in an unusable state. In any case, possible insertions or deletions should be carefully planned before the broadcast.

13. *Time signals.*   As the program nears its conclusion, the announcer often must be aware of the exact number of minutes or seconds remaining. The signals are as follows:

Three minutes. The director holds up three fingers to the announcer.
Two minutes. He holds up two fingers.
One minute. He holds up one finger.
Thirty seconds. He crosses the index finger of one hand with the index finger of the other into a plus (+) sign.
Fifteen seconds. He raises a clenched fist away from but beside his head.

14. *O.K.*   This signal is used to indicate that everything is proceeding nicely. It is made by forming an "o" with the thumb and index finger.

Two more signals are used exclusively in television. Because the television announcer usually looks directly into the on-the-air camera, and because most television productions use more than one camera, the announcer must know which camera to look at at any given time. Of course, the red light on the "hot" camera tells him this after the fact, but he needs to know in advance when the director intends to cut from one camera to another. When the floor manager, who is responsible for throwing all cues during a performance, hears the camera director say over the intercom, "Ready 2"—or whatever number the next camera is—he points first to the camera currently on the air. Then, when he hears the camera director say, "Take 2," he moves his hand in the direction of Camera 2. The announcer switches from one camera to the other as rapidly as possible.

The second signal used exclusively in television is for cueing film (discussed in Chapter 9).

Nearly all announcers operate broadcast equipment at one time or another. A thorough knowledge of microphones, consoles, turntables, tape machines, and tape cartridges will help you qualify for an announcing job. Both radio and television announcers should know the hand signals used in broadcast production, and television announcers should be familiar with television production techniques. You may not get an announcing job if you have a poor voice, but even the best voice will get you nowhere if you do not know the technical side of broadcasting.

Seven FCC Rules and Regulations

The Federal Communications Commission (FCC) was created in 1934 to protect the airwaves for the "public convenience, interest, or necessity." The FCC, which succeeded the Federal Radio Commission created in 1927, is composed of seven Commissioners and has its headquarters in Washington, D. C. Its functions are generally to license and regulate domestic broadcasting and to enforce the provisions of international radio agreements in the United States. Among its particular functions are (1) licensing and classifying radio and television stations and operators, (2) requiring stations to keep records of their operations, and (3) coordinating the use of radio and television during national emergencies. Aspects of these three areas of FCC jurisdiction are the subject of this chapter, because they affect announcers more directly than others.[1]

FCC Operator's Licenses

If you are seriously considering a career as either a radio or a television announcer, you are strongly advised to get an FCC operator's license. Though the license is not required of announcers on most television and large radio stations, there are several reasons for having this credential: first, the knowledge you acquire in working for your license will be invaluable as long as you are in broadcasting; second, unless you are unusually talented or lucky, you will begin your announcing career on a small-market radio station where a first- or second-class

[1] Material in this chapter was drawn from the FCC *Rules and Regulations Governing Broadcast Services,* 1968 edition, updated to 1970. Wherever possible, direct quotes are used; in other instances, brief passages have been translated into English from the original Governmentese, a language not widely understood outside the District of Columbia. A National Association of Broadcasters pamphlet, "NAB Radio-Television Program Log Recommendations," was helpful in clarifying some points, and their sample program log has been included (Figure 21) as an excellent illustration of log keeping.

operator's license is practically mandatory; third, an increasing number of small-market television stations, as well as some Community Antenna Television (CATV) operations, expect the announcer on duty to operate broadcast equipment, and a license is necessary for this; fourth, the often understaffed educational radio or television station and the instructional television fixed-service operation will welcome anyone to their staffs who has the knowledge and the licensed authority to operate broadcast equipment. The FCC does not require anyone to get a license; it *does* require, with insignificant exceptions, that the holder of a first-class operator's license be on duty at all times of broadcast by AM and FM radio stations, commercial and educational television stations, and educational FM radio stations with power above twenty-five kilowatts.

There are two classes of FCC broadcast licenses—radiotelephone first-class operator license and radiotelephone second-class operator license—and two classes of permits—radiotelephone third-class operator permit and restricted radiotelephone operator permit. All but the restricted permit, issued for the lifetime of the holder, must be renewed every five years. To be eligible for any of these licenses or permits, you must be at least fourteen years of age and an American citizen. No license will be issued or reissued to anyone (a) whose license is under suspension or who is involved in a suspension proceeding; (b) who is involved in any pending litigation based on an alleged violation of the Communications Act of 1934, as amended; (c) who is afflicted with complete deafness or complete muteness or complete inability for any other reason to transmit correctly and to receive correctly by telephone spoken messages in English. The ensuing section of the FCC *Rules and Regulations* on eligibility for FCC licenses, although tedious to read, is reproduced verbatim because of its importance to anyone with a severe physical disability:

(c) No applicant who is eligible to apply for any commercial radio operator license shall, by reason of any physical handicap, other than as set forth in paragraph (b)[2] of this section, be denied the privilege of applying and being permitted to attempt to prove his qualifications (by examination if examination is required) for such commercial radio operator license in accordance with established procedure; nor, subject to the following conditions, shall such applicant be denied the issuance of any commercial radio operator license for which he is found qualified:

(1) If the applicant is afflicted with uncorrected physical handicap which would clearly prevent the performance of all or any part of the duties of a radio operator, under the license for which application is made, at a station under emergency conditions involving the safety of life or property, he may be issued the license for which he is found qualified: *Provided,* That any license so received, if of the diploma-form (as distinguished from such document of the card-form), shall bear a restrictive endorsement as follows:

This license is not valid for the performance of any operating duties other than installation, service and maintenance duties, at any station licensed by the Federal Com-

[2] Deafness, muteness, or other inability to receive correctly telephone messages in English.

munications Commission which is required, directly or indirectly, by any treaty, statute or rule or regulation pursuant to statute, to be provided for safety purposes.

Provided further, That in the case of a diploma-form license for which no examination in technical radio matters is required, the endorsement will be modified by deleting the reference therein to installation, service and maintenance duties.

(2) If an applicant afflicted with blindness is afforded a waiver of the written examination requirement and is found qualified for a radiotelephone third class operator permit. he may be issued the permit: *Provided,* That the license so received shall bear an endorsement as follows:

This license is not valid for the operation of any station licensed by the Commission unless the station has been adapted for operation by a blind person and the equipment to be used in such station for that purpose is capable of providing for operation in compliance with the Commission's rules.

(3) In any case where an applicant, who normally would receive or has received a commercial radio operator license bearing the endorsement prescribed by subparagraph (1) of this paragraph, indicates his desire to operate a station falling within the prohibitive terms of the endorsement, he may request in writing that such endorsement not be placed upon, or be removed from, his license, and may submit in support of his request any written comment or statement of himself or any interested party.

(4) An applicant who shows that he has theretofore performed satisfactorily (by means of the service record appearing on the appropriate license document of the applicant or such other proof as may be appropriate under the circumstances of the particular case) the duties of a radio operator at a station required, directly or indirectly, by any treaty, statute, or rule or regulation pursuant to statute to be provided for safety purposes, during a period when he was afflicted by uncorrected physical handicaps of the same kind and to the same degree as the physical handicaps shown by his current application (this showing may be made by means of the applicant's written, sworn statement or such other documentary proof as may be appropriate under the circumstances of the particular case), shall not be deemed to be within the provisions of subparagraph (1) of this paragraph.

Application forms for permits and licenses may be obtained from FCC field offices, which also administer examinations.[3] Following are the cities in which the field offices are located; street addresses can be found in local telephone directories.

Alabama, Mobile   36602
Alaska, Anchorage (P.O. Box 644)   99501
California, Los Angeles   90014
California, San Diego   92101
California, San Francisco   94111
California, San Pedro   90731
Colorado, Denver   80202
District of Columbia, Washington   20554
Florida, Miami   33130
Florida, Tampa   33602

[3] The restricted operator permit requires no examination and may be obtained from the FCC field office at Gettysburg, Pennsylvania 17325. If the applicant lives in Alaska, Hawaii, Puerto Rico, or the Virgin Islands, or if the need for the permit is immediate, it may be obtained from the nearest field office.

Georgia, Atlanta   30303
Georgia, Savannah (P.O. Box 77)
   31402
Hawaii, Honolulu   96808
Illinois, Chicago   60604
Louisiana, New Orleans   70130
Maryland, Baltimore   21202
Massachusetts, Boston   02109
Michigan, Detroit   48226
Minnesota, St. Paul   55102
Missouri, Kansas City   64106

New York, Buffalo   14203
New York, New York   10014
Oregon, Portland   97205
Pennsylvania, Philadelphia   19106
Puerto Rico, San Juan (P.O. Box
   2987)   00903
Texas, Beaumont   77701
Texas, Dallas   75202
Texas, Houston   77002
Virginia, Norfolk   23510
Washington, Seattle   98104

The examination requirements for permits and licenses, as set forth in the FCC
Rules and Regulations, are: [4]

§ 13.21   Examination elements.

Written examinations will comprise questions from one or more of the following examination elements:

1. *Basic law.* Provisions of laws, treaties and regulations with which every operator should be familiar.
2. *Basic operating practice.* Radio operating procedures and practices generally followed or required in communicating by means of radiotelephone stations.
3. *Basic radiotelephone.* Technical, legal and other matters applicable to the operation of radiotelephone stations other than broadcast.
4. *Advanced radiotelephone.* Advanced technical, legal and other matters particularly applicable to the operation of the various classes of broadcast stations.

Elements 5–8 refer to requirements for nonbroadcast licenses. Since 1964, a holder of the third-class permit can receive a "Basic Broadcast Endorsement" entitling him to operate certain kinds of low-power stations by passing Element 9:

9. *Basic broadcast.* Basic regulatory matters applicable to the operation of standard commercial FM, and noncommercial educational FM broadcast stations.

§ 13.22   Examination requirements.

Applicants for original licenses will be required to pass examinations as follows:

  (a) *Radiotelephone second-class operator license:*
      (1) Ability to transmit and receive spoken messages in English
      (2) Written examination elements: 1, 2, and 3.
  (b) *Radiotelephone first-class operator license:*
      (1) Ability to transmit and receive spoken messages in English.
      (2) Written examination elements: 1, 2, 3, and 4.

                .   .   .   .   .

  (f) *Radiotelephone third-class operator permit:*
      (1) Ability to transmit and receive spoken messages in English.
      (2) Written examination elements: 1 and 2.

                .   .   .   .   .

[4] The portions of this section dealing with radio*telegraph* operator licenses have been omitted.

(h) *Restricted radiotelephone operator permit:*

No oral or written examination is required for this permit. In lieu thereof, applicants will be required to certify in writing to a declaration which states that the applicant has need for the requested permit; can receive and transmit spoken messages in English; can keep at least a rough written log in English or in some other language in general use that can be readily translated into English; is familiar with the provisions of treaties, laws, and rules and regulations governing the authority granted under the requested permit; and understands that it is his responsibility to keep currently familiar with all such provisions.

§ 13.23 Form of writing.

Written examination shall be in English and shall be written by the applicant in longhand in ink, except that diagrams may be in pencil.

§ 13.24 Passing mark.

A passing mark of 75 percent of a possible 100 percent will be required on each element of a written examination.

The FCC also imposes several responsibilities on the announcer-engineer:

§ 13.63 Operator's responsibility.

The licensed operator responsible for the maintenance of a transmitter may permit other persons to adjust a transmitter in his presence for the purpose of carrying out tests or making adjustments requiring specialized knowledge or skill, provided that he shall not be relieved thereby from responsibility for the proper operation of the equipment.

§ 13.64 Obedience to lawful orders.

All licensed radio operators shall obey and carry out the lawful orders of the master or person lawfully in charge of the ship or aircraft on which they are employed.

§ 13.65 Damage to apparatus.

No licensed radio operator shall willfully damage, or cause or permit to be damaged, any radio apparatus or installation in any licensed radio station.

§ 13.66 Unnecessary, unidentified, or superfluous communications.

No licensed radio operator shall transmit unnecessary, unidentified, or superfluous radio communications or signals.

§ 13.67 Obscenity, indecency, profanity.

No licensed radio operator or other person shall transmit communications containing obscene, indecent, or profane words, language, or meaning.

§ 13.68 False signals.

No licensed radio operator shall transmit false or deceptive signals or communications by radio, or any call letter or signal which has not been assigned by proper authority to the radio station he is operating.

§ 13.69 Interference.

No licensed radio operator shall willfully or maliciously interfere with or cause interference to any radio communication or signal.

§ 13.70 Fraudulent licenses.

No licensed radio operator or other person shall alter, duplicate, or fraudulently obtain, or assist another to alter, duplicate, or fraudulently obtain an operator license. Nor shall any person use a license issued to another or a license which he knows to have been altered, duplicated, or fraudulently obtained.

The FCC *Study Guide* indicating the nature and scope of its licensing examinations will be less valuable to you than several commercially published question-and-answer manuals. Most of these books can be found in school and community libraries, or they may be ordered from any bookstore. The FCC guide may be obtained from The Superintendent of Documents, U. S. Government Printing Office, Washington, D. C. 20402. Before sending for it, check its current cost with the nearest FCC field office, since your order must be accompanied by a check or money order.

FCC Rules and Regulations Pertaining to the Announcer

The FCC publications setting forth the rules and regulations governing radio and television broadcasting include the requirements of logging, station identification, operating a broadcast facility during an emergency, and several other matters of importance. The regulations undergo sporadic but unending revision; the current ones will be outdated before this book is released, so they will not be reprinted here. The following overview will acquaint you with their general provisions, but before taking it as gospel truth, be sure the regulations have not been changed.

The FCC requires each broadcast station to keep program, operating, and maintenance logs. Radio and television announcers usually keep the program log; those who double as announcer-engineers on radio stations may be responsible for the other two. Only program logs (Figure 21) will be discussed here, since the operating and maintenance logs are too complex technically for the scope of this book.

FCC regulations state that "each log shall be kept by the station employee or employees competent to do so, having actual knowledge of the facts required, who in the case of program and operating logs shall sign the appropriate log when starting duty, and again when going off duty." At most radio and some television stations, this means the announcer. The sample log sheet (Figure 21) illustrates the way in which a log is to be kept. The FCC accepts a simple check mark (✔) as an indication by the operator that the indicated material was broadcast. No log or any part of it may be erased, obliterated, or willfully destroyed for two years. Logs involving communications about a disaster or an investigation by the FCC must be retained until the FCC authorizes their destruction. Corrections may be made only by striking out the erroneous portion, not by erasing it, and the person who does so must initial the correction if it is made during his shift or must write and sign an explanation if it is done later. The FCC allows logs to include "additional information such as that needed for billing purposes or for the cueing of automatic equipment" and it exempts these entries from FCC restrictions on correcting and changing logs.

The FCC requires in a program log specific information in each of four categories: programs, commercial matters, public-service announcements, and other announcements:

A. For each program, enter:
1. Program name or title (Column 4 on sample log)
2. Time program begins and ends (Columns 2 and 3 on sample log)
3. Type of program (Column 6 on sample log). The FCC acknowledges eight types of programs and three subcategories.[5] Here are the current definitions of the eight program types:

(a) AGRICULTURAL PROGRAMS (A) include market reports, farming or other information specifically addressed, or primarily of interest, to the agricultural population.

(b) ENTERTAINMENT PROGRAMS (E) include all programs intended primarily as entertainment, such as music, drama, variety, comedy, quiz, etc.

(c) NEWS PROGRAMS (N) include reports dealing with current local, national, and international events, including weather and stock market reports; and when an integral part of a news program, commentary, analysis, and sports news.

(d) PUBLIC AFFAIRS PROGRAMS (PA) include talks, commentaries, discussions, speeches, editorials, political programs, documentaries, forums, panels, round tables, and similar programs primarily concerning local, national, and international public affairs.

(e) RELIGIOUS PROGRAMS (R) include sermons or devotionals; religious news; and music, drama, and other types of programs designed primarily for religious purposes.

(f) INSTRUCTIONAL PROGRAMS (I) include programs (other than those classified under Agricultural, News, Public Affairs, Religious or Sports) involving the discussion of, or primarily designed to further an appreciation or understanding of, literature, music, fine arts, history, geography, and the natural and social sciences; and programs devoted to occupational and vocational instruction, instruction with respect to hobbies, and similar programs intended primarily to instruct.

(g) SPORTS PROGRAM (S) include play-by-play and pre- or post-game related activities and separate programs of sports instruction, news or information (e.g., fishing opportunities, golfing instructions, etc.)

(h) OTHER PROGRAMS (O) include all programs not falling within definitions (a) through (g).

The three subcategories are:

(i) EDITORIAL (EDIT) include programs presented for the purpose of stating opinions of the licensee.

[5] The letter or letters in parentheses following the name of each program type is the authorized abbreviation of the type for log entries.

(j) POLITICAL PROGRAMS (POL) include those which present candidates for public office or which give expressions (other than in station editorials) to views on such candidates or on issues subject to public ballot.

(k) EDUCATIONAL INSTITUTION PROGRAMS (ED) include any program prepared by, in behalf of, or in cooperation with, educational institutions, educational organizations, libraries, museums, PTA's or similar organizations. Sports programs shall not be included.

The rules state that these subcategories are to be indicated, when appropriate, under one or another of the eight major types. Types (i) through (k) may be duplicated, *"e.g.,* a program presenting a candidate for public office, prepared by an educational institution, would be classified as Public Affairs (PA), Political (POL), and Educational Institution (ED)."

4. Source of program (Column 7 on sample log).[6] The FCC instructions on program source are:

(a) A LOCAL PROGRAM (L) is any program originated or produced by the station, or for the production of which the station is substantially responsible, and employing live talent more than 50% of the time. Such a program, taped, recorded, or filmed for later broadcast shall be classified by the station as local. A local program fed to a network shall be classified by the originating station as local. All non-network news programs may be classified as local. Programs primarily featuring syndicated or feature films or other nonlocally recorded programs shall be classified as "Recorded" (REC) even though a station personality appears in connection with such material. However, identifiable units of such programs which are live and separately logged as such may be classified as local (*e.g.,* if during the course of a feature film program, a non-network 2-minute news report is given and logged as a news program, the report may be classified as local).

(b) A NETWORK PROGRAM (NET) is any program furnished to the station by a network (national, regional or special). Delayed broadcasts of programs originated by networks are classified as network.

(c) A RECORDED PROGRAM (REC) is any program not defined in (a), (b), (c) above, including without limitation, syndicated programs, taped or transcribed programs, and feature films.

5. Name and political affiliation of the program if it presents a political candidate (Column 4, Line 15 on sample log)

B. For commercial matter, enter:

1. Name of sponsor(s) (Column 4 on sample log)
2. Names of person(s) who paid for the announcement (Column 4 on sample log)
3. Name of person(s) who furnished materials or services (Column 4 on sample log)

---

[6] The abbreviations in parentheses are the approved FCC code for log entry.

If the title of a sponsored program includes the name of the sponsor, a separate entry for the sponsor is not required.

Commercial matter is defined by the FCC as commercial continuity and commercial announcements (both network and non-network). Further:

> (1) Included are (i) "bonus spots"; (ii) tradeout spots, and (iii) promotional announcements of a future program where consideration is received for such an announcement or where such announcement identifies the sponsor of a future program beyond mention of the sponsor's name as a integral part of the title of the program. (*E.g.,* where the agreement for the sale of time provides that the sponsor will receive promotional announcements, or when the promotional announcement contains a statement such as "LISTEN TOMORROW FOR THE—[NAME OF PROGRAM]—BROUGHT TO YOU BY—[SPONSOR'S NAME]—.")

This section of the FCC rules also stipulates six types of announcements *not* considered commercial matter:

1. Promotional announcements which are not advertising messages for which a charge is made or other consideration is received
2. Station identification announcements for which no charge is made
3. Mechanical reproduction announcements (announcements that a program is mechanically reproduced)
4. Public-service announcements
5. Announcements that materials or services have been furnished as an inducement to broadcast a political program or a program involving the discussion of public issues, *if* the service or property furnished is given free or with nominal charge and if the agency providing the support does not expect anything beyond a simple identification of its help
6. Announcements required by the FCC of station pre-grant and renewal hearings [7]

C. For public-service announcements, enter:

1. A statement that a PSA has been broadcast and the name of the organization or interest in whose behalf it was made (Column 4, Line 6 on sample log)

The FCC definition of a public-service announcement is:

> . . . an announcement for which no charge is made and which promotes programs, activities, or services of federal, state or local governments (*e.g.,* recruiting, sales of bonds, etc.) or the programs, activities or services of non-profit organizations (*e.g.,* UGF, Red Cross Blood Donations, etc.), and other announcements regarded as serving community interests, excluding time signals, routine weather announcements and promotional announcements.

---

[7] The FCC holds hearings before granting or renewing station licenses.

AM FM TV
☐ ☐ ☐

STATION WXXX DAILY PROGRAM LOG

Chevrolac Broadcasting Co., Inc.
Littletown, Plainstate

6. Commercial Matter or Announcement Type: Commercial Matter (CM); Public Service Announcement (PSA); Mechanical Reproduction Announcement (MRA); Announced as Sponsored (V).
7. Program Source: Local (L); Network (Identify); Recorded (REC).
8. Program Type: Agricultural (A); Entertainment (E); News (N); Public Affairs (PA); Religious (R); Instructional (I); Sports (S); Other (O); Editorials (EDIT); Political (POL); Educational (ED).

page 1
day Monday
date 10/6/69
time EST

Station Identification Time 1	Program Time Begin 2	Program Time End 3	Program Title — Sponsor 4	Commercial Matter or Announcement Duration 5	Type 6	Program Source 7	Program Type 8
1– 8:00	8:00	9:00	RHYTHM MELODIES			REC	E
2–			James Brothers	60	✓ CM		
3–			XYZ Laundry	60	✓ CM		
4–			Alan Tires	60	✓ CM		
5–			~~ABC Ice Cream~~	~~30~~	~~✓ CM~~		
6–			Red Cross		PSA		
7–			Sureway Food	60	✓ CM		
8–			Stop-Start Driver Training School	60	✓ CM		
9–			Shady Hill Summer Theatre	60	✓ CM		
10– 8:30	8:30	8:35	NEWS HEADLINES - Country Journal	1:30	✓ CM	L	N
11–			John's Donut Shop	60	✓ CM		
12–			Blackacre Real Estate	60	✓ CM		
13–			Wright Insurance	60	✓ CM		
14–			Rong Shoe Store	60	✓ CM		
15– 9:00	9:00	9:14	JOE SMITH DEM. County Democratic Com.			L	PA-POL
16–			Cosmo Drugs	30	✓ CM		
17–	9:15	9:28	FARM REPORT Coles' Tractor Co.	3:00	✓ CM	L	A
18–	9:29		Local Notice per Sec. 1.580				
19– 9:30	9:30	9:59	LITTLE ORPHAN PUNJAB			MBS	
20–			Mechanical Reproduction Announcement		MRA		
21– 10:00	10:00	10:29	LITTLETOWN LIBRARY TOPICS			L	I-ED
22–			Petite Clothes	60	✓ CM		
23– 10:30	10:30	10:44	HEAVENLY MOMENTS - Coun. of Churches			L	R
24–			Lehi Beverage Co.	EM ✗60	✓ CM		
25–	10:45	10:59	MAN ON THE STREET Ford's Used Cars	3:00	✓ CM	L	PA
26–			John's Garage	60	✓ CM		
27– 11:00	11:00	11:24	COKE MELODIES	3:30	✓ CM	REC	E
28–			Tony's Pizzeria	60	✓ CM		
29–	11:25	11:29	MORNING HEADLINES -			L	N
30–			Sta. Promo - Sports Windup (Schmaltz Beer)	10	✓ CM		
31– 11:30	11:30	11:59	JOHN'S OTHER LIFE			MBS	
32–			Ray Hay Rep. Back Hay Com.	20	✓ CM		
33–			Weekday Religious Education		PSA		
34– 12:00	12:00	12:14	MID-DAY NEWS			MBS	
35–	12:15	12:30	AIR FORCE TUNE TIME			REC	E
36–			Air Force Recruiting		PSA		
37– 12:30			Air Force Recruiting		PSA		

On	9. Operator or Announcer *[signature]*	Off 9:00	On 9:00	9. Operator or Announcer *[signature]*	Off
On	9. Operator or Announcer	Off	On	9. Operator or Announcer	Off

Comments: ABC Ice Cream spot was not run during Rhythm Melodies and log-keeper forgot to delete entry. *Bob West, Program Manager WXXX 10/7/69*

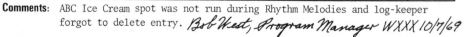

Figure 21. Sample program log showing application of logging procedures described in this section. (Courtesy National Association of Broadcasters)

D. For other announcements, enter:

1. The time each required station identification announcement is made (Column 1 on sample log)
2. The name and political affiliation of each candidate for whom an announcement is made (Column 4 on sample log)
3. The time each announcement of pre-grant and renewal hearings is made (Column 4, Line 18 on sample log)
4. The time of each announcement that preceding or following material was mechanically reproduced (Column 6, Line 20 on sample program log)

All transcribed announcements lasting more than one minute and all recorded programs in which timeliness is of special significance must carry with them a statement that they have been mechanically reproduced, and a notation that such an announcement has been made must be entered in the log. The FCC is especially concerned about time of origin of certain types of programs—speeches, news events, forums, panel discussions, special events, and commentaries. The FCC does not prescribe the exact form to be followed in making these announcements, but it demands that "the language shall be clear and in terms commonly used and understood."

Network programs rebroadcast at later times for the convenience of the public are exempt from this provision unless they are delayed more than the time-zone differential between the place the broadcast originates and where it is rebroadcast. Stations which delay broadcast within this limitation must announce this fact at least once each broadcast day between the hours of 10:00 A.M. and 10:00 P.M. Mechanical reproduction announcements are logged as "MRA," while the recorded program or announcement is logged as "REC" under "source."

Station identification requirements are subject to change by the FCC, and you should check them frequently. Despite modification of minute details, though, they probably will remain essentially the same. They require that stations give their call letters and location at the beginning and end of each broadcast day and at some point during each hour of operation. Television stations must identify "by both aural and visual means" at the beginning and end of each time of operation. Hourly identification "may be made by either aural or visual means."

Logging and station identification requirements are much simpler for educational and international broadcast stations. Since they, too, are susceptible to change, you should keep up with the current rules if you work for a station of this type.

Section 315 and the Fairness Doctrine

Section 315 of the Communications Act of 1934 was an attempt to guarantee freedom of the airwaves to all legally qualified candidates for public office:

SEC. 315. (a) If any licensee shall permit any person who is a legally qualified candidate for any public office to use a broadcasting station, he shall afford equal opportunities to all other such candidates for that office in the use of such broadcasting station: *Provided,* That such licensee shall have no power of censorship over the material broadcast under the provisions of this section. No obligation is hereby imposed upon any licensee to allow the use of its station by any such candidate. Appearance by a legally qualified candidate on any—

(1) bona fide newscast,

(2) bona fide news interview,

(3) bona fide news documentary (if the appearance of the candidate is incidental to the presentation of the subject or subjects covered by the news documentary), or

(4) on-the-spot coverage of bona fide news events (including but not limited to political conventions and activities incidental thereto),

shall not be deemed to be use of a broadcasting station within the meaning of this subsection. Nothing in the foregoing sentence shall be construed as relieving broadcasters, in connection with the presentation of newscasts, news interviews, news documentaries, and on-the-spot coverage of news events, from the obligation imposed upon them under this Act to operate in the public interest and to afford reasonable opportunity for the discussion of conflicting views on issues of public importance.

(b) The charges made for the use of any broadcasting station for any of the purposes set forth in this section shall not exceed the charges made for comparable use of such station for other purposes.

(c) The Commission shall prescribe appropriate rules and regulations to carry out the provisions of this section.

The interpretations and reinterpretations of this brief section are anything but brief. In 1949, the FCC reversed its famous 1941 "Mayflower Decision," which had strongly condemned editorializing by broadcast licensees, and laid down guidelines for fair coverage of news and political campaigns and for editorials.[8] In so doing, the FCC applied the spirit of Section 315 to much more than political matters. The Commission summarized its 1949 interpretation as follows:

21. To recapitulate, the Commission believes that under the American system of broadcasting the individual licensees of radio stations have the responsibility for determining the specific program material to be broadcast over their stations. This choice, however, must be exercised in a manner consistent with the basic policy of the Congress that radio be maintained as a medium of free speech for the general public as a whole rather than as an outlet for the purely personal or private interests of the licensee. This requires that licensees devote a reasonable percentage of their broadcasting time to the discussion of public issues of interest in the community served by their stations and that such programs be designed so that the public has a reasonable opportunity to hear differ-

---

[8] The entire Communications Act of 1934, as well as the bulk of FCC interpretations of Section 315, may be found in Frank J. Kahn, ed., *Documents of American Broadcasting* (New York: Appleton-Century-Crofts, 1968). "The Section 315 Primer," beginning on page 410, should be studied by all announcers engaged in news and special events reporting, interviewing, or ad-lib announcing.

ent opposing positions on the public issues of interest and importance in the community. The particular format best suited for the presentation of such programs in a manner consistent with the public interest must be determined by the licensee in the light of the facts of each individual situation. Such presentation may include the identified expression of the licensee's personal viewpoint as part of the more general presentation of views or comments on the various issues, but the opportunity of licensees to present such views as they may have on matters of controversy may not be utilized to achieve a partisan or one-sided presentation of issues. Licensee editorialization is but one aspect of freedom of expression by means of radio. Only insofar as it is exercised in conformity with the paramount right of the public to hear a reasonably balanced presentation of all responsible viewpoints on particular issues can such editorialization be considered to be consistent with the licensee's duty to operate in the public interest. For the licensee is a trustee impressed with the duty of preserving for the public generally radio as a medium of free expression and fair presentation.

The distinctions between the "equal opportunities requirement" and the "fairness doctrine" were indicated by the FCC in 1964:

While Section 315 thus embodies both the "equal opportunities" requirement and the fairness doctrine, they apply to different situations and in different ways. The "equal opportunities" requirement relates solely to use of broadcast facilities by candidates for public office. With certain exceptions involving specified news-type programs, the law provides that if a licensee permits a person who is a legally qualified candidate for public office to use a broadcast station, he shall afford equal opportunities to all other such candidates for that office in the use of the station. The Commission's Public Notice on Use of Broadcast Facilities by Candidates for Public Office, 27 Fed. Reg. 10063 (October 12, 1962), should be consulted with respect to "equal opportunities" questions involving political candidates.

The fairness doctrine deals with the broader question of affording reasonable opportunity for the presentation of contrasting viewpoints on controversial issues of public importance. Generally speaking, it does not apply with the precision of the "equal opportunities" requirement. Rather, the licensee, in applying the fairness doctrine, is called upon to make reasonable judgments in good faith on the facts of each situation—as to whether a controversial issue of public importance is involved, as to what viewpoints have been or should be presented, as to the format and spokesmen to present the viewpoints, and all the other facets of such programming. See par. 9, Editorializing Report. In passing on any complaint in this area, the Commission's role is not to substitute its judgment for that of the licensee as to any of the above programming decisions, but rather to determine whether the licensee can be said to have acted reasonably and in good faith. There is thus room for considerably more discretion on the part of the licensee under the fairness doctrine than under the "equal opportunities" requirement.

The relevance of the "fairness doctrine" to the announcer should be clear, but because of its importance, an indication of how it might some day apply to you may be helpful. You would have to know something about it in any of the following situations:

1. You are the host on a telephone-talk show, and you "sound off" against a particular political candidate; or you indicate support or opposition to a bond issue.
2. You are interviewing a guest on your program, and you make derogatory remarks about the organization he represents.
3. You are a news commentator (or analyst), and you make partisan remarks about a controversial issue of public importance.
4. You are a disc jockey, and your ad-lib remarks about a figure in the news are judged by others to be sarcastic and demeaning.

In any of these examples (unless there are mitigating circumstances), the FCC would require your station to notify those who have been attacked or whose cause has been criticized, provide them with the text of the broadcast, and offer equal time for a rebuttal. In certain instances, these same measures must be taken by a station because of controversial material broadcast during news programs or on-the-spot news reports. Of course, the invocation of the fairness doctrine is not automatic, and, as the FCC pointed out, "it does not apply with the precision of the 'equal opportunities' requirement." It must also be said—and *underscored*—that the purpose of this résumé of the fairness doctrine is not to discourage you from engaging in controversy over the air; it is, rather, to make you aware of the pertinent FCC rules and regulations you must follow.

Emergency Action Notification and Emergency Broadcast Systems

The broadcasting stations of the United States have an important role in national emergencies or local disasters. The FCC *Rules and Regulations* devote eight double-column pages to the scope, purposes, and procedures of two warning systems, and you should be completely familiar with all provisions. Because evolving technology undoubtedly will result in modifications of procedures, a basic outline of the systems rather than detailed instructions will be given here.

The Emergency Action Notification System (EANS) is intended "to provide an expeditious means for the dissemination of an Emergency Action Notification . . . to licensees and regulated services of the Federal Communications Commission and to the general public during conditions of a grave national crisis or war." Participation in this program is mandatory for all licensees; participation in the Emergency Broadcast System (EBS) is voluntary, but it is organized and controlled to guarantee effective nationwide broadcast communication in time of emergency.

Selected stations are given one of four kinds of National Defense Emergency Authorization (NDEA): (1) Primary Station NDEA, issued to one or more stations in a given operational area "for broadcasting a common emergency program for the initial period of, or for the duration of, an Emergency Action Condition"; (2) Alternate Station NDEA, issued to one or more licensees in a given area to provide back-up protection for the primary station; (3) Primary Relay NDEA, used to relay messages to primary or alternate stations rather than the public; (4) Alternate Relay NDEA, which backs up a primary relay station. All licensed stations are provided with color-coded cards which specify the procedures to be followed on receipt of an Emergency Action Notification. Stations not granted an NDEA and not voluntarily participating in the EBS are required to discontinue operations for the duration of an Emergency Action Condition.

The section of the *Rules and Regulations* dealing with the declaration of an Emergency Action Condition is worth quoting in full, since it reveals the importance of the broadcaster in time of national emergency:

§ 73.931   Notification of Emergency Action Condition.

(a) Authority for release of the Emergency Action Notification rests solely with the President of the United States. This authority has not been delegated, except as set forth in paragraph (b) of this section.

(b) Under the President's responsibility to activate the Emergency Broadcast System (EBS), he has directed that in the event an enemy attack has been detected, the White House Communications Agency shall be authorized to activate the Emergency Broadcast System (EBS) and the Office of Civil Defense shall be authorized to follow with the dissemination of appropriate warning messages.

(c) The Emergency Action Notification will be released by direction of the President and will be disseminated only via the Four Methods of the Emergency Action Notification System in one of the following two forms:

(1) The Emergency Action Notification only without Attack Warning Message.

(2) The Emergency Action Notification with Attack Warning Message.

An attention signal may be transmitted by any AM, FM, or television station, and all broadcast licensees are required to install and maintain equipment capable of receiving such signals. Though the highest priority for using the EBS is given to the President of the United States, the system may also be used by state and local authorities. Under certain circumstances, any broadcast station may, without specific authorization, initiate an emergency broadcast:

DAY-TO-DAY EMERGENCY OPERATION

§ 73.971   Day-to-day emergencies posing a threat to the safety of life and property; use of Attention Signal.

(a) The Emergency Action Notification Attention Signal may be transmitted for the following purposes by all standard, FM and television broadcast stations, at their discretion, in connection with day-to-day emergency situations posing a threat to the safety of life and property:.

(1) Activation of State program distribution interconnecting systems and facilities for the origination of emergency cueing announcements and broadcasts by the management of the State Network Primary Control Station in accordance with previous arrangements and agreement of the State Industry Advisory Committee in day-to-day emergency situations in the public interest. These include both situations where the time element is short, and those which develop slowly. (For example: Tornado warnings or tornado sightings; toxic gases threatening a community; flash floods; widespread fires threatening populated

areas; tidal waves; earthquakes; widespread commercial electric power failures; large scale industrial explosions and fires; tornado watches, hurricane watches, and hurricane warnings; civil disorders; heavy rains—developing dangerous flood conditions; icing conditions—developing dangerous road hazards; heavy snows—developing blizzard conditions; appeals for medical assistance and facilities; appeals for emergency food and housing; call-back of off-duty police personnel; call-back of off-duty fire personnel; call-back of off-duty military personnel.)

(2) Activation of Operational Area interconnecting systems and facilities for the origination of emergency cueing announcements and broadcasts by the management of the Primary Broadcast Stations for the Operational Area in accordance with previous arrangements and agreement of the Operational Area Industry Advisory Committee and the State Industry Advisory Committee in day-to-day emergency situations in the public interest. (Examples set forth in subparagraph (1) of this paragraph.)

Any broadcasting station should have up-to-date information on the EBS.

Though the FCC rigidly controls every aspect of American broadcasting, its intent is not restrictive. In fact, the Commission bends over backwards to keep the airwaves a public medium of free expression: it does not censor programs; it is loath to take the final step of revoking a license; it encourages innovations and improvements. Its standards for broadcasting are high, and they have served to make the ethical and technical quality of American broadcasting the highest in the world.

Eight Commercial Announcements

The commercial message is the lifeblood of the American broadcast system. Both radio and television would have developed differently had it not been for commercial sponsorship. Almost all radio and television programs are canceled when they fail to sell the sponsor's product; announcers frequently lose their positions for the same reason. The announcer of today must, therefore, be a salesman in the best sense of the term.

In recent years, television has moved farther and farther away from radio in the style and production techniques of commercials. For this reason, the two media must be discussed separately.

Radio Commercials

Following the rock-bottom days of radio around 1950–1952, when television seemed destined to wipe it out altogether, radio executives initiated fundamental changes in program service. Their efforts have been so successful that radio today is actually in a stronger financial position than at any time in its history. In the last few years more radio sets have been built and sold in the United States than ever before, and their sales are perhaps greater than the sales of new television sets. As television viewing has gradually declined, radio listening, especially during the daylight hours, has increased. The reason for this comeback is quite basic and simple: radio was willing and able to change its program service from what it had been and from what television now is. Radio today is, in this sense, a newer medium than television. The days of sponsored dramatic shows, costly variety and comedy programs, and Arch Oboler and Norman Corwin are gone, apparently forever. The order of the day is recorded music, news, telephone talk, and sports. Perhaps the most important effect of these changes on the announcer is that he now has become almost exclusively a staff announcer. Very few announcers today receive the bulk of their income from advertising agencies or work exclusively for one sponsor, as did Ken Carpenter for Kraft Foods or Don Wilson for Jell-O. Now the announcer works for the station and reads (or ad-libs) commercials for every product or service for which time has been sold. To understand how this works in practice, we shall examine the way commercial time on radio was and is bought and sold.

In the days before television, most of the time segments of the broadcast day were purchased by time buyers representing advertising agencies who, in turn, represented the manufacturers of products. If, for example, Chase and Sanborn purchased a one-hour segment during Class AA time (7:00 P.M. to 10:30 P.M.) one night a week, the agency, in cooperation with the sponsor, was then able to develop the entire program (within certain quite flexible limits) and commercials, limited only by the restrictions on commercial time laid down by the network. In this system, the agency interviewed, auditioned, and hired its commercial announcer for the program. Once established in such a position, an outstanding announcer could earn a comfortable living from his work on that program alone. If the sponsor had no objection, he was free to take on other similar positions and thus increase his income. From the established announcer's standpoint, these were the "good old days" of radio.

Today few such positions are available, and most of them do not pay what they once did. The broadcast day of most radio stations now consists of music, sports, or talk programs, frequently lasting three or four hours. The disc jockey program varies in length from one to four hours; sportscasts run as long as three hours; shopping news, cooking programs, or "handy hints" programs frequently last an hour. These programs seldom have a single sponsor. They are, instead, "announcement" programs, meaning that time for individual announcements must be purchased from the station. This system is called *spot radio advertising*. A time buyer representing an advertising agency buys one or several brief periods of time at stipulated points in the broadcast day for presenting advertising messages. This may result in any of the following means of delivering commercials:

1. The advertising agency sends a commercial script to the local station and the script is read or ad-libbed live by the announcer on duty.

2. The agency sends the script to the station and it is then produced and recorded for future use by station personnel.

3. The agency sends a script and a recording—the announcer reads part of the commercial live and plays the recording for the rest (see the commercial on pages 155–156).

4. The agency sends a completely produced and recorded commercial to the station and the engineer on duty simply plays it at the appropriate time.

In smaller markets, ad agencies are often not involved; local merchants purchase advertising time, and a commercial, written by the merchant himself or by a station employee, is then delivered live or prerecorded by station personnel for later use.

What changes has this new system of time sales caused in the work of the radio announcer? First of all, it has meant that a radio announcer today must read copy for dozens and dozens of different products and services. The possibility of sincerely believing in all the products he advertises is, therefore, slight; the same announcer may read copy for as many as five competing products in one four-hour shift, necessarily lessening his selling ability.

In the second place, radio has improved its financial position not so much by charging higher rates as by announcing more commercials. On certain music stations throughout the country it is not uncommon to hear as many as twenty or twenty-five commercials per hour. These commercials are often "double-spotted"—that is, one follows another with no program material intervening. Under such conditions it is small wonder that many announcers sound the same whether they are advertising cheese or automobiles!

Third, on many smaller stations, announcers double as time salesmen and must write their own commercial copy. You would thus do well to take a course in commercial copywriting.

One important exception to the general pattern of radio commercial announcing today is the announcer who has established such a loyal following that he may pick and choose advertisers for his program. Certain disc jockeys are in this enviable position. The advertisers pay a higher rate, so the announcer can hold down the total number of commercials on the program. This type of program is called a *participating program,* and the "personality" usually writes or ad-libs his own commercials. But the most realistic way of practicing for commercial radio delivery is by working with every type of commercial exercise, regardless of personal preference.

More and more often, announcers are faced with the split-second timing and technological complexities of commercials like those mentioned under (3) on page 154. The following script is an example:

ACCOUNT: <u>PSA Airlines</u>   CARTRIDGE #: <u>L-46, L-47 (cues are same)</u>

LENGTH: <u>(60)</u>   COPY #: <u>Tag 2 (rev 6/30)</u>

TYPE: <u>Cart with live tag</u>   BEGIN: <u>6/17</u>   BY: <u>PS</u>

CART: <u>L-46, L-47 open</u>

LEAD: (5)

VOICE: "Ladies and Gentlemen"

CART CLOSE & TAG CUE

VOICE: "Crack to it."

SFX: (1)

TAG IN AT: (45)

LIVE TAG: That's right. Now PSA jets fly every 90

minutes between Oakland and Los Angeles.

With eleven-hundred PSA flights a week

connecting 8 Northern and Southern Cali-

fornia cities, it's hardly worth bothering

with a reservation. But if you insist,

call your travel agent. PSA gives you a

lift.

How do you work from such a script? First of all, you must know the symbols. "CART" means an audio-tape cartridge, and the numbers identify the particular cartridges to be used. "Cart with live tag" means that the commercial is a combination of recorded material on a cartridge with the closing, or "tag," read live by the booth announcer. "LENGTH: (60)" means that this is a sixty-second commercial. "TAG IN AT: (45)" tells the announcer that he is to come in with the tag at the forty-five-second mark and that he has fifteen seconds to read the copy. "SFX" is the symbol for sound effects. Some announce booths are equipped with an electronic clock which starts counting off the seconds the moment the engineer starts a tape cartridge or a transcription. By keeping track of the seconds elapsed on the clock, the announcer can come in at the precise split second called for by the script without waiting for an aural cue or a signal from the engineer. Exercise 3 below will give you practice in this type of commercial delivery.

Radio Commercial Exercises

These exercises will provide practice in most of the types of commercial presentation outlined above. Although some commercial scripts are included in the drill section, you are encouraged to find or write more yourself.

1. Practice reading aloud ten-, thirty-, and sixty-second radio commercials from Part Two of this book, alone and in pairs. Public service announcements, though not technically commercials, need the same techniques of salesmanship and should, therefore, be included in this assignment.

2. Produce on audio tape some commercials and PSA's requiring "production"—sound effects, music, dramatization.

3. Practice some commercials with a recorded lead-in and close and a precisely timed live announcement in between until your timing becomes razor sharp.

4. Write and deliver thirty- or sixty-second commercials based on the following fact sheets. Write some for live delivery, others with production effects for taping.

FACT SHEET 1

    CLIENT: Millerson's Hardware Store

    OCCASION: Special Fall sale

    MERCHANDISE: Prefabricated cement incinerators,
            $14.95 (reg. $19.95)
        Snow shovels, $2.98 (reg. $3.49)
        Galvanized roof guttering, ten-foot
            strips, $1.29 (reg. $1.79)
        Acrylic latex house paint, $6.44
            gal. (reg. $7.99)
        7-piece brass-finish fireplace set,
            incl. screen, $39.99 (reg. $44.99)

        (NOTE: Choose three items for each
        commercial.)

    SALE DATES: Starting Sat., Sept. 3, and ending
            Sept. 10

    ADDRESS: Westgate Shopping Center, opposite
        Post Office

FACT SHEET 2

CLIENT: Café International

OCCASION: Weekend features

MERCHANDISE: From Italy, <u>stufato di manzo alla Genovese</u>
From Germany, <u>gewürztes Rindfleisch</u>
From Mexico, <u>carne in salza negra</u>
From France, <u>ragout de queue de boeuf</u>
Wines of the week: Cabernet Sauvignon 1949 and Liebfraumilch 1954
Complete dinners from $3.00

(NOTE: Try to awaken curiosity about these dishes.)

DATES: This Fri. and Sat. eve., and Sun. from noon, Mar. 14, 15, 16

ADDRESS: 118 Central, between Jefferson and Adams

FACT SHEET 3

CLIENT: S & F Drive-In

OCCASION: Regular weekly spots

MERCHANDISE: Hot pastrami
Chiliburgers
Fishy-burgers
Corny-dogs
French fried potatoes and onion rings
Supershakes
Nothing over 39¢

ADDRESS: Just outside town on Highway 44

FACT SHEET 4

    CLIENT: Heimberger's Pet Store

    OCCASION: Special sale

    MERCHANDISE: Aquariums, 5-gal., heated and
                   filtered, $12.95 (reg. $19.95)
               Guppies and gold fish, 9¢ each
               Squirrel monkey, $25.00
               White mice, 25¢ each
               Land tortoises, $1.99 each

               (NOTE: Client wants humorous
                commercial.)

    SALE DATES: Weekend only, Sat. from 9:30, Sun.
               from 10:30, May 21 and 22

    ADDRESS: 142 Fulton Street, near Mariposa

5. Practice ad-libbing one-minute commercials from fact sheets. Because it is extremely difficult to ad-lib intelligently about products or services you do not know, select your own merchants or products, become familiar with the stores or merchandise, and then write your own fact sheets.

In practicing with the commercial copy in Part Two, try to sound genuinely enthusiastic even though honest conviction may be hard to generate; effective commercial announcing is the surest and fastest way of moving up in the industry. And be scrupulous about time: *read a one-minute commercial in no more than sixty seconds and no less than fifty-nine; read a thirty-second commercial in no more than thirty seconds; read a twenty-second commercial in exactly twenty seconds.*

Television Commercials

Television commercials, because they use both aural and visual production devices, are far more complex than radio commercials. In the early days of television, many commercials were performed live at both local-station and network levels. Gradually, because of the difficulties and uncertainties involved in live production, filmed and videotaped commercials took over. The advantages are many: first, film allows for special effects not possible in live production, including slow motion, optical effects, and animation; second, both film and video

Figure 22. Shooting a Clorox commercial in a supermarket. Commercials are no longer produced exclusively in television and film studios. Sensitive, miniaturized microphones and high-quality tape recorders have made location shooting practical and inexpensive. (Courtesy Vista Productions, Inc., and Clorox Co.)

tape can be edited and/or reshot to eliminate production errors; third, the reusability of film or tape represents an economy, despite a high initial cost; fourth, the portability of film and remote television taping equipment means that commercials may be shot in a variety of attractive locations, rather than in the often sterile atmosphere of a studio.

The move away from live television commercials has changed the work of the television commercial announcer. Memorizing copy—once a requirement—no longer is very important. Muffed lines or dropped cues can be eliminated in editing or reshooting. Because film allows the controlled creation of a visually stimulating picture, more and more narration is off-camera; this, of course, means that the announcer can read from a script. Finally, prompting devices have made memorizing copy almost unnecessary even for on-camera work. However, this does not mean you should not familiarize yourself with your script.

Television commercials may be classified according to how they are produced. Following are the chief types of commercial production for television:

1. *Live studio presentation.* This type of commercial—increasingly rare—usually is a demonstration. The studio announcer, who may be the host of a children's show or the hostess for the afternoon movie, makes a straight, presentational address to the viewers. Sometimes the announcer ad-libs the commercial; sometimes he reads it from a prompting device. Often he holds or points to the product being advertised. Usually the commercial includes one or more slides telling the viewer how the product may be obtained.

2. *Live remote presentation.* In rare cases, the sponsor wants his commercial produced live from his car lot or drive-in restaurant. The difficulties of remote production are obvious, and the costs are considerable. The sponsor usually acts as his own announcer or hires someone other than a station employee for the purpose.

3. *Live voice over slides.* This is about the simplest and cheapest method of commercial presentation on television; perhaps for that reason its popularity with advertisers is growing rapidly. In this kind of production, the staff announcer reads from a script which supplements a series of slides. A common arrangement for a slide presentation is: Slide 1: Name of sponsor superimposed over photograph of the sponsor's place of business; Slide 2: Photograph of specific product being offered; Slide 3: Superimposed slide showing price of product; Slide 4: Superimposed slide replacing price slide showing address of store; Slide 5: Return to opening slide. The main challenge to the announcer is properly synchronizing his delivery with the slides.

4. *Live voice over silent film.* Although rarely seen, this is another inexpensive method of commercial production. It combines silent 16mm film with live voice-over narration. Its advantage over the slide-and-voice presentation should be obvious, and its cost is not significantly higher. Since no "studio time" (involving lights, cameras, etc.) is required for its on-air presentation, it is as inexpensive for the station to play as the slide commercial; both are inexpensively broadcast with telecine (televised motion-picture) equipment. The problem of synchronizing image and voice is similar to that of any off-camera narration over film.

5. *Off-camera narration over film or video tape.* As in Types 3 and 4, the announcer is heard but not seen; however, the voiced announcement is recorded on film or tape. Either animated cartoon characters or live actors may demonstrate a product, while an off-camera announcer reads the commercial script. The filming or videotaping may take place in a studio or in one or more remote locations. Slow motion, special effects, montages, and similar visual devices are often used, and tight editing and careful synchronization are essential.

6. *On-camera narration on film or video tape.* This is usually a demonstration commercial, and it differs from the live studio or remote presentation only in the care and expense of production. When recorded in a studio, the final recording of the announcer's voice is almost always made as the commercial is taped or filmed. When filmed (but not videotaped) on location, his voice may be recorded on a cue track intended only as a guide for postsynchronous dialogue dubbing—looping with the cue track—performed under ideal audio conditions in a recording studio. In this procedure, the announcer listens to his own voice on the cue track while he watches the film of his performance and ultimately synchronizes his studio reading with his lip movements on the film. With the

perfection of highly directional microphones and such miniaturized synchronous tape recorders as the Nagra, postsynchronous dialogue dubbing is used less and less in producing television commercials.

7. *Combinations of two or more of the above.* Some commercials combine filmed on-camera delivery with animation, voice over slides, voice over film, etc. (see Exercise 8 on page 163 for a sample script).

Television Commercial Exercises

1. Practice on-camera delivery with some of the simple, presentational commercials in the drill material in Part Two. Use demonstration commercials and commercials incorporating studio cards or one or two slides instead of commercials involving elaborate production. Work for exact timing as well as camera "presence." Practice using cue cards, "idiot sheets," and a prompting device.

2. Practice ad-libbing live on-camera television commercials from fact sheets. Some slides or studio cards may be used, but do not overdo the production. (NOTE: Any of the fact sheets on pages 157–159 may be used for this assignment.)

3. Prepare slides or studio cards for voice-over-slide presentation of any of the twenty-, thirty-, or sixty-second radio commercials or PSA's in Part Two, and practice synchronizing your off-camera delivery with the visual images as they appear on the screen.

4. If you have access to a 16mm sound commercial, make a written script from the sound track and then, with the sound on the projector turned off, practice reading the script with the film.

5. Visit a cooperative merchant or manufacturer and shoot silent film for editing into a commercial. Eight, Super 8, or 16mm film may be used for this assignment, as long as you can project it. After you shoot the film, write a script for off-camera delivery and then edit your film accordingly. Practice reading the script with the film.

6. Produce a demonstration commercial with one person on camera demonstrating the product and one off camera delivering the voice-over narration.

7. (Marginally recommended) If the appropriate equipment is available, practice postsynchronous dialogue dubbing. Since this method of commercial production is increasingly rare, no space will be devoted here to the procedures involved. Several current film production books explain this complex process in detail, but the keys to learning it are a knowledgeable and experienced instructor and the necessary equipment. Any of the on-camera commercials in Part Two may be used for this project.

8. Work up your own combination commercials from the exercises in Part Two. The following script may be helpful as a guide:

VIDEO	AUDIO
OPEN ON SLIDE 1: "BRONSON'S PLUMBING AND HEATING PRESENTS."	MUSIC: WINTER STORM MUSIC. SOUND: WHISTLING WIND, LOW BUT INCREASING THROUGHOUT
SLIDE 2: "THE COLD WINTER."	MUSIC: DOWN BUT NOT OUT
DISS. TO ANNCR WEARING HEAVY COAT AND EAR MUFFS. BEGIN LOW ON LARGE FAN, BLOWING ANNCR.	ANNCR: Hi! Well, here it is just about wintertime again. Remember last winter?
CUT TO FILM OR SLIDE OF DOG SLED TEAM IN HEAVY STORM.	Remember how much trouble the mail had getting through?
CUT TO SLIDE OR FILM OF ESKIMO ENTERING IGLOO.	Remember how relieved you were to see Dad making it home from work?
CUT TO SLIDE OR FILM OF BEAR CUBS ROLLING IN SNOW.	And how grateful you were when the storms let up and you could send the little ones out to play?
START CONFETTI IN FRONT OF FAN.	

FAST DISS. TO ANNCR.	Well, the weatherman tells us that we can expect more of the same this winter. So now is the time to have Bronson's expert furnace men visit you. Maybe you only need simple adjust-ments, or maybe you would like an appraisal of your heating system and an esti-mate of what it would cost to replace it with some-thing that really does the job. Minor adjustments are free, and estimates are fair and honest. Bronson's has been serving the county for 43 years, and the name BRONSON has come to mean quality at reasonable prices.
CUT TO SLIDE 3: "BRONSON'S HEATING AND PLUMBING,"	Call first thing in the

SUPERED OVER PHOTO OF BIG HOME FURNACE.	morning, and Chet Bronson promises to have a man at your house before the end of the week.
	SOUND: WIND SOUND UP.
CUT TO ANNCR.	ANNCR: Call 453-5550 -- that's 453-5550 -- for that special Bronson's service.
ANNCR GLANCES OFF-CAMERA.	Huh? (PAUSE.) I can't hear a blasted thing with these silly earmuffs on.
DISCARDS EARMUFFS.	That's better. What? Oh, time's up.
STARTS TO WALK AWAY FROM SET AND CAMERA. CAMERA DOLLIES BACK TO SHOW WIND MACHINE, TECHNICIAN WITH CONFETTI, LIGHTS, ETC.	Well, it's about time -- I'm sweating to ever-loving death in this dumb outfit. Don't you know those tele- vision lights are hot!
CUT TO SLIDE 4: "BRONSON'S -- FAIRMONT SHOPPING CENTER -- PHONE 453-5550."	I'll think twice before I do a commercial like this again . . .

```
SOUND:  OUT.


MUSIC:  UP TO CLOSE.
```

The following general suggestions should help you with the exercises:

1. *Dress for the final performances of these commercials as if you had been hired to deliver them.*

2. Try in each one to *understand and convey the impression the sponsor wants to create.*

3. *Make your movements* in handling props or pointing to signs or products *slow, deliberate, and economical.*

4. If television equipment is available, try to *simulate actual broadcast conditions.*

5. Some of the practice commercials call for animation, film inserts, or properties which will not be available. There is no ideal way of working out such commercials, but they are included here because it would be unrealistic to exclude them: they form a large part of broadcast commercials today. Animated cartoons may be simulated by flipping a series of still drawings, showing the major points in the original cartoon, to estimate the amount of time for this part of the commercial. Film inserts may be handled in the same way, or still photographs may be substituted for the original motion pictures. Properties, including the sponsor's product, should be simulated only if they are truly unobtainable.

6. *Make sure you adhere scrupulously to the time limits* of the commercials.

7. *Make sure you speak conversationally and directly into the camera lens.*

8. *Practice switching smoothly from one camera to another* as the director makes a cut.

9. *Communicate!*

As you practice radio and television commercial delivery, try to reflect your own personality. Some commercials call for a slow, relaxed delivery, others for a hard-sell approach; often sponsors will ask for a particular style of delivery. But appropriately changing pace, volume, and level of energy does not mean you have to transform yourself totally each time the style or mood of a commercial changes. If you do not maintain and project your own personality, you will run the risk of sounding like an impersonator rather than an announcer.

Nine Broadcast Journalism

As recently as the early 1960's one kind of announcer was called a "newscaster." Today he has been replaced by a highly trained specialist who might better be called a "broadcast journalist." Changes in broadcast news have been dramatic, even though they have probably been imperceptible to people outside the field. The newscaster usually read news items gathered, written, and arranged by others. In some cases, the news items were straight copy from one of the wire services; in others, the script was written or rewritten by professional writers employed by the station or network. The newscaster himself seldom covered events as a working reporter, and his journalistic abilities were often underdeveloped; since his script was written by newswriters and editorial judgments were made by a news editor, he frequently was responsible only for reading the news effectively. There were, of course, significant exceptions to this type of announcer, like Eric Sevareid and Howard K. Smith, and the exceptions have become our most respected broadcast journalists.

Today's broadcast journalist is far more than an efficient reader of scripts. Both radio and television news personnel are hired today chiefly for their journalistic ability. Although such skills as good articulation, phonation, and pronunciation are still important for on-the-air work, they guarantee neither a first job nor success in this field. Several popular broadcast journalists have pronounced regional accents, and some have downright unpleasant voices; they have succeeded in a highly competitive profession because their news ability outweighs their vocal inadequacies. The moral is clear: if you want to specialize in broadcast news, become a first-rate newsman as well as a good oral communicator.

The gradual change from the newscaster to broadcast journalist can be clearly seen in retrospect. From the very beginning, newspapers saw radio as a serious threat and used their considerable power to keep radio stations on a slim ration of news. Once or twice a day, a radio staff announcer was allowed to read without embellishments a few news items furnished by Associated Press (AP), United Press (UP), or a local newspaper. By 1940, with the settlement of the "press-radio war," radio stations had full access to news stories from all existing wire services, but the typical radio newscast was still little more than the oral reading of wire-service copy. The more prosperous radio stations supplemented wire-service stories with local news items gathered and written up by station employees. At the national network level, considerable money and effort went into preparing some news broadcasts like the Walter Winchell and Edwin C. Hill programs, but, despite varying degrees of effort or excellence, radio news remained almost exclusively an oral recitation by an announcer.

In the late 1930's, with wars raging in China, Spain, and Ethiopia, radio networks perceived a growing hunger for international news and, with the help of short-wave transmission, began to broadcast regular reports from foreign correspondents. H. V. Kaltenborn, Edward R. Murrow, Cecil Brown, William L. Shirer, and a dozen equally talented journalists finally succeeded in breaking the dominant pattern of radio news. They sometimes ad-libbed their reports from the scene of the action; they often interviewed newsmakers on the air; they succeeded because of their excellence as broadcast journalists, not as announcers. When the war ended, most of the outstanding foreign correspondents continued to be heard on radio, some as on-the-scene reporters, but most as home-based analysts and commentators. Then came television!

During the 1950's, television undermined the financial base of network radio. Local radio stations relied increasingly on their own news programming resources rather than network originations. The global news organizations so painstakingly built by the radio networks were gradually disassembled. At the time of the 1956 Hungarian revolt, American network radio found itself unable to provide even minimal on-the-scene coverage of the events. And television, still in its technical infancy, was unable to offer an acceptable substitute for the rapid, accurate, and dynamic news coverage radio had developed and then abandoned. For this brief transitional period, both radio and television relied heavily on studio-based news announcers. At that time, television news directors at both the local and national levels sought announcers with the physical appearance and vocal apparatus traditionally associated with "good announcing." News specialists were engaged to back up the newscaster, some as newswriters and others as commentators, analysts, and field reporters. Much the same pattern was repeated in radio, even though radio was generally moving away from national network programming and television was moving toward it. The old-fashioned newscaster —an anonymous voice reading stories gathered and written by anonymous reporters—was still dominant in both radio and television at this time.

Gradually, as evolving technology introduced new possibilities in both radio and television communication, the newscaster began to be replaced by the modern broadcast journalist. Miniaturized audio-tape recorders, telephone beeper systems, video-tape recorders, microwave relay systems, and communication satellites made possible rapid, on-the-scene coverage of news events. On network television, men like Chet Huntley, Walter Cronkite, David Brinkley, and Frank Reynolds rose to the top of their profession. All offered announcing skill, but each was a top-notch journalist, too, and knew how to work with production personnel to make the best possible use of his medium. Back-up teams included such outstanding journalists as Eric Sevareid, Howard K. Smith, Frank McGee, Sander Vanocur, Harry Reasoner, John Chancellor, and Charles Kuralt.

During this same period, local television news coverage underwent a comparable transformation. News film, delivered to subscribing stations rapidly and inexpensively by United Press International (UPI), gave even independent television stations a "network look." Both AP and UPI developed means of transmitting still black-and-white photographs over telephone lines, and now they can send color photographs this way. Stations affiliated with national networks receive extensive videotaped news material daily to be screened, edited, retaped, and incorporated into local news programs. Whether the local station is independent or affiliated with a network, the chances are it can afford at least one news cameraman to cover local events. With the availability of miniaturized video- and audio-tape recorders, the news department no longer needs to put up with the delay or cost of processing film.

All these added resources have tended to make the television studio newscaster a kind of video traffic conductor; during a thirty-minute news broadcast, as few as five minutes of air time may be devoted to direct studio presentation of news. The studio newscaster is called an *anchor man,* and his chief function is giving overall continuity to the program. He opens the program with news headlines, and he introduces filmed and videotaped reports from on-the-scene news reporters. Every effort is made to keep the news items read by the anchor man to a minimum.

Because of considerably lower costs, radio news has benefited from new technology even more than television news. It is hard to imagine a radio station so impoverished that it cannot afford a "beeper phone" and a tape recorder. Without leaving his desk, a newsman can record interviews, public statements, police bulletins, weather forecasts, and any number of other newsworthy items. Relatively inexpensive battery-operated tape recorders make it possible for an on-the-scene reporter to record and transmit news via telephone within minutes of its occurrence. The news wire services provide audio feeds for taping and replaying by subscribing stations. To summarize, radio and television stations, whether independent or affiliated with a network, have access to many sophisticated resources for responsible and competitive news coverage which can be fully exploited only by a well-prepared broadcast journalist.

Up to this point the term "broadcast journalist" has been used to describe the modern radio and television newsman. It should be noted that the term "newscaster" is still in common use, however, and will be used in subsequent portions of this book. The distinction was made in the opening paragraphs of this chapter to underscore the significant fact that the "newscaster" of the 1970's is by no means the "newscaster" of the 1950's.

Special Areas of Broadcast Journalism

Increased diversification in broadcast news service has spawned a number of specializations for news announcers. The chief types of news announcer are (1) anchor man, (2) field or general assignment reporter, (3) correspondent, (4) news analyst, (5) news commentator, (6) farm reporter, (7) weather reporter, (8) sports reporter, (9) women's feature reporter. A description of their duties follows.

Anchor Man

The term "newscaster" is still in widespread use to describe this newsman. The American Broadcasting Company defines a newscaster as "a person who reads factual news items written and edited by qualified news writers and editors." [1] At both local and network levels, although subject to the supervision of a news editor, the newscaster usually writes or rewrites his own copy. This practice has several advantages: first, anyone can give a more conversational interpretation to copy he himself has written; second, since many newscasters do not use prompting devices, it is easier for them to remember their own words than someone else's; third, writing a newscast allows the newscaster a greater and more rewarding involvement in the creative process; fourth, the newscaster who writes his own script will generate a greater feeling of authority as he delivers the news to his audience.

Prerequisites. The newscaster should possess a number of special qualities, among them:

1. *A genuine sense of the newsworthy.* Far too many newscasters today are guilty of poor judgment in selecting and ordering stories.
2. *A broad background of general knowledge* so that he can spot an important story and its implications and possible consequences at the time it is first mentioned by the wire services.
3. *A built-in curiosity* to probe for facts behind stories.
4. *Good taste.* Some newscasters today show incredibly poor judgment in padding their newscasts with unnecessary details of violent deaths, accidents of all kinds, and illnesses of famous people. Certainly no one would argue against reporting such events if they are important and pertinent, but they should not

[1] American Broadcasting Company, *Manual of Standards and Policies* (1966 revision), quoted in I. E. Fang, *Television News* (New York: Hastings House, 1968), p. 222.

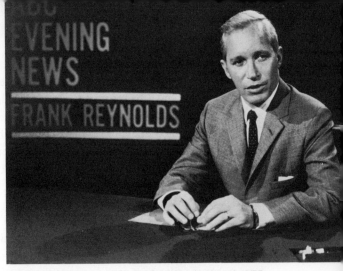

Figure 23. Anchor man Frank Reynolds of ABC. (Courtesy ABC)

be belabored or savored. The point here is not to suppress legitimate news; it *is* to advise balanced reporting rather than morbid sensationalism. Luckily, the good taste of most newscasters may be relied on to determine which sensational stories are truly news and how much detail should be supplied.

5. *An ability to write.* The smaller, frequently understaffed stations often rely on press wire copy for all their news and broadcast the copy with no important changes. Many of the small stations and almost all the larger stations, however, rewrite this news, and it is the newscaster himself who usually does it. If you want to specialize in newscasting, you will undoubtedly find your progress limited if you cannot write well. Some suggestions on newswriting will be found on pages 173–176.

Methods. There are several ways of reading television news. On many local-station programs, the newscaster merely reads from a script. This places a burden on him: since he is expected to keep good eye contact with the camera, he must be able to read well ahead of his voice and be willing to spend time preparing and studying his material. On some newscasts the copy is unfolded to the newscaster on a mechanical prompter, making him far freer to concentrate on interpretation and delivery.

One of the skills commonly expected of the television newscaster is cueing and narrating over film inserts. This problem in timing demands careful coordination between newscaster and director. Almost all film inserts are preceded by "academy leader," a strip of blank film twelve feet long. Numbers from 12 to 5 are printed in reverse order at each of the first eight feet. Beyond the number 5 the film is "black." The projectionist, in cueing up the film, customarily runs the leader until he reaches the 5 and then turns off his machine. At a signal from the director—"Roll film"—he starts the machine; there are just enough seconds left on the leader to enable the projector to get up to speed. To avoid a period of nothingness on the screen, the director must give the "Roll film" cue a few seconds before the picture is needed. He takes his cue from the newscaster, who is thus expected to say just the right words (the cue) at just the right time and at just the right speed in order to have everything come out on time. When the newscaster says the prearranged phrase, the director tells the projectionist to roll the film and then counts "Four, three, two, one, cut." As he says these numbers, the floor manager passes them on to the newscaster by first holding up four fingers, then three, then two, then one, and then giving him the cut signal. The newscaster thus has four feet of film or approximately seven or eight seconds in which to close his remarks—unless, of course, he is to narrate over the film. When working from a script, timing film is not very difficult. In narrating over film inserts, the newscaster usually has a monitor before him on which he watches the film as it goes out over the air, thus simplifying timing even more.

Resources. As indicated earlier, the anchor man frequently writes his own news copy; on small or low-budget stations, he invariably must do so. The following section lists some of the resources he usually has at his disposal:

For radio or television newscasts:

1. *AP and/or UPI news wires.* Both major news agencies furnish essentially the same kind of news material, so a brief run-down of the UPI services will introduce both. UPI maintains a radio wire; an "A" wire, intended chiefly for newspapers but subscribed to by many broadcasting stations, providing fast and detailed national and international news; a "B" wire, again newspaper oriented, transmitting state and regional news; a full-time sports wire; a financial wire. UPI also supplies the following daily schedule: [2]
   (a) eighteen five-minute "World in Brief" news summaries
   (b) six ten- to fifteen-minute "World News Roundups"
   (c) twenty-four one-minute "News Headlines"
   (d) six weather reports
   (e) twenty-four ten- to twenty-five-minute regional news feeds
   (f) sixteen sports news reports
   (g) five news feature programs, *e.g.,* "The Almanac," "Flashback," etc.
   (h) seven or more specialized in-depth reports, *e.g.,* "The Farm Show," "The Woman's World," "Business World"

UPI also furnishes subscribers with seasonal features such as income-tax news, fall fashions, election news, gardening tips, year-end reports, etc. During the appropriate times of the year, lengthy sports features are provided. Special reports on business, religion, science, and agriculture are usually sent out for weekend broadcasts.

2. *Receivers for monitoring police, sheriff, highway-patrol, and fire-department broadcast frequencies.*

3. *A teletype machine for receiving the weather wire* maintained by the United States Department of Commerce through its Environmental Science Services Administration (ESSA).

---

[2] The weekend schedule varies slightly from the Monday-through-Friday schedule.

4. *A city wire service.* In some markets the major news bureaus supervise this service; in others it is independently owned and operated.

For radio newscasts:

1. *Audio reports from general and special assignment reporters.*
2. *Interviews or news reports by beeper phone.* This news material is usually tape recorded before broadcasting since it almost always needs editing.
3. *The UPI Audio Network.* This is a full-period telephone-line hookup and transmits between sixty and one hundred audio "cuts" daily. These cuts are audio reports from correspondents scattered over the world and provide a small local radio station with network-like news coverage. Metromedia has a similar service, and stations belonging to a broadcast chain (*e.g.,* Westinghouse or Avco) feed news items to one another.

For television newscasts:

1. *Filmed or videotaped reports from general or special assignment reporters.*
2. *Filmed or videotaped news reports fed to local affiliates by the network.*
3. *UPI newsfilm.* Between 3,000 to 4,500 feet of film, in color and black and white, are sent out weekly.
4. *Still photographs* transmitted over telephone lines by AP (Wirephoto) or UPI (Unifax). Although transmitting color photographs is possible, most photographs sent are a brownish-black and white. Artists in the graphics department of some stations sometimes add color.

These, then, are the major sources of news available to the radio or television news department. But collecting the items is only half the story. The quality of a news broadcast depends on how the items are selected, arranged, and presented.

Newswriting. For the newscaster who writes or rewrites his own copy, these suggestions are offered:

1. *Write for the ear rather than the eye.* Your audience does not see the script; it only hears it. Sentences should be relatively short, the vocabulary should be geared to a heterogeneous audience, potentially confusing statistics should be simplified. Chet Casselman, Director of News and Public Affairs for KSFO–AM, San Francisco, has these important tips for newswriters:

(a) *Trim all fat.* Fat to us consists of unnecessary ages, middle initials, addresses, occupations, unfamiliar or obscure names, precise, involved numbers, incidental information, and stories of relatively little interest or importance.
(b) *Precise, involved numbers should be converted* to a simplified form to make them easily understood by the listener; unless the number is an essential part of the story, it should be dropped. Change a number like 1,572 to "15 hundred," a number like 2.6 million to "2½ million," and 35.7 per cent to "nearly 36 per cent."
(c) *Names of the famous and their relatives should be handled carefully* to avoid any confusion. For instance, "Mary Nolan is dead in Chicago at the age of 67. She was the wife of famed architect Sydney Nolan" is much clearer than

"Mary Nolan, 67, wife of famed architect Sydney Nolan, died today in Chicago."

(d) *Avoid the indiscriminate use of personal pronouns*, repeating the name of the person involved in the story rather than using "he," "she," or "they" if there is the slightest chance that the reference may be misunderstood.

(e) *Report that a person pleads "innocent" rather than "not guilty";* the latter may be too easily misunderstood as just the opposite.

(f) *"Latter," "former,"* and *"respectively"* are excellent print words but *should not be used on the air* since the listener has no way of referring back to the original comment.

(g) *Avoid a number of weak words that are more suitable for print:* say "looking for," "asking for," or "trying to get" instead of *"seek";* "run," "leaving," or "racing away" instead of *"flee";* "kill" or "murder" instead of *"slay."* [3]

A simple but excellent method of checking the clarity of your broadcast newswriting has been developed by Dr. Irving Fang of ABC News. Dr. Fang calls his method the "Easy Listening Formula" (ELF), and it is applied as follows: *"In any sentence, count each syllable above one per word.* For example, 'The quick brown fox jumped over the lazy dog' has an ELF score of 2: 1 for the second syllable in 'over,' 1 for the second syllable in 'lazy.' " [4] To find your total ELF score, compute the ELF scores of all sentences in your news script and average them. Dr. Fang's investigation of a wide variety of broadcast news scripts showed that the ELF scores of the most highly rated newswriters average less than twelve. If your sentences are consistently above that figure, the chances are you are not writing well for aural comprehension. A word of caution: as Dr. Fang points out, no mechanical system of measuring language is infallible. Common sense must be applied at all times in using his formula, since "it is easy to devise a confusing sentence with a low ELF score, just as it is easy to devise a simple sentence with a high ELF score. . . . What the Easy Listening Formula shows is tendency and trend." [5]

2. *Avoid confusing words or statements.* For example, listeners often interpret a report that a bill has cleared a particular congressional committee as the enactment of the bill into law. Saying that a victory in a primary campaign is "tantamount to election" tells many people that the candidate has been elected. Another confusion comes from using a word pronounced like a quite different word—*e.g.,* the word "expatriate" can easily be interpreted "ex-patriot," and the consequences could be embarrassing.

3. *Avoid undue redundancy.* Repeating salient facts once or twice is advisable, but too frequent repetition is dull. Example: In his headlines, a newscaster makes the statement "Senator Muncey declares himself opposed to the recent hike in interest rates." Later, in the body of the newscast, we hear this:

[3] Chet Casselman, *KSFO News Style Book* (San Francisco: Golden West Broadcasters, 1967), pp. 4–7.

[4] Irving E. Fang, "The Easy Listening Formula," *Journal of Broadcasting,* XI (Winter, 1967), 65.

[5] *Ibid.,* p. 67.

NEWSCASTER:	In Washington today, Senator Muncey blasted away at those responsible for the recent hike in interest rates. We go now to Washington for this special report from Vic Webb.
WEBB:	Here in Washington, Senator Muncey has attacked those responsible for the recent hike in interest rates. Here is the Senator speaking at a special news conference.
MUNCEY:	I have called this news conference to express my outrage toward those responsible for the recent hike in interest rates.
WEBB:	This has been Vic Webb in Washington, covering the special news conference called today by Senator Muncey.

"On-the-scene" reports such as this are a service to no one and are sure to be resented for their inanity.

4. *Don't forget the good news.* Though newsmen generally feel that the public thrives on stories of disasters, murders, miscarriages of justice, and similar unpleasantness, the truth is that the average person is equally interested in stories of success, heroism, and unusually productive human activities. Without being a Pollyanna, the newscaster can easily find room for such stories; indeed, he should—without them, he gives an unrepresentative and misleading picture of reality.

5. *Use the present tense.* As Chet Casselman puts it, "Since we can report events as they happen, the present tense is our natural tense. In using the present tense, we automatically give the news an air of immediacy and the listener a sense of participation." [6]

6. *Avoid using initials* except where they are so well known that no ambiguity is possible. To cite Chet Casselman, "Only a few standard abbreviations are well enough known to be used on broadcasts; for example, FBI, US, UN, YMCA, and NATO. Most abbreviations should be avoided in favor of a recognizable title, followed up later in the story with a qualifying phrase such as 'the teachers' association,' or 'the service group.'" [7]

7. *Be wary of badly cast sentences* which innocently distort what you want to say. An example from a wire service bulletin shows the perils of careless writing: "DETECTIVES FOUND 2½ POUNDS OF ORIENTAL AND MEXICAN HEROIN IN A LARGE WOMAN'S HANDBAG WHEN THE CAR WAS STOPPED IN SOUTH CENTRAL LOS ANGELES." Listeners probably missed the next two news items trying to decide whether the heroin was found in the handbag of a large woman or in a woman's large handbag.

When practicing newscasting, write or rewrite all your copy. When you use wire-service copy, read it carefully for errors. If you use the AP and UPI drill material in Part Two, combine stories to make five- and fifteen-minute newscasts. This will give you experience in judging the relative importance of news stories. If film and television equipment is available, assemble a team of news-

[6] Casselman, *op. cit.,* p. 5.
[7] *Ibid.,* p. 7.

men—anchor man, field reporters, weather girl, sports reporter—and produce a complete news program. Try a variety of approaches rather than sticking with the conventional format now in vogue.

Timing. In preparing material for a newscast, you must have an idea of the number of lines or pages you can read in the time allotted. Time yourself as you read aloud at your most comfortable and effective speed. Determine how many words per minute you averaged, and gauge from the following chart the number of words you need for five- and fifteen-minute newscasts.

TIME CHART

	NUMBER OF WORDS	
RATE OF READING	*4:30 newscast*	*14:30 newscast*
150 wpm	675	2,175
155 wpm	698	2,248
160 wpm	720	2,320
165 wpm	743	2,393
170 wpm	765	2,465
175 wpm	788	2,538
180 wpm	810	2,610

Wire-service copy runs about eleven words per line; copy composed with out-size type may average only six or seven. Divide the number of words per line into your figures on the time chart to arrive at the number of lines you can read during your newscast. Keep in mind that you will want to read some stories more slowly than your usual rate, that you will slow down for headlines, and that you must deduct from the total the time taken out for commercials or reports from other newsmen.

General Assignment Reporter

Both radio and television have come to rely heavily on the general assignment or field reporter. His duties are the same for the two media, even though their different technologies require slightly different approaches. The general assignment reporter for radio works alone. He may use a mobile transmitting unit to broadcast his reports back to the station for taping or for live airing. More commonly, however, he records interviews or his report with a small battery-operated tape recorder and then transmits the taped material back to the station by telephone. Because the television general assignment reporter works with a cameraman, remote television reporting is both more expensive and more difficult than remote radio reporting.

The general assignment reporter must be extremely versatile, for he is respon-

Figure 24. News "nests" at KNEW–AM, Oakland, California. Each nest includes tape and tape-cartridge machines, a microphone for recording news stories, telephone lines to receive reports from the field or to interview newsmakers, and a typewriter. (Courtesy KNEW)

sible for reporting accurately, clearly, and authoritatively any event his news director considers worth covering. Mike Forrest, a reporter for KNEW–AM, Oakland, was given the following assignment by News Director Gil Haar:

7:00A —Check demonstration in support of first seminary student to be inducted into the army. Oakland Induction Center.

10:00A —Undersecretary of Labor news conference (BG ATT).[8] Room 10064, Federal Bldg., SF.

11:00A —Mental health and Nick Petris [9] (BG ATT). U. C. Med. Ctr., 3rd and Parnassus, SF.

12:00M—Dr. Paul Seabury [10] addresses World Affairs Council on "Western Europe in Search of a Future." 406 Sutter, SF.

1:00P —Hit Mayor with businessmen.

2:00P —Hit executive committee of SPUR.[11] (What are they doing in Exec. Board mtg.?) 126 Post St., SF.

3:00P —Hit Mayor with businessmen at end.[12]

[8] "Background of person named is attached."
[9] California State Senator Nicholas Petris.
[10] A professor of political science at the University of California.
[11] San Francisco Planning and Urban Renewal Association.
[12] Assignment sheet courtesy of KNEW–AM, Oakland.

A demonstration, labor affairs, mental health, Western European politics, business problems, urban renewal—all were part of one day's challenge. When the reporter receives concise, accurate, and informative background material far enough in advance to digest it, he may be able to turn in an adequate report even if his previous knowledge of a subject is limited; yet the very nature of news dictates that it cannot be fully predicted or prepared for. At any time during working hours, the general assignment reporter may be told to drop his tentative assignment schedule and hurry to the scene of a more important news event. Meeting any imaginable contingency and performing at a high level of professionalism demands a very special kind of reporter.

A television reporter usually covers fewer stories during a working day than a radio reporter. The technical complexities of the visual medium require more equipment, more time, and more expense than radio. For this reason, on-the-scene television news reports are selected with great care and given more air time. An audio report for radio will become part of a five-minute newscast. while a filmed report for television will be integrated into a half-hour news program. The radio report, then, may be as brief as fifteen seconds, while a television report of the same news event may last for several minutes.

Both radio and television general assignment reporters are essentially ad-lib announcers. Though they may make a few notes before recording their reports, the pressures of time and the lack of office facilities in the field preclude much writing. Because of this, the reporter must have a grasp of the story he is presenting; no amount of ad-lib experience can compensate for ignorance.

Much reporting done from remote locations is interviewing, perhaps the easiest task for the reporter, since the newsmaker does most of the talking. The news conference is especially kind to reporters, since people call conferences to reach the public with a message; they therefore patiently repeat and rephrase answers and submit to the glare of flashbulbs and television lights. The reluctant interviewee who does not feel that media exposure is to his advantage is, of course, a greater problem for the reporter. Yet, even an endless string of "No comment" responses or visible hostility can, in some cases, be newsworthy.

The greatest challenge to the general assignment reporter is covering a story in depth. This "special assignment" reporting, as it is usually called, demands real journalistic ability. To be specific, let us suppose you are to visit a small town, recently condemned by the Government because of its proximity to a potentially dangerous arms depot, and report on the views of representative townspeople and Government spokesmen. You must interview, obtain factual information, evaluate everything, and then deliver a five-part special report which is clear, concise, documented, and responsible. An assignment like this is a challenge any broadcast reporter can expect to face. Large well-financed news departments sometimes employ a number of special assignment reporters, each of whom has a "beat"—City Hall, ethnic minority neighborhoods, educational institutions, etc. Such news departments are, unfortunately, rather rare.

In practicing both general and special assignment reporting, begin with actual news events which interest you. Nothing is more difficult to bring off or more tedious for others to hear than an uninteresting taped report or interview. A report on the operations of a college admissions office is far more difficult to make exciting than a special feature on public attitudes toward policemen.

Civil disorders. Civil disorders are usually covered by general assignment reporters. Because radio and television—alone of all mass communication media —are able to report events as they happen, they are obviously capable of adversely affecting or prolonging disturbances. Accusations of just such negative effects were leveled at the conduct of radio and television news personnel during the severe civil disorders in Selma, Watts, Chicago, and Cleveland in 1965 and 1966. In July of 1966, Professors Kenneth Harwood and Theodore Kruglak of the University of Southern California drew up a set of suggestions for reporting civil disorders, subsequently circulated to stations by the National Association of Broadcasters. The suggestions are reproduced here in their entirety.

The following are suggestions for reporting of civil disorders and other events that may reflect public tension. These reminders to newsmen are based on experience in various cities of the United States, including Los Angeles.

1. Avoid emphasizing stories on public tensions while the tensions of a particular incident are developing. Ask the law enforcement agency involved whether the developing incident is designated as a disturbance of the peace or otherwise. Report the official designation of the incident.
2. Public reports should not state exact location, intersection, street name or number, until authorities have sufficient personnel on hand to maintain control.
3. Immediate or direct reporting should minimize interpretation, eliminate airing of rumors, and avoid using unverified statements.
4. Avoid the reporting of trivial incidents.
5. Because inexpert use of cameras, bright lights, or microphones may stir exhibitionism of some people, great care should be exercised by crews at scenes of public disorders. Because, too, of the danger of injury and even death to news personnel, their presence should be as unobtrusive as possible. Unmarked vehicles should be used for initial evaluation of events of this nature.
6. Cruising in an area of potential crisis may invite trouble. It is suggested that reporters make full use of the law enforcement headquarters nearest such an area until a newsworthy event occurs.
7. Reporters who are at the scene of an explosive or potentially explosive situation should avoid reporting of interviews with obvious "inciters."
8. Reporters should inform in advance any person who is interviewed that the interview may be made public.
9. Scare headlines, scare bulletins and sensationalism of other kinds should be avoided in magazines, newspapers, radio, and television.

10. All news media should make every effort to assure that only seasoned reporters are sent to the scene of a disaster.
11. No report should use superlatives or adjectives which might incite or enlarge a conflict, or cause a renewal of trouble in areas where disturbances have quieted.
12. Advisory data for discretionary use by newsmen should be written in calm, matter-of-fact sentences. This is for the purpose of avoiding inflammatory results from unintended public report of discretionary information. Honest and dispassionate reporting is the best reporting.
13. Reporters should not detail how any weapon is obtained, made or used.
14. Reporters should not identify precise locations of command posts of public officials, police, fire units, or military units.
15. Every reporter and technician should be governed by the rules of good taste and common sense. The potential for inciting public disorders demands that competition be secondary to the cause of public safety.[13]

Some television field reporters have unwittingly contributed more to public misunderstanding than to enlightenment. In a word, they have inadvertently misrepresented the broader realities of an event through misguided judgments about what is "newsworthy." Television is a visual medium, and it is tempting to concentrate on visually interesting activity. For example, a field reporter covering a multifaceted event, such as a demonstration, riot, or war, directs his cameraman to take shots showing a maximum amount of physical movement. Both reporters and their editors are pleased when the footage shows people in action—throwing rocks, shooting guns, setting fires, or making threatening gestures. But the significant nonphysical aspects of the event go unreported because they are not visually exciting. The outstanding general assignment reporter will shun this simplistic and superficial approach and report significant developments even when they are not dramatic. Violence must be reported, but it should be reported clearly, objectively, responsibly, *and in context*. Unfortunately, television reporting of violence has not been particularly good in recent years. Its tendency to play up sensational details and ignore the nonviolent aspects of events has angered, misled, or confused millions of people, and the consequences will be with us for many years.

A final word of advice for prospective television general or special assignment reporters: learn how to remain silent when the event you are covering speaks for itself. During the last critical moments of countdown for a manned space flight, a view of the space vehicle with the electronic countdown clock superimposed tells the story better than all the explanation in the world. Similarly, the reporter covering a political convention or comparable "actuality" should refrain from telling the audience how it ought to interpret what it has just seen and heard. Radio and newspaper journalists have left television news personnel a bothersome legacy: an irresistible urge to explain every detail of the event they are

---

[13] These suggestions are in the public domain and may be reproduced freely.

Figure 25. NBC reporter Lem Tucker reporting from the floor during the 1968 Democratic National Convention in Chicago. (Courtesy NBC)

covering. Overly careful explanation may be appropriate for radio and newspaper reporting, but it is unnecessary for television: the television audience often sees and hears essentially the same thing as the reporter.

Correspondent

The broadcast correspondent is similar to the special assignment reporter, but he works for a network rather than a local station and more often comes from the field of print journalism than broadcasting. He may be a congressional correspondent, White House correspondent, foreign correspondent, United Nations correspondent, etc. Frequently, he works for more than one news medium: both radio and television, or radio, television, and newspapers. His daily reports on national newscasts show how important he is, but employment opportunities are limited. The best way to become a radio or television correspondent is to become first an excellent general or special assignment reporter; knowledge of politics, government operations, journalism, and international affairs is essential.

News Analyst

The American Broadcasting Company describes a news analyst in the following terms: "a qualified person who broadcasts factual and balanced analyses of the news without direct personal opinions." [14] As you can detect from this description, there are far fewer news analysts on radio and television than meet the ear and eye, for despite their billing as analysts, most *do* give direct personal editorial comment. A true analyst does not reveal his position on a given question. Instead, he investigates all possible approaches to the problem and reports his findings impartially, thus rendering a great public service. Here are the steps in preparing a news analysis:

1. *Select the subject.* The news copy in Part Two suggests many areas of research.

2. *Begin your research in the library.* The card catalogue lists books by author, title, and subject, but you will probably want to start with briefer and more general information. Here are some of the more helpful reference books:

> *The New York Times Index.* Index to news items which have appeared in *The New York Times.* Published annually, with bi-monthly supplements.
>
> *The Readers' Guide to Periodical Literature* (New York: H. W. Wilson). An index by author, title, and subject to articles in periodicals. Published at regular intervals, with an annual cumulative volume.
>
> *Facts on File.* Facts on many different subjects, ranging from the pig-iron output of Czechoslovakia to the crop statistics of Pakistan. Published weekly, with a bound annual volume.
>
> *The New York Times Encyclopedic Almanac* (New York: The New York Times Company). Covers a vast array of topics, with major contributions by members of the *Times* staff and selected academic specialists. Published annually.
>
> *The World Almanac* (New York: Doubleday). Tremendous range of current statistics on a great many subjects. By referring to earlier issues, you can trace a year-by-year development. Published annually.
>
> *The Encyclopædia Britannica,* the *Encyclopedia Americana,* other encyclopedias, both American and foreign. Frequently the best starting point, since most entries carry bibliographies. The supplemental yearbooks for the *Britannica* are also helpful.
>
> *The Reference Shelf* (New York: H. W. Wilson). Articles and bibliographies on timely topics. Each volume takes up one major issue. Published irregularly.
>
> *Who's Who* (various publishers). Available for almost every major country and profession (art, music, education, science, etc.). Brief biographies of famous persons. Similar information can also be found in *World Biography* and *Current Biography.*
>
> *Who's Who in American Politics,* Second Edition (New York: R. R. Bowker Company, 1969). Contains approximately 19,000 biographical sketches of political figures, from the President to prominent local politicians. Published biennially.
>
> For brief biographies of deceased Americans, *The Dictionary of American Biography* (New York: Scribner) and *Who Was Who in America, 1607–1968,* five volumes (Chicago: Marquis) are recommended; for deceased

[14] American Broadcasting Company, *op. cit.,* p. 222.

Britons, *The Dictionary of National Biography* (London: Oxford University Press).

Pocket Data Book, U.S.A. 1969 (Washington, D.C.: U.S. Bureau of the Census). Contains vital statistics on all aspects of American life from area and climate to foreign commerce. Published biennially.

Statistical Abstract of the United States (Washington, D.C.: United States Department of Commerce). A summary of statistics on the United States. Data on population, health, vital statistics, immigration and naturalization, education, law enforcement, agriculture, business, construction and housing, etc. Published annually by the U.S. Bureau of the Census.

Statistical Yearbook (New York: Statistical Office of the United Nations). World statistics somewhat comparable to those in *Statistical Abstract of the United States*. Published annually.

Background Notes on the Countries of the World (Washington, D.C.: Bureau of Public Affairs, Department of State). Short pamphlets about various countries and territories, including facts on the country's land, people, history, government, political conditions, economy, and foreign relations. Most notes contain a map and a brief bibliography. Revised and updated continually.

Worldmark Encyclopedia of the Nations, Third Edition (New York: Harper & Row, 1967). Five volumes of basic information—about all nations of the world—historical, economic, and geographical.

The Middle East and North Africa (London: Europa). Geographical, historical, economic, political, industrial, financial, cultural, and educational information. Includes *Who's Who in the Middle East and Africa*. Published irregularly, but usually on an annual basis.

The Europa Yearbook, 2 vols. (London: Europa). Volume I deals with Europe, Volume II with Africa, the Americas, Asia, Australasia, the United Nations, and regional organizations like SEATO, the Arab League, etc. Information on each country's constitution, government, politics, legal system, and religion. Directories of the press, publishers, banks, industrial organizations, unions, learned societies, research institutes, libraries, museums, and universities. Published annually.

The South American Handbook (London: Trade and Travel). Information on travel, natural resources, governments, communications, and transportation of the Latin American nations and the West Indies. Published annually.

Current World Leaders Almanac (Pasadena, Cal.: Almanac of Current World Leaders). Up-to-date information on all leaders of the world. Published three times a year.

The United States in World Affairs (New York: Simon and Schuster), published annually.

The American Negro Reference Book (Englewood Cliffs, N.J.: Prentice-Hall, 1966). Twenty-five chapters provide "a reliable summary of current information on the main aspects of Negro life in America. . . ."

The Negro Almanac (New York: Bellwether, 1967). Historical, biographical, economic, social, scientific, cultural, and educational facts about American Negroes.

The Negro Handbook, compiled by the editors of *Ebony* (Chicago: Johnson Publishing Company, 1966). Covers much of the same ground as *The*

American Negro Reference Book, but contains "directory-type information" and more statistical tables.

United States Government Organization Manual (Washington, D.C.: General Services Administration). Describes all agencies of the Federal Government, giving date of creation, authority, principal activities, chief officials, and brief history of expired, transferred, and terminated agencies. Published annually.

Official Congressional Directory (Washington, D.C.: Joint Committee on Printing). Biographical sketches of all members of Congress, memberships of all committees, outlines of congressional commissions and boards, lists of administrative assistants and secretaries, names of the officers of the Senate and the House, and names of Executive and Judiciary personnel, including Cabinet members and their staffs. Foreign diplomatic representatives and U.S. diplomatic and consular officials are also listed. Published irregularly.

Decisions of the United States Supreme Court (Rochester, N.Y.: The Lawyers Co-operative Publishing Company). Review of all Supreme Court decisions. Published annually.

The Municipal Yearbook (Chicago: International City Manager's Association). Review of city personnel, municipal finance, activities, and salaries. Statistical information on all cities larger than 10,000. Published annually.

The Book of the States (Chicago: Council of State Governments). State constitutions; information about elections, legislation, the judiciary, administrative organization, finance, intergovernmental relations, major state services, statistics; directory of officers; general information. Published biennially, with annual supplements.

Nearly every state publishes an annual directory of state legislators and key administrative personnel.

Applied Science and Technology Index (New York: H. W. Wilson). For locating articles in these fields. Published monthly.

Social Sciences and Humanities Index (New York: H. W. Wilson). An index of articles in academic journals on the subjects indicated. Published monthly.

The Encyclopedia of Sports, Fourth Edition, by Frank G. Menke (New York: A. S. Barnes, 1969). History, rules, records, and statistics of all recognized sports.

These standard reference works should help you acquire solid factual information for sound analyses. With the obvious exception of those too bulky, rarefied, or expensive, they would form an excellent nucleus for any newsroom's private reference library.

3. After researching your subject, *decide on the ideas, facts, or opinions (of others, not yourself) most pertinent to the analysis.*

4. *Organize the material* into a clear, logical sequence.

5. *Write your analysis.*

6. *Read your analysis aloud.* Make any changes in sentence structure needed to eliminate awkward phrasing or incomprehensible statements.

7. If the analysis is for television, *collect material for visual effects* such as maps, charts, or photographs.

News Commentator

The American Broadcasting Company defines a news commentator as "a qualified person who broadcasts analyses of the news with personal opinions and comments." [15] On the theory that a variety of responsible news interpretations contributes to public understanding and decision making, ABC allows personal comment by "qualified" persons but does not define this term; obviously, the criteria are imprecise, and no set political, educational, or experiential background will qualify you for unfettered comment in the name of a network. Commentators range all the way from conservative to extremely liberal, with the majority somewhere between.

There is no easy way to prepare for a position as a news commentator. Most successful commentators "arrive" purely by chance. After years of work in radio news reporting, government service, newspaper feature writing, or professional public platform speaking, they suddenly find themselves respected for their knowledge and opinions. From there it is a natural if not easy step to a position as a news commentator. Of the total number of radio and television announcers, news commentators account for only a small percentage. If you want to become a commentator, you had best plan to serve a lengthy apprenticeship, not only because of the few opportunities but because most people are reluctant to accept the opinions of the young and inexperienced, however sound they may be.

If you want to practice commenting on the news, you should follow the suggestions given for analyzing news, omitting some of the arguments at variance with your position and taking a direct editorial stand on the subject.

Farm Reporter

Because most radio stations and many television stations reach into rural areas, farm reporting has become a standard feature in their program schedules. Obviously, anyone who deals with farm news ought to know and like farming. Frequently, however, small stations are unable to afford a full-time farm reporter, and announcers take turns reporting farm news and attending fairs and other agricultural events where they meet and talk with the farm audience and answer questions. If you feel that farm reporting may constitute at least part of your future work, you should make every effort to take at least one agriculture course. You should also subscribe to a farm journal and ask to be put on the mailing list of the United States Department of Agriculture by writing to the Superintendent of Documents, United States Government Printing Office, Washington, D. C.

Today's farmer is better trained and more specialized than his forebears. He has often attended an agricultural college, he subscribes to farm journals, and

[15] *Ibid.*, p. 222.

he sends for all pertinent publications of the Department of Agriculture. He also recognizes that radio and television are both oriented to the city population—largely, in fact, to New York and Hollywood—and he is quick to detect and resent bluff, ignorance, and condescension on the part of the farm reporter. He is also an individualist, neither predominantly Republican nor chiefly Democratic. He does not necessarily agree with his fellow farmer on farm subsidies, flexible price supports, soil banks, the policies of the Secretary of Agriculture, or new versus traditional methods of farming. The farm reporter must therefore be sure not to alienate large sections of his audience by assuming that there is a "farmer's position" on specific issues. Unlike the news commentator, who is free to take a stand, the farm reporter must present all sides of an issue; he is frequently the only person in his area providing his particular service. His chief functions are (1) disclosing new discoveries or developments in fertilizers, sprays, seeds, machinery, etc.; (2) publicizing farm events such as fairs, expositions, plowing contests, auctions, etc.; (3) giving up-to-date, accurate, and comprehensive weather reports; (4) giving market prices, including futures; (5) encouraging farm activities like 4–H, Future Farmers, or the Grange.

In Part Two (pages 346–350) you will find drill material for farm programs for both radio and television. Most of the copy is not regional in nature, for obvious reasons. You may want to supplement it with local farm news.

Weather Reporter

Weather reports have always played a small part on radio news programs, but they have come into their own on television for two reasons: first, most people are interested in the weather; second, weather programs are visually interesting. Aside from tornado warnings or frost warnings for fruit growers, radio coverage of weather information tends to be routine and unexciting. Most radio stations broadcast periodic round-ups of regional weather conditions, including current temperatures, predictions for the ensuing twelve to twenty-four hours, and sometimes long-range weather bureau forecasts. Both UPI and AP carry national weather reports on their general teletype services, and both also offer regional feeds to most areas of the country. Radio stations placing unusual stress on weather information generally receive the free weather wire of the United States Department of Commerce (see pages 335–337).

Television has three primary ways of handling weather information in regularly scheduled newscasts. In the first, most often used on small or low-budget stations, the anchor man delivers the report. Larger stations retain a professional meteorologist who not only reports the weather but explains the causes of meteorological phenomena, subtly and continually educating his audience. Many meteorologists engage in television reporting as only one part of their professional careers. Third, a professional announcer, though not a trained meteorologist, may become a specialist in weather reporting.

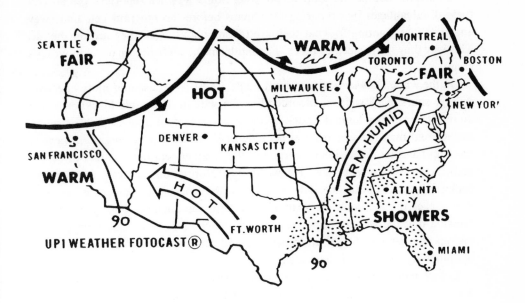

For Period Ending 7:00 P.M. EST

During Saturday, shower and thunderstorm activity will occur
the Gulf coastal area and the Southern Atlantic states.
Mostly sunny skies will dominate the remainder of the nation.
Warm and humid temperatures will continued over much of the
Eastern third of the country, while hot weather is expected
in the Plains and Plateaus. Maximum temperature forecast
includes: Atlanta 86, Boston 85, Chicago 87, Cleveland 89,
Denver 90, Duluth 85, Ft. Worth 100, Jacksonville 86, Little Rock 87, Los Angeles 80, Miami 88, New York 84, Phoenix
96, San Francisco 75, Seattle 66, St. Louis 85 and Washington 86.

Figure 26. ESSA weather map sent by UPI Unifax. (Courtesy UPI)

There are several ways of staging weather programs for television, all involving a map. The simplest kind of map is the outline variety used in geography
classes. Rubbing it with charcoal dust or spraying it lightly and evenly with dull
black paint reduces glare. A felt-tipped pen may then be used to emphasize the
borders. The map is pinned to a wall and weather information is marked in
with a felt-tipped pen during the telecast. A similar but somewhat less effective
method is tracing an outline of the area being discussed on a blackboard and
chalking in information. Opaque or blackboard maps have at least two important
disadvantages: the weather reporter usually blocks at least part of the map from

the television audience, and he must write awkwardly because he is crowded as far to one side of the map as possible. Some weather reporters get around these disadvantages by preparing their maps before the program gets underway and then just pointing to what they are talking about when they are on the air. This way they never need to block the map from the audience or develop writer's cramp.

On the whole, however, transparent maps are easier to use and more effective. A large sheet of Plexiglas is mounted like the slate in a portable blackboard. An outline map of the United States or the reporter's local area is painted on its surface and may be seen from either side of the plastic. The *backward* view of the map faces the television camera, and the weather reporter stands behind the map facing the correct view. He writes his information correctly for him but backwards for the audience. The trick is that the scan on the camera is reversed. This makes the map and the writing correct for the audience and gives the impression that the weather reporter is writing backwards. With this kind of map, the reporter can stand right up to the map and write with complete freedom without blocking the view of the audience.

Unfortunately, this effective and simple way of posting weather information is no longer possible at some television stations. Color television cameras, most of which use either three or four pickup tubes, are extremely difficult to adjust to reverse sweep. Unless the station can afford the luxury of maintaining one camera for this purpose only or unless it is a monochrome station, the weather reporter must either write on the Plexiglas map from the front or learn to write backwards. Backward writing for weather reporting is not as difficult as it sounds: the reporter really needs to learn only the digits 1 through 9 and a few words such as "low," "high," and "fair."

In portraying the weather on a map, the following symbols have become more or less standard:

1. A bold line to mark off any section of the country with uniform weather
2. A round circle with radiating lines to indicate a sunny area
3. Short diagonal lines to suggest rain
4. An asterisk to suggest snow
5. An arrow to point the way a wind is blowing, with the velocity written in in figures
6. A puffy cloud for cloudy skies
7. An "X" for a tornado
8. A large circle encompassing an area for a hurricane
9. A large "H" or "L" indicating a high or low pressure area
10. A figure and a degree mark for temperature

You will find drill material for radio and television weather programs in Part Two (pages 333–337).

Sports Reporter

Many radio stations feature five-minute sports reports, and both radio and television stations customarily include sports news as part of regularly scheduled newscasts. Most larger stations employ sports specialists; radio stations will use sports authorities on all but routine newscasts, while television stations may have three to five minutes of sports news on each half-hour newscast. Generally speaking, the sports specialist is also a play-by-play sportscaster. A career as a sports *reporter* begins with sound background as a sports*caster*.

On smaller stations, the anchor man must deliver the sports news. He may not be especially knowledgeable about sports, but handy resources should enable him to perform adequately: both AP and UPI sports wires carry more news than any station could possibly broadcast; both wire services also feature sports news on their regular radio wires. An important contribution of the wire services is sports features which, with slight editing, can become the basis of entire five-minute sports programs. For example, here are the sports features supplied by UPI:

1. Baseball season—"Along the Baseball Trail," twenty-two scripts
   "Sizing Up the Majors," twenty-two scripts
   "Sizing Up the World Series," three scripts
2. Horse racing   —"Sizing Up the Kentucky Derby," three scripts
3. Football season—"Sizing Up College Football," ten scripts
   "Sizing Up Pro Football," seven scripts
   "Sizing Up the Bowls," six scripts
   "Football Prophet," every Thursday
   "Pro Football Prophet," every Friday
4. General sports —"Speaking of Sports" and "Great Moments in Sports," each
   sent five days a week throughout the year. Both contain
   stories about golf, tennis, swimming, hockey, basketball,
   and other sports not included above.

Wirephoto and Unifax transmit still photographs of sports events, and networks supply films or video tapes.

Women's Feature Reporter

AP and UPI both carry a number of items each day for women. Typical stories sent by AP under the generic title "Listen, Ladies" are "Entertainment," "Fashions," "Capsule Book Reviews," "Beauty Hints," "Budgeting," "Menu and Cooking Cues," "Hints for the Homemaker," "Gardening," "Camping Out," and "Women in the News." Also available for women's feature programs are numerous reports not designed specifically for women, *e.g.,* UPI's "Of Human Interest," "Flashback," or "The Week in Religion."

The women's feature show varies considerably from one station to another, and general observations are therefore not too helpful. Obviously, the essence of this type of program is its emphasis on stories appealing to women: fashions, make-up, recipes, biographies of famous people, and so on. Most incorporate live or taped interviews with interesting people passing through town. The integrated commercial is another feature of most of these shows. The woman announcer is often given permission to endorse products and services advertised, and most stations likewise allow far more commercial time on these programs than on any others. Shopping news, a popular part of many of these programs, is frequently little else but commercials. And far from resenting the commercials, most women consider them a public service.

If you are a woman student of announcing, you are encouraged to practice largely with the women's feature program material in Part Two (pages 350–357), bearing in mind the following suggestions:

1. In addition to reading individual stories from the women's feature section, *produce a complete program* or at least a complete program format. You may want to include a taped interview with someone not a student in the class; a report on the latest fashions in clothing and accessories; a history of some item or event of interest to women; news from Hollywood or from radio or television; some of the feature stories to be found in the drill material in Part Two; advice on grocery shopping; advice on make-up; integrated commercials; a musical selection other than the opening and closing theme; some notes on child rearing.

2. *Project a real "personality."* The audience must come to know you as an individual, not as an impersonal voice.

3. *Avoid condescension.* Many professional women feel superior to the "homemakers" who are their typical listeners and talk down to them; nothing will be more readily detected and sincerely resented by a female audience.

4. As you will see from the drill material, all the women's features are aimed at middle- to upper-middle-class women. None of the copy has been designed to help the educationally, culturally, or economically deprived housewife. Perhaps you would rather *build a program* not from the drill material but from information obtained from a variety of governmental and private agencies on nutrition, budgeting, product comparison, legal aid, medical aid, and similar subjects *geared to the needs of women not in the middle of our society*.

5. Don't make the mistake of thinking that the limits of a woman's interests have been adequately calculated by the wire services. Today's woman is interested in much more than fashions and recipes. *Include in your program science news, political news, sports reports, and anything else that interests* YOU.

Philosophies of Broadcast Journalism

As a broadcast journalist, you will make important decisions daily. Your choice of stories and means of reporting them will undoubtedly affect the attitudes and actions of your listeners. For this reason it is imperative that you develop a working philosophy of broadcast journalism. Wilbur Schramm, in his book *Responsibility in Mass Communication*, discusses four divergent theories of journalism.[16] They are a good starting point for developing an individual, functional, and consciously held philosophy of broadcast journalism. You will reexamine your philosophy, of course, as your perceptions mature and society and technology change. You may revise your ideas many times in the next dozen years, but you cannot wait until middle age to formulate them. You should have a clear idea of your principles the first day you work in broadcast journalism.

Schramm outlines the four chief theories this way:

1. The Authoritarian Theory

In the oldest and most persistent concept of mass communication, the "establishment"—state, church, the intellectual elite, and the wealthy—controls all media of information. In earlier times control was vested in the Catholic church, the Protestant church, the Medici, the Tudors, or some similar authority. Today in many countries of the world religion has been suppressed if not abolished, royalty has been exiled, the intellectual and artistic elite has been stripped of power, and no one can be called "wealthy." But the prevailing "establishment," no matter what it is, still controls the press. As Schramm puts it, "In many parts of the world [authoritarianism] continues today, even though it may be disguised in democratic verbiage and in protestation of press freedom. Wherever a government operates in an authoritarian fashion, there you may expect to find some authoritarian controls over public communication." [17] Although Schramm does not specifically say so, the persistence of authoritarianism in mass communication shows that it is not tied to any particular religion, form of government, or economic system: authoritarianism flourishes wherever those who control communications lack faith in the ability of man to govern himself. Such people, whether official censors in a totalitarian state or news editors in a democracy, make editorial judgments to serve a predetermined end. Having access to information and having decided how it ought to be interpreted, the authoritarian then selects, arranges, exaggerates, plays down, and/or slants it for the public. In many instances the authoritarian journalist is naively unaware of his modus operandi and justifies his editorial decisions as being "in the public interest."

2. The Libertarian Theory

As Schramm describes it, the libertarian theory of the press is the inevitable by-product of seventeenth- and eighteenth-century rationalism. As the ancient

[16] Wilbur Schramm, *Responsibility in Mass Communication* (New York: Harper & Brothers, 1957), Chapter 5.
[17] *Ibid.*, p. 66.

idea of the divine right of kings gave way to the social contract theory of government, more and more dependence was placed on the ability of man, as a rational animal, to make wise decisions concerning his own governance. Central to the exercise of good judgment, however, was the availability of relevant information. A free press, free speech, and an active "marketplace of ideas" were deemed essential to democratic government. John Locke at the end of the seventeenth century and Thomas Paine, Jefferson, and other American revolutionaries a hundred years later all emphasized the importance of a free and vigorous press. "If a nation expects to be ignorant and free, wrote Jefferson in 1816, ". . . it expects what never was and never will be." [18] Except for defamation, obscenity, or wartime sedition, the libertarian demands that no information be censored or suppressed for whatever exalted motives. John Stuart Mill gave four sound reasons against censorship of opinion, which the libertarian applies also to information: "First, if we silence an opinion, for all we know we may be silencing the truth. Second, even a wrong opinion may contain the grain of truth that helps us find the whole truth. Third, even if the commonly held opinion is the whole truth, that opinion will not be held on rational grounds until it has been tested and defended. Fourth, unless a commonly held opinion is challenged from time to time, it loses its vitality and its effect." [19] It is safe to say that in the United States the libertarian theory of the press predominates. Some uphold it from sincere conviction, others for less salutary reasons—because an absolutist doctrine makes day-to-day judgments unnecessary, or because the competitive drive dictates that all news be disseminated.

3. The Soviet Communist Theory

The communist theory of the press, although marked by a fundamental strain of authoritarianism, does have some interesting new aspects. First, in the Soviet scheme of things, the media of information and opinion are an integral part of the state and exist only to further the cause of the state. The notion of the journalist as one who watches, reports, and criticizes the state is anathema; the Soviet journalist consciously works to bring about the objectives of the decision makers in the Kremlin. Second, the Soviets reward journalists for their propagandistic skill rather than their commercial appeal. Third, where the old authoritarianism was designed to preserve the status quo, Soviet authoritarianism is designed to achieve planned and specified change. And fourth, while the operating criterion of the press in a typical authoritarian society is what it cannot speak or print, the Soviet journalist is guided by what he is required to produce. In America and other democracies, surprisingly enough, some broadcast journalists sub-

[18] Thomas Jefferson, letter to Colonel Charles Yancey, January 6, 1816, in *The Writings of Thomas Jefferson* (Washington: Thomas Jefferson Memorial Association of the United States, 1904), XLV, 384.
[19] John Stuart Mill, *On Liberty,* quoted in Schramm, *op. cit.,* p. 72.

scribe to similar practices. Like the Soviets, they have adopted a blind faith in their particular value system; they propagandize in order to bring about planned change; they consider the broadcast media instruments of persuasion rather than channels of free and open communication.

4. The Social Responsibility Theory

A number of developments during the last part of the nineteenth century and the early part of the twentieth undermined the effectiveness and the rationale of the libertarian theory of the press. Most important was a growing disenchantment with laissez-faire theories of economics and government. The basic premise of the libertarians was that free men in full possession of the facts would act responsibly; to some extent events bore out this premise during the eighteenth and nineteenth centuries. By 1900, however, it had become quite clear that both the optimism and idealism of the Enlightenment had been tarnished by greedy politicians, businessmen, and journalists, and a feeling developed that the performance of the press in a free society ought to be examined and, if necessary, controlled. The weakness of the libertarian philosophy is succinctly stated by Schramm: "Under libertarianism, the media were expected to reflect the world as their owners saw it. They were permitted to distort, to lie, to vilify, all with the confidence that when all the distortions, the lies, the vilifications were put together, then rational man could discern truth among the falsehoods." [20] In practice, rational decision making—difficult under any circumstances because of man's tendency to be subjective and emotional—was consistently frustrated because truths were not being presented on which to base sound decisions.

In 1947, a privately endowed Commission on Freedom of the Press concluded that "it is no longer enough to report the *fact* truthfully; it is now necessary to report the *truth about the fact.*" [21] If we apply this statement to an important news event—to a severe and continuing civil disorder, for example—its meaning is clear and its significance apparent: though the *facts* of the moment may be the rioting, sniping, looting, and police action, the important *truths* underlying the facts may be quite obscure and go unreported. The Kerner report summarizes this point: "Disorders are only one aspect of the dilemmas and difficulties of race relations in America. In defining, explaining, and reporting this broader, more complex and ultimately far more fundamental subject, the communications media, ironically, have failed to communicate." [22] All too often journalists have, like Pontius Pilate, attempted to wash away their sins by shunning responsibility for their deeds. "Look," they tell us, "everything we reported actually happened.

[20] Schramm, *op. cit.,* p. 91.
[21] Commission on Freedom of the Press, *A Free and Responsible Press* (Chicago: University of Chicago Press, 1947), quoted in Schramm, *op. cit.,* p. 92.
[22] *Report of the National Advisory Commission on Civil Disorders* (New York: Bantam, 1968), pp. 382–383.

Don't blame us if you can't take the truth." Yet the truth may be that the reported fact was an exceptional rather than a typical incident; disclosing the fact may have caused even more serious incidents; the reported fact may have indeed happened, but it may have occurred only because the news media were encouraging extreme actions by their very presence on the scene.

The social responsibility theory of journalism is, of course, the most difficult to practice. It falls between the authoritarian and libertarian theories, thus requiring an exercise of judgment that the other theories do not. In them, decisions about the function of news dictate the way news will be covered or ignored; the broadcast journalist who subscribes to the social responsibility philosophy must constantly weigh his conduct as a mass communicator. As Schramm concludes, the social responsibility theory is "still tentative, still rather rootless, retaining many of the doctrines and goals of libertarianism, but turning away from individualism toward social responsibility, from rationalism toward a social and religious ethic. The new concept is still emerging, still not quite clear, but clearly a creature of our own time, and likely to be with us for the rest of the century." [23]

The National Association of Broadcasters' program standards for radio news reflect the undeniable paternalism underlying the social responsibility theory of the press:

> *Radio is unique in its capacity to reach the largest number of people first with reports on current events. This competitive advantage bespeaks caution— being first is not as important as being right. The following Standards are predicated upon that viewpoint.*

1. NEWS SOURCES. Those responsible for news on radio should exercise constant professional care in the selection of sources—for the integrity of the news and the consequent good reputation of radio as a dominant news medium depend largely upon the reliability of such sources.

2. NEWS REPORTING. News reporting shall be factual and objective. Good taste shall prevail in the selection and handling of news. Morbid, sensational, or alarming details not essential to factual reporting should be avoided. News should be broadcast in such a manner as to avoid creation of panic and unnecessary alarm. Broadcasters shall be diligent in their supervision of content, format, and presentation of news broadcasts. Equal diligence should be exercised in selection of editors and reporters who direct news gathering and dissemination, since the station's performance in this vital informational field depends largely upon them.

3. COMMENTARIES AND ANALYSES. Special obligations devolve upon those who analyze and/or comment upon news developments, and management should be satisfied completely that the task is to be performed in the best interest of the listening public. Programs of news analysis and commentary shall be clearly identified as such, distinguishing them from straight news reporting.

4. EDITORIALIZING. Broadcasts in which stations express their own opinions about issues of general public interest should be clearly identified as editorials and should be clearly distinguished from news and other program material.

[23] Schramm, *op. cit.,* p. 97.

5. COVERAGE OF NEWS AND PUBLIC EVENTS. In the coverage of news and public events the broadcaster has the right to exercise his judgment consonant with the accepted standards of ethical journalism and especially the requirements for decency and decorum in the broadcast of public and court proceedings.

6. PLACEMENT OF ADVERTISING. A broadcaster should exercise particular discrimination in the acceptance, placement and presentation of advertising in news programs so that such advertising should be clearly distinguishable from the news content.[24]

Dr. Frank Stanton, president of the Columbia Broadcasting System, seemed to place himself against the social responsibility theory of the press at Sigma Delta Chi's 1968 convention:

Discipline is breaking down in our homes, our schools and our churches. Our cities are in disarray. Assassins plot against our public officials. At a time when science is literally lifting us to the stars, the major issues of our election came down to the deceptively simple question of law and order, and man's relentless inhumanity to man. This turmoil is tragic. But it is also, as James Reston wrote, "the biggest story in the world today."

As journalists, it is our job to tell that story—*all* of it, the good and the bad, the beautiful and the ugly, the noble and the ignoble. Yet increasingly, attempts are being made to block us in that job. The people behind these attempts feel that something other than professional news judgment should control the flow of information to the public.

They would have us suppress anything which they find disagreeable, troublesome or embarrassing, and publish or broadcast only that which serves some loftier social or ethical purpose—as they see it.[25]

Dr. Stanton seemed most concerned about governmentally imposed rules for news coverage—the shadow of authoritarianism—and basically upheld the libertarian theory of the press. He applauded Walter Lippmann's statement that "the theory of a free press is that the truth will *emerge* from free reporting and free discussion, not that it will be presented perfectly and instantly in any one account." [26] Thomas Jefferson did not present the libertarian case more clearly.

A 1969 UNESCO publication succinctly outlines an international code of journalistic ethics combining the libertarian and social responsibility theories:

PREAMBLE: Freedom of information and of the press is a fundamental human right and is the touchstone of all the freedoms consecrated in the Charter of the United Nations and proclaimed in the Universal Declaration of Human Rights; and it is essential to the promotion and to the preservation of peace.

That freedom will be the better safeguarded when the personnel of the press and of all other media of information constantly and voluntarily strive to main-

[24] *The Radio Code* (Washington: National Association of Broadcasters, 1968), pp. 4–5.

[25] Frank Stanton, "If We Bury the First Amendment Will We Rest in Peace?" Keynote address to Sigma Delta Chi National Convention, Atlanta, Georgia, November 21, 1968 (printed and distributed by CBS, Inc.), pp. 3–4.

[26] Walter Lippmann, quoted in Stanton, *op. cit.,* p. 14.

tain the highest sense of responsibility, being deeply imbued with the moral obligation to be truthful and to search for the truth in reporting, in explaining and in interpreting facts.

This International Code of Ethics is therefore proclaimed as a standard of professional conduct for all engaged in gathering, transmitting, disseminating and commenting on news and information and in describing contemporary events by the written word, by word of mouth or by any other means of expression.

ARTICLE I: The personnel of the press and of all other media of information should do all in their power to ensure that the information the public receives is factually accurate. They should check all items of information to the best of their ability. No fact should be wilfully distorted and no essential fact should be deliberately suppressed.

ARTICLE II: A high standard of professional conduct requires devotion to the public interest. The seeking of personal advantage and the promotion of any private interest contrary to the general welfare, for whatever reason, is not compatible with such professional conduct.

Wilful calumny, slander, libel and unfounded accusations are serious professional offenses; so also is plagiarism.

Good faith with the public is the foundation of good journalism. Any published information which is found to be harmfully inaccurate should be spontaneously and immediately rectified. Rumor and unconfirmed news should be identified and treated as such.

ARTICLE III: Only such tasks as are compatible with the integrity and dignity of the profession should be assigned or accepted by personnel of the press and other media of information, as also by those participating in the economic and commercial activities of information enterprises.

Those who make public any information or comment should assume full responsibility for what is published unless such responsibility is explicitly disclaimed at the time.

The reputation of individuals should be respected and information and comment on their private lives likely to harm their reputation should not be published unless it serves the public interest, as distinguished from public curiosity. If charges against reputation or moral character are made, opportunity should be given for reply.

Discretion should be observed concerning sources of information. Professional secrecy should be observed in matters revealed in confidence; and this privilege may always be invoked to the furthest limits of law.

ARTICLE IV: It is the duty of those who describe and comment upon events relating to a foreign country to acquire the necessary knowledge of such country which will enable them to report and comment accurately and fairly thereon.

ARTICLE V: This Code is based on the principle that the responsibility for ensuring the faithful observance of professional ethics rests upon those who are engaged in the profession, and not upon any government. Nothing herein may therefore be interpreted as implying any justification for intervention by a government in any manner whatsoever to enforce observance of the moral obligations set forth in this Code. [27]

---

[27] "A Draft International Code of Ethics," *Professional Association in the Mass Media* (New York: UNESCO, 1969), pp. 23–24.

Here, then, are some of the considerations you will want to ponder in forming your own philosophy. It seems clear that more than a single position can be justified; perhaps a combination of expressed views plus some insights of your own will lead you to your own working philosophy of broadcast journalism.

A fifth view, not worthy of inclusion in Schramm's analysis, must be introduced since it is actually practiced and defended by some broadcast journalists. It is the "show-biz" theory. The rationale is best expressed in a syllogism: "Television is an entertainment medium; news is presented on television; therefore, news must entertain." The supporter of this philosophy consistently selects news stories not for significance or balance but for audience appeal. He ignores 99 per cent of the reality of an event to concentrate on the atypical 1 per cent that is sensational, sexy, gory, or blasphemous. If 6,000 students are graduated from a university, he selects the one student who wears shorts, tennis shoes, and a crash helmet to represent the entire graduating class. He edits the statements of people he does not like or does not agree with to make them seem ridiculous. He "jazzes up" voice-over narration to make unexciting news footage more entertaining. In interviewing newsmakers, he uses every trick to force them into making more extreme comments than they intended to make. On asking a prominent person "Do you intend to run for public office?" and receiving the response "I haven't given that any thought," the "show-biz" newscaster will report that "business tycoon Roger Steiner states that he has not ruled out the possibility of a political career."

Of course, there is a competitive aspect to radio and television, and newscasts share in it. Furthermore, newscasts are not automatically bad if they entertain. Only when he sacrifices responsibility, objectivity, accuracy, and fairness for entertainment can a newscaster be accused of unprofessional conduct in the interest of "show biz." Experience has shown that important news accurately and effectively reported is compelling enough to attract and hold a sizable audience.

Ten The Disc Jockey

American radio is oriented toward recorded popular music, and the man who introduces it is called a disc jockey. The term is not well chosen—the disc jockey may or may not "jockey" his own music, and the music may be on disc or tape—but it has caught on and seems to have stuck. The announcer on the so-called "good" music station is not called by this name. This chapter will discuss both the radio disc jockey and the good music announcer and will, as well, give passing notice to their television counterpart, the "sprocket jockey."

The Disc Jockey

Preparing and presenting popular music programs varies from station to station. A few top disc jockeys, earning as much as a quarter of a million dollars a year, have assistants, secretaries, and engineers to help them and are free to spend much of their time on profitable outside activities, as well as in lining up "hit" records, on which part of their success hinges. On most smaller radio stations, the disc jockey has a rigorous job. He is on the air as much as four or five hours a day; he performs all the work connected with his broadcast without assistance; he is expected to build a loyal audience, yet finds that he has only brief moments in which he can speak as anything other than a salesman; he is expected to perform off-shift duties like time selling, copywriting, or news reporting; he must make appearances at supermarkets, teen dances, and record stores; and for this he may receive the lordly salary of one hundred dollars a week. Although he does receive invitations to cocktail parties at which new recordings or new stars are to be introduced, his work load often prevents or curtails his appearance there.

The small-station disc jockey usually works not in a studio but in a small control room. Although an engineer may be in master control to play taped commercials and adjust the quality of the outgoing signal, the disc jockey is almost always responsible for selecting, cueing up, and playing his records. His selections are made not with an eye to determining public taste in music but in answer to two practical questions: (1) Is the song popular and do I like it? (2) How long does the record play? The pressure of commercials has forced a reduction in time spent playing music; the once-standard music segment of three minutes has been reduced to two and a half and more recently two minutes to allow as many as twenty-five commercials per hour. In watching the hard-pressed disc jockey at work, one is amazed at the skill necessary to bring off an apparently simple program. Here is a sample of a few minutes in the broadcast day of the disc jockey at a small station:

10:00 A.M. — Gives correct time and identifies station.

10:00:45 — Makes a few general comments about program for listeners who have just tuned in.

10:02 — Sight-reads one-minute commercial for tire-recapping company.

10:03 — Sight-reads one-minute commercial for supermarket.

10:04 — Introduces next record.

10:04:30 — Plays record. During next two minutes, changes turntable not in use from 33⅓ to 45 rpm; places next selection on turntable and cues it up; shuffles through commercial copy and lays out the two he will read when current record has ended; makes entries in program log; looks at record label of next selection for name of song, name of performer, name of manufacturer, and something interesting to say about it.

10:06:30 — Turns on mike; stops record turntable; announces last selection; reads first one-minute commercial.

10:08 — Reads next one-minute commercial.

10:09 — Turns off mike; starts next record; goes through approximately the same procedure as during last record.

With this sort of schedule to maintain, the disc jockey has little time to ramble on about interesting aspects of popular music or anything else which might help establish his personality and build up a personal audience.

The disc jockey on a larger station has some of the problems of his counterpart on the very small station, but he is likely to have more help and fewer commercials to present. His work begins to be enjoyable, and he is free to spend more time in leisurely discussions with visiting singers and musicians. One of the most important qualities a disc jockey on the medium or large station can possess is a superior ability to interview (see Chapter 12). Musicians and singers are often available for interviews; record companies and agents believe such appearances are good publicity for their artists and see to it that they visit disc jockeys frequently. But it takes a master interviewer to change a publicity gimmick into an interesting and revealing discussion.

Popular music stations are usually characterized by one type of music: "middle-of-the-road (MOR)," "hard rock," "acid rock," "chicken rock," "soul," "rhythm and blues," "country and western," "jazz," "semiclassical," or "super-market pop." Some so-called "underground" stations feature all types of music.

The disc jockey is concerned about the music policy of his station, but he is even more concerned about its operating policy. Generally speaking, the disc jockey may (1) work combo (combine engineering with announcing) or (2) work with engineering help. If he has engineering help, he is not, in a literal sense, a disc jockey, since he does not play the discs; to emphasize his emancipation from turntables, cartridge machines, and consoles, this announcer usually calls himself a "personality" or "talent." But whether he is a "jock" or a "personality," the popular music announcer is subject to variable policies governing his work: (1) he may not be allowed to ad-lib or otherwise reflect his own personality on the air, or he may be expected to project his individuality and build a personal following; (2) he may be allowed to select his own music, he may have to follow a scripted "playlist," he may have a playlist but be allowed to arrange the sequence of records, or he may be expected to choose his own favorites from a larger master list; (3) when he is not on the air, he may or may not have other duties of varying kinds.

It was said in Chapter 1 that there is no such thing as a typical radio station. This general premise holds true for popular music stations. The following hypothetical stations represent some of the more common radio operations as they affect the disc jockey.

1. *WZZZ*.   This station, located in a small resort community in the eastern part of the country, is a daytime-only station, operates with 500 watts of power, and is completely automated. The station is run by three employees, each of

Figure 27. Typical control-room arrangement for combo operation. Equipment includes a Gates Dualux audio console, an E–V 665 dynamic microphone, a Gates turntable, and a Gates Spot Tape cartridge unit. (Courtesy KTIM–AM and FM, San Rafael, California)

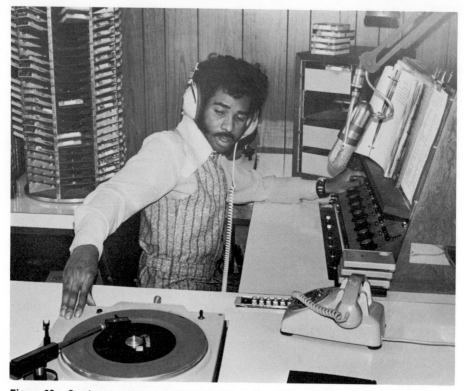

Figure 28. Combo operator at work. Tony King, disc jockey at KSOL–AM, San Francisco, operates a Sparta console, a QRK turntable, and an RCA 77–DX ribbon microphone. (Courtesy KSOL)

whom has his first phone. The three have essentially the same duties: they sell time, write commercials, record commercials and much program material, program and service the automated equipment, keep the various logs, and function as newscasters or, when an important local story breaks, as news reporters.

2. *WKKK.* This station is located thirty-five miles from a major market and is the only station serving the southern county in which it is located. It is an automated, 1,000-watt, daytime-only station. It has a larger staff than WZZZ, and this permits somewhat greater specialization. Some of its employees are salesmen who do not announce on the air, but one announcer who wants to move into sales does both. The other announcers have FCC licenses and spend their off-shift time on two jobs: preparing and delivering newscasts and preparing and recording local commercials. They work on routine maintenance but are not expected to make major repairs.

3. *KFFF.* This station is located in a community of 25,000, about sixty miles from a major market. Although it receives some competition from the high-power stations in the large city, the sometimes poor reception from them gives

Figure 29. Jack Ballance, combo operator at KSRO–AM, Santa Rosa, California, making entries in the program log. He works with a Western Electric console and an Altec microphone. (Courtesy KSRO)

KFFF an advantage over WKKK. The station is not automated. It has power of 1,000 watts, and it is licensed for full operation, though it must beam its signal in one direction only after sundown. The announcers work three-hour board shifts six days a week. They spend another three hours a day in a variety of ways: one is the weather specialist and also writes commercial copy for local merchants; another records commercials on audio-tape cartridges; a third specializes in news when he is not on the air as the "personality" disc jockey. All the announcers operate their own boards and play music and commercials on turntables and cartridge machines. Although the station is prosperous, the announcers, as matters of personal preference, continue to use RCA–77 and 44 microphones, a rebuilt Western Electric board, and a vintage Gates turntable.

4. *KPPP.* This is a 5,000-watt station in a major western market. It has high audience ratings, and its prosperity allows considerable specialization. It maintains a news staff of five, its sales staff never appears on the air, and it has programming, traffic, and engineering departments. The announcers do not work combo and do not need FCC licenses; an engineer plays the records and tapes. The on-duty announcer maintains the program log, but the engineer keeps the

operating log. The "personalities" do not select their own music, but they may play the selections in any order they choose. At this station announcers are known by name, but they are not encouraged to ad-lib at any length. Each record on the playlist is timed so that the announcer knows exactly how many seconds will elapse between the start of the instrumental and the beginning of the vocal; an electronic clock starts the moment a record is begun, and the announcer is expected to time his introductory remarks so that they will end the split second the vocal begins. Communicative energy and skill in timing are required for this kind of announcing.

5. *WDDD*. This is a 50,000-watt station in a major market. It has an MOR format, and its announcers are expected to talk at some length and project an engaging personality. At this station, as at KPPP, announcers are on the air only three hours a day and have few off-the-air duties. Occasionally they will be asked to make personal appearances and to record commercials, but they receive an extra fee whenever their commercials are played on air shifts other than their own. They must, of course, spend time preparing their ad-lib commentary, previewing records, and studying the commercials they will read during their shift. They do not operate broadcast equipment and therefore do not need FCC licenses. They are responsible for maintaining the program log. Some announcers on this station are paid by the week, others by the shift. Some stations in this category pay on-the-air announcers for each commercial programmed during their shift.

Figure 30. Control room and announce booth at KNBR–AM and FM, San Francisco. Announcer Dave Niles speaks into an RCA 77–DX ribbon microphone, while engineer Diane Smithem operates an RCA BC–7 consolette. (Courtesy KNBR)

6. *KHHH.* This station is located in a large California city. It operates at 5,000 watts during the day and 1,000 watts at night. A highly rated station, it maintains a staff of between seventy and seventy-five employees, including eight newsmen and six announcers. Some of the announcers work three-hour shifts and some work four; the night man works a six-hour shift. The news personnel are all staff announcers, but all the disc jockeys have individually negotiated contracts. The station features MOR music, but each announcer selects his own records, so semiclassical, jazz, or rock music are occasionally heard. The station expects each announcer to spend at least one hour preparing for each hour on the air; aside from this, the only off-the-air duty required is participation in a minimum of twelve public-service projects each year. Because this station emphasizes the personalities of the disc jockeys, advertisers usually request that commercials be ad-libbed.

7. *WSSS.* This 5,000-watt station is located in a large midwestern city. The music is chosen by the program director, and nearly all selections are semiclassical instrumentals; Mantovani, the Singing Strings, and André Kostelanetz typify the sound of this station. The announcers have engineering help, and none is known by name to the audience. Each announcer is hired to sound like those already employed by the station: soft, mellifluous, and slow-paced to echo the soft, mellifluous, slow-paced music.

8. *WUUU–FM.* This is a relaxed station featuring whatever music happens to appeal to the on-duty announcer. The station hires disc jockeys who do not sound "announcerish," who know and love music, and who are able to speak engagingly on a variety of topics; hence, many of them are not professionals. Because these announcers so often lack training, engineers operate and maintain the equipment, and the announcers are free to concentrate on selecting music and planning commentary.

Aside from practicing obvious skills and developing a good air personality, you are advised, if you want to become a disc jockey, to concentrate on the chapters in this book dealing with operating equipment (Chapter 6), interpreting copy (Chapter 2), improving voice and diction (Chapter 3), commercial announcing (Chapter 8), newswriting and delivery (Chapter 9), and interviewing (Chapter 12). When you practice disc jockeying, these suggestions may also prove useful:

1. In selecting music, *choose pieces you like and can talk about.* Even though it may be years before you will be able to do this professionally, it is good practice.
2. Every half hour or so, *"headline" some of the songs coming up.* This will help hold an audience even though they don't particularly like the next song.
3. *Give the name of the song and the performers at either the start or the conclusion of each record.*
4. *Practice commercials and PSA's.* It is unrealistic not to do so.

5. *Practice cueing up your own records and working your own console.* Spend less time with tape cartridges; you can learn to play them in a few minutes.

6. *Practice ad-libbing about the music, the day's events, or ideas that intrigue you.*

7. *Introduce your records ad lib.* Scripts are unknown to the disc jockey.

8. *Avoid corny clichés.* Do not use "render" or "rendition," "the boys in the band," "songbird," "platter," "spin a disc," or other similar expressions. Try to develop your own style. The idiosyncrasies in an outstanding disc jockey's expression become the clichés of unimaginative and unoriginal disc jockeys.

9. *Balance your program.* On most music stations, some of the songs will be fast and some slow, some loud and some soft. When you can, arrange the records for your program for variety and build.

The Announcer on the Good Music Station

The past several years have seen the rise of radio stations in all parts of the country specializing in what is called "good," "classical," or "serious" music. The term "good" snobbishly implies that other kinds of music are not good; most of the music on these stations is not truly classical, except in a narrow sense of the term; a good portion of it is not serious. However, inasmuch as most stations accept the term "good," we will follow that practice here.

Although the announcer on the good music station has much in common with the disc jockey, some important differences exist: (1) the good music announcer is not concerned with hit records; (2) he is seldom concerned with developing a personal following; (3) no ladder extends from the small good music station to the "big time"; (4) the good music announcer has fewer commercials to read, and the selections he plays are longer, often lasting thirty minutes or more; (5) he must have a different kind of musical knowledge; (6) he must be able to pronounce French, Spanish, German, Italian, and Russian names and titles of musical compositions.

Like the disc jockey, the good music announcer must usually (1) cue up and spin his own records; (2) read commercials; (3) make entries in the program log; (4) operate his own audio console; (5) ad-lib most of his musical introductions. His job, however, is usually somewhat more relaxed than the disc jockey's, and although he may have a "special" program—featuring pre-Bach composers or opera—he spends most of his on-the-air time announcing more general programs—for example, a Bach fugue followed by a Strauss tone poem, a Rossini overture, a Wagner operatic aria, and a Beethoven symphony. Seldom does the announcer select the music or the specific version played. Because the number of new compositions to appear each year is small—probably fewer than twenty—the same pieces are played over and over again. To avoid too much repetition, the station keeps a record of the exact date and time each composition is played and often insists on a lapse of a certain number of weeks or months between playings.

To obtain a position on a good music station, the most important prerequisite is a thorough understanding and appreciation of good music. If you hope to specialize in this type of announcing, enroll in as many general music courses as possible, listen to good music broadcasts, collect records, practice foreign pronunciation, and buy and learn to use the majority of the following source- books:

Willi Apel. *Harvard Dictionary of Music,* Second Edition. Cambridge, Mass.: Harvard University Press, 1969.

Theodore Baker. *Biographical Dictionary of Musicians,* Fifth Edition. New York: Schirmer, 1958.

Martin Bernstein and M. Picker. *Introduction to Music,* Third Edition. New York: Prentice-Hall, 1966.

Eric Blom (ed.). *Grove's Dictionary of Music and Musicians,* Fifth Edition. 9 vols. New York: St. Martin's Press, 1954. (A tenth volume was published in 1961.)

Howard Brofsky and Jeanne Bamberger. *Art of Listening: Developing Musical Perception.* New York: Harper & Row, 1969.

David Ewen. *Encyclopedia of the Opera.* New York: Hill & Wang, 1963.

David Ewen. *The World of Twentieth-Century Music.* Englewood Cliffs, N.J.: Prentice-Hall, 1968.

Gustave Kobbe. *Complete Opera Book.* Edited and revised by the Earl of Harewood. New York: G. P. Putnam's Sons, 1964.

Joseph Machlis. *Music: Adventures in Listening.* New York: W. W. Norton, 1968.

Percy A. Scholes. *The Oxford Companion to Music,* Tenth Edition. New York: Oxford University Press, 1970.

An excellent guide to pronouncing musical terms is:

W. J. Smith. *A Dictionary of Musical Terms in Four Languages.* London: Hutchinson, 1961. (The four languages are English, French, German, and Italian. All words are transcribed into the International Phonetic Alphabet only.)

If continuity must be written for introducing musical compositions on the good music station, the announcer is frequently given the assignment; he often writes introductions to twenty selections every day. For this reason, you should take a course in continuity writing and note the kind of continuity being written for the good music stations in your area.

If there is no script for continuity, the good music announcer ad-libs introductions from the dust jackets of records. Unlike the disc jockey, however, he does not ramble or try for an intimate, relaxed style of delivery. His audiences tend to take their music seriously, and station managers believe that this demands a reserved, rather formal delivery. Though some stations encourage their good music announcers to display a sense of humor and reflect their individual personalities, most do not. In ad-libbing introductions, you are normally expected to: (1) be fluent and unfaltering; (2) avoid clichés; (3) be dignified, though not necessarily sober; and (4) display a knowledge of the music and the artists.

Because nearly all good music stations are commercial enterprises, the commentary and introductions are almost always held to a minimum. Long selections—even symphonies or concertos—cannot be broken up, so most of the time between selections, especially on AM stations, must be spent on commercials. The problem is made doubly acute by the typical good music audience's intolerance for double-spotted commercials, transcribed jingles, or commercials for certain products advertised with impunity on other stations.

The FM good music station is frequently under less commercial pressure than the AM station, chiefly because it has resigned itself to a smaller income. This still does not free the announcer to make extended remarks about the music to be played, however, for the smaller income means fewer employees, which means, in turn, that the announcer has duties other than his announcing chores. And in any case, most good music stations have discovered that their listeners prefer music to chatter. The old days of prolonged discussions of composers, artists, compositions, or recording technology are apparently gone forever.

For this reason, the drill material in Part Two concentrates on short, general introductions. In working with them, bear in mind the following suggestions:

1. *Perfect your foreign pronunciation* (Chapter 5).
2. *Practice commercials* (Chapter 8).
3. *Practice cueing up and playing the records you introduce* (Chapter 6).
4. *Create a program, including title, written opening, and theme music, which features a special type of good music.*
5. *Practice ad-libbing introductions* with only the record jackets as your source of information.

The Sprocket Jockey

Most television stations run film programs using live announcers, usually spotted at times other than Class AA. These programs may be reruns of old Hollywood motion pictures, reruns of filmed television programs, screenings of ancient one-reel comedies or cartoons, or new films of exploration and real-life adventure. Although some of the details will vary, the announcer, or *sprocket jockey,* usually operates under the following general conditions:

1. *He has very little preparation and no rehearsal at all.* But because the announcer and his crew do this kind of program as often as once a day, a smooth job is possible even without rehearsal time.
2. *He delivers commercials or introduces filmed commercials.* He is also responsible for (a) introducing the film; (b) briefly mentioning the film before and after its screening; (c) providing a running commentary over silent comedies, cartoons, and real-life adventure films; (d) on children's programs, chatting about any number of subjects interesting to children.
3. *On a children's show, he may have to enact a character*—fireman, policeman, cowboy, naval captain, inventor, or whatever—and be able to talk wisely about the character's profession.

4. With the usual exception of commercials, *he ad-libs.*

5. *He cues the director.* As on a television newscast (Chapter 9, pages 171–172), the director must know at exactly what moment to give the projectionist the signal to "Roll film." For a smooth job, he wants the film to come up on his monitor a scant moment after the announcer has finished talking. He wants neither an overlap nor a dead period. When he hears a prearranged remark from the announcer, the director must be confident that the announcer will bring his remarks to a logical and satisfying close in exactly seven seconds. To help the announcer time these seconds, the floor manager first holds up his hand with all fingers extended, and as the director counts "Five, four, three, two, one, cut," he lowers one finger at a time, finishing with the "cut" signal.

In practicing the skills of the sprocket jockey, concentrate on the following:

1. *Decide on a particular format*—Hollywood motion picture, children's show, etc.—and build your program and your "character," if any, around it.

2. If motion picture equipment or, better still, television equipment with film chain is available, *practice cueing film.*

3. *Include commercials,* since they constitute a large segment of the sprocket jockey's time on the air.

4. *Develop an easygoing manner* and learn to project your personality effortlessly.

Styles in disc jockeys are as changeable as the music they play. If you have a career as a disc jockey in mind, you are advised to work hard at all types of announcing; the type of disc jockey you want to become may not be around in five or ten years. If you practice commercial delivery, narration, good music announcing, sportscasting—as well as announcing today's popular music—you will be assured of a continuing career despite changes in music and music announcing styles.

Eleven Sports Announcing

Most announcers spend hours of hard work in return for moments of satisfying achievement, and the dichotomy is nowhere so exaggerated as in sports announcing. A small number of topflight sportscasters are "celebrities." They receive excellent salaries, their opinions on sports are solicited by fans and professional athletes alike, they associate with exciting people, and their work is generally as stimulating as the sports events they describe. But they have paid a price to reach the top: they have put in many years of rigorous apprenticeship; grueling travel schedules may have impaired both health and family relationships; the pressure of stiff competition for the small number of prestigious jobs has not allowed them much career security. If you are determined to become a professional sportscaster in spite of the hazards, weigh carefully the advice of Russ Hodges: [1] (1) You will not succeed unless you love sports and broadcasting and commit yourself to both. (2) You must truly believe you *will* be successful. (3) Prepare yourself educationally for a different career just in case you are one of the ninety-five out of a hundred who do not succeed in sports announcing.

The Sports Announcer's Job

Some sportscasters are employed by stations or regional networks, some by athletic teams, and some by national networks. If you are under contract to a national network, you will risk your job if you show favoritism toward a team. If you announce games between home and visiting teams for a local station, the station probably will discourage you from obviously preferring the home team, even

---

[1] Russ Hodges has been sports announcer for the Washington Senators and Redskins, the Cincinnati Reds, the Chicago Cubs and White Sox, the New York Yankees and Giants, and the San Francisco Giants and 49ers. He called the CBS Wednesday Night Fights for seven years and has covered horse racing, hockey, polo, golf, and nearly every other major and minor sport. His sportscasting career began in 1929.

though local listeners may try to pressure you to show more team spirit. If you are employed by an athletic organization, you will be under the supervision of the team's management. You may not have to substitute your employer's perceptions and feelings for your own, but the chances are good that you will be expected to slant your commentary slightly in favor of your organization. Sometimes this means out-and-out rooting for your team, but more often it merely means making dull games seem a little more exciting than they are. Most sports announcers who work for an athletic organization are as loyal to their team as the players or the owners; the problem, then, is preserving some semblance of neutrality. Regardless of who pays your salary, though, you should avoid home-team bias; only the most avid and unsportsmanlike listeners enjoy obviously slanted sportscasts.

The typical staff for radio coverage of sports is made up of two announcers, a producer who may also act as statistician, and an engineer. A television sports staff includes a camera director, cameramen, a video-tape engineer, an instant-replay technician, a lighting man, a stage manager, and many others—yet it, too, uses only two announcers. Some announcing teams assign one member to call the game and the other to provide color; others alternate roles during the course of each game. Both systems are effective, depending on the talents and preferences of the announcing team.

Many sportscasters still use spotters, but the top announcers usually perform without them. They feel that a middleman increases the risk of mistakes in identifying players and calling plays; consequently, they spend many hours memorizing the names, numbers, and appearance of players so they can instantly recognize

Figure 31. Tony Kubek, Curt Gowdy, and statistician Allan Roth covering a baseball game. Before the two sportcasters are Shure Unidyne microphones with foam-rubber wind screens. (Courtesy NBC)

the man who made the tackle, the goal, or the putout. In practicing sportscasting, you are advised to work without a spotter. If only one person is helping you, he can be more useful as a statistician and color man than a spotter.

If you become the regular announcer for a professional baseball or basketball team, your life will be like that of the athletes in many respects. You can expect to make twenty-five road trips a year with a baseball team, some lasting as long as two weeks with visits to five cities. Although the basketball season is shorter, its travel schedule is even more rigorous. A baseball team will remain in one town for two to four days, but basketball teams are plagued by one-night stands in order to cram in the seventy-two games before the playoffs. Football sportscasters are free to return to their homes between road games, so their travel is less grueling.

Since each professional team has a traveling secretary who makes all arrangements for the tours, as team announcer you will not need to bother with flight arrangements, tickets, hotel reservations, or handling luggage. The secretary will hand you your seat reservation for each flight, provide you with hotel information, and arrange for chartered buses to take you from airport to hotel to stadium or ballpark. Your wife and children will be able to accompany you on some regular commercial flights but not on chartered flights. You will receive a per-diem allowance while traveling, either from the team or the station. There will be no "training table," but you probably will want to eat with the players since mealtime conversations often yield valuable information.

Sports announcers for major professional teams usually have a close relationship with sponsoring companies. If you become a sportscaster and call 162 baseball games during a season, your audience will come to identify you with sponsors whose messages you broadcast again and again and again. You probably will deliver the commercials yourself, and most sponsors will want you to sound as though you like and use the product. This, in turn, means that you must be able to deliver commercials well no matter how good you are at play-by-play announcing. And beyond this obvious conclusion is another, equally important. In the fifty to seventy-five personal appearances you will make each year before civic clubs, youth groups, or booster organizations, you will represent not only the team and the station but your long-term sponsors as well. Although you will not make a sales pitch before the Rotary Club, you cannot escape your obvious connection with those who pay for your broadcasts.

Covering the Major Sports

If you are the sportscaster for a team playing many games during a long season, you will easily accumulate the kind of information you need for intelligent ad-lib commentary. Your association with league players will make player identification routine, and your exclusive involvement with a single sport should give you plenty of material for illuminating analyses of tactics and strategies. At the highest levels of amateur and professional sports broadcasting, you will have help from your broadcast staff and the team management. Each day of broadcast, you will be given a press information kit updating all relevant statistics. During the game, a Western Union leased wire will give you the scores of other games. Perhaps a full-time statistician will work with you, unearthing and bringing to your attention significant records, dates, or events which you can incorporate into your running commentary. An engineer will continuously balance your voice with crowd sounds to add drama to your narrative. If you telecast a game, you probably will have instant replay to enrich the coverage. A famous athlete may be at your side, whose evaluations and predictions will add another dimension to the broadcast. It is still difficult and demanding work, but at least you have budget, personnel, and working conditions in your favor.

If you work for a smaller station and must announce a wide variety of games—high school, college, semipro, etc.—your job will be much more difficult. Rules of play may not be standardized, players may be unknown to you, press information kits may not exist, and you can expect little help and a low budget.

If you begin your sportscasting career, as most do, with a small station, you can expect to cover all major sports. In the "big leagues," however, overlapping and ever-expanding seasons as well as the competition of single-sport specialists

Figure 32. Chris Schenkel coordinates coverage of a golf tournament. (Courtesy ABC)

will require you to focus on no more than three major sports. Practice sports-casting for a small-station job by covering the easiest sports first and moving to the others in order of difficulty. Russ Hodges suggests this order as a guide:

1. *Boxing.* You are close to the athletes, so identification is no problem. You must remember only two names and detect only a few strategies.

2. *Basketball and hockey.* Though any fast sport demands a facile tongue, the small number of players and your proximity to them make basketball and hockey fairly easy sports to cover.

3. *Football and baseball.* These sports are different in many respects, but covering them well takes about the same degree of skill. Both require the ability to recognize a large number of players from a considerable distance. Both have periods when little is happening and moments of exceedingly rapid movement.

4. *Golf.* Golf is subject to even longer delays than baseball; consequently, you must be able to ad-lib extensively. Unless you are steeped in the lore of the game, you will have difficulty holding the attention of your audience.

5. *Horse racing.* Rapid shifts in the positions of horses, the speed and brevity of the event, and your distance from the action make horse racing the most difficult of all sports to cover.

You should also practice covering tennis, track and field, polo, auto racing, and other less popular sports if they are important in your geographical area.

Preparing for the Broadcast

Each sport requires different preparation and performance. The following suggestions do not apply to all sports and cannot anticipate every circumstance. You should not hesitate to challenge or change any of them as better ones emerge from your experience.

1. *Procure from each team, if possible, a yearbook or information kit* containing team statistics and data about the players, the coaches, and the institution represented.

2. *Condense information* from all sources and organize it on index cards or sheets of heavy paper for handy reference during your sportscast.

3. *Prepare scoring and spotting charts.*

4. *Memorize the names, positions, and numbers of the starting players* on both teams.

5. *Review the rules* in force for the game being played.

6. Arrive at the stadium, gymnasium, or playing field early, and *check starting lineups, pronunciation of players' names,* and any other relevant data with

assistant managers or team captains. (The International Phonetic Alphabet is helpful for transcribing difficult names.)

7. During the game, *keep* these *resources before you:* spotting and scoring charts, color information, and blank paper for note-taking. "Color information" includes biographical sketches of the athletes, statistics about the teams and players, the rules of the game, a list of significant records, interesting facts about the history of the sport, data about the field, court, gymnasium, or stadium, and similar pieces of information which might help you amplify and give "color" to your sportscast.

Tips on Sportscasting

Whether you have much or little help during a sportscast, you may benefit from these suggestions.

1. On radio, *report anything of importance to an audience which cannot see the game:* the size of the crowd, the configuration and dimensions of the stadium, the weather, the right- or left-handedness of players, etc.

2. On television, *concentrate on interpreting the events and adding comments about anything not clearly shown by the television camera.* Do not assume that your television audience is seeing the game as clearly as you are. If a television receiver is available to you, look at it whenever you wonder whether you are telling your viewers too little. It will keep you from getting yourself into the following frustrating situation:

Video	*Audio*
Brown comes out of his corner, and meets Green in the center of the ring. They clinch. The referee separates them, and they move away from each other. Green, in moving away, throws a punch which is not clearly seen on the home screen. The crowd yells—is it an illegal punch? a low punch? a near miss?	That's Green in the white trunks.
The boxers now turn to the side; Green's back is to us, and Brown is almost completely unseen. We see a glove fly, and hear a tremendous roar from the crowd.	Brown's a college boy, y'know—a graduate of Northwestern. He makes his home in New Jersey now.
Still in the same position, we hear another roar from the crowd.	Ooooh! That one hurt.

At the same time, avoid extraneous comments; if the events speak for themselves, silence is far better than irrelevant chatter.

3. *Do not keep telling the audience how great the game is.* If it *is* a great game, the events and the way you report them will speak for themselves. If it isn't, no amount of wishful talking on your part will make it exciting. You are a reporter, not a raconteur.

4. *Don't ignore fights and injuries, but don't oversensationalize them either.* Injuries to players or spectators could culminate in lawsuits, and your interpretations during the broadcast could influence the eventual decision.

5. *Repeat the score of the game at frequent intervals.* Tell a baseball audience what inning it is, and tell football, basketball, and hockey audiences which period it is and how much time is left. Football audiences need to be reminded frequently of who has the ball, where the ball is, and what down is coming up. It is almost impossible to give this information too often.

6. *If you aren't sure about your information, don't guess.* Wait as long as necessary to give official verdicts on whether a ball was fair or foul, whether a goal was scored, or whether a first down was made. Constant corrections of even minor errors are annoying to sports fans.

7. Likewise, *if you can't immediately identify a player making an important play, cover the play without mentioning names and give the information when you have it correctly.*

Figure 33. Color man Jack Twyman and sportscaster Chris Schenkel covering a basketball game. (Courtesy ABC)

Poor example:

ANNCR: The ball is taken by Richards. . . . He's back in the pocket to pass. . . . He's being rushed. . . . He just barely gets it away and it's intercepted by Pappas . . . no, wait, I think it's Harrison. . . . He has it on the twenty-five, the thirty, the thirty-five . . . and he's brought down on the thirty-seven. Yes, that *was* Pappas, the All-American defensive back . . .

Better example:

ANNCR: The ball is taken by Richards. . . . He's back in the pocket to pass. . . . He's being rushed. . . . He just barely gets it away and it's intercepted on the twenty . . . back to the thirty . . . the thirty-five . . . and all the way to the thirty-seven. A beautiful interception by Charley Pappas, the All-American defensive back . . .

8. *Give available scores of other games when this information won't intrude on the game you are covering, i.e.,* in moments of inactivity. Read only the numbers of scores you can give slowly and clearly. A jumble of hastily read scores is enlightening to no one.

9. *Learn where to look for the information you need.* In football, watch the official rather than the athlete when you want to know whether a first down has been made, who recovered a fumble, or if a pass was caught on or off the playing field. In baseball, watch the outfielders instead of a fly ball to see if the ball will be caught, fielded, or lost over the fence.

10. *Do not rely on scoreboard information.* Keep your own data—balls and strikes, number of downs, number of fouls, etc.—and when the scoreboard does not agree, check with the official scorer.

11. *Give statistics and records.* Baseball fans are always interested in batting and earned-run averages, fielding percentages, strikeout records, and similar data. Track and field followers are obsessed with distance and speed records. Football, basketball, and hockey fans are showing increasing interest in statistical information. The contribution to sportscasts of supporting statisticians becomes more important each season.

12. In calling horse races, *learn to identify horses by the stable colors* worn by the jockeys. Your distance from the track, the speed and brevity of the race, and the bunching of the horses preclude identifying them by number; the colors are nearly always visible.

13. *Don't give the order of horses during a race unless you are absolutely sure you are correct.* This information is vital to racing fans; you will not easily be forgiven for mistakes. And you can be checked up on: newspapers show the position of each horse at the end of each quarter or furlong.

14. *Avoid calling athletes "boys."* This title is appropriate to Little League or even high school players; college and professional athletes often consider it condescending.

15. *Deliver commercials effectively.* When you practice sportscasting, always work commercials into your coverage.

16. *Build your own library of sports books.* Many excellent books on major-league sports are available from the Sporting News Publishing Company, St. Louis, Missouri. Keep for reference the team yearbooks and press information kits you collect.

These suggestions may or may not help you become a competent sports announcer, but it should be emphasized that they are no substitute for extensive practice. If you are serious about a sportscasting career, buy a battery-operated tape recorder and take it with you to all the sports events you can cover. Practice calling the game, and then spend even more time evaluating the results at home. If you can, wait until you have forgotten the specifics of the game before listening to your tape. If you find yourself frustrated by an incomplete, inaccurate, or tedious narrative, you will at least know how much work lies ahead of you. This kind of practice need not be costly: Little League, Babe Ruth, and Pop Warner games have no admission fee; high school and college games seldom cost more than one dollar. After several hours of practice and evaluation, you should know whether or not to pursue your interest in sportscasting.

Twelve Interviewing

Interviews are important features of radio and television. They have an intrinsic audience appeal because people interviewed usually are the famous or the infamous. They are inexpensive since they entail no scriptwriting costs or overhead; guests are paid either a token amount or nothing. And interviews are appropriate to a wide range of program types—news, special events, sports, women's features, talk shows, panel discussions, science programs, etc.

The word "interview" comes from the French and means, roughly, "to see one another." We recognize as interviews question-and-answer sessions with newsmakers but sometimes fail to see that a relaxed conversation between a program host and his guest is equally an interview; the difference is in *technique,* and technique is determined by *purpose*.

Ernie Kreiling, syndicated television columnist and part-time instructor of broadcasting at Long Beach and Los Angeles State Colleges, has culled a helpful list of interviewing do's, don't's, ideas, and pitfalls from a variety of sources, including his personal experiences and the first edition of this book. Because they provide a splendid framework for our discussion of interviewing, his suggestions will be listed below with appropriate amplification. You should understand at the outset that you need not memorize these points or follow them as you would a countdown checklist for a space launch. The suggestions should be read, pondered, worked into practice sessions whenever possible, and then referred to after each dry run to help you discover where things went wrong. Some of the suggestions apply to any kind of interview; others refer only to special cases.

CONCERNING YOUR GUEST:

1. *Carefully research the guest's background, career, accomplishments, attitudes, positions, beliefs, and immediate concern with the topic of the interview.*

The list of reference works in Chapter 9 (pages 182–184) will help if the interviewee is well known. If you are interviewing a local citizen who is not nationally known, the problem is more difficult. Try the files of your local newspaper and cooperative members of the interviewee's family.

To facilitate acquiring background information on people who are not nationally known, most stations maintain a "futures file," a repository of biographical information about people who might some day be newsworthy. (Of course, information about the great also may be kept here.) If you hope to become a general or special assignment reporter, you probably ought to begin your own futures file. Approach it as follows:

a. List every agency, activity, or arena of potential news you can think of, for example, police department, fire department, city schools, local representatives of political parties, various ethnic and/or religious groups, labor unions.

b. Check into them and compile lists of "authoritative" spokesmen. Check your lists against others; be prepared to settle for something less than unanimous agreement.

c. Index your "morgue" by subject matter and names of individuals.

d. Systematically clip every news report, biographical sketch, or similar piece of potentially useful data, file in the appropriate place, and enter the information in your index. Revise your file and your index as you need to. In time, your information will enable you to select (or reject) people to be interviewed on nearly any subject and to go to your interview armed with at least rudimentary background information on your guest.

This first suggestion is as important as all the others combined. Style, personality, smooth production, and perfect timing cannot compensate for lack of preparation.

2. *Make your guest feel at home.* Introduce him to production personnel when convenient. Show him the studios and control rooms, if that's where you are, and give him an idea of what's going to happen. This hospitality will prove especially valuable if subsequent production problems delay a taping session. But:

3. *Do not submit questions to a guest in advance.* Discuss the broad areas to be covered, and possibly give him the gist of your first question so that he can plunge right in. The inexperienced guest will ask for more information about the line of questioning, but spontaneity demands that he know only the general areas of discussion.

4. *Never refer to conversations held prior to air time.* An audience will feel excluded by a question like, "Well, Joe, I'm sure the folks would find interesting that new hobby you were telling me about just before we went on the air. Will you tell them about it?" They want to feel "in" on the interview, not as if most of it has already taken place.

5. *Establish the guest's credentials at the start of the interview.* Station personnel have usually selected the guest because they believe him to be knowledgeable and responsible, and it follows that the audience should know how and

why he is qualified to speak on his subject. The significance of a partisan statement about heart transplants differs when the statement is made by (a) a heart surgeon, (b) a religious leader, (c) a heart recipient, or (d) a politician. This is not to say that one opinion is necessarily better or more newsworthy than another; it simply means that your audience needs to be aware of the specific credentials of the speaker in order to assess his statement in a meaningful way.

At times, an interviewee will appear not because he is called or chosen but because he has appointed himself a knowledgeable spokesman. It is crucial to retain an open mind toward the volunteer but not automatically assume that his statements reflect the opinions of those he claims to represent. No specific suggestions for determining the qualifications of volunteer speakers can be given; experience will help you sense the more obvious phonies, crackpots, or publicity seekers. When time permits, check credentials after the interview but before broadcasting the statements. Incalculable harm has come from irresponsibly broadcasting interviews with self-appointed spokesmen involved in campus or civil disorders.

6. *Occasionally but indirectly reestablish the guest's name and credentials.* On television this is frequently done with supers at the bottom of the screen. On radio, of course, it must be done aurally; since listeners cannot see the guest, frequent reintroductions are especially important. Because the television audience can see the guest, frequent reintroductions are unnecessary if the guest is well known.

7. *Seek out the guest's deep convictions.* Don't settle for his mentally rehearsed platitudes and clichés. Probing usually means that you must reveal something of yourself; your guest is not likely to lower his guard unless you do. Then, if you are successful in getting him to reveal his deep convictions, and they seem to be quite different from his stated position, don't ridicule them or imply that your guest is lying. He has granted you a privilege, and you would be inhumane to abuse it.

8. *Be tenacious.* Don't be put off with evasive answers. Keep probing until you see you can't get any further; then drop the line of questioning and turn to something else.

9. *Listen attentively to your guest's replies* and react with appropriate interest. Don't feign interest; if your interest is not genuine, you are either conducting a bad interview or not listening to your guest's responses.

10. *Don't interrupt with meaningless comments* like "I see," "Uh huh," "Oh, yes." An attentive mien gives the guest all the encouragement he needs; verbal interpolations while he is talking only distract him.

11. *Don't patronize your guest and don't be obsequious.* Avoid phrases like "I'm sure our viewers would like to know . . ." and "Do you mind if I ask . . . ?" Some interviewees are reluctant or hostile, to be sure, but most come to be interviewed and need no coddling.

12. *Keep cool.* Your milieu is interviewing, and you should feel at ease. The

odds are that your guest is not a professional speaker and is a stranger to the interviewing situation. He will be awed by the equipment, a bit afraid of you, and frightened to death of saying something wrong. If you are distracted by the signals of producers or floor managers or are preoccupied with timing the show, you will only further rattle your guest and lower the quality of the interview.

13. *Discuss the subject with your guest.* Don't cross-examine or otherwise bully him. Because he is probably nervous, it is up to you, no matter how much you may dislike or disagree with him, to put your guest at ease. If you show hostility, unfairness, or lack of common hospitality, both your guest and your audience will resent it.

14. *Remember, the guest is the star.* In few instances is the interviewer actually of more interest to the audience than his guest. One famous wit and raconteur consistently upstaged his guests and the audience loved it. In general, however, it is not only contrary to the purpose of the interview—drawing the guest out—it is simply rude.

15. *Remember, the guest is the expert.* At times, of course, you will be an authority on the subject under discussion and will be able to debate it with your guest. Under most circumstances, though, your guest will be the expert and you will do well to keep your uninformed opinions to yourself. However:

16. *Keep control of the interview.* Experienced guests, particularly politicians,

Figure 34. General assignment reporter Belva Davis conducts a street interview, while cameraman Tony Frazitta records both sound and picture. (Courtesy KPIX–TV, San Francisco)

can take it away and use it for their own purposes. Keep the questions coming so that the guest does not have time to diverge from the subject.

17. On television, *don't have your guest address the camera.* The best television interview gives the illusion that the two participants are so absorbed in their conversation that the camera is eavesdropping.

18. At the conclusion of the interview, *thank your guest warmly but briefly.* Don't be effusive. Then move directly to your concluding moments.

CONCERNING YOUR SUBJECT:

19. *Be sure the subject to be discussed is of interest or importance.* Although a dull guest can make even the most exciting subject boring, and vice versa, your chances of bringing off a good interview are infinitely greater if the topic itself is truly interesting or important. An interview with a university president beleaguered with a student strike will probably be of greater audience interest than one with a student about life in a college dormitory.

20. *Limit the topic so you can cover it in the allotted time.* Most newsworthy guests are multidimensional in their activities, experience, and beliefs. Avoid skimming the surface of ten topics; instead, explore one or two in depth.

21. *Establish the importance of the topic.* Although obviously important topics need no special buildup, the importance of others may benefit from brief and subtle amplification. One simple way of doing this is to ask the interviewee early in the session why he is so concerned about the issue.

CONCERNING YOUR QUESTIONS AND COMMENTARY:

22. *Write out your introduction and conclusion.* This is not possible in spontaneous interviewing situations, but when you can plan ahead, prescripting the beginning and end of the interview will free you during air time to focus on the body of the interview.

23. If you do preplan your interview and establish its length, *build it toward a high point or climax.* Hold back an especially important question for the end of the interview; if your skill allows you to lead up to that question, so much the better.

24. *Preplan at least a few questions* to get the interview started and to fill awkward gaps. Few sights are more pathetic than an interviewer at a loss for a question. However:

25. *In general, base questions on the guest's previous statements.* Don't hesitate to dispense with preplanned questions if more interesting ones arise naturally from the discussion. An exaggeratedly poor example will illustrate the problem:

ANNCR: Now, Mayor, your opponent has charged you with a willful and illegal conflict of interest in the city's purchase of the new park. What is your answer to him?

MAYOR:	Well, it hasn't been revealed yet, but I have evidence that my opponent is a parole violator from Louisiana. He served five years as a common purse-snatcher.
ANNCR:	*The News-Democrat* claims to have copies of the deeds of sale and is ready to ask for your resignation. Will you tell us your side of the story on the park purchase?

Clinging to a preselected question when a far more interesting one clamors for recognition may result from inattention to your guest's answers, insensitivity, or undue rigidity. In assessing your taped practice interviews, watch carefully for moments when you sacrifice common sense to a previously determined plan. Have a plan, but don't be a slave to it.

26. *In particular, follow up on important contradictions.* Many public figures, especially politicians, make contradictory statements which can be used as the basis for good dialogue. A word of warning, however: if you perceive that your guest is going to evade his contradictions, adopt another line of questioning. (Also refer to Number 8.)

27. *Make logical, smooth transitions to new subjects.*

Bad example:

ANNCR:	Billy, you were RBI champ last year. Do you think you can repeat this season?
BILLY:	It all depends on how my trick knee holds up. I'm having it x-rayed tomorrow.
ANNCR:	How do you and your teammates feel about players forming or joining a labor union?

Better example:

ANNCR:	Billy, last season you were a hold-out. When you finally signed, did you get everything you asked for?
BILLY:	Well, the front office and I have an agreement, but I'm not supposed to talk about it.
ANNCR:	Secrecy about salaries has always puzzled me, but I guess you have your reasons for it. Secrecy about trade negotiations puzzles me, too. Do you think much or worry much about the possibility of being traded?

28. *Always be ready with the next question,* but don't allow this to distract you from the comments your guest is making at the time. The problem of thinking ahead to the next question without "tuning out" the present can be solved only with practice and experience.

29. *Check your notes for the next question openly* rather than furtively. It would be better if you didn't do it in front of the television audience at all, but if you must, do it unselfconsciously. The best time is after your guest has completed his statement, not while he is finishing.

30. *Make your questions brief and to the point,* but not rude or brusque.

Don't be afraid to ask a more detailed question when the circumstances warrant, but try to avoid this kind:

ANNCR: George, I remember when you won the Academy Award for *Broken Hearts*—that was '54, I believe—and at that time you said you wanted to give up motion picture directing and do something with the Broadway stage. That's when you got involved in the production of *Butch,* and I guess they won't ever let you forget that disaster. Well, looking back on the years that have intervened, is there any one moment you consider to be the turning point in your life? Any moment when you should have done something other than what you did?

GEORGE: Zzzzzzzzzzzz.

31. *Don't ask questions that lend themselves easily to "Yes" or "No" answers.* Try instead to draw the guest into a discussion.

Poor example:

ANNCR: Are you working on a book now?

AUTHOR: Yes.

Much better example:

ANNCR: Tell me about the present. Are you working on a book, an article, or what?

AUTHOR: I've almost finished the first draft of a novel about migratory farm workers, but as soon as that's done, I want to write one or more fact pieces for magazine publication.

In this example, even if the author had *not* been writing at the time, he would not have been able to respond with a simple "Yes" or "No."

32. *Ask questions a layman would ask if he were interviewing,* but

33. Go a step farther and *ask interesting questions the layman probably wouldn't think of.* The knowledgeable interviewer should be able to elicit information his audience wants but doesn't know it wants.

34. *Avoid obvious questions.* Don't ask Sandy Koufax: "You were a baseball player, weren't you?" It's an unintelligent waste of time.

35. *Avoid predictable questions.* Word some of them from a point of view opposed to the guest's. Fresh and unexpected questions are called for in two common circumstances: first, when the guest regularly appears on interview shows and his opinions on nearly everything are already known; second, when the topic has been so thoroughly chewed over by expert and layman alike that the audience can anticipate exactly what questions are going to be asked.

36. *Point up and underscore important answers,* but don't parrot.

Good example:

ANNCR: Senator, if you were offered your party's nomination for the Presidency, would you accept?

| SENATOR: | I have given much thought to that question, and at present my inclination would be to accept such a call, assuming, of course, that it were truly a mandate from the rank and file as well as the party leaders. |
| ANNCR: | Senator, you have just said—for the first time, I believe—that you would run for the Presidency if the nomination were offered. That sounds firm and unconditional. Am I right in drawing that conclusion? |

Poor example:

ANNCR:	Miss Millar, you have been married five times. If you had your life to live over again, would you try to stick it out with one husband?
MILLAR:	No, I wouldn't do anything differently.
ANNCR:	You wouldn't do anything differently. Well, which of your five husbands did you love the most?
MILLAR:	I loved them all in the beginning.
ANNCR:	You loved them all in the beginning. Does that include Husband Number Three, with whom you lived but two days?

Obviously, the first example shows proper use of the repeated or paraphrased response; it leads naturally to the next question. The repetitions in the second example are simply monotonous.

37. *Don't follow your guest's statements with meaningless comments* before launching into your next question. Example:

ANNCR:	How old are you now, Fred?
FRED:	Fifteen.
ANNCR:	I see. And yet you've just graduated from college?
FRED:	Yep.
ANNCR:	I see. And what are your plans for the future?

The "I see's" only clutter the interview.

38. *Don't answer the question as you ask it.* Example:

| ANNCR: | Congressman, you voted against the treaty. Just what are your feelings about it? Your statement to the press indicated that you felt we were giving up more than we were gaining. |

What could the Congressman say except "That's right"? The interview would be dead.

39. *Never end an interview with "Well, I see our time is up."* This broadcasting cliché went out with flappers and bootleg gin. Your audience knows you are concluding because the time is up!

Kreiling concludes his suggestions with a reminder that his first point is central to all others: *Careful research into your guest's background, career, accomplishments, attitudes, positions, and beliefs, and his immediate concern with the topic of the interview is as important as the other thirty-eight points combined.*

Style, timing, personality, smooth production, and similar attributes of a good interview cannot compensate for lack of preparation.

Kreiling's suggestions are necessarily quite general. For specific interviewing situations, these additional pointers may be useful.

Interviewing Musical Talent on Disc Jockey Shows

A recording star appears on disc jockey programs chiefly because his agent or recording company feels that the appearance will be good publicity. You as the disc jockey must therefore resign yourself to a certain amount of "plugging"; this is the artist's price for his appearance (and if the artist is popular, your audience will be legitimately interested in facts about his new records or latest personal appearances). Beyond this, however, it is your skill alone that will turn a routine appearance into an outstanding interview.

1. *Stretch the interview* with records and commercials between segments. Talking with your guest off the air while his records are being played may turn up interesting facets of his life and experience to bring up on the air. It also puts him at ease and encourages him to be open and frank. The records being played can themselves be something to discuss. The segmented interview can act as a "hook" to keep the audience tuned to your program.

2. *Meet and know as many musicians as possible* in other than broadcast situations. This will make it easier to converse with visitors in an interview and will keep you abreast of the musical idiom. Disc jockeys are often invited to receptions and parties for recording stars; make it a habit to drop in on these events, for it is through them that you will come to know the people you may be interviewing at a later date.

Interviewing Athletes

Pre- and post-game interviews are common features of both radio and television sportscasts. Interviews with athletes are particularly difficult to handle. First, some athletes are inarticulate. Second, the code of the locker room seems to demand that athletes, except wrestlers and roller-derby participants, be modest about their own accomplishments and praise their teammates or opponents regardless of the facts. Third, athletes are preoccupied before a game and exhausted afterward. Fourth, the noise and confusion in dugouts or locker rooms and on the playing field can make sensible, coherent conversation impossible.

When interviewing sports stars, keep these points in mind:

1. *Assume that your audience is interested in and capable of understanding complex, precise discussions about training and technique.* Avoid asking superficial, predictable questions; your audience probably knows a lot about the sport and the athlete and wants to find out more, not the same old things.

2. *Work up to controversial or critical questions with care.* If you "pop" a big question without some preparation, you are likely to get a routine statement "for the record" from the athletes and coaches. Sports figures are interviewed so often that most of them could supply the questions as well as the answers. They tend to rely on safe, pat explanations for most common questions. If you want more than this, lead up to big questions with a sequence of less controversial ones. If you begin an interview with a football coach by asking if he approves of a trade recently made by the club's owners, he is naturally going to say "Yes" and avoid elaborating on his answer. Begin instead by talking about the team, its strengths and weaknesses. Move to a question about the playing abilities of the traded player. Ask specific questions about the player's strong and weak points. Finally, ask the coach to explain how he thinks the loss of this player will affect the team. A coach will seldom criticize the capricious decisions of the club's owners, but if you want a better than vague response, don't ask the big question straight out. Give him a chance to comment informatively as well as loyally.

3. *Get to know the athletes* likely to appear on your interview show so that you have some idea of the kinds of questions they can and cannot handle. Some sportscasters travel with teams, visit locker rooms, and are invited to opening day parties, victory celebrations, and promotional luncheons. If you have such opportunities, use them to meet and remeet the atheletes who attend.

4. *Listen to conversations among athletes and coaches.* A good way to discover what they think is timely and important is simply listening to their conversations. Though time pressures sometimes require you to enter into the conversation yourself in order to come up with a story or anecdote for your program, you can often learn more by just listening. If you are lucky enough to have meals with athletes and are accepted in clubhouse or locker room, try to be a silent observer; you will be amazed at the spontaneous insights that emerge.

Television Talk Shows

A phenomenon of our time is the proliferation of television talk shows. Once a late-night offering for insomniacs, talk shows now can be seen during all but prime time. Dick Cavett, David Frost, Mike Douglas, Merv Griffin, David Susskind, Johnny Carson—these are among the best who offer up to an hour and a half of daily conversation. Some shows alternate between interviews and performances by singers or comedians, others concentrate on discussion; some feature several guests at a time and some only one.

Talk shows of this kind are a "natural" for television. Their intimacy suits the medium well; they deal with contemporary issues, a most appropriate use of television's immediacy; they are informative, which hardly is true of most prime-time entertainment shows; they have variety, since they offer a broad spectrum of guests of all degrees of sobriety and shades of opinion.

Figure 35. Talk-show host David Frost interviewing Mrs. Coretta Scott King. (Courtesy Group W Productions)

If you develop this announcing specialty, keep these points in mind:

1. *Try to have good conversationalists on your show*. The skill, knowledge, and wit of even the best program host cannot compensate for a dull guest, or one who replies in grunts and monosyllables.

2. *Research your guest* according to the suggestions given earlier in this chapter. An hour can be an excruciatingly long time to spend with someone about whom you know very little; when the hour is spent before television cameras, it seems even longer. Make notes as you do your research, and refer to them whenever the conversation begins to pall.

3. *Don't try to match wits with a comedian* unless you are clearly his equal. And don't upstage him if you are his superior.

4. *Don't constantly interrupt your guest*. Some talk program hosts operate on the premise that thirty or so seconds of uninterrupted monologue makes their show drag. They constantly chime in, add unnecessary comments, throw unwelcome witticisms into the midst of serious reflections, and even break in to change the subject. If your guest is personable and his conversation good, and if you have established a calm but vibrant atmosphere, uninterrupted monologues can entertain for many minutes (to wit, Peter Ustinov's virtuoso one-man appearances with David Susskind). Nothing will make your audience more impatient with your guest's stories than indications from you that he is going on too long.

5. *Avoid displaying extreme feelings about your guest*. Sometimes your guests will be people you idolize and sometimes people you despise. It is certainly ac-

ceptable to reveal controlled feelings of approval or disapproval, but do not simper and fawn over those you like, or gratuitously insult those you dislike. Honest emotions, appropriate to an intimate television program, will probably exclude these extremes automatically.

6. *Try to elicit anecdotes from your guest.* Anecdotes are short narratives which may range in mood from the tragic to the comic. Good anecdotes are both structured and complete—they have a beginning, middle, and end. Usually they have been developed by their teller long after the incident being described. Time has brought objectivity and insight, and a process of clarification and intensification has sharpened the tale. Anecdotes are necessary ingredients of lengthy conversations; the rapid-fire question-and-answer type of interview has its place—occasionally in a television talk show—but more leisurely, anecdotal discussions are the mainstay of good talk programs.

7. *Match your guests.* If you have more than one guest on your show, and if you control guest selection, try to choose them so that they complement each other. If, for example, you have one guest who is a well-known concert artist, invite as well an articulate rock musician and lead them in a discussion of musical taste. Sometimes complementary pairing means choosing opposites; at others, it suggests inviting two people who are very much alike. There is no formula for this; let what you hope to bring out in the conversation guide you.

8. *Go outside your guest's special area of competency.* Naturally, you will ask many questions within the field of your guest's expertise, but don't limit the conversation there. If your guest is a famous conductor, his views on politics, religion, sports, and similar broad topics will be of enough interest to touch on them lightly. Avoid, however, staying away from his own area of expertise too long; after all, it is as a musician that he is appearing on your show.

Interviewing Political Figures

Politicians are frequently difficult to interview. Most believe that they must consistently cling to the positions which won them election. They all must seek office at frequent intervals, and a careless statement on any of a thousand issues could alienate an important bloc of voters. Further, an elected official may have two opinions on certain issues: one representing the will of his constituents, the other his personal conviction. By the demands of his profession he must watch his tongue, so he discovers effective ways of turning aside questions he does not wish to answer. Seldom does a politician reveal a changed or newly acquired position in an interview; such newsmaking events are generally confined to news conferences which consist largely of carefully worded written statements.

The purpose of interviewing politicians is not to catch them out in inconsistencies but to clarify issues and stands. Some interviewers carefully research all past statements made by an official, look into current and anticipated political issues, and then try to "corner" their guest. Sometimes this means pursuing him

Figure 36. NBC correspondent Frank McGee interviewing under the difficult conditions of the 1968 Republican National Convention at Miami Beach. (Courtesy NBC)

with apparently contradictory statements in the hope that he will admit an inconsistency; at other times it develops into an attempt to force the guest into an extreme, controversial, or careless statement. Politicians know this game well and can easily escape unscathed from such combat. When interviewing a politician well known as a white supremacist, there is little point in trying to get him to admit that he is a racist. He can easily fill a half-hour with bland, unsensational ambiguities. The relentless pursuit of a headline-making statement is not only fruitless and purposeless, but boring as well. Let this be your guide: when interviewing a politician who holds extreme but covert positions, try to help him express clearly the beliefs he is willing to state publicly; do not waste your time trying to force, goad, or trick him into making statements that common sense tells you he will not make.

No drill material accompanies this chapter, of course, but you should practice interviewing nonetheless. Use broadcasting equipment when you can: at most, radio or television equipment, including recording and playback units; at the least, an audio-tape recorder. Spend as much time as possible preparing and evaluating your work; conducting dozens of practice interviews will not help you if you repeat the same mistakes. If you have motion-picture or videotaping equipment with sound, practice filming and editing brief interviews.

Because interviews are basic to so many different kinds of broadcast programs, you should practice this skill at every opportunity. Good interviewing is the result of practice and diligent research. Do not be misled by the apparent ease with which David Frost or Dick Cavett bring off their interviews; part of the skill of any first-rate performer is the ability to make a professional job seem effortless. Your first few interviews should help build respect for those who excel in broadcast interviewing, and extensive practice will inevitably move you toward competency in this demanding job.

Thirteen Television and Film Narration

Even though "narrate" simply means "tell," not all announcing is considered narration. Both broadcasting and film have developed a narrow but imprecise definition of narration which excludes sportscasting, newscasting, and almost all on-camera television announcing. In brief, a narrator works from a script and is usually unseen; his purpose is to amplify and clarify the visual images.

Since the radio narrative has virtually vanished from the American scene, the term "narrator" has become the unchallenged property of the visual media. Though not all types of film and television narration will be considered in this chapter, a list of the major genres will show the range of job opportunities available to the professional narrator:

1. *Film documentaries.* Whether designed for theatre or television viewing, most "pure" documentaries are filmed. The narration is exclusively voice-over.

2. *Television "documented reports."* Reports may include filmed and video-taped documentation, but if the narrator is seen from time to time, they are not, strictly speaking, documentaries.

3. *Instructional films.* These range from studio-produced how-to-do-it lessons to anthropological films shot on location.

4. *Promotional films.* Many companies and institutions produce films to explain their work and promote their image.

5. *Filmed and animated commercials.* In recent years the on-camera commercial announcer has largely been replaced by off-camera announcers, actors, or musical groups voicing over the film.

6. *Travel-adventure films.* Most films of this type are shot with silent 16mm cameras. Some have music, sound effects, and narration added later, while others are broadcast with ad-libbed commentary only.

Figure 37. Frank Reynolds narrating the first in a five-part series of reports on Soviet education. (Courtesy ABC)

The narrator of the "artistic" *documentary* is not seen and usually is not known by his listeners. Sometimes an easily recognized voice is considered advantageous; a low-keyed documentary about the work of the Goodwill Industries, for example, may be more effective if the voice of a popular movie star is used. A documentary aiming for dramatic impact, however, will be more successful if the narrator's voice cannot be identified. The creators of "artistic" documentaries feel that visual images, music, and voiced commentary should blend and focus sharply on the topic explored. A familiar voice may easily divert attention from other elements in a documentary; at the worst, it may alienate those who do not like the speaker.

As a documentary narrator you are not expected to be a working member of the production team until the film is shot and edited and sound effects and music are recorded and mixed. This does not mean that you can then come in "cold" to synchronize the voice track. Most documentary scripts require study and research before they can be read effectively; investigating the subject carefully may not contribute to the filming or scripting, but it obviously will enhance your spoken interpretation and the quality of the finished product.

The object of most documentaries is dramatic impact. To be sure, documentary producers try to make their works factually accurate and objectively balanced; staged scenes, once acceptable in documentaries, are now passé. But a documentary is more than an objective fact piece. It is a dramatic presentation. The producer arranges his material just as carefully as a playwright structures a play; he orchestrates its various rhythms; he adds music and sound effects to heighten emotion; he develops a script which is precise in its language, appropriate to the meaning and mood of the visual images, and, in many instances, enhanced by poetic imagery.

Because of this, you as narrator should think of yourself as an actor rather than a journalist. This does not mean that you should *sound* "actorish"; good acting never seems like acting to an audience. It does mean that you should devote as much effort to analyzing the script as a professional actor would. You must thoroughly understand its meaning, mood, and dynamics, and you must plan and practice ways to project them effectively. The suggestions in Chapter 2 under "Interpreting the Copy" will be useful in analyzing a documentary script, and the checklist at the end of this chapter should help you evaluate your performance. But the script itself and the director will help you determine best how to interpret the mood of a documentary. It may be happy, sad, witty, whimsical, angry, or placid; in other words, documentaries are as varied in mood as dramas. In some, a straightforward objective reading will be best; in others, emotional involvement will be appropriate.

Modern production techniques make sensitive narration fairly difficult. The narrator is allowed no planned rehearsals and typically reads his script into an audio-tape recorder. The film is not projected as he reads, and he is not expected to match his delivery with the frames. If he makes mistakes, he simply stops and picks up the narrative at the last definite pause. Mistakes or unwanted takes are edited out later, and the remaining segments are matched with the film footage. If you want to perform well under these unfavorable conditions, you must devote time and thought to your delivery before making the recording. If you can, view the film several times so that you can visualize it as you read.

The *documented report* is often called a documentary, but it is different enough to warrant separate consideration. The documented report may include more than one story; it is strictly a television production; it is often broadcast live, with recorded inserts; the narrator is seen from time to time, and he almost always opens and closes the program. The narrator of a report usually is a well-known newsman, and for a very good reason: he can best convey the reportorial quality needed to explain, investigate, or evaluate an event or situation. When the viewers hear him speculate, editorialize, or recommend, they assume that he has personally researched the subject and that the conclusions are his own. To be effective in this kind of narration, therefore, you really *should* research the subject and form some opinions on it. You should be associated with the production from its earliest stages, even where others perform all production tasks. You may not do your own filming, but you may well supervise the shooting and editing and write the script.

Figure 38. Sander Vanocur introducing a documented report. (Courtesy NBC)

A short documented report called "Man's Uglification of the Landscape" has been included in the drill section of this book (pages 539–546). It was selected because it can be produced for television at small cost and with little effort. For additional practice, write and produce your own scripts. The following topics can be researched, documented, scripted, and produced in any part of the country. If you cannot film these reports, substitute still shots on easel cards or slides.

1. *How your city government works:* elective offices and their functions; appointive offices and their functions; sources and distribution of revenue; preparing, screening, modifying, and approving budgets; legal machinery and its relation to state and federal law agencies; police operations and selection of officers; how elections are supervised; how a citizen can appeal for redress of grievances; etc.

2. *How your city handles and controls the problem of waste disposal:* agencies responsible for garbage, sewage, industrial waste, litter, air pollutants; current dangers and hope for the future; etc.

3. *How welfare is administered in your area:* agencies and competition among them; kinds of people on welfare and amounts they receive; opinions of the welfare workers and the recipients on the effectiveness of the present system; alternatives; funding; etc.

4. *A day in the life of someone of interest* (policeman, judge, probation officer, factory worker, baseball player, teacher, musician, minister. etc.)

5. *How a product is manufactured* (tires, potato chips, shoes, beer, etc.)
6. *How electricity is generated* and transmitted, and how and why it works.

Instructional films are of many kinds, but few require more than straightforward delivery. Most high-school or college-level films include unfamiliar medical, scientific, sociological, anthropological, or legal terms; a few minutes with an authority in the subject will allow you to hear and transcribe into the International Phonetic Alphabet any difficult words in your script. An instructional film recently produced by the Film Production Office of the University of California points up the problem. It included these words:

amorphous	[ə'mɔrfəs]
nucleation	['nuklɪ'eʃən] *or* ['njuklɪ'eʃən]
nuclei	['nuklɪaɪ] *or* ['njuklɪaɪ]
tensile	['tɛnsl̩]
viscous	['vɪskəs]
Li_2O_3	['lɪθɪəm 'ɑksaɪd] (lithium oxide)
Al_2O_3	[ə'lumɪnəm 'ɑksaɪd] (aluminum oxide)
SiO_2	['sɪlɪkən daɪ'ɑksaɪd] (silicon dioxide)
TiO_2	[taɪ'tenɪəm 'ɑksaɪd] *or* [tɪ'tenɪəm 'ɑksaɪd] (titanium oxide)

The audiences for instructional films tolerate no margin of error; often "in-group" pronunciations develop within a field of specialization which bear no resemblance to conventional lay pronunciation. The U.S. Navy pronounces *tackle* ['tekl] (TAKE'-EL), and it pronounces *oblique* [ə'blaik] (UH-BLIKE'). If you were narrating an instructional film for the Navy and mispronounced these words, you would be *keelhauled* ['kilhɔld] (KEEL'-HAULED).

Promotional films serve many purposes and are aimed at various target audiences, but for the most part they are much like instructional films. They share the problems of specialized vocabulary and the atypical pronunciation of certain key terms. A chamber of commerce hiring you to narrate a film to boost tourism would be outraged if you mispronounced local place and street names. Similarly, an institutional banking film would be unacceptable if you mispronounced *liquidity* [lɪ'kwɪdətɪ] (LIH-KWID'-UH-TEE), *exchequer* ['ɛkstʃɛkɚ] (EX'-CHECK-ER) or [ɪks'tʃɛkɚ] (IKS-CHECK'-ER), or *arbitrage* ['ɑrbətrɪdʒ] (AR'-BUH-TRIDGE).

Unlike instructional films, promotional films are seldom designed for captive audiences; this means that they often try to be amusing—or at least entertaining—and you may, therefore, be expected to give a whimsical, mock-serious, or dialectal-narrative performance demanding real acting ability.

Filmed and animated commercials. When a performer delivers a commercial on camera, he calls himself an announcer; when he provides an off-camera voice over slides, film, or animation he usually insists that he is a "voice-over narrator." Status seeking aside, the production techniques of on- and off-camera commercial work differ considerably. The on-camera announcer prepares for his assignment exactly as if he were doing the commercial live: he studies and memorizes the script, learns movements and gestures, and practices the commercial as a nonstop performance. He pays careful attention to grooming, makeup, and clothing. An off-camera announcer prepares as he would for a documentary or an instructional film: he need not memorize his lines since he can work with the script before him, and he is unconcerned about his appearance. He will sit behind a microphone and watch the filmed commercial as he tries to coordinate his performance with it. Off-camera commercial announcers are the most pampered and overpaid performers in the industry. Many earn more than $100,000 a year for a few hours of work each week. But most jobs of this sort are monopolized by New York and Hollywood actors and actresses. If you enjoy this work, practice it as time permits, but under no circumstances should you plan your career around it. Think of it as a wel-paying but precarious sideline.

Travel-adventure films are nearly always narrated by the people who made the trip and took the films. Few use a script, and nearly all would suffer if they did: explorers and adventurers are seldom accomplished actors and perform better when they ad-lib during a screening of their film. If you find yourself as a program host on a travel-adventure film series, your chief contributions will be: (1) opening the show and awakening audience interest; (2) introducing your guest and interviewing him briefly; (3) keeping your guest's narrative flowing during the screening of his films; (4) making bridges between the program and the commercials; (5) conducting a concluding interview with your guest; (6) closing the show with some comments about the next one. Travel-adventure show hosts are always best when they themselves have traveled widely. There are few opportunities for this announcing specialization, and it would be unwise to plan your career around it.

In practicing the narrative productions discussed in this chapter, exploit every available facility. You can benefit from just reading scripts into a tape recorder and judging the purely auditory results, but it is far more practical to use filmed, taped, or photographed materials. Even if you cannot make your own, you can probably borrow some. Most audio-visual centers collect documentary, promotional, and instructional films. You can make a typescript of the narration, turn off the sound, project the film, and practice voice-over narration. You will have some problems in synchronization if you record your voice and play it back as you project the film, but a little practice should make the variations between voice track and film negligible.

Dr. George Wilson of the State University of Iowa has compiled a comprehensive checklist for narrators. It should help you spot your major problems and measure your growth as you practice narration.[1]

---

[1] Published in *Radio-Television-Film Composite Course Outlines,* prepared and issued by the Association for Professional Broadcasting Education. Copies of this publication, which includes outlines of eleven broadcasting courses, may be obtained for $2.00 by writing to the Association at 1771 N Street, N.W., Washington, D.C.

CIRCLE: 0 for does not apply; 1 for present to some degree, to 5 for present in great degree.

POSITIVE POINTS:

INTELLECTUAL MEANING

A. *Central theme* or theme or thesis clear?   0 1 2 3 4 5
B. *Vocal shift* or transition to indicate various
   parts?   0 1 2 3 4 5
C. Correct emphasis on *key words* and ideas?   0 1 2 3 4 5
D. Makes listener aware of relationship of ideas?
   cause and effect   0 1 2 3 4 5
   parenthetical   0 1 2 3 4 5
   comparison   0 1 2 3 4 5
   contrast, etc.   0 1 2 3 4 5
E. *Realization of meaning* of:
   groupings as read   0 1 2 3 4 5
   connotative words   0 1 2 3 4 5
   allusions   0 1 2 3 4 5
   symbols   0 1 2 3 4 5

ATTITUDE, MOOD, AND/OR EMOTION

A. *Main attitude,* mood, or emotion clearly pre-
   sented?   0 1 2 3 4 5
B. Presents *changes in attitude,* mood, or emo-
   tion?   0 1 2 3 4 5
C. Presents his *own attitude,* mood, or emotion?   0 1 2 3 4 5
D. Wants *to share* his material with the listeners?   0 1 2 3 4 5
E. Indicates a desire *to communicate* to listeners?   0 1 2 3 4 5
F. Indicates *an appreciation* of the material?   0 1 2 3 4 5
G. Maintains a *one-to-one relationship* with the
   listener?   0 1 2 3 4 5
H. Seems *sincere* and straightforward?   0 1 2 3 4 5
I. Exhibits a commendable degree of *warmth*
   and cordiality?   0 1 2 3 4 5
J. Has *vitality* and enthusiasm?   0 1 2 3 4 5
K. *Poised,* assured, in command?   0 1 2 3 4 5
L. *Ethical* appeal?   0 1 2 3 4 5

VIVIDNESS

A. Presentation indicates *reader involvement?*   0 1 2 3 4 5
B. Makes the listener see *mental pictures* of ac-
   tion, scenes, people?   0 1 2 3 4 5
C. Uses *sound values* to reinforce meaning,
   mood, *pictures?*
   alliteration   0 1 2 3 4 5
   assonance   0 1 2 3 4 5
   rhythm   0 1 2 3 4 5
   onomatopoeia   0 1 2 3 4 5
   stressing of vowel & consonant combinations   0 1 2 3 4 5
D. Preparation is complete and reader has as-
   similated material?   0 1 2 3 4 5

ADAPTATION TO MICROPHONE

A. Timing of: titles, punch lines, end-of-scene
   lines, humor, words to video materials?   0 1 2 3 4 5
B. Conversational?   0 1 2 3 4 5
C. Intimate?   0 1 2 3 4 5
D. Illusion of the first time?   0 1 2 3 4 5
E. Casual articulation?   0 1 2 3 4 5
F. Esthetic distance correct for content?   0 1 2 3 4 5

ADDITIONAL DELIVERY POINTS

A. Variety in length of groupings—"*ebb and
   flow*"?
B. Effective *use of pauses*?   0 1 2 3 4 5
C. Variety of emphasis techniques?
   pause before   0 1 2 3 4 5
   pause after   0 1 2 3 4 5
   attenuation of words   0 1 2 3 4 5
   volume-pitch increase   0 1 2 3 4 5
   change of quality   0 1 2 3 4 5

NEGATIVE POINTS:

INTELLECTUAL MEANING

A. Superficial reading for meaning?   0 1 2 3 4 5
B. Careless reading for meaning?   0 1 2 3 4 5
C. Incorrect reading for meaning?   0 1 2 3 4 5
D. Too much emphasis on form and throw-away
   words and phrases?   0 1 2 3 4 5
E. Incorrect emphasis?   0 1 2 3 4 5
F. Incorrect groupings?   0 1 2 3 4 5
G. Incorrect pauses?   0 1 2 3 4 5
H. Group relationships neglected (ignored)?   0 1 2 3 4 5

ATTITUDE, MOOD AND/OR EMOTION

A. Tense, nervous, apprehensive?   0 1 2 3 4 5
B. Self-centered, narcissistic, exhibitionistic? 0 1 2 3 4 5
C. Incorrect attitudes, moods, or emotions?   0 1 2 3 4 5
D. Superficial presentation?   0 1 2 3 4 5
E. Style and level of communication too formal? 0 1 2 3 4 5

VIVIDNESS

A. Lacking in vividness?   0 1 2 3 4 5
B. Word color overdone?   0 1 2 3 4 5

ADAPTATION TO MICROPHONE

A. Mike faux pas:
   distance off?   0 1 2 3 4 5
   offbeam?   0 1 2 3 4 5
   paper rattle?   0 1 2 3 4 5
B. Esthetic distance not recognized?   0 1 2 3 4 5

ADDITIONAL DELIVERY POINTS

A. Stereotype delivery pattern?   0 1 2 3 4 5
B. Mono-syndrome: rate, quality, tone, pitch?   0 1 2 3 4 5

C. Hypnotic pattern: repetitive pattern of rate, quality, tone, or inflection?	0 1 2 3 4 5
D. "Fluffs"	0 1 2 3 4 5
E. Incorrect pronunciations?	0 1 2 3 4 5
F. Incorrect pause?	0 1 2 3 4 5
G. Too fast (slow) rate?	0 1 2 3 4 5
H. Poor quality? (Specify: dull, breathy, nasal, etc.)	0 1 2 3 4 5
I. Syllabic duration neglected (overdone)?	0 1 2 3 4 5
J. "Read-ie" quality?	0 1 2 3 4 5
K. Announcer's hold?	0 1 2 3 4 5

Though the market for television and film narrators is not large, it is good to practice this skill. Mastering both live and recorded narration will help you in all other areas of oral communication. Try to select scripts which offer challenges in interpretation and pronunciation. Short educational film scripts and longer "mood pieces" are especially good for practice. You may never earn your living as a narrator, but if you become a broadcast journalist, a sportscaster, or even a staff announcer, you may be able to increase your income through an ocasional free-lance job of narration.

Answers to Drill on Page 56

1. ten	tɛn		11. caught	kɔt
2. goat	got		12. looking	ˈlʊkɪŋ
3. sat	sæt		13. easy	ˈizi(ɪ)
4. wait	wet		14. awhile	əˈhwaɪl
5. which	hwɪtʃ		15. louder	ˈlaʊdɚ
6. shoot	ʃut		16. usable	ˈjuzəˌbl̩
7. whither	ˈhwɪðɚ		17. loiter	ˈlɔɪtɚ
8. murder	ˈmɝdɚ		18. about	əˈbaʊt
9. church	tʃɝtʃ		19. bombing	ˈbɑmˌɪŋ
10. mutter	ˈmʌtɚ		20. moisten	ˈmɔɪsən(n̩)

Part Two **Practice**

Commercial Announcements

Permission to reproduce these commercials was generously granted by the sponsors and agencies indicated. Sponsors are credited in the upper left-hand corner of each commercial and agencies in the upper right. If no agency is listed, the commercial was prepared by the sponsoring company. The public-service announcements were contributed by a variety of non-profit organizations, including The Advertising Council, Inc.

Ad-lib fact sheets are featured not because they are common, but because they will help you improve your ability to communicate a sales message. It is easy to read a script; with an ad-lib fact sheet you must think about what you are saying or you will not be able to perform.

Several radio commercials require coordination with tape-recorded material. It is suggested that you tape an approximation of the indicated recorded sound and practice coordinating your live delivery with it. Also note that many commercials need local names and addresses.

Television commercials were selected for quality, stylistic variety, and simplicity of production. Some require slides or film; it will be up to you to decide what visuals are needed and to procure or make them.

If time limits are indicated, try to be no more than one second off in either direction.

TACO BELL   Wyman/Anderson-McConnell Advertising

FACT SHEET FOR LIVE PORTION OF   :60 TV SPOTS
(CHILDREN'S SHOWS)

THE FOLLOWING IS A LIST OF FACTUAL INFORMATION, INCLUDING
MENU COPY, TO BE AD-LIBBED BY THE CHILDREN'S SHOW'S HOST.
WE INVITE AS MUCH LATITUDE AS THE HOST DESIRES, AND URGE
HE INJECT HIS OWN PERSONALITY INTO ITS DELIVERY.

NOW FOR A LIMITED TIME TACO BELL IS GIVING AWAY A FREE
KIANG HAND PUPPET WITH ANY PURCHASE.

ANNOUNCE THAT THE PUPPETS ARE LIMITED AT TACO BELL STANDS
AUGUST 8TH, 9TH, AND 10TH ONLY!!!

DEMONSTRATE THE PUPPET AND TALK TO IT ABOUT TACO BELL, THE
MENUS, SLOGANS, ETC. MAKE THE FOOD SOUND AS APPETIZING AS
POSSIBLE: PARTICULARLY TELL THEM HOW GOOD THE PURE PRIME
BEEF IS THAT IS USED IN THE TACOS AND THE BELLBURGERS.

MENU: Taco Bell offers a real taste treat. It's delicious Mexican-American food and features:

1) THE TACO (TAH'-COH): A crackly deep-fried corn tortilla containing pure ground beef, shredded cheese, and crisp, fresh lettuce.

2) THE BELLBURGER: A warm fresh hamburger bun containing a large portion of pure ground beef. Also contains tasty shredded cheese and crisp, fresh lettuce.

3) THE TOSTADA (TOAST-TAH'-DAH): Deep-fried corn tortilla served open-faced. Contains refried beans, shredded cheese, and lettuce.

4) THE BURRITO (BURR-EE'-TOH): A delicious combination of refried beans, cheese, and tasty sauce rolled in a long flour tortilla.

It is important that the description of these items be rotated. We would like to establish the names of the items in markets where Mexican food has not yet been recognized.

SLOGANS, ETC.: In the recorded part of these commercials, the spokesmen for Taco Bell are Ralph, the Taco Bell crewman, and "Klang," a blue gourmet monster who is constantly gulping tacos, burritos, tostadas, the cash register, and practically everything in sight. Klang's line "Taco Bell is a nice place to eat" was born out of the :10 film ID where he consumes the entire building. This is more or

less the official slogan.

KEN BETTS CHEVRON

FACT SHEET
60 SECONDS; LIVE

1. Ken does major and minor mechanical repairs

2. <u>Open 24 hours</u>

3. For prompt automobile or heavy duty truck towing,

    call 893-9212

4. Stop in and see his Kenworth diesel tow truck

5. Have your car repaired while you're at your office

6. Official California Brake Station
    "   "   Smog Station
    "   "   Light Station
    "   "   Tune-up Station

7. Has been in downtown Oakland 15 years

8. Journeyman mechanics

9. Standard Oil products

10. Most credit cards accepted for repairs

11. Will drive customers to their offices and pick them up after work

12. Loan cars

13. Professional service and estimates

14. Services offered:

Brake relining	Generator and starter
Tune-ups	Radiator repair
Air conditioning	Electrical repair
Front-end alignment	Bearings and seals
Mufflers	Carburetors
Universal joints	Car rentals
Ball joints	

15. Address: 925 Webster Street, Oakland; or say 10th and Webster, downtown Oakland

16. Telephone: 893-9212

MJB ELECTRIC PERCOLATOR COFFEE   Batten, Barton,
                                   Durstine & Osborn, Inc.

FACT SHEET: LOCAL D.J.'s
(*To be used in every commercial)
(**To be used twice in every commercial)

**1. MJB Electric Percolator Coffee is the one coffee that was made to be timed. (USE AS NEAR BEGINNING AS POSSIBLE AND AT END.)

2. MJB has designed a new coffee especially for electric percolators: MJB Electric Percolator Coffee.

3. MJB Electric Percolator Coffee tastes <u>extra</u> rich
   because it was made to be <u>timed</u> -- actually <u>designed</u>
   to match the automatic perking cycle of your electric
   percolator.

4. MJB Electric Percolator Coffee gives you delicious
   coffee <u>consistently,</u> pot after pot.

5. Now your electric percolator can give you the kind
   of coffee it was <u>engineered</u> to make.

6. Electric percolators are automatically timed to perk
   a certain length of time -- and there was nothing
   you could do about it -- until now.

7. Look for the electric green MJB can -- with the
   words: "New Electric Percolator Coffee."

*8. <u>Good</u> things start with MJB -- and this is one of the
    best!

OPTIONAL LINES:

1. Do you have the "Oh-I-goofed-the-coffee-again" blues?

253

You need the coffee that's <u>made</u> to be <u>timed</u> -- MJB
Electric Percolator Coffee.

2. Here's news from MJB that'll make you perk up.

3. The time is 7:45 (OR WHATEVER), time for the <u>timed</u>
    coffee. MJB Electric Percolator Coffee. It's the
    ONE THAT'S <u>MADE</u> TO BE <u>TIMED</u>. (BUILD A WHOLE COM-
    MERCIAL AROUND THIS IF YOU LIKE.)

4. It's electric!

5. Look for the electric green can that says MJB.

6. Look into my electric green eyes . . . and tell me
    you'll buy MJB! It's <u>MADE</u> to be <u>TIMED</u>, you know.

THE TONI COMPANY   Clinton E. Frank, Inc.
(SUN-IN)

FACT SHEET

BASIC PRODUCT FACTS

Starred (*) items <u>must</u> be included in every commercial.
Other facts are optional, and should be rotated.

(*) Once it took all summer to give your hair that true
    sun-lightened look. But now there's SUN-IN, Toni's

brand-new sun lightener for your hair.

(*) SUN-IN works a new way--it works <u>with</u> the sun to speed up the sun lightening of your hair.

(*) SUN-IN works on drab brown hair as well as dishwater blonde and darkening blonde.

(*) Just spray on--and go sunning.

(*) SUN-IN works gradually--so you can lighten hair as much or as little as you like.

(*) Use SUN-IN for streaking, for tipping, or for overall lightening. Because SUN-IN conditions and protects your hair, you can use it up to four times in one day. You can use it day after day.

(*) When you've finished each sunning with SUN-IN, simply shampoo the way you always do. And admire the results.

What could be easier?

Now you have no excuse to be dishwater blonde or mousey brown. With SUN-IN you can have the natural sun-lightened look you want without waiting all summer!

Know how some tanning lotions work with the sun to speed up a tan? Well, new SUN-IN works with the sun to speed up the lightening of your hair! So you can lighten your hair while you tan. SUN-IN is sun-sational!

ALTERNATE OPENINGS

1. Hey dishwater blondes and mousey browns--come to a sun-in! SUN-IN is Toni's fabulous new idea--a sun lightener for your hair.

2. Know what can make a great suntan look even greater? Sun-lightened hair. And now there's a new way to get it--SUN-IN, Toni's brand-new sun lightener for your hair.

3. If you've ever wanted to lighten your hair, but were afraid it wouldn't look natural, try fabulous new SUN-IN, Toni's brand-new sun lightener for your hair.

4. Hey you, out sittin' in the sun -- wish you could speed up that slow-poke sun to hurry and sun-lighten your hair? You can -- SUN-IN is here! SUN-IN. Toni's brand-new sun lightener for your hair.

5. Hey sun-lovers! Have you discovered SUN-IN? SUN-IN
    is Toni's brand-new sun lightener for your hair. And
    it's great! Now, while you tan, SUN-IN speeds up the
    sun lightening of your hair.

6. This summer it's not gonna be enough to have a sensa-
    tional tan. If you're really with it, you'll set off
    that tan with sun-lightened hair. Because now there's
    SUN-IN from Toni. SUN-IN speeds up the sun lightening
    of your hair, so you can have the naturally lightened
    look you want -- without waiting all summer.

SEQUOIA VACUUM CLEANERS

FACT SHEET

1. Perhaps you've seen Sequoia Built-In Cleaning Systems
    in homes you have visited -- because Sequoia has more
    than 20,000 installations in the Bay Area alone.

2. Sequoia is the recognized built-in cleaning system for
    homes, hospitals, motels, apartments, offices, res-
    taurants, dental labs, schools, and churches.

3. The electronics industry knows the value of Sequoia
    systems -- specifying Sequoia for their immaculate
    "Clean Rooms," where dust must be kept from delicate
    parts.

4. Sequoia is FAST . . . one-stroke vacuuming on rugs,
    floors, drapes, furniture.

5. Neat -- no messy filter bags to empty or replace.

6. Virtually eliminates dusting after vacuuming.

7. Sequoia is LIGHT: no heavy machine or tank to push
    or pull.

8. Complete set of attachments included . . . including
    rug tool, floor tool, crevice tool, upholstery tool,
    dusting brush.

9. We call it "Plug-and-Go Magic" -- just plug in . . .
    and vacuum.

10. Easy to install in new or existing homes.

11. Cost may be as low as $475.00. Bet you have 2 or 3
    vacuums around the house that cost that much. And
    none of them will do the job of Sequoia (has 3 times

the suction of ordinary vacuums!)

12. Sequoia ADDS RESALE VALUE to your home.

13. Headquartered right here in the Bay Area.

14. Call 322-7281 collect . . . or write Sequoia, care of KSFO, San Francisco.

GENERAL TIME, WESTCLOX DIVISION
(WESTCLOX 24-HOUR SWITCH TIMER)

FACT SHEET

1. Fully automatic . . . turns lights and appliances on or off at designated times. Operates on regular house circuit.

2. Just plug it in . . . set it and forget it.

3. Can be used for turning house lights on and off during vacation, to make home appear occupied.

4. When beside lamp is plugged in, the timer can act as a "silent alarm" clock, waking you without disturbing the rest of the household by turning on the lamp at desired times.

5. Start the coffee perking . . . turn on the air conditioner.

6. Turn on your TV.

7. Attractive compact case available in Antique White or Woodtone.

8. Shatterproof Crystal

2 | Short Radio Commercials and Public-Service Announcements

CARLSBERG BEER   Edward J. McElroy, Inc.

30 SECONDS

You know, there's something rather rare about the Danish people. They are bright, lighthearted people. Lovers of beautiful things. So it's not so surprising that they created Carlsberg, the bright, lighthearted beer of Copenhagen. They did it with fine European hops, barley, and malt. They added the crystal purity of Danish artesian water. And when they were through, they poured all that mellowness into a tall, tapering bottle. For you. So if you can't make it to Denmark this year . . . bring Denmark to you. With a bottle of Carlsberg . . . the bright, lighthearted beer of Copenhagen. It's delightfully Danish!

BEATRICE FOOD   Campbell-Mithun, Inc.
(LA CHOY)

30 SECONDS

What do you serve a late-working husband? Something

quick . . . something easy . . . but it's got to be

good . . . like LA CHOY Beef Chow Mein. LA CHOY Beef

Chow Mein comes in a Bi-Pack can . . . hearty beef in a

rich gravy on top . . . with water chestnuts, bean

sprouts, bamboo shoots and more in the bottom. Just mix

the two cans, heat and serve in six minutes flat. Great

for late-working husbands . . . even when they come home

on time.

NORTH PACIFIC CANNERS AND PACKERS, INC.   Ralph P. Coleman
(FLAV-R-PAC)   and Associates

30 SECONDS

(Dinner gong) There is one good way to save on fancy

frozen fruits, vegetables, and juices . . . buy FLAV-R-

PAC Frozen Foods in the bright yellow package with the

blue FLAV-R-PAC shield. Unlike many other foods you buy, many FLAV-R-PAC Frozen Foods cost about the same as they did ten years ago . . . and you'll find them at bargain prices every day. FLAV-R-PAC Frozen Foods with the red, white, and blue Government Grade A Fancy shield on the package.

FORD DEALERS   J. Walter Thompson Company

30 SECONDS

The latest word from Ford Country: The Official Ford Dealer Clearance Sale is just getting underway. Your Ford Dealer has to move 'em all out to make room for the new models, and he knows that nothing encourages action as fast as big savings. Savings on every car in stock . . . including Galaxies, Falcons, Fairlanes, and even Ford trucks. All at their lowest prices. Now's the time to take advantage of your Ford Dealer's once-a-year, end-of-year savings. See him today!

SEALY MATTRESS COMPANY   Bernard B. Schnitzer, Inc.

45 SECONDS

It's their eighty-sixth anniversary . . . And, naturally,
you'd <u>expect</u> the Sealy Posturepedic people to make a <u>big</u>
<u>thing</u> out of this event. Well . . . they have. They've
taken the same expensive cover formerly used on their
nationally advertised eighty-nine fifty mattress and put
it on the new Sealy-Rest mattress. And . . . because the
Sealy people believe you should get value plus, they've
added even more quality features to the Sealy-Rest . . .
like costliest deep quilting for surface luxury . . . and
patented Edge Guards to keep your mattress firm. Then
Sealy did the nicest thing of all . . . they priced the
elegant Sealy-Rest at a modest forty-nine ninety-five, in
twin or full size. How can you <u>beat</u> such value?

BOB OSTROW

30 SECONDS

FOLLOWS TAPE CART . . . VOCAL JINGLE FULL . . . 8 SECONDS
(Read over musical bg . . . 22 seconds)

263

If you're a salami expert, we'd like to suggest BOB
OSTROW Italian Salami. If you're not, we'd like to suggest it anyway! Finely spiced and flavored to a sausage
gourmet's taste; it's thin-sliced for easy sandwich making. Use it to top off pizza for a special treat! BOB
OSTROW Italian Salami. Another fresh, convenience food
available at _____.
                    (name and address of store)

JOS. SCHLITZ BREWING COMPANY   Post-Keyes-Gardner, Inc.
(BURGERMEISTER BEER)

30 SECONDS

Right now, Burgie has a friendly special offer going for
you on the comfortable beer. You can save yourself ten
cents on every six-pack of twelve-ounce cans. Now a
dollar-fifteen a six-pack, for Burgie . . . the comfortable beer. Burgie's comfortable because it's soft-water
brewed to refresh you and keep right on refreshing. That
special price again? Only a dollar-fifteen a six-pack.
Limited time only. Get acquainted with the comfortable
beer. Dollar-fifteen a six-pack. That's Burgie!

If you can get something good for less money than usual --
that's a bargain. Right? Okay -- if you can get something good and comfortable for less money than usual --
what's that? That's Burgie, the comfortable beer. The
brewers of Burgie want everybody to try comfortable beer,
so, for a limited time only, you can pick up a six-pack of
twelve-ounce cans for just a dollar-fifteen. You save ten
cents on every six-pack. That's a real comfortable
bargain for you, because it's Burgie . . . the comfortable
beer. Get several six-packs of Burgie . . . and save even
more.

VISTA   Office of Economic Opportunity

30 SECONDS

A child hugs the first picture book he has ever seen. A
man learns to read. A dropout gives school another
chance. These are the hard tasks . . . small miracles
performed by Volunteers in Service to America. If you
want the chance to change the future for someone who never
had a chance, see the VISTA representatives at _____.
                                                (address)

20 SECONDS

Looking for low pay, long hours, and an immense amount of personal satisfaction? If you are and want to spend a year of your life helping others help themselves, see the VISTA representatives at _____.

(address)

REHABILITATION FOR THE MENTALLY
AND PHYSICALLY DISABLED CAMPAIGN

The Advertising
Council, Inc.

30 SECONDS

Maybe you have a disability. And maybe you're giving it the best years of your life. It doesn't have to be that way. Today, with proper guidance and medical aid, you can be taught to take care of yourself. And learn a job you like. If you're disabled, or concerned about someone who is, write to this address. Write: HELP, H-E-L-P . . . Box 1200, Washington, D.C., 20013. You've got nothing to lose but your disability.

AID TO HIGHER EDUCATION CAMPAIGN   The Advertising
                                          Council, Inc.

                          30 SECONDS

Scientific knowledge is one of America's keys to progress.

To keep it growing we'll need more and more brilliant

young scientific leaders. Where will we get them? From

college. Because that's where most of them come from

today. But colleges need help. They need contributions

from business, foundations, and people like you. So give

to the college of your choice. And if you don't have a

favorite, adopt a college, and give regularly. Your gift

may help one of America's future leaders get his start.

_____

TRAFFIC SAFETY CAMPAIGN   The Advertising Council, Inc.

                          30 SECONDS

Different people find different excuses for not wearing

their safety belts when they drive. Mrs. Gordon never

wore them when she was just going down to the beauty shop.

Now she's not so beautiful anymore. Bob Watson used to

say they made him feel confined. Now he's confined for

good. To a wheelchair. Mike Cammuso thought safety belts

were for kids. Now his six kids have no father. Almost anyone can find an excuse for not wearing safety belts. What's <u>your</u> excuse?

KEEP AMERICA BEAUTIFUL CAMPAIGN

The Advertising Council, Inc.

30 SECONDS

One discarded wrapper helps ruin the scenery. And a steady splash of trash -- carelessly dropped by many people -- really piles up the damage. Our parks and high-ways and waterways and beaches belong to all of us. Litter spoils the view . . . threatens highway safety and boating fun. Litter costs tax dollars . . . when there's rubbish to pick up, the taxpayers pick up the check. Carry a litter bag in car and boat, and hold your trash for the first container. Living in litter is not for people. Help Keep America Beautiful.

POST-U-CHAIR

60 SECONDS

Orthopedic specialists will tell you that backaches are often the result of poor posture. Standing or sitting with the spine in a curved position can weaken muscles and cartilage and make you susceptible to backache and spinal injury. The POST-U-CHAIR has been designed to help avoid an unnatural curvature of your sacroiliac. POST-U-CHAIR and regular exercise can help prevent lumbago, sciatica, and other aches and pains associated with back trouble. Of course, POST-U-CHAIR can't do the job alone--knowing the correct way to stand, walk, and lift are important too--but, POST-U-CHAIR can keep your back in a straight line while resting, reading, or watching television. Send for our free booklet, "Caring for the Back," and see how the POST-U-CHAIR can combine with exercise and common sense to give you a strong, trouble-free back. Send a card to _____,
(address)
and POST-U-CHAIR will get the booklet to you by return mail. The address, once again, is _____,
(address)
for the booklet "Caring for the Back."

269

60 SECONDS

Here's a chance to help your youngster improve his school work and get yourself a great camera in the bargain. If you buy a Smith-Corona electric portable now, you can have your choice of either an Anscomatic (Ans-co-matic) movie camera with an electric eye and electric drive . . . or a Minolta (Mi-nol-ta) sub-miniature camera for only $8.95 or $10.95. Each of these cameras is worth more than $30.00, so it's another good reason for you to choose Smith-Corona, the typewriter that has introduced more features to make it easier to type than any other portable. Send your youngster back to school this fall with America's best-selling portable typewriter and get yourself either an Anscomatic movie camera or a Minolta sub-miniature camera for only $8.95. Act now! This offer expires soon, at participating Smith-Corona dealers.

CAFE L'EUROPA

60 SECONDS

When you think of good food, you probably think of Paris,
Copenhagen, or Rome. But, now, right here in the center
of America, you can find the best of European and Asian
cuisine at a price that will surprise you. The CAFE
L'EUROPA, on Highway 40 at White's Road, is under the
supervision of Chef Aristide Framboise. Chef Framboise
earned his Cordon Bleu at the famous Ecole des Quatre
Gourmandes in Cannes, France. The Chef's staff of
European and Oriental cooks have been personally trained
for the exacting work of pleasing you, regardless of your
culinary preferences. Whether you like poulet sauté
marseillais or gedämpfte Brust, spaghetti all' amatriciana
or calamares en su tinta, you'll thrill to your candlelight dinner at CAFE L'EUROPA. Dial 777-3434, and ask our
Maître D for a reservation soon. That's 777-3434, the
CAFE L'EUROPA, at White's Road on Highway 40.

60 SECONDS

How long since you've taken your wife out for a special
occasion of your own making? Not a birthday, anniversary,

271

or holiday, but an evening you've set aside to tell her you appreciate her. The CAFE L'EUROPA is the perfect restaurant for this and all other very special celebrations. The CAFE L'EUROPA, on Highway 40 at White's Road, features delicacies from around the world. Mahi-mahi from Hawaii, sukiyaki from Japan, nasi goereng from Indonesia. European cuisine includes Pfannekoeken from Holland, cochifrito from Spain, and ratatouille from France. If you like less exotic dishes, try English Welsh rabbit or German Sauerbraten. Whatever your taste, you're sure to enjoy candlelight dining at CAFE L'EUROPA. Make a date with your wife now, and call our Maitre D for dining reservations. Dial 777-3434, and prepare yourself for an unforgettable evening of dining at the CAFE L'EUROPA. Your wife will appreciate your thoughtfulness.

THE GENERAL TIRE AND RUBBER COMPANY

60 SECONDS

The famous General Jet! It's a tire built to take it, with a slim white sidewall and a famous dual-tread design built from rugged Duragen rubber, that racks up long, safe mileage. Four full plies of strong nylon cord help the General Jet run fast and cool . . . mile after mile

. . . no matter what the terrain. Right now the General

Jet is on sale for only fourteen-ninety-five . . . only

fourteen-ninety-five plus one-seventy-eight Federal

Excise Tax for the popular six-fifty by thirteen size that

fits most compact cars. Larger sizes are available at

extra cost. The four-ply nylon cord whitewall General Jet

tire . . . on sale right now at your General Tire

Specialist's. Drive in today and get set . . . with the

famous General Jet . . . at surprisingly low sale prices

for General whitewall tires. See the Yellow Pages for

your nearest General Tire dealer or store.

GALLO SALAME, INC.   Edward J. McElroy, Inc.

60 SECONDS

In this day and age when everybody seems to be in a hurry,

maybe you'd like to hear about a food that takes its own

sweet time. That food is Gallo Italian Dry Salame. Gallo

is made the fine old Italian way . . . with no spices or

herbs added. It starts with superb beef and pork, mixed

together, then slowly and patiently aged to develop its

unique, tantalizing flavor . . . a flavor you simply can't

get in a hurry. Maybe that's why Gallo Italian Dry
Salame is the choice of people who take the time to appreciate the finer things in life. Maybe that's why
Gallo Italian Dry Salame adds so much pleasure to that
quiet hour before dinner. Tomorrow night, when your husband comes home, serve him a tray of thin Gallo Italian
Dry Salame slices with his favorite beverage. It's a
beautiful Italian way to relax and unwind. Gallo Italian
Dry Salame is waiting in the deli case . . . waiting
patiently for you . . . very patiently.

DRAPER'S MEAT LOCKER

60 SECONDS

How would you like to save dollars, while serving your
family the very best in beef, pork, chicken, and lamb?
Sound impossible? Well, it isn't, if you own a home
freezer and buy your meats wholesale at Draper's Meat
Locker. Hundreds of families have discovered that it
actually costs less to serve prime steaks, roasts, and
chops than it does to scrimp along on hamburger and tough
cuts -- IF you buy your meat in quantity from Draper's.
Imagine. One hundred pounds of prime beef steaks and

roasts for only 99¢ a pound! Or, save even more by buy-

ing a quarter or a side. With every purchase of a side

of beef, Draper's throws in twenty pounds of chicken, ten

pounds of bacon, and five legs of spring lamb absolutely

free! If you don't own a freezer, Draper's will get you

started in style. Buy any of their 300 pound freezers,

and Draper's will give you a freezer full of frozen food

free! Meat, vegetables, even frozen gourmet casseroles,

all free with the purchase of a new freezer. Prices

start at $199, and terms can be arranged. So, why don't

you decide to beat the high cost of living? Come into

Draper's soon and see which plan is best for your family.

Draper's has two locations -- in the Lakeport Shopping

Center, and downtown at 1338 Kraemer Street.

WISEMAN'S INTERNATIONAL CIRCUS

60 SECONDS

(IMITATING A CARNIVAL BARKER) HURRY, HURRY, HURRY! The

world's greatest show is about to begin! Yes, Wiseman's

International Circus will be visiting _____
                                     (name of city)

for ten gala performances during the week of _____

_____. See the death-defying space shot of
(inclusive dates)
Spain's Julio Zurrapiento, two hundred feet to a splash-

down! Thrill to the daring Skladanowski Brothers, high

wire artists from Poland! You'll hold your breath as

Georges Cinquataine, sensational French animal trainer,

performs with fierce lions, tigers, leopards, and grizzly

bears, all in the ring at the same time! For beauty, see

the Satyajit Koomarswami dancers from Hindustan in their

"Kashmiri Love Dance." And for the children, Wiseman's

famous circus clowns under the leadership of internation-

ally renowned Alois Schicklgruber, the greatest clown of

them all! So, HURRY, HURRY, HURRY. Seven big circus

days, beginning Monday, _____. It's Wiseman's
                         (date)
International Circus. Tickets are now on sale at all

_____ Drug, and _____ Grocery stores.

Call or write now, for the World's Greatest Circus!

Note: Mr. James A. Richardson, the writer of the follow-
       ing three commercials, offers them to you with
       this advice:

    Too often, the live announcer gives the commercial
only brief study and is tempted to rely solely on his
individual style of delivery to the detriment of the
thought behind the message. This seems to hold true
for a newscaster whose elocutionary hangup is to accent every word in the sentence, as much as it does
for the talk-show MC who tries to ad-lib his way
through the commercial in striving for his own emotional rapport with his listeners. The three American
Plan commercials should be an excellent test for the
student to demonstrate his understanding of the degree
of hard or soft sell intended by the author; all deliver the same basic message, yet the imagery should
change for the announcer as each commercial obviously
is planned to evoke its major response from a different profile within the spectrum of listeners.

60 SECONDS

You know - everybody needs some money sometime. And when

that time comes, more and more home owners who need money

are calling the Man at American Plan. They know they're

on solid ground, because only American Plan has the key

to low-cost borrowing . . . even less than your local

bank. Best of all, American Plan is a personal and con-

fidential service . . . that solves money problems right

at home. Forget about artificial limits on credit, age

or occupation. If you own property, paid for or not, you can borrow five hundred, five thousand, ten thousand dollars to pay taxes; to pay bills; to let you relax about money. There's no obligation at all when you call American Plan. The telephone is 434-1383. Call collect, anytime, for prompt, friendly, and accurate information. 434-1383. Or see the Yellow Pages under Real Estate Loans. Remember: You're not alone. Everybody needs some money sometime. Maybe right now is the time for you to call the Man at American Plan.

60 SECONDS

One of today's leading financial services for property owners is American Plan. Why? Because American Plan is the key to the fastest, easiest way for home owners to borrow at low rates . . . even less than your local bank. American Plan helps you relax about money by solving money problems. It's as simple as that. Best of all . . . American Plan makes cash available without cosigners; without credit investigation; without artificial limits on age or occupation. If you own property, paid for or not, you can borrow five hundred, five thousand, ten thousand dollars for any purpose you wish. The thing to

do is call the Man at <u>American</u> Plan. Just tell him how
much money you need. Chances are he can say "Yes" right
over the telephone. Call now -- without cost or obligation. 434-1383. Yes, the key to money problems is as
near as your telephone. Call the man with the <u>key</u> at
<u>American</u> Plan. Call collect -- 434-1383. Or see the
Yellow Pages of your local phone book.

60 SECONDS

Here is something worth thinking about. The day you
bought your home you started a <u>built-in</u> savings account.
That's <u>true!</u> Your share of home ownership began to grow
month after month, year after year. This is <u>your</u> money,
believe it . . . and it's yours to <u>use</u> for any purpose.
The Man at <u>American</u> Plan has the <u>key</u> . . . <u>American</u> Plan
<u>is</u> the key . . . to making your built-in cash available.
What could be more sensible than borrowing <u>your own money</u>
at the most favorable rate -- even less than your local
bank -- and paying it back to <u>yourself</u> through <u>American</u>
Plan! If you own property, paid for or not, you can bor-
row <u>five hundred,</u> <u>five thousand,</u> <u>ten thousand</u> dollars to
pay taxes; to pay bills; to help you <u>relax</u> about money.
There's no obligation at all when you call <u>American</u> Plan

. . . not even the cost of the phone call. The number is 434-1383. Call collect, anytime, 434-1383. Or, see your local Yellow Pages under Real Estate Loans. Remember: You're not alone. Everybody needs some money sometime. Think about it. Maybe it's time for you to call the Man at American Plan.

SEQUOIA VACUUM CLEANERS

60 SECONDS

Do you sometimes get tired of pushing a heavy vacuum cleaner around your home? Well, thanks to Sequoia Built-In Systems, you need do this no longer. Sequoia . . . the pioneer producer of BUILT-IN cleaning systems, with installations in more than 20,000 Bay Area homes . . . would like to put this amazing system in your home. With Sequoia there's no tank to pull, no bag to empty. Just plug in . . . and vacuum. Dirt, dust, and even odors are whisked out of the house into a central container you empty only once every 6 to 8 months. It's quiet . . . so powerful it removes deep-down hidden dirt . . . and healthful, eliminating redistribution of germ-laden dust. Depending on the size of your home, your Sequoia built-in

system can be installed for as low as $475.00 . . . even
less if you install it yourself. Learn how you can enjoy
Sequoia Built-In Cleaning in your own home. For a free
brochure or estimate, just call 322-7281 collect . . . or
write Sequoia, care of KSFO, San Francisco. For a short
time Sequoia will give you a Japanese electric teapot if
you call for an estimate.

MONTGOMERY WARD   Lufrano Associates

60 SECONDS

Now is the time to replace those lumpy bed pillows and
old, worn blankets during Montgomery Ward's <u>gigantic</u>
PILLOW AND BLANKET SALE. All sizes--pillows and blankets
--at <u>gigantic</u> savings! Fluffy Kodel Polyester pillows--
cloud-soft goosedown pillows--Acrilan <u>regular</u> blankets,
nonallergenic, machine washable, dramatic colors, and
Acrilan <u>thermal</u> blankets, cool in summer, warm in winter.
Also, automatic constant-heat electric blankets--com-
forters--and bedspreads. All bargains! Savings of up to
33 per cent! For example, Kodel bed pillows, superb for
sleeping comfort, regularly priced at 2 for $12, regular
size, <u>now</u> on sale 2 for 7.99! That's one-third off! And

all pillows are on sale! Ward's Kodel Polyester pillows
are nonallergenic, dustless, moth and mildew-proof, and
machine washable. Don't miss this sale! It's Montgomery
Ward's PILLOW AND BLANKET SALE--going on right NOW-- with
UNUSUAL SAVINGS--up to ONE-THIRD OFF on pillows and
blankets--at all Montgomery Ward Stores.

HOUGH'S HOUSE OF FABRICS

60 SECONDS

Hough's House of Fabrics announces its annual spring
fashion yardage sale. Beginning this Thursday and running for one full week, you can save dollars while you
prepare for a colorful spring and summer. Synthetic
fabrics that never need ironing, in a variety of textures
and patterns -- appliqué puff, crêpe de chine, etched
peau di luna, your choice, only $2.49 a yard. Or, look
for summertime sheers -- batiste, voile, or crushed crepe,
at just $1.09 a yard. Hough's has a complete collection
of dazzling Hawaiian prints, too. Wahini poplin, Kahului
broadcloth, or Niihau jacquard weave -- with prices ranging from 99¢ to $2.89 a yard. And, yes, Hough's has pat-
terns, notions, and everything else you need to create

your wardrobe for the coming season. So, why don't you
save money and get started on your own versatile and
original spring and summer wardrobe right now? Remember,
Hough's House of Fabrics, in the Northfield Shopping
Center, just out of town on Marsh Road. That's Hough's --
on Marsh Road. Sale ends a week from Thursday.

KUYUMJIAN'S RUG BAZAAR

60 SECONDS

Kuyumjian's has just received a large shipment of new and
used oriental rugs which must be sold at once. These
rugs are being sold to settle tax liens against a major
import firm. So, their misfortune is your gain. Here is
your chance to own a genuine oriental rug at a fraction of
its regular cost. Gulistan, Kerman, Sarouk, Shiraz, and
Baktiary rugs at unheard-of prices. Time does not permit
a complete listing, but here are a few specials: a five-
by-seven Faridombeh rug in antique gold, only $288. A
three-by-five Feraghan in ivory and pistachio, just $375.
An extra-large, nine-by-fourteen virgin wool Ispahan
Ivory, $1,000. Small Yezd, Oushak, and Belouj scatter
rugs at less than $100. All sizes are approximate, and

quantities of each style are limited. Visit Kuyumjian's
this week, and become the proud owner of an original,
hand-woven, virgin wool oriental rug. Kuyumjian's Rug
Bazaar, on the downtown mall opposite the State Theatre.

GALBRAITH'S DRAPERY SHOP

60 SECONDS

Any time of the year is a good time for sprucing up your
home, and Galbraith's Drapery Shop wants to help you get
started right now. Galbraith's has the most complete line
of drapery materials in the county. Galbraith's also has
ready- and custom-made drapes at prices that will please
you. See their custom-made flameproof, stainproof, moth-
and mildew-proof draperies made of spun glass. Only
$12.99 a pair, with your choice of scalloped or pinch-
pleated valances. Or, look for their elegant jacquard
tapestries with woven matte patterns. Ready-made sizes,
as low as $9.99 a pair. For the boudoir, Galbraith's has
Austrian pouff pull-ups made of machine-washable batiste,
and this luxury can be yours for just $8.99 a panel. What-
ever your drapery needs, drive to Galbraith's Drapery Shop
now, while styles and fabrics are at their most complete.

Galbraith's is located at First and Mandan Streets, right in the heart of town. Jot down your window measurements and your color scheme, and visit Galbraith's today.

WHITE FRONT STORES   Recht and Company, Inc.

60 SECONDS

CART 601 . . . BUGLE CHARGE . . . 4 SECONDS

This week, WHITE FRONT has the back-to-school bike you've been looking for. At a fantastic savings! The Golden Arrow Italian Import . . . sports a new low profile, features a long, slim supercharger, white sidewalls, contour seat, front-end and coaster brakes, and hi-rise handle bars. Styled for boys or girls. And now the surprise! This model, which usually sells at WHITE FRONT's regular low discount price of just 39.97, is specially priced this week at just 35.97! And . . .

CART 601 . . . BELL . . . 2 SECONDS

as the Bell-Ringer Bonus this week, with this purchase you receive absolutely free a Whamo Wheelie Bar . . . the hottest item for the bike set! WHITE FRONT has sold hundreds of the Whamo Wheelie Bars at 9.97 each . . . but you get yours _free_ when you purchase the Golden Arrow Italian Bike this week. 'Til Sunday at 7 p.m. at WHITE FRONT! And Tommy T. Tire says to remind you that September is Tire Month . . . for outstanding savings and values at WHITE FRONT.

MERCURY/COMET   Kenyon and Eckhardt, Inc.

60 SECONDS

Note: This commercial requires elaborate production and is intended for recorded rather than live delivery.

ANNCR: Right now, the hottest spot in the West is
              your Mercury-Comet dealer's.

SOUND/MUSIC: KEY INTO SPANISH FLAMENCO CABARET TYPE OF
              SCENE. ALREADY IN PROGRESS ARE GUITAR AND
              JOSE GRECO FOOT STOMPING. OLE'S AND MUI
              BIEN'S AND BUENO'S ARE HEARD IN BG. SUSTAIN
              FOR :07 THEN VOICES OUT AS HEELS DOMINATE.

ANNCR: He's hot for that old car of yours. He
              needs that old car of yours.

SOUND/MUSIC:	OLD CAR BACKFIRES TWICE IN TEMPO TO HEELS. HEELS AND GUITAR LAY OUT AS SOUND OF OLD MOTOR REVS UP. THIS X-FADES TO CASTANETS RATTLING. CASTANETS AND GUITAR LAY RHYTHM UNDER FOR:
ANNCR:	Any old car is worth more right now on a hot new Mercury or Comet. That's because these cars are selling like hotcakes. So your Mercury Man can afford to make the hottest deals in this town . . . or any other town.
SOUND/MUSIC:	FADES ON LAST WORD. MERC FADES IN ON TOP OF LINE AT HIGH SPEED. CASTANETS ECHO IT (AS WITH OLD CAR) AS FLAMENCO SCENE BEGINS FULL BLOWN. HOLD, THEN UNDER FOR:
ANNCR:	So what are you waiting for? Those hot new Comets and Mercs have never been easier to pay for.
SOUND/MUSIC:	FINISH WITH HEELS PREDOMINATING.
ANNCR:	That's something to kick up your heels about.

PABCO PAINT   Wyman/Anderson-McConnell Advertising

60 SECONDS

Here's a long-range forecast from Pabco, the paint people:
Rain Stain weather . . . for many years to come. Rain
Stain weather means rain, sun, salt air, and storm. And
Pabco Rain Stain is the one stain finish that shields
wood -- beautifully -- in any climate. Your Pabco Paint
dealer, _____ ,has the full story. But
             (dealer name and address)
here it is in a word: Acrylic. Modern chemistry developed a versatile, tough resin and called it acrylic.
Pabco uses acrylic as a base for outdoor/indoor rustic
stain and calls it the Rain Stain. It's tough as all outdoors. Glides on smoothly right out of the can . . .
dries in two hours and cleans up with soap and water.
Pabco Paint dealers have actual wood samples showing
Pabco Acrylic Rustic Stain in a wide range of contemporary
colors and neutral tones. See them at _____
                                        (dealer name and
_____ .
address)

60 SECONDS

(MUSIC KEYED TO SCRIPT)

For sheer brass, nothing can touch it. Houston. The big
rich. Brash. Confident. A brawler. That just opened
the finest opera house in the Southwest. That calls itself one of the world's fashion centers. And is. Houston.
It's oil. Hard cash. Enchilladas in the Mexican quarter.
It's a fast quip. A millionaire who rode before he could
walk. The NASA space center. If ever there was a frontier, Houston is it. If ever there was a cosmopolitan
city, call it Houston. But mostly, call it guts.

(SOUND OF JET TAKEOFF)

Houston . . . an Eastern address. Eastern Airlines has 3
nonstop jets going there every business day -- throughout
the business day. A lot of people want to get to Houston.
We'd like to make it easier for every one of them. We
want everyone to fly.

---

60 SECONDS

ANNCR: Excedrin Headache #24, "What's for Dinner?"

HUSBAND: We've had liver so many times in the last month
           that I'm . . .

WIFE: Are you gonna eat your liver?

HUSBAND: Negative. I'm not gonna eat it. Zero liver is
           going into my mouth.

WIFE: Liver is good for you. With liver you can live.

HUSBAND: I'm gonna live without . . . I'm gonna risk my
           life by not eating liver for three days.

WIFE: If you're not like strong and healthy, I mean,
           what do I need you for, right?

HUSBAND: Well, I've been strong and healthy. You don't
           see me collapsing and falling down and . . .

WIFE: But you will be.

HUSBAND: Somebody has to take a stand on this thing, and

I'm gonna. . . . I'd rather stand on it than
eat it. I'm just not gonna take this liver. I
look in the mirror -- I see liver, I look like
liver.

WIFE: Oh, that's funny.

HUSBAND: Uh-oh. What are you taking that little bottle
of aspirin for?

WIFE: This is not aspirin, this is Excedrin.

HUSBAND: Ya have a headache, huh?

WIFE: I don't have just a headache, you've given me
an Excedrin headache.

HUSBAND: Oh, honey . . . (FADE)

ANNCR: Life is full of Excedrin headaches. That's why
you should get a bottleful of Excedrin tablets--
each 50 per cent stronger than an aspirin tablet
for relief of headache pain. If you get
Excedrin headaches -- why take anything else?

HUSBAND: (FADE UP) . . . have a funnel put in my mouth
like a Strasbourg goose   (FADE)

BIRR, WILSON & CO.   Albert Frank-Guenther Law, Inc.

60 SECONDS

Do you find it nearly impossible to keep abreast of the latest stock market conditions? If that's the case, Birr, Wilson & Company has a suggestion. If you act now you can receive for the asking, every two weeks, a helpful report entitled "Birr, Wilson Guideline." The guideline, published by Birr, Wilson's research department, gives you at a glance a brief summary on the current market. You'll also find an in-depth study of one recommended stock, as well as other stocks selected under the "Buying Guide" section. Every investor will find the "Birr, Wilson Guideline" an important and informative look at the market. If you write today, you'll receive a current biweekly issue to be studied in the privacy of your home. For your regular copy, send your name and address to "Birr, Wilson Guideline," _____.
                                          (station address)
Sit down and write today to "Birr, Wilson Guideline," ___

_____.   Remember, this offer is avail-
  (station address)
able only from Birr, Wilson & Company, members New York

Stock Exchange. In _____, Birr, Wilson's
                          (town)
office is located at _____.
                                (address)

MOTOROLA, INC.   Clinton E. Frank, Inc.
(COLOR TV)

60 SECONDS

Most people seem to think there's not much difference in
color TV. But Motorola Color TV has a big difference . . .
and _____ has a wide selection of Motorolas.
        (dealer name)
How does Motorola differ? Motorola Color TV has solid-
state components at 17 vital points for extra reliable
performance. How important is this solid-state difference to you? It means that the most critical points in
Motorola Color TV have no tubes to weaken or burn out.
Because solid-state devices are designed to keep working
without burning out. If you've been looking for the big
difference in color TV, plan on seeing the full line of
Motorolas at _____. You'll find everything
            (dealer name)
from a 14-inch color portable for only _____ . . . to
                                        (price)
a big selection of luxurious 23-inch console models in
prices ranging from _____ to _____. At _____
                    (price)   (price)   (dealer
_____ you'll find a Motorola Color TV in a style and
name)
price to please everyone.

_____

60 SECONDS

It's jam and jelly-making time again . . . and there's no better way to make perfect homemade jam and jelly than with Pen-Jel, the natural apple pectin. Pen-Jel assures you of perfect old-fashioned jam or jelly, without old-fashioned hard work, boiling, and skimming. You save up to half the cost with Pen-Jel, too, because you need less sugar and fruit. It's the quick, easy way to make delicious jams and jellies, with less work and less cost. Pen-Jel works wonders with any fruit or fruit juice -- fresh, canned, frozen, or bottled. Try Pen-Jel soon . . . with fresh berries, peaches, or whatever fruit you'd like. There are tested recipes in every box . . . for favorite berry jams, apple jelly, grape jelly . . . and even for unusual treats like mint or orange jelly and spiced tomato jam. Look for the bright yellow Pen-Jel box and get up a jam session! It's easy with Pen-Jel, the natural apple pectin.

60 SECONDS

Changing the future for someone who never had a chance before is the work of VISTA, the strong right arm of the war against poverty. It may be on an Indian reservation, in a migrant worker's camp, or the slum areas of a large city. But the work . . . the people . . . the experiences will make up a year you'll remember for the rest of your life. If you're 18 or over, if you really want to do something for your country and your less privileged fellow countrymen, see or call the VISTA representatives at

_____, _____.
    (address)   (phone)

REHABILITATION FOR THE MENTALLY
AND PHYSICALLY DISABLED CAMPAIGN

The Advertising
Council, Inc.

60 SECONDS

Maybe you have a disability. Maybe you've accepted it.
Maybe you're giving it the best years of your life. It
doesn't have to be that way. Not today. Today you can
get medical aid . . . you can be taught to take care of

yourself . . . and you can learn to do a job you like.
There's just one little catch. Before we can help you,
we have to find you. Last year we managed to find and
give hope to 200,000 people. But while we were doing
that . . . 300,000 more became disabled. And the gap gets
wider and wider every year. So if you're disabled, or
concerned about someone who is, do something about it.
And do it soon. Write: HELP, Box 1200, Washington, D.C.
H-E-L-P, Box 1200, Washington, D.C. 20013. You've got
nothing to lose but your disability.

4 | Television Commercials and Public-Service Announcements

HOUGHTON MIFFLIN COMPANY
(AMERICAN HERITAGE DICTIONARY)

Quinn & Johnson, Inc.

VIDEO	AUDIO
MCU DOWNS SEATED AT DESK WITH BOOK.	On September 15, a new college dictionary is coming out. It won't be just another dictionary. In fact, it's being hailed as the first really new college dictionary to come along this century.

HOLDS UP BOOK. CAMERA ZOOMS TO ECU.	This is it. The American Heritage Dictionary of the English Language.
AS OPENS BOOK. 2nd CAMERA PICKS UP ECU OF PAGE AS DOWNS FLIPS THROUGH.	Now here's why it's new. A bigger page with wider margins and larger type. And look at the illustrations. More than twice as many as you'll find in any other college dictionary. 4,000 in all.
CLOSES BOOK. CAMERA 1 PULLS BACK TO MCU.	In terms of scholarship, you'll find more information on word usage, exceptional coverage of the history of words, a new approach to definitions and synonyms. And lots more. If you have a son or daughter in high school or college, this is the dictionary they should have. Or if you already have a dic-

tionary, good. It's worth
a dollar when you trade it
in on this one. Just check
participating book and sta-
tionery stores for details.

DISSOLVE TO LIMBO SHOT OF
DICTIONARY.

The American Heritage Dictionary. Only $8.95 for
the thumb-indexed edition.

MASTER CHARGE

Quinn & Johnson, Inc.

60 SECONDS

<u>VIDEO</u>

<u>AUDIO</u>

CAMERA OPENS ON MEDIUM SHOT
OF BOB AND RAY.
CAMERA SIMPLY FOLLOWS THEM
AS THEY GO THROUGH THEIR
MOTIONS.
CAMERA MOVEMENTS TO BE EX-
AGGERATED TO GIVE THE IM-
PRESSION OF A 1950 LOW-
BUDGET COMMERCIAL.

RAY (Edwin C. Hill type):
Friends, Master Charge, the
biggest card around with
nearly two million card-
holders, in New England,
presents . . . "THINGS."
BOB (Van Voorhees): Things
you can buy, do, see, eat,
and smell by presenting a

Master-Charge card at any
of the thirty thousand
local retailers who honor
it.

RAY: You can charge two by
fours, four by sixes, and
four by eight panels at The
Purple Thumb Lumber Yard.

BOB: Or gloxinia, nastur-
tium, periwinkle and creep-
ing arbutus at The Green
Thumb Greenhouse.

RAY: A fun-filled evening
in The Pokey, the new dis-
cotheque built in an abandoned jailhouse. Sit in a
cell and enjoy the music
of Warden Jokes and The
Turnkeys.

BOB: Get a bleach, cut,
and set at "The Lovely Person" beauty shoppe.

RAY: Galoshes, raincoats,

and umbrellas at The Rain
King.

BOB: Not to mention . . .
cymbals, bongos and an
electric kettle drum at Per-
cussion Palace -- The Music
Shop. That's hard to beat.

RAY: And friends, if
there's a businessman
around who will not, as yet,
honor a Master-Charge card
. . . charge money at more
than 600 offices where you
can get a cash advance.

BOB: We're sure he'll
honor cash. Master Charge
. . . Let's you buy what
you want . . . when you
want it.

RAY: Do you suppose someone could charge the Light
Brigade? (LAUGHS)

BOB (LAUGHING STIFFLY):

Very funny . . .

RAY (LAUGHING . . . FAD-
ING): I tried to lighten

up this commercial a bit . . .

BOB & RAY (LAUGHTER FADES

OUT)

GENERAL FOODS   Young and Rubicam, Inc.
(JELL-O)

60 SECONDS

VIDEO	AUDIO
MOTHER NATURE SEATED IN PARLOR WITH FRUIT GATHERED IN FRONT OF HER ON TABLE.	MOTHER NATURE (TO AUDI-ENCE): Hello, I'm Mother Nature and these are my children. Beautiful, right? Rotten. You know what one of them did? Told Jell-O our family secret. About our just-picked taste.

(TO FRUIT)

Now, how many times have I |

told you, you don't repeat
what you hear in the house
to strangers.

(TO AUDIENCE)
Kids!

(TO FRUIT)
Who told Jell-O? Tell
Mother Nature. I won't
punish.

(TO AUDIENCE)
You know, just because
you're over 30 million years
old, kids today, they don't
trust you.

(TO FRUIT)
I'll give you one more
chance. Was it you darling?
You? This is the way you
treat your mother? Where
have I failed?

CROSS-FADE TO PACKAGE SHOT.   ANNCR (VO): The only way

left to make Jell-O better
was to give it the taste of
just-picked fruit.

CROSS-FADE TO TITLE:
"NOW JELL-O TASTES LIKE
JUST-PICKED FRUIT."

And we did it. Now there's
a new Jell-O gelatin that
tastes like just-picked
fruit. Even the powder's
different--darker.
We found a way, but we're
not telling.

AMERICAN HOME FOODS
(CHEF BOY-AR-DEE)

Young and Rubicam, Inc.

VIDEO

AUDIO

OPEN ON MEDIUM CU OF BOY
SITTING AT TABLE.

ANNCR (VO): Michael James
Wixted, you stand at the
crossroads of young man-
hood. Do you have the
courage to stop eating the
kind of spaghetti you eat
with a spoon?

BOY NODS.

We ask you, sir, are you

303

	ready for the real thing --
	Chef Boy-Ar-Dee's Spaghetti
	and Meatballs?
HANDS GIVE BOY A FORK.	Very well. Your fork.
GIVE BOY PLATE OF SPA-GHETTI.	And this plate of protein-packed, full-length spa-ghetti, and big, beefy meatballs.
BOY BEGINS TO EAT.	Eat, sir, and know the pure joy of mastering the twirly, whirly, full-length spaghet-ti and meatballs from Chef Boy-Ar-Dee.

PPG INDUSTRIES
(PITTSBURGH PAINTS)

Young and Rubicam, Inc.

60 SECONDS

VIDEO	AUDIO
OPENING BILLBOARD: PITTS-BURGH PAINTS PRESENTS THE BREATHING HOUSE.	Pittsburgh Paints presents the breathing house.
HOUSE BREATHING. CON-TRACTING AND EXPANDING. CONTINUE.	Your house is breathing all the time. It expands when

it's hot and humid. Con-
tracts when it's cool and
dry. Inhales and exhales.
Stretches and shrinks.
That's why ordinary oil-
base paint cracks and blis-
ters and peels. So we made
a new paint--that stretches
and breathes . . .

DISS TO CAN BREATHING.

New Pittsburgh Sunproof
Latex Housepaint. It has
much more stretchability
than ordinary housepaint.
It breathes and expands and
contracts with your house.
So it resists cracking and
blistering and peeling.
Pittsburgh Sunproof Latex
Housepaint.

DISS TO HOUSE.

Lasts years longer than
ordinary housepaint. Try
it. Give your house a
breather.

305

LOGO.   Pittsburgh Paints. A

                                   product of PPG INDUSTRIES.

_____

ARROW SHIRTS   Young and Rubicam, Inc.

                          60 SECONDS

        <u>VIDEO</u>   <u>AUDIO</u>

OPEN ON CHORUS GIRLS IN   ANNCR (VO): Some guys
DRESSING ROOM.
                                   never know how good they

                                   have it.

CUT TO EDDIE THE STAGE   Take Eddie.
MGR. ENTERING.

DISS TO VARIOUS BACKSTAGE   Day after day, a stranger
SCENES: EDDIE LIGHTING
CIGARETTES FOR GIRLS, ETC.   in paradise. And nobody
HE EXITS.
                                   notices him. It's "Eddie

                                   hand me this." And "Eddie

                                   get me that." And nobody

                                   knows he's there.

EDDIE RE-ENTERS VIA HALL-   Then one day, Eddie wears
WAY, WEARING NEW SHIRT.
                                   a new shirt. A blue and

                                   orange striped number --

                                   from Arrow.

HE KNOCKS, OPENS DOOR AND GIRLS SCREAM AS THEY NOTICE HIM. HE EXITS HURRIEDLY.	All of a sudden, _everybody_ notices Eddie.
EDDIE HESITATES, WALKS OVER TO LOCKER, AND LOOKS AT HIS OLD SHIRT. SCENE DISS TO BLACK, FADES UP ON EDDIE WALKING TO DOOR IN OLD SHIRT. HE ENTERS.	Well, that's show biz-- maybe Arrow shirts aren't for everybody after all. Especially if you have a job like Eddie's.
CUT BACK TO NEW SHIRT HANG- ING IN LOCKER.	But if you have a job like Eddie's . . . who needs Arrow?

JOS. SCHLITZ BREWING COMPANY
(BURGERMEISTER BEER)

Post-Keyes-Gardner, Inc.

20 SECONDS

VIDEO	AUDIO
OPEN ON STORE INTERIOR AS CUSTOMER WALKS UP TO COUNTER AND SPEAKS TO CLERK.	CUSTOMER: Do you have Burgie in cans? CLERK: Yes, sir. CUSTOMER: I'll take one.
CUT TO CU OF CLERK.	CLERK: Everybody buys six.
CUT TO CU OF CUSTOMER.	CUSTOMER: One, please.
CUT TO CU OF CLERK.	CLERK: You want it in a

bag?

VIDEO	AUDIO
CUT TO CU OF CUSTOMER.	CUSTOMER: Please.
CLERK OPENS CAN OF BEER, POURS IT INTO PAPER BAG.	
CLERK HANDS BAG TO CUS- TOMER.	
CUT TO CU OF CUSTOMER	CUSTOMER: Thanks.
CUSTOMER TURNS AND WALKS OUT WITH BAG.	CLERK: Enjoy yourself.
MOVE IN TO TCU OF CAN.	CLERK: Take along Burgie -- the take-along beer.

LOCAL GROCERY STORE

60 SECONDS

Note: To produce this commercial, you should first visit
a local grocery store, obtain their permission to
shoot still photos or silent film, and fill in the
missing information.

VIDEO	AUDIO
COVER SHOT OF EXTERIOR OF GROCERY STORE, SHOWING NAME OF STORE.	For grocery specials all through the week, visit _____, located (name of store) at _____, (address)

SHOT OF STORE MANAGER AT CHECK-OUT STAND	Here's _____, (name of manager) store manager. He can't stop the rising cost of liv- ing, but he has helped slow it down a bit.
CUT TO PRODUCE SECTION. SHOW ITEMS AS THEY ARE INTRODUCED.	For instance, check the price on these baking pota- toes. You'd expect to pay much more, but they are only _____ for a ten- (cost) pound sack this week at _____. How (name of store) about Florida's best juice and eating oranges? Just _____ a pound, and even (cost) less for a five-pound sack.
CUT TO DISPLAY OF CANNED ITEMS.	Chile con carne, usually 49¢ a can, now only _____ (cost) for three cans. Tomato sauce, three cans for _____. And, _____ (cost) (brand _____ instant coffee, name) only _____ for the ____- (cost) (no.)

309

CUT TO SHOT OF ENTIRE
STORE.

 SHOT OF CHECKSTAND WITH
CUSTOMERS AND CLERK.

REPEAT OF OPENING SHOT.

ounce size.

Bargains in every department,

and a money-back guarantee

if you're not satisfied.

Friendly people shop at

_____, and they
(name of store)
enjoy the relaxed, unhurried

atmosphere of the store that

wants to please. No ques-

tion about it, you'll enjoy

shopping at _____.
                (name of store)

For all your grocery needs,

visit _____, the
       (name of store)
friendly market, located at

_____.
(address)

THE HOOVER COMPANY

60 SECONDS

<u>VIDEO</u>   <u>AUDIO</u>

<u>Note</u>: This commercial was   Now, Hoover and the Emporium
originally produced with
eight slides. You may make   combine to give you a sensa-
your own slides, studio
cards, or silent film, or   tional buy on this Hoover
you may perform this as a
demonstration commercial.   704 Convertible. World re-

                                  knowned, the Hoover Deluxe

                                  Convertible upright is

                                  priced during the Emporium

                                  October home sale for less

                                  than $50. Here is the fa-

                                  mous Hoover with features

                                  like the "Dirt-Finder" head-

                                  light which illuminates a

                                  large area in front of the

                                  cleaner . . . a nonmarking

                                  furniture guard . . . and

                                  modern-styled hood that

                                  <u>really</u> gets under low fur-

                                  niture. The vinyl outer

                                  bag that encloses a large

311

throw-away bag . . . easy to change . . . your hands never touch dirt. Plus the famous triple-action cleaning . . . it beats as it sweeps as it cleans. The Hoover Convertible 704, a regular $79.95 value, is sale-priced right now for just $49.88. Hurry, supply is limited . . . first come, first served. Come to the Emporium during the annual store-wide October sale and save $30.07 on this GREAT HOOVER CONVERTIBLE. Sale ends October 14, so hurry to any Emporium store for your Hoover Convertible 704 now.

PEACE CORPS VOLUNTEER CAMPAIGN   The Advertising
                                     Council, Inc.

                        60 SECONDS

            VIDEO   AUDIO

SLIDE: "HOW MUCH CAN YOU   There are days when you love
GIVE? HOW MUCH CAN YOU
TAKE?   FIND OUT IN THE   teaching science. When you
PEACE CORPS."
                              know you're giving a great

                              class because the kids are

                              responding . . . the lesson

                              finally sinking in. Then

                              there are other days. Like

                              before Christmas vacation.

                              When you have to spend the

                              whole class trying to keep

                              them awake. Because their

                              minds are everywhere except

                              on inertia. Wouldn't it be

                              great to teach kids who are

                              wide-eyed and full of ques-

                              tions every day? Kids who

                              come to you . . . not be-

                              cause they have to . . . but

because they want to. Then
come teach in a country
like Khatmandu. In a village where poverty and disease make kids eager to get
rid of it. Where they sense
coming to you will help.
Where you'll be the best
teacher in the world . . .
because they want you to be.
Teach science in Khatmandu.
Watch Galileo come alive.
And Khatmandu along with it.
Write the Peace Corps,
Washington, D.C.

30 SECONDS

VIDEO	AUDIO

SLIDE: "HOW MUCH CAN YOU GIVE? HOW MUCH CAN YOU TAKE? FIND OUT IN THE PEACE CORPS."

You don't have to be a me-
chanic to teach people about
mechanical things in the
Peace Corps. If you just

tinker around with the car
on weekends you can do a
lot to stop hunger . . .
kill disease. Important
things . . . that you don't
need all kinds of diplomas
to do. If you know some-
thing about machines . . .
if you're a do-it-yourself-
er . . . especially if
you're a full-fledged me-
chanic, the Peace Corps
needs you. To get some
wheels going. To fix up
the world. Write the Peace
Corps. Washington, D.C.

KEEP AMERICA BEAUTIFUL CAMPAIGN

The Advertising
Council, Inc.

30 SECONDS

<u>VIDEO</u>

<u>AUDIO</u>

SLIDE: "LITTER. IT'S
ENOUGH TO MAKE YOU SICK.
ISN'T IT ENOUGH TO MAKE
YOU STOP?"

It seems like such a simple
thing to carry a litter bag
in your car and boat. Or
to drop your trash in the
nearest litter basket. And
it is simple . . . if you'd
just think. Think of litter.
It's ugly. And it makes
other things ugly. Every
year it costs <u>you</u> millions
of tax dollars to clean up.
It's a source of disease, a
haven of insects and rats.
And it causes highway and
boating accidents. In short,
litter is enough to make you
sick. But isn't it enough to
make you stop? Let's Keep
America Clean. Let's Keep
America Beautiful.

316

Wire-Service Copy for Newcasts

The Associated Press and United Press International supplied all copy in this section and generously granted permission for its verbatim reproduction. All errors have been retained exactly as they came over the wire to give you practice in detecting and correcting mistakes.

All the news items were selected to give you practice in pronunciation, interpretation, and news editing. You can get further practice from rewriting them to suit your own announcing style.

Most of the copy would be classified as "soft" news by broadcast journalists; sensational "headline" news tends to be too time-bound to retain interest for long. When you begin to assemble five-, fifteen-, and thirty-minute newscasts, you should supplement your choices from this section with current news stories.

SAN FRANCISCO (UPI)--AN EXPERT ON DRUGS SAYS THE
GOVERNMENT'S TEMPORARY SUCESS IN LIMITING THE AVAILABILITY
OF MARIJUANA IS HAVING AN ADVERSE EFFECT.

DR. JOEL FORT OF SAN FRANCISCO BELIEVES THAT THE LACK
OF MARIJUANA IS PROMPTING MANY YOUNG PEOPLE TO SWITCH TO
THE USE OF DANGEROUS DRUGS.

FORT IS A DOCTOR OF MEDICINE WHO HAS SERVED AS A
CONSULTANT ON DRUG ABUSE FOR THE WORLD HEALTH ORGANIZATION
AND THE UNITED NATIONS. HE'S A PROFESSOR AT THE
UNIVERSITY OF CALIFORNIA AT BERKELEY.

FORT SAYS ONE OF THE PRINCIPAL ARGUMENTS AGAINST THE
USE OF MARIJUANA HAS BEEN THAT IT SUPPOSEDLY CAUSES THE
USER TO GRADUATE TO "HARDER DRUGS". HE DESCRIBES THAT
ARGUMENT AS A MYTH, AND DECLARES IT'S WORKING IN REVERSE
IN CALIFORNIA. ACCORDING TO FORT, NUMBERS OF YOUNG PEOPLE
ARE USING DRUGS BECAUSE MARIJUANA IS TEMPORARILY
UNAVAILABLE.

FORT BELIEVES THE AVERAGE AMERICAN MUST CHANGE HIS
ATTITUDE DRASTICALLY TOWARDS MARIJUANA AND DRUGS BEFORE
THE CRISIS CAN BE SOLVED. HE SAYS PASSING MORE AND MORE
STRINGENT CRIMINAL LAWS HAS NOT WORKED...AND WILL NOT
WORK...TO STOP DRUG ABUSE. INSTEAD, HE BELIEVES THE

APPROACH SHOULD BE PREVENTION AND EDUCATION--AND AN
ATTEMPT TO OVERCOME ALIENATING FORCES IN SOCIETY.

LONDON (AP)--ANNE HUGESSEN IS BATTLING WITH OFFICIALS
OVER A QUESTION OF TAXATION. AUTHORITIES SAY A PRODUCT
MADE BY MISS HUGESSEN'S COMPANY MUST CARRY A SALES TAX
BECAUSE IT IS IN THE SAME CLASS AS FURNITURE AND BOOK
ENDS. BUT SHE INSISTS THE PRODUCT COMES UNDER THE
HEADING OF SAFETY EQUIPMENT AND THEREFORE IS TAX EXEMPT.

WHAT ARE THEY ARGUING ABOUT? MISS HUGESSEN'S
COMPANY IS TURNING OUT REPRODUCTIONS OF MEDIEVAL CHASTITY
BELTS.

RED BANK, N.J. (UPI)--PHYSICIST NATHANIEL B. WALES,
JR., 54, WHO DEVELOPED THE FIRST NUCLEAR ION ACCELERATOR
AND MADE THE PRODUCTION OF ISOTOPES POSSIBLE, DIED
THURSDAY AT RIVERSIDE HOSPITAL AFTER A LONG ILLNESS.

A GRADUATE OF HARVARD AND STEVENS INSTITUTE, WALES
HELD MORE THAN 75 PATENTS IN THE NUCLEAR PHYSICS,
MECHANICAL, BUSINESS MACHINE AND MILITARY FIELDS.

IN WORLD WAR II HE DEVELOPED THE SUPER-BAZOOKA AND
THE PRIMACHORD TRIPLINE, BOTH OF WHICH CONTRIBUTED TO THE
ALLIES' DEFENSE CAPABILITIES.

HE IS SURVIVED BY HIS WIDOW, THE FORMER ANNE L.
PEACOCK.

WASHINGTON (AP)--THE HEAD OF ARMY MEDICAL RESEARCH
REPORTS GOOD PROGRESS IN DEVELOPMENT OF A VACCINE TO
COMBAT MENINGITIS, A DISEASE THAT HAS BROKEN OUT AT
MILITARY CAMPS. MAJOR-GENERAL JOE BLUMBERG TOLD NEWSMEN
IN WASHINGTON THE VACCINE--STILL BEING TESTED--IS
BEGINNING TO LOOK "LIKE SOMETHING THAT'S EFFECTIVE."
OTHER MEDICAL OFFICERS ESTIMATED ANOTHER THREE YEARS OF
TESTING WILL BE NEEDED BEFORE THE VACCINE CAN BE
CONSIDERED READY.

SPOKANE, WASH. (UPI)--FIFTEEN INLAND EMPIRE RESIDENTS
FRIDAY BECAME THE FIRST CIVILIAN GRADUATES OF A TWO-YEAR
COURSE IN CARDIO-PULMONARY TECHNOLOGY.

THE GRADUATES WERE THE FIRST IN A PROGRAM INSTITUTED
IN THE FALL OF 1967 AT SPOKANE COMMUNITY COLLEGE HERE, AS
ONE OF 14 HEALTH PROJECTS ADMINISTERED BY THE WASHINGTON-
ALASKA REGIONAL MEDICAL PROGRAM.

UNTIL THE GROUP BEGAN STUDYING FOR THE MEDICAL
SPECIALTY, THE ONLY PLACES A DEGREE COULD BE OBTAINED

WERE AT THE U.S. HOSPITALS AT BETHESDA, MD., AND SAN
DIEGO, CALIF.

THE CARDIO PULMONARY TECHNICIANS DIVIDED THEIR STUDIES
EQUALLY BETWEEN THEORY AND CLINICAL EXPERIENCE. UPON
GRADUATION, THEY WERE QUALIFIED TO TAKE ELECTROCARDIOGRAMS,
ASSIST IN HEART CATHETERIZATION, OPERATE HEART-LUNG
MACHINES DURING OPEN HEART SURGERY AND MONITOR HEARTS OF
SURGERY PATIENTS.

THE FOUR MEN AND 11 WOMEN GRADUATES HAVE ALREADY
SIGNED CONTRACTS TO WORK FOR NORTHWEST HOSPITALS,
ATTESTING TO THE NEED FOR THEIR SERVICES.

LEADING THE CLASS WAS KEREN WHITMAN, 20, SPOKANE, WHO
ACCUMULATED A 3.53 GRADE POINT AVERAGE DURING THE TWO-
YEAR COURSE.

SCHOOL OFFICIALS SAID THERE WERE 12 STUDENTS
PRESENTLY COMPLETING THEIR FIRST YEAR OF THE COURSE,
WHICH IS RUN BOTH AT THE SCC CAMPUS AND IN LOCAL
HOSPITALS.

HOWEVER, THE COLLEGE HOPES TO EXPAND THE ENROLLMENT
TO 20-25 FOR NEXT FALL'S STARTING CLASS.

SAN FRANCISCO (UPI)--CRY CALIFORNIA, A PERIODICAL
PUBLISHED BY THE CONSERVATION ORGANIZATION CALIFORNIA

PROUDER.

JONES, A FORMER TEACHER NOW IN REAL ESTATE, IS THIS CITY'S FIRST MAN TO ADOPT A CHILD AS A SINGLE PARENT UNDER THE DEPARTMENT OF SOCIAL SERVICE.

THE OBJECT OF JONES' PRIDE AND JOY IS AARON HUNTER JONES, A BLUE-EYED, BUTTON-NOSED THREE YEAR OLD.

SUNDAY WILL BE JONES' FIRST FATHER'S DAY SINCE THE ADOPTION WAS FINALIZED.

"MY LIFE IS REALLY BEGINNING AT 40," JONES SAID.

BEFORE THE ADOPTION JONES WAS WORKING 12 to 14 HOURS A DAY.

"I WAS UNMARRIED, I HAD NO CHILDREN. AND I WAS ASKING MYSELF, 'WHAT AM I DOING?'"

HE RECALLS VIVIDLY THE FIRST TIME HE SAW AARON, THE DAY BEFORE HIS SECOND BIRTHDAY.

"IT WAS CRUSHING," HE SAID.

AARON BROUGHT IN FROM HIS FOSTER HOME, JUST SAT. HIS SKIN WAS TANNED VERY DARK, DIRTY IN SPOTS, AND HIS HAIR WAS CLIPPED TOO CLOSE.

"I REALLY EXPECTED SHIRLEY TEMPLE TO COME OUT SINGING," JONES SAID.

HE BROODED FOR A FEW DAYS, THINKING "ABOUT THAT SMELLY, BROWN, BALD KID. I KNEW NOBODY WOULD EVER ADOPT

323

HIM."

JONES WAS ARMED WITH A TEDDY BEAR THE NEXT TIME HE
VISITED AARON.

"HE CAME RUNNING OUT OF THE NEXT ROOM AND THREW HIS
ARMS AROUND MY LEG. THAT DID IT. I WAS HOOKED. I JUST
STOOD THERE AND CRIED. THAT WAS IT. HE WAS MY BOY."

ST. LOUIS (UPI)--FOR MONTHS, IRRITATED MOTORISTS
HAVE PLEADED FOR THE REPAIR OF AN INTERSECTION ON THE
SOUTH SIDE OF ST. LOUIS.

FINALLY, A STREET DEPARTMENT CREW APPEARED LAST WEEK
AND LAID NEW PAVING AT THE INTERSECTION.

ONLY A FEW MINUTES AFTER THEY HAD FINISHED THE JOB,
ANOTHER CREW...THIS ONE FROM THE TELEPHONE COMPANY...
ARRIVED AT THE CORNER AND UNLOADED JACKHAMMERS. THAT'S
RIGHT. THEY RIPPED UP THE NEW PAVEMENT TO LAY A PHONE
CABLE.

IN THE WORDS OF ONE MOTORIST: "WE JUST CAN'T WIN."

LOS ANGELES (UPI)--A REPUBLICAN CANDIDATE FOR STATE
ATTORNEY GENERAL TOLD A GRADUATING LAW CLASS IN LOS
ANGELES TONIGHT HE HOPED THEY WOULD DEFEND AS WELL AS
KPRACTICE LAW. SENATOR GEORGE DEUKMEJIAN OF LONG BEACH

STRONGLY ATTACKED MILITANT DISSENTERS AT THE

COMMENCEMENT EXERCISES OF THE WEST LOS ANGELES SCHOOL OF

LAW. HE SAID...QUOTE..."THOSE WHO ARE ATTEMPTING TO

EQUATE THE CURRENT WAVE OF BLATANT LAWLESSNESS WITH THE

EXPRESSION OF BASIC CONSTITUTIONAL RIGHTS...ARE DOING

NOTHING BUT TO DEFAME, DEFILE AND DISTORT THE

CONSTITUTION OF THE UNITED STATES."

WASHINGTON (AP)--A NEW STUDY SAYS THE QUALITY OF LIFE

IN THE NATION'S METROPOLITAN CENTERS WILL CONTINUE TO

DECLINE UNLESS THERE IS AN IMMEDIATE EFFORT TO IMPROVE

THEIR DESIGN AND LIVABILITY. THE STUDY IS BASED ON A

MANUSCRIPT BY JOHN HIRTEN, FORMER EXECUTIVE DIRECTOR OF

THE SAN FRANCISCO PLANNING AND URBAN RENEWAL ASSOCIATION.

IT SAYS CONSTANT DETERIORATION OF THE CITIES LEADS

DIRECTLY TO HIGHER CRIME RATES, SOARING WELFARE ROLLS AND

OTHER URBAN PROBLEMS. THE STUDY ALSO ASSERTS THAT URBAN

DECAY CAN CAUSE THE LOSS OF (B) BILLIONS OF DOLLARS IN

REAL ESTATE, TRANSPORTATION SYSTEMS AND FACILITIES OF ALL

KINDS.

WASHINGTON (UPI)--AN ORGANIZATION REPRESENTING THE
NATION'S LAND-GRANT COLLEGES AND STATE UNIVERSITIES
SATURDAY CAME TO THE DEFENSE OF TMTAIYESERVE OFFICER
TRAINING CORPS (ROTC), WHICH HAS BEEN THE TARGET OF
STUDENT DISSENT ON SEVERAL CAMPUSES.

THE NATIONAL ASSOCIATION OF STATE UNIVERSITIES AND
LAND-GRANT COLLEGES, SAYING IT WAS SPEAKING FOR 113
MAJOR SCHOOLS, ISSUED A STATEMENT SAYING THIS CAMPUS
MILITARY TRAINING WAS "MOST APPROPRIATE."

THE STATEMENT, APPROVED BY THE ASSOCIATION'S 15-
MEMBER EXECUTIVE COMMITTEE, SAID:

"SOCIETY DEPENDS ON ITS INSTITUTIONS OF HIGHER
EDUCATION TO FURNISH EDUCATED LEADERSHIP IN A WIDE
VARIETY OF ROLES AND OCCUPATIONS. THESE INCLUDE
PROFESSIONALLY TRAINED INDIVIDUALS FOR SERVICE IN
GOVERNMENT AT ALL LEVELS, LOCAL, STATE AND NATIONAL....

"THE BASIC ISSUE, AS THIS COMMITTEE SEES IT, IS
WHETHER OR NOT IT IS APPROPRIATE FOR STATE UNIVERSITIES
AND LAND-GRANT COLLEGES, WHICH HAVE TRADITIONALLY TAKEN
LEADERSHIP IN OFFERING OPPORTUNITIES FOR BOTH
PROFESSIONAL AND GENERAL EDUCATION FOR THOSE ENTERING THE
VARIOUS 'PURSUITS AND PROFESSIONS OF LIFE IN OUR COUNTRY,
TO INCLUDE AMONG THEM OPPORTUNITIES FOR THOSE WHO WISH TO

PREPARE THEMSELVES FOR SERVICE IN THE ARMED FORCES.

"WE BELIEVE IT IS MOST APPROPRIATE."

PROVISION FOR MILITARY TRAINING ON CAMPUS WAS MADE WHEN THE LAND-GRANT SCHOOLS AND STATE UNIVERSITIES WERE CHARTERED. THE ROTC SYSTEM IS THE LARGEST SINGLE SUPPLIER OF COMMISSIONED OFFICERS FOR THE SERVICES, AND THE ARMY IN PARTICULAR RELIES HEAVILY ON IT.

DEMANDS THAT ROTC BE ABOLISHED HAVE BEEN A LEADING FACTOR IN CAMPUS UNREST OVER THE PAST SCHOOL YEAR.

VALLEY FORGE, PA. (UPI)--LIONEL F. BAXTER, VICE PRESIDENT FOR RADIO DIVISION OF STORER BROADCASTING CO., DEPLORED IN A FLAG DAY ADDRESS SATURDAY THE WAVES OF VIOLENCE, REBELLION AND DISSENT WHICH FOR THE MOST PART "HAS NO CONSTRUCTIVE VALUE WHATEVER."

BAXTER TOLD A CEREMONY OF THE FREEDOMS FOUNDATION, DEDICATING A "FREEDOM WALL," THAT MOST OF THE DISSENT "IS ACTUALLY DESTRUCTIVE BF THE VALUES WHICH MADE OUR NATION POSSIBLE."

"TOO MANY OF US HAVE FORGOTTEN THE ADMONITION OF DANIEL WEBSTER THAT 'GOD GRANTS LIBERTY ONLY TO THOSE WHO LOVE IT, AND

RE ALWAYS

READY TO GUARD AND DEFEND IT.'

"ANY CITIZEN WHO IS NOT WILLING TODAY TO SACRIFICE
FOR HIS COUNTRY DOES NOT DESERVE HIS CITIZENSHIP,"
BAXTER SAID. "HE IS A PARASITE RESTING ON THE SHOULDERS
OF OUR HEROIC FOREBEARS AND EATING AWAY AT THE VITAL
FABRIC ON WHICH OUR FUTURE DEPENDS."

THE CEREMONY DEDICATED THE INITIAL PILLAR OF A
"FREEDOM WALL" IN TRIBUTE TO FORMER PRESIDENT DWIGHT D.
EISENHOWER, WHO SERVED JS THE FREEDOM FOUNDATION'S
CHAIRMAN AND HONORARY CHAIRMAN FROM 1949 TO 1969.

A PILLAR NEXT TO EISENHOWER'S WAS DEDICATED IN MEMORY
OF BAXTER'S BROTHER, 1ST LT. HERMAN M. BAXTER, BAY SXT.
LOUIS, MISS., KILLED IN EUROPE IN WORLD WAR II.

JACKSON, MISS. (UPI)--CIVIL RIGHTS LEADER CHARLES
EVERS SAID SUNDAY NEGROES HAD USED BALLOTS AND DOLLARS
INSTEAD OF GUNS AND BULLETS TO MAKE SIGNIFICANT GAINS
SINCE THE ASSASSINATION OF HIS BROTHER SIX YEARS AGO.

EVERS, MISSISSIPPI'S ONLY NEGRO MAYOR, SPOKE AT
MEMORIAL SERVICES FOR HIS BROTHER, MEDGAR, SHOT TO DEATH
JUNE 12, 1963 IN FRONT OF HIS HOME HERE DURING A VOTER
REGISTRATION CAMPAIGN.

EVERS SUCCEEDED HIS SLAIN BROTHER AS FIELD DIRECTOR

OF THE MISSISSIPPI CHAPTER OF THE NATIONAL ASSOCIATION FOR THE ADVANCEMENT OF COLORED PEOPLE AND ONLY RECENTLY WON ELECTION AS MAYOR OF FAYETTE, MISS.

A GROUP OF ABOUT 150 PERSONS MARCHED A MILE FROM A NEGRO HIGH SCHOOL TO A SMALL CHURCH TO HIGHLIGHT THE MEMORIAL. THEN, IN THE CHURCH WHERE THEY WERE JOINED BY ABOUT 150 MORE, THEY HEARD EVERS RECALL THE BOYHOOD DAYS AND DREAMS HE HAD SHARED WITH HIS YOUNGER BROTHER.

EVERS SAID MANY OF HIS DREAMS HAD BECOME A REALITY, INCLUDING THE ELECTION OF 81 NEGROES TO STATE, COUNTY AND MUNICIPAL OFFICES, DESEGREGATION OF SCHOOLS AND PUBLIC FACILITIES AND EMPLOYMENT OF NEGROES AS POLICEMEN IN MANY MISSISSIPPI TOWNS.

"WHITE RACISTS CAN NEVER SAY THEY'RE GOING TO KILL ONE NEGRO AND STOP THE MOVEMENT," EVERS SAID. "ONE THEY HATED WORST HAS NOW BECOME THE MAYOR OF A LITTLE TOWN."

WASHINGTON (UPI)--TOBACCO MANUFACTURERS GOT THEIR WAY IN THE HOUSE OF REPRESENTATIVES TODAY...THE HOUSE VOTED TO FORBID ANY FEDERAL AGENCY TO REQUIRE A HEALTH WARNING IN CIGARETTE ADVERTISING.

THE BAN WILL LAST FOR THE NEXT SIX YEARS. THE BILL ALSO INCLUDES A SLIGHTLY STRONGER HEALTH WARNING ON

CIGARETTE PACKAGES. THE NEW WARNING WILL READ "THE

SURGEON GENERAL HAS DETERMINED THAT CIGARETTE SMOKING IS

DANGEROUS TO YOUR HEALTH AND MAY CAUSE LUNG CANCER OR

OTHER DISEASES."

THE BILL FACES AN UNCERTAIN FUTURE IN THE SENATE,

WHERE IT IS POSSIBLE IT WILL BE REVERSED.

JACKSONVILLE, FLA. (UPI)--SHERIFF DALE CARSON ANNOUNCED

FRIDAY HE WAS STARTING A "POLICE YOUTH PATROL" TO

DEMONSTRATE TO ANTI-ESTABLISHMENT YOUNGSTERS THAT OFFICERS

SPEND MORE TIME HELPING PEOPLE THAN MAKING ARRESTS.

BEGINNING NEXT WEEK, YOUNGSTERS WILL BE ASSIGNED TO

RIDE WITH OFFICERS ON PATROL FOR PERIODS OF FOUR HOURS

EACH ON THE MIDNIGHT SHIFT.

"ONE OF THE MAJOR PROBLEMS WE FACE TODAY IN LAW

ENFORCEMENT," CARSON SAID, "IS THAT OF WORKING WITH OUR

YOUNG PEOPLE.

"THEIR QUESTIONING OF THE SO-CALLED 'ESTABLISHMENT'

HAS PUT US SQUARELY IN THE MIDDLE OF STUDENT DISORDERS,

PROTEST MARCHES AND SOCIAL UPHEAVAL."

CARSON SAID THE PROGRAM WAS DEVELOPED WITH THE IDEA

THAT IF YOUNG PEOPLE COULD SEE THAT POLICEMEN SPEND 90

PER CENT OF THEIR TIME HELPING PEOPLE AND LESS THAN 10

PER CENT ARRESTING PEOPLE "THEY WOULD HAVE A CLEARER
UNDERSTANDING OF OUR POSITION IN SOCIETY."

THE PROGRAM IS THE FIRST MAJOR EFFORT OF THE NEWLY-
FORMED POLICE COMMUNITY RELATIONS TEAM HEADED BY LT. JOHN
GOODE.

ANYONE BETWEEN THE AGES OF 16 AND 21 CAN APPLY.
THERE WILL BE NO RESTRICTIONS BECAUSE OF RACE, CREED OR
BACKGROUND--ESPECIALLY BACKGROUND.

NEW YORK (AP)--HERE'S NEWS FROM THE WORLD OF SCIENCE
AND HEALTH:

A STUDY JUST OUT SHOWS THAT MEN WHO MOVE THEIR LEGS
AND MUSCLES DOUBLE THEIR ODDS OF ESCAPING HEART ATTACKS
-- COMPARED WITH SITTERS.

AND -- IF HEART ATTACKS DO COME -- THE SITTERS ARE
FOUR TIMES MORE LIKELY TO DIE THAN MEN WHO ARE
PHYSICALLY ACTIVE.

THE STUDY ALSO SHOWS:

FOR WOMEN AS WELL AS MEN, THE RISK OF HAVING AN
INITIAL HEART ATTACK IS TWICE AS GREAT IF THEY SMOKE
CIGARETTES AS COMPARED WITH NON-SMOKERS.

THE ODDS OF HAVING A HEART ATTACK RISE AMONG
PERSONS WHO GAIN WEIGHT IN ADULT LIFE.

MEN WHOSE BODY WEIGHT WAS 15 PER CENT OR MORE ABOVE
AVERAGE HAD ABOUT A 50 PER CENT GREATER RISK OF A FIRST
ATTACK THAN MEN WITH A RELATIVE WEIGHT JUST UNDER
AVERAGE.

FOR WOMEN, WEIGHT GAINS ALSO INCREASED THE RISK OF
HEART ATTACKS AND OF DEVELOPING ANGINA PECTORIS, THE
PAINS COMING FROM A HEART BEING STARVED FOR OXYGEN
BECAUSE OF CLOGGED HEART ARTERIES.

THE FINDINGS WERE FROM A NINE-YEAR CONTINUING STUDY
AMONG 110,000 ADULTS, AGE 35 TO 64.

THE RESULTS WERE REPORTED IN THE JUNE ISSUE OF THE
AMERICAN JOURNAL OF PUBLIC HEALTH.

HANOVER, N.H. (UPI)--DARTMOUTH COLLEGE CELEBRATED ITS
200TH BIRTHDAY SATURDAY WITH FIREWORKS, SPEECHES AND A
PARADE LED BY GERALD HUMPHREY LEGGE, THE NINTH EARL OF
DARTMOUTH, WHO CAME FROM ENGLAND FOR THE OCCASION.

LEGGE GAVE THE COLLEGE A TWO-FOOT HIGH SILVER CUP
BEARING THE COLLEGE CREST AND DARTMOUTH PRESIDENT JOHN
SLOAN DICKEY GAVE LEGGE A GOLD MEDAL, ONE OF TWO STRUCK
BY THE U.S. MINT TO MARK THE OCCASION.

DARTMOUTH WAS CHARTERED UNDER KING GEORGE III AND
NAMED AFTER THE SECOND EARL OF DARTMOUTH.

THE DAY ALSO MARKED THE 150TH ANNIVERSARY OF THE

"DARTMOUTH COLLEGE CASE," IN WHICH THE SUPREME COURT

UPHELD THE ORIGINAL CHARTER AND DISMISSED LEGISLATIVE

ATTEMPTS TO OVERRIDE IT AND APPOINT NEW TRUSTEES.

IN ARGUING THE CASE BEFORE THE HIGH COURT, DANIEL

WEBSTER, SAID:

"IT'S A SMALL COLLEGE SIR, BUT THERE ARE THOSE WHO

LOVE IT."

NEARLY 1,000 STUDENTS WILL RECEIVE DEGREES AT THE

COMMENCEMENT EXERCISES SUNDAY.

AP 29

-FORECAST SUMMARY- (330)

VIOLENT THUNDERSTORMS ARE LASHING A LARGE PORTION OF

THE NATION'S MID-SECTION.

THE HEAVIEST ACTIVITY HAS OCCURRED ALONG AND AHEAD OF

A COLD FRONT FROM THE SOUTHERN MID-WEST TO OKLAHOMA, WITH

NUMEROUS REPORTS OF TORNADOES, FUNNEL CLOUDS, HAIL, HEAVY

RAINS AND STRONG WINDS.

TWO PERSONS WERE KILLED AND MANY INJURED SUNDAY

EVENING AS A TWISTER HIT THE TOWN OF OLD MINES IN EAST

CENTRAL MISSOURI, ABOUT 50 MILES SOUTHWEST OF ST. LOUIS.

AND THE NEARBY TOWN OF DOE RUN REPORTED THREE FATALITIES,

333

APPRECIABLE DAMAGE AND SOME INJURIES.

AREAS HARD HIT BY THE SEVERE THUNDERSTORMS INCLUDE ILLINOIS COUNTIES EAST OF ST. LOUIS AND THE SOUTHEAST INDIANA COUNTIES NORTH OF LOUISVILLE WHERE TREES AND POWER LINES WERE DOWNED.

A TORNADO ALSO WAS REPORTED NEAR HARTFORD, ARKANSAS. HARTFORD IS IN WEST CENTRAL ARKANSAS, ABOUT 25 MILES SOUTH OF FORT SMITH.

GOLF BALL SIZE HAIL BATTERED PORTIONS OF CENTRAL AND NORTHERN OKLAHOMA BETWEEN OKLAHOMA CITY AND TULSA, AND SOME FUNNEL CLOUDS WERE SIGHTED.

A CLOUDBURST VIRTUALLY INUNDATED PORTIONS OF IROQUOIS COUNTY IN EAST CENTRAL ILLINOIS ABOUT 75 MILES SOUTH OF CHICAGO YESTERDAY EVENING. UP TO THREE INCHES OF RAIN REPORTEDLY FELL IN ONLY 15 MINUTES, MAKING ALL HIGHWAYS IN THE AREA NEARLY IMPASSIBLE.

A SEVERE THUNDERSTORM WATCH REMAINS IN EFFECT UNTIL SIX A.M. (EDT) FOR PORTIONS OF EAST CENTRAL OKLAHOMA AND NORTHWEST ARKANSAS.

ELSEWHERE AROUND THE NATION MORE TRANQUIL WEATHER PREVAILS, WITH PRECIPITATION LIMITED MAINLY TO SOME LIGHT SHOWER ACTIVITY IN THE NORTHERN ROCKIES AND THE PACIFIC NORTHWEST.

TEMPERATURES CONTINUE QUITE WARM EARLY THIS MORNING ACROSS THE SOUTHERN SECTIONS OF THE NATION WHILE CONTRASTING COOLNESS IS THE RULE IN THE NORTH.

READINGS AROUND THE NATION EARLY TODAY RANGED FROM 46 AT HANCOCK, MICHIGAN TO 89 AT NEEDLES, CALIFORNIA.

THE NATIONAL WEATHER OUTLOOK FOR TODAY: SHOWER AND THUNDERSHOWER ACTIVITY WILL OCCUR ACROSS MOST OF THE EASTERN HALF OF THE NATION AS WELL AS FROM THE NORTHERN PLANS AND THE NORTHERN AND CENTRAL ROCKIES TTO THE NORTHWEST. SUNNY AND DRY WEATHER WILL BE CONFINED MAINLY TO THE PLAINS, THE SOUTHWEST AND THE WESTERN MID-WEST. WARM WEATHER WILL BE THE RULE, WITH HOT CONDITIONS ACROSS MOST OF THE SOUTHERN STATES.

NATIONAL WEATHER SUMMARY

ESSA...WEATHER BUREAU

SATURDAY JUNE 14TH 1969

TIME...252PM CDT

A LARGE MOUND OF POLAR AIR DOMINATES MOST OF THE MIDDLE PART OF THE NATION.

THIS UNSEASONABLY COOL HIGH NOW COVERS THE AREA FROM THE GREAT LAKES AND OHIO VALLEY THROUGH THE ROCKY MOUNTAIN REGION. TEMPERATURES IN THIS AREA ARE 10 TO 20

DEGREES BELOW NORMAL AND AS MUCH AS 30 DEGREES BELOW
NORMAL IN PORTIONS OF THE CENTRAL PLAINS.

MEANWHILE...CONTRASTING WARM AND HUMID TROPICAL AIR
IS STILL HOLDING FORTH OVER THE ATLANTIC AND GULX STATES.

THE WEATHER IS RATHER CLOUDY AND SHOWERY FROM THE
EAST PORTIONS OF THE SOUTH AND CENTRAL PLAINS TO THE
GREAT LAKES AND THE ATLANTIC.

MORE THAN AN INCH OF RAIN FELL AT WINDSOR KANSAS/1.85/
...CLIFTON CITY KANSAS/1.48/...MINERAL WELLS TEXAS/1.27/
...LEXINGTON KENTUCKY/1.25/ AND JOPLIN MISSOURI/1.23/ IN
THE LAST SIX HOURS. AND NEARLY AN INCH WAS REPORTED AT
CHANUTE KANSAS/.98/AND FORT WAYNE INDIANA/.86/ IN THE
SAME SIX HOUR PERIOD.

ONE INCH HAIL WAS REPORTED NORTHEAST OF LEXINGTON
KENTUCKY DURING A HEAVY THUNDERSTORM LATE THIS MORNING.

A WEAK TROPICAL DEPRESSION IS LOCATED JUST NORTH OF
THE YUCATAN PENINSULA AND IS DRIFTING SLOWLY
NORTHEASTWARD. THERE IS CONSIDERABLE SHOWER ACTIVITY
NORTHEAST OF THE DEPRESSION THROUGH THE FLORIDA STRAITS
AND THE BAHAMAS.

TWO INCHES OF RAIN FELL AT KEY WEST FLORIDA IN A HALF
AN HOUR PERIOD DURING THE FORENOON AND THEY HAD A TOTAL
OF 2.71 INCHES IN THE LAST SIX HOURS.

THE WEATHER IS MOSTLY SUNNY FROM THE ROCKIES WESTWARD EXCEPT FOR LOW CLOUDINESS ALONG THE IMMEDIATE PACIFIC COAST.

TEMPERATURES AT 2PM CDT RANGED FROM 42 AT COLORADO SPRINGS COLORADO TO 96 AT NEEDLES CALIFORNIA.

CHICO (UPI)--AGRICULTURAL OFFICIALS ARE MAPPING PLANS TO DEAL WITH A WASP-LIKE MITE WHICH HAS ATTACKED THE PISTACHIO CROP IN BUTTE COUNTY.

THE PISTACHIO SEED CHALCID WAS FOUND EARLIER THIS MONTH AT SEVERAL LOCATIONS AROUND CHICO.

COUNTY AGRICULTURAL COMMISSIONER DON BLACK SAYS IF THE PEST IS ALLOWED TO SPREAD, IT COULD DESTROY CALIFORNIA'S 50-THOUSAND DOLLAR PISTACHIO CROP. MOST OF IT IS GROWN IN TULARE COUNTY.

BLACK SAYS IT HAS BEEN DECIDED TO EXPAND THE TRAPPING PROGRAM TO OTHER AREAS OF BUTTE COUNTY AND THE STATE TO DETERMINE THE EXTENT OF THE INFESTATION. THE PEST IS ABOUT TWICE THE SIZE OF A PINHEAD.

BLACK SAYS THERE IS NO ADEQUATE SAFE, COMMERCIAL CONTROL FOR THE CHALCID AT THE MOMENT.

337

ST. LOUIS (UPI)--PLANNED UNDERGROUND NUCLEAR TESTS COULD CAUSE TIDAL WAVES THAT MIGHT DEVASTATE THE COASTS OF CALIFORNIA, HAWAII, AND JAPAN, THE COMMITTEE FOR ENVIRONMENTAL INFORMATION SAID SUNDAY.

THE PROPOSED TESTS ARE SCHEDULED FOR KAMCHITKA ISLAND, ALASKA, IN OCTOBER. THE COMMITTEE URGED THAT THE TESTS BE POSTPONED BECAUSE OF THE DANGER OF EARTHQUAKES WHICH IN TURN WOULD TRIGGER THE TIDAL WAVES. THEY ALSO CITED POSSIBLE READIATION FROM THE TESTS.

A REPORT RELEASED BY THE COMMITTEE SAID THAT "ANY EARTHQUAKE TRIGGERED ON OR NEAR THE ISLAND WOULD BE ALMOST CERTAIN TO RESULT IN MOVEMENT OF THE SEA FLOOR, AND THEREFORE, POSSIBLY, IN A TSUNAMI (TIDAL WAVE)."

"IF IN THIS EARTHQUAKE REGION," THE REPORT CONTINUED, "A TEST WERE TO PRECIPITATE A QUAKE NO LARGER IN MAGNITUDE THAN THE TEST ITSELF BUT RESULTING IN FAULT MOVEMENT OVER MANY MILES, THE RESULT MIGHT BE A TSUNAMI WHICH DID DAMAGE THOUSANDS OF MILES AWAY."

SCIENCE TODAY

BY WILLIAM H. GORISHEK

GUYAQUIL, ECUADOR (UPI)--A U.S. AIR FORCE OPERATION IN ECUADOR NICKNAMED "COMBAT MOSQUITO" IS HELPING BREAK

THE CYCLE OF NATURE RESPONSIBLE FOR THE WORST EPIDEMIC
OF ENCEPHALITIS HERE IN SEVERAL YEARS.

TWO AIR FORCE UC-123 PROVIDER AIRCRAFT FROM LANGLEY
AFB, VA., ARE BEING USED TO SPRAY A QUARTER-MILLION
ACRES OF THE MOST POPULATED COASTAL AREAS OF THE COUNTRY.
THEY ARE TRYING TO KILL ENCEPHALITIS CARRYING MOSQUITOES
WHICH HAVE CAUSED OVER 500 DEATHS SINCE THE FIRST OF THE
YEAR.

MANY OF THOSE STRICKEN BY THE BRAIN-DAMAGING DISEASE
ARE CHILDREN UNDER FIVE-YEARS-OLD. MOST OF THE
FATALITIES HAVE BEEN FROM THIS AGE GROUP.

ECUADORIAN GOVERNMENT HEALTH OFFICIALS SAY THAT
ANOTHER 50,000 PEOPLE AND COUNTLESS HORSES, MULES AND
BURROS HAVE CONTRACTED THE DISEASE.

MORE THAN 25 TONS OF MALATHION INSECTICIDE HAS BEEN
AIRLIFTED TO ECUADOR. THE INSECTICIDE WAS DONATED BY
THE STATE DEPARTMENT UNDER ITS AGENCY FOR INTERNATIONAL
DEVELOPMENT (AID) PROGRAM.

TWO ENTOMOLOGISTS FROM THE U.S. PUBLIC HEALTH SERVICE'S
COMMUNICABLE DISEASE CENTER SAID THE TWO PRIMARY FACTORS
RESPONSIBLE FOR SUCH EPIDEMICS ARE PRESENT IN ABUNDANCE
IN ECUADOR -- MANY ECUADORIAN ANIMALS ARE INFECTED BY
VENEZUELAN EQUINE ENCEPHALITIS VIRUS, AND CONDITIONS ARE

SUITABLE FOR ENCEPHALITIS CARRYING MOSQUITOES TO BREED.

THE VIRUS REMAINS IN THE BLOOD STREAMS FOR INFECTED
ANIMALS AND IS AVAILABLE TO MOSQUITOES FOR ONLY A FEW
DAYS. IT IS THEN ABSORBED INTO THE ANIMALS' INTERNAL
ORGANS. THEREFORE, THE DISEASE CAN BE HALTED IF THE
MOSQUITO POPULATION IS SUFFICIENTLY REDUCED DURING THE
PERIOD THE VIRUS IS BEING ABSORBED.

EXPERTS ESTIMATE THEY HAVE KILLED 95 PER CENT OF THE
MOSQUITOES IN THE GUAYAQUIL AREA AND THEY EXPECT SIMILAR
RESULTS IN THE OUTLYING AREAS NOW BEING SPRAYED.

ECUADORIAN GOVERNMENT OFFICIALS HAD PREVIOUSLY TRIED
TO CONDUCT A MOSQUITO SPRAYING PROGRAM BUT WERE UNABLE TO
SUSTAIN IT EFFECTIVELY BECAUSE THEY LACKED SPRAY AIRCRAFT
WITH ENOUGH INSECTICIDE CARRYING CAPACITY.

WASHINGTON (UPI)--DECLARING THAT COMBINATION DRUGS
OFFER A "SHOTGUN" APPROACH TO CURING DISEASE WHEN WHAT IS
NEEDED IS A "RIFLE," THE FOOD AND DRUG ADMINISTRATION (FDA)
HAS ORDERED 49 OF THE DRUGS OFF THE MARKET.

AT THE SAME TIME, THE FDA REPEALED REGULATIONS FOR
CERTIFYING COMBINATIONS OF PENICILLIN AND STREPTOMYCIN
AND PENICILLIN AND SULFA FOR HUMAN USE.

COMMISSIONER HERBERT L. LEY, JR., SAID THURSDAY THAT

48 OF THE BANNED DRUGS ARE COMBINATIONS OF PENICILLIN-
STREPTOMYCIN AND PENICILLIN-SULFA. THE OTHER ORDER
APPLIED TO THE COMBINATION DRUG, MYSTECLIN F, WHICH
CONTAINS TETRACYCLINE PLUS THE FUNGICIDE, AMPHOTERICIN B.

"THE PENICILLIN-SULFA AND THE PENICILLIN-STREPTOMYCIN
COMBINATIONS DO NOT OFFER ANY THERAPEUTIC BENEFIT THAT
CANNOT BE ACHIEVED BY USING THESE DRUGS SINGLY," SAID
LEY.

THE ORDERS ON THE 49 DRUGS WILL BECOME EFFECTIVE IN
40 DAYS. OPPONENTS OF THE ORDER HAVE 30 DAYS TO FILE
OBJECTIONS AND REQUEST A PUBLIC HEARING.

FDA HAD ANNOUNCED ITS INTENTIONS APRIL 2 TO TAKE
ACTION ON THE PENICILLIN COMBINATIONS BASED ON THE
FINDING OF A NATIONAL AACADEMY OF SCIENCE-NATIONAL
RESEARCH COUNCIL STUDY OF MORE THAN 3,000 DRUGS.

LAST DEC. 24, FDA ANNOUNCED THE NAS-NRC FINDING THAT
THE FOUR FORMS OF MYSTECLIN F WERE INEFFECTIVE FOR
PREVENTING DISEASE DUE TO AN OVERGROWTH OF FUNGUS.

(WITH BORADCAST ROW---FARM)

CHICAGO (UPI)---A PANEL OF FARM BROADCASTERS AGREED
GENERALLY TODAY THEIR PROFESSION IS CHANGING...BUT THEY
TOLD A MEETING OF THE NATIONAL ASSOCIATION OF FARM

341

BROADCASTERS (NAFB) THE FUTURE IS BRIGHT.

"THERE IS NO DOUBT THAT BROADCAST MEDIA WILL BECOME MORE IMPORTANT IN THE AGRI-BUSINESS FIELD," SAID ARNOLD W. PETERSON, FARM DIRECTOR OF WOW RADIO AND T-V, OMAHA, NEBRASKA.

PETERSON WAS ONE OF A DOZEN FARM SPECIALISTS FROM LARGE AND SMALL RADIO AND T-V STATIONS DISCUSSING PROSPECTS FOR FARM BROADCASTING IN THE 1970'S AT THE NAFB CONVENTION IN CHICAGO TODAY. MORE THAN 250 BROADCASTERS AND ASSOCIATES ARE ATTENDING THE MEETING.

DEWEY P. COMPTON, OF KTRH, KTRK-TV AND KRLD, HOUSTON, TEXAS, TOLD THE MEETING THAT FARM TELEVISION IN METROPOLITAN AREAS CAN BE USEFUL IN THE NEXT DECADE BY GIVING INCREASING EMPHASIS TO HOME AND CONSUMER SERVICE AND BY TELLING "THE FARMERS' STORY" TO CONSUMERS.

DEREK ROOKE OF WMC, MEMPHIS, TENNESSEE, RECOMMENDED THAT IN FARM RADIO SERVICE BROADCASTERS SHOULD STUDY THE PRACTICE, ALREADY USED IN SOME AREAS, OF CREATING SPECIALIZED FARM PROGRAM NETWORKS.

LONDON (AP)--THE LONDON ZOO HAS A NEW GNU. SPELLED G-N-U, THE ANIMAL IS AN ANTELOPE THAT COMES FROM EAST AFRICA. IT IS THE FIRST TO BE BORN IN THE ZOO SINCE 1966.

UP TO SEVEN MILLION AMERICANS HAVE USED MARIJUANA

BY CRAIG PALMER

WASHINGTON (UPI)--DRUG ABUSE IN THE UNITED STATES, PARTICULARLY THAT INVOLVING MARIJUANA, HAS REACHED EPIDEMIC PROPORTIONS, ACCORDING TO THE DEPARTMENT OF HEALTH, EDUCATION AND WELFARE.

IN A JUNE NEWSLETTER, THE DEPARTMENT ESTIMATED THAT FIVE MILLION TO SEVEN MILLION PERSONS IN THE UNITED STATES HAVE USED MARIJUANA AT LEAST ONCE. BUT IT ALSO REVEALED T

IN A JUNE NEWSLETTER, THE DEPARTMENT ESTIMATED THAT FIVE MILLION TO SEVEN MILLION PERSONS IN THE UNITED STATES HAVE USED MARIJUANA AT LEAST ONCE. BUT IT ALSO REVEALED USE OF LSD, SO-CALLED "ACID," HAS DECLINED IN THE PAST TWO YEARS.

HEW LISTS THESE OTHERS DRUG-USE STAT SESHDSPV: ONE MILLION PERSONS

HEW LISTS THESE OTHER DRUG-USE STATISTICS: ONE MILLION PERSONS HAVE USED NON BARTIBURATE SEDATIVES, INCLUDING LSD: 400,000 HAVE USED BARTITURATES AND AMPHE

HEW LISTS THESE OTHER DRUG-USE STATISTICS: ONE MILLION

PERSONS HAVE USED NON BARBITURATE SEDATIVES, INCLUDING

LSD: 400,000 HAVE USED BARBITURATES AND AMPHETAMINES AND

100,000 ARE KNOWN NARCOTICS ADDICTS.

"THE TOTAL SOCIAL COST IS $541 MILLION A YEAR," HEW

SAID.

SOME OF THE INFORMATION CAME APRIL 22 IN

CONGRESSIONAL TESTIMONY BY DR. STANLEY F. YOLLES,

DIRECTOR OF THE NATIONAL INSTITUTE OF MENTAL HEALTH.

"MARIJUANA USE HAS BEEN RAPIDLY INCREASING IN THE

PAST FIVE YEARS," YOLLES SAID. "ALTHOUGH ORIGINALLY

RESTRICTED TO CERTAIN JAZZ MUSICIANS, ARTISTS AND GHETTO

DWELLERS, IT HAS NOW APPEARED AMONG THE MIDDLE AND UPPER

CLASS."

A NIMH INFORMATION SHEET ON MARIJUANA SAYS IT IS NOT

NARCOTIC. IT DOES NOT CAUSE PHYSICAL DEPENDENCY AS DO

HEROIN AND OTHER NARCOTICS, THE PUBLICATION SAYS.

"A NUMBER OF SCIENTISTS THINK THE DRUG CAN CAUSE

PHYCHOLOGICAL DEPENDENCY, HOWEVER, IF ITS USERS TAKE IT

REGULARLY," IT SAID.

YOLLES DID NOT USE THE TERM EPIDEMIC IN HIS TESTIMONY.

BUT A MAY 15 MEMORANDUM FROM NIMH OFFICE OF COMMUNICATIONS

DIRECTOR GERALD N. KURTZ TO THE EDITORS OF THE HEW

NEWSLETTER QUOTED YOLLES AS SAYING DRUG ABUSE HAS REACHED

EPIDEMIC PROPORTIONS.

IN HIS TESTIMONY, YOLLES SAID," ...DRUG ABUSE AND
NARCOTIC ADDICTION ARE MAJOR AND GROWING PUBLIC HEALTH
PROBLEMS OF MAJOR NATIONAL CONCERN."

HE ALSO SAID THE USE OF LSD HAS DECLINED DURING THE
LAST TWO YEARS.

"IN PART IT MAY BE DUE TO THE INFORMATION
DISSEMINATED ABOUT ITS DANGER AND THE FACT THAT IT DOES
NOT PROVIDE INSTANT INSIGHT OR MAGICAL SOLUTIONS TO ONE'S
PROBLEM," HE SAID.

"IT REMAINS A DRUG OF ABUSE ESSENTIALLY FOR YOUNG
MIDDLE-CLASS PERSONS," HE SAID.

NIMH HAS LAUNCHED AN INTENSIVE PUBLIC INFORMATION
CAMPAIGN WITH RADIO, TELEVISION AND NEWSPAPER
ANNOUNCEMENTS "AS A FIRST LINE OF DEFENSE AGAINST
CONTINUED DRUG ABUSE."

BOSTON (UPI)--AQUA-CHEM, INC., THURSDAY CONVERTED
DIRTY BOSTON HARBOR SEA WATER INTO BACTERIA-FREE FRESH
WATER BY ITS RESERVE OSMOSIS PROCESS IN A DEMONSTRATION
FOR A TECHNOLOGY SEMINAR OF INSTITUTIONAL INVESTORS
SPONSORED BY COLLINS SECURITIES CO. OF DENVER. THE
REVERSE OSMOSIS SYSTEM OF DE-SALTING REQUIRES NO HEAT

ENERGY. THECOMPANY IS PRESENTING AN 80,000 GALLONS A
DAY UNIT USING THE PROCESS FOR THE NAVY.

THE NEWS OF THE WEEK IN AGRICULTURE

BY BERNARD BRENNER, UPI FARM EDITOR IN WASHINGTON

THE AGRICULTURE DEPARTMENT'S MONTHLY CROP REPORT
SHOWS WINTER WHEAT PRODUCTION UP FROM LAST MONTH...AND
FARM SOURCES PREDICT THE U-S-D-A WILL CUT THE 1970 WHEAT
ACREAGE ALLOTMENT.

AND...A FORMER JOHNSON ADMINISTRATION FARM OFFICIAL
RECOMMENDS REDUCING GOVERNMENT SUPPORT PAYMENTS TO WHEAT
AND COTTON GROWERS.

NOW, A LOOK AT THE HIGHLIGHTS OF THESE AND OTHER TOP
STORIES OF THE PAST WEEK ON THE NATIONAL FARM SCENE.

THE U-S-D-A'S JUNE CROP REPORT ESTIMATED THE WINTER
WHEAT CROP AT ONE BILLION, 161 MILLION BUSHELS...DOWN
FIVE PER CENT FROM LAST YEAR, BUT NOT DOWN FAR ENOUGH TO
HEAD OFF THE PROBABILITY OF SOME FURTHER INCREASE IN THE
NATIONAL WHEAT SURPLUS. AS A RESULT, FARM EXPERTS IN
WASHINGTON ARE PREDICTING THE 1970 WHEAT ACREAGE ALLOTMENT
WILL BE REDUCED. THE QUESTION OF HOW FAR IT WILL BE CUT
IS REPORTED UNDER CLOSE STUDY AT THE U-S-D-A.

FARM POLICY EXPERTS IN THE CAPITAL THIS WEEK WERE

346

ALSO LOOKING OVER A RECENT STATEMENT BY JOHN A. SCHNITTKER, UNDERSECRETARY OF AGRICULTURE DURING THE JOHNSON ADMINISTRATION.

SCHNITTKER SAID THE MONEY SPENT ON SUPPORT PAYMENTS FOR COTTON AND WHEAT COULD BE CUT IN HALF WITHOUT DAMAGING THE FARM ECONOMY.

ALSO ON THE NATIONAL FARM SCENE THIS WEEK...THE NATIONAL GRANGE AND THE AMERICAN FARM BUREAU FEDERATION HAVE URGED THE SENATE TO KILL A HOUSE-APPROVED CEILING ON GOVERNMENT FARM PAYMENTS..THE U-S-D-A PREDICTS THAT EGG PRICES WILL RISE THIS SUMMER, MOVING UP CLOSE TO LAST SUMMER'S LEVELS...AND AN AGRICULTURE DEPARTMENT REPORT SHOWS THAT MILK PRODUCTION FOR THE FIRST FIVE MONTHS OF 1969 HAS BEEN ABOUT ONE-AND-A-HALF PER CENT BELOW LAST YEAR'S OUTPUT...A DECLINE WHICH COMES IN FACE OF THE FACT THAT MILK PRICES HAVE BEEN HIGHER THAN THEY WERE A YEAR AGO.

FARM POLICY SPECIALISTS, MEANWHILE, WERE TAKING A CLOSE LOOK THIS PAST WEEK AT A NEW REPORT RECOMMENDING A SO-CALLED "EASEMENT" PROGRAM FOR CONTROLLING FARM SURPLUSES. UNDER THIS PROGRAM, THE GOVERNMENT WOULD BUY UP CROP-PRODUCING RIGHTS ON MARGINAL FARMS FOR PERIODS OF 20 YEARS. THE PLAN WOULD BE AIMED AT TAKING ABOUT 73

MILLION ACRES OUT OF CROP PRODUCTION, WITH HALF OF THE

ACREAGE TO BE USED FOR INCREASING PRODUCTION OF BEEF.

(END SUNDAY FARM)

CHICAGO (UPI)--PRICES OF SLAUGHTER STEERS AND HEIFERS

GENERALLY WERE STEADY TO SLIGHTLY EASIER AT MIDWEST

MARKETS TODAY, BUT THE BULK OF THE HOGS TRENDED LOWER.

TWELVE MARKETS RECEIVED ABOUT 29,000 CATTLE, 47,000

HOGS AND 5,000 SHEEP AND LAMBS.

TRADING SHOWED SOME UNEVENNESS, BUT SLAUGHTER STEERS

GENERALLY SOLD STEADY TO WEAK AND HEIFERS AT LEAST

STEADY. AT CHICAGO, PRIME 1,225-1,400 POUND STEERS, YIELD

GRADES 3-4, BROUGHT 35.75 TO 36.25. GOOD AND CHOICE

STEERS AT CHICAGO CLEARED FROM 30.50 TO 35.00.

THE AVERAGE PRICE OF SLAUGHTER STEERS AT CHICAGO WAS

ESTIMATED TO BE 34.60 PER HUNDREDWEIGHT COMPARED WITH

27.01 A YEAR AGO.

HOGS IN THE EASTERN CORNBELT SOLD STEADY TO 25 CENTS

HIGHER, EXCEPT FOR A STEADY TO 25 CENTS LOWER TREND AT

EAST ST. LOUIS. IN THE WESTERN CORNBELT, HOG PRICES

WERE STEADY TO 50 CENTS LOWER. U-S NUMBER 2-4 GRADE

HOGS WEIGHING 200-260 POUNDS MAINLY BROUGHT 24.75 TO

25.75 AND 270-280 POUND BUTCHERS 24.00 TO 25.00.

348

SLAUGHTER LAMBS GENERALLY SOLD STEADY TO 50 CENTS
HIGHER. MOST CHOICE AND PRIME SPRING LAMBS BROUGHT 28.50
TO 30.25.

STEER BEEF CARCASSES WERE STEADY TO 50 CENTS LOWER
THAN TUESDAY'S CLOSE AND CHOICE HEIFER BEEF 50 CENTS
LOWER IN WHOLEXALE CARLOT MEAT TRADING AT NEW YORK.
LAMB WAS MOSTLY STEADY, INSTANCES 1.00 HIGHER.

COMPARED WITH TUESDAY'S CLOSE AT CHICAGO, WHOLESALE
CARLOT PRICES WERE STEADY FOR STEER AND HEIFER BEEF.
CHOICE 500-900 POUND STEER CARCASSES, YIELD GRADES 2-4,
BROUGHT 54.00. CHOICE 500-700 POUND HEIFER CARCASSES
WERE REPORTED AT 53.50. PORK LOINS WERE STEADY.

CASH GRAINS WERE MIXED AT CHICAGO WEDNESDAY. SOYBEANS
ADVANCED 1 CENT, ON A NOMINAL BASIS, WHEAT PRICES WERE
UNCHANGED, CORN 1 1/4 CENTS HIGHER AND OATS 1/4 CENT
LOWER.

CLOSING QUOTATIONS FOR CASH GRAINS AT CHICAGO BASED
ON TODAY'S TRADE AND AVAILABLE BIDS WERE 1.31 TO 1.31 1/4
FOR NUMBER 2 YELLOW HARD WINTER WHEAT, 2.68 3/4 TO 2.69
FOR NUMBER 1 YELLOW SOYBEANS, NUMBER 2 YELLOW CORN WAS
QUOTED FROM 1.30 TO 1.30 1/4 AND NUMBER 2 HEAVY WHITE
OATS FROM 61 3/4 TO 62 CENTS.

NUMBER 1 YELLOW SOYBEANS WERE BID 2.56 TO 2.65 1/2 A
BUSHEL ON TRACK AT ILLINOIS COUNTRY STATIONS.

WHOLESALE PRICES FOR EGGS DELIVERED TO CHICAGO WERE UNCHANGED TO 1 1/2 CENTS LOWER. LARGE WHITES 80 PER CENT OR BETTER GRADE A BROUGHT 33 1/2 TO 36 1/2 CENTS PER DOZEN AND MEDIUM WHITES 25 to 26 CENTS.

CHICAGO WHOLESALE BUTTER VALUES WERE UNCHANGED TO 1/2 CENTS HIGHER. BOTH AA AND A GRADE BUTTER WERE REPORTED AT SLIGHTLY LESS THAN 67 3/4 CENTS PER POUND.

CHEESE PRICES AT CHICAGO WERE UNCHANGED.

AP21

ADVANCE FOR USE FRIDAY, JUNE 20TH

-LISTEN, LADIES-

BY KAY LAWRENCE

ONE OF THE MOST UNIQUE FIGURES IN SPORTS, MAUREEN ORCOTT, OUTSTANDING WOMAN GOLFER FOR HALF A CENTURY, HAS BEEN HONORED IN NEW YORK--AND SHE SAYS SHE PLANS TO CONTINUE PLAYING.

SUNGLASSES--FROM TINY BEN FRANKLIN "SPECS" TO THE NEW GIANT SIZE GLASSES THAT PRACTICALLY COVER THE FACE, ARE MAKING BIG FASHION NEWS HERE AND ABROAD.

FOR TODAY'S COOKOUT WE SUGGEST YOU TRY GRILLED FRESH PEACH AND PLUM KEBOBS--THEY'RE DELICIOUS, AND DIFFERENT.

WOMEN IN THE NEWS

ONE OF THE MOST UNIQUE FIGURES IN SPORTS, AND AN
OUTSTANDING WOMAN GOLFER FOR HALF A CENTURY, MAUREEN
ORCUTT, ALSO IS ONE OF THE BUSIEST, FOR SHE HAS ANOTHER
CAREER--AS A SPORTS WRITER.

WHILE GOLF IS HER FIRST LOVE, MAUREEN ENJOYS HER
SPORTSWRITING CAREER TOO, ALTHOUGH SHE ADMITS THERE ARE
TIMES WHEN THE COMBINATION PUTS HER UNDER SOMEWHAT OF A
STRAIN. FOR INSTANCE,WHEN SHE COMPLETES A COMPETITIVE
ROUND OF GOLF, AS SHE WILL NEXT WEEK IN DEFENDING HER
TITLE IN THE WOMEN'S METROPOLITAN CHAMPIONSHIP, SHE HAS
TO RUSH TO THE PRESS ROOM AND BAT OUT A STORY OFTEN
EATURING MAUREEN ORCUTT. IT IS A STRAIN ON HER MODESTY.

SHE HAS WON THE WOMEN'S METROPOLITAN CHAMPIONSHIP
TEN TIMES, BEGINNING IN 1926. IN WINNIG IT LAST YEAR
SHE ACCOMPLISHED ONE OF THE MOST REMARKABLE ACHIEVEMENTS
IN SPORTS. AS USUAL, HER EDITOR HAD ASSIGNED HER TO
COVER THE TOURNAMENT SHE COMPETED IN, AND SHE PLANNED TO
DO IT. BUT SHE SAYS: "WHEN I GOT TO THE FINAL LAST
YEAR, I CALLED THE OFFICE AND SAID, 'I WANT HELP.' "
THE REASON WAS, OF COURSE, THAT SHE HAD SHOT HERSELF

INTO THE FINAL OF THE METROPOLITAN CHAMPIONSHIP.

SHE RECALLED THIS, AND OTHER MEMORABLE INCIDENTS IN HER LONG AND BRILLIANT GOLFING CAREER, WHEN SHE WAS HONORED WEDNESDAY IN NEW YORK FOR HER MANY CONTRIBUTIONS TO THE GAME, RECEIVING THE FIRST ANNUAL TANQUERAY AWARD. FRIENDS GATHERED AT A MIDTOWN STEAK HOUSE TO WITNESS THE PRESENTATION AND LISTEN TO MAUREEN REMINISCE.

A TREMENDOUSLY LONG DRIVER, THE BLONDE GOLFER FREQUENTLY PLAYED WITH SUCH MALE STARS AS WALTER HAGEN AND BOBBY JONES. ONCE IN FLORIDA SHE DEFEATED THE LATE BABE DIDRIKSON ZAHARIAS, RATED THE BEST WOMAN GOLFER OF ALL TIME, IN AN EXHIBITION MATCH.

MAURREN ALSO VIVIDLY REMEMBERS THE DAY--FOUR DECADES AGO--WHEN HAGEN, THEN GOLF'S MOST COLORFUL PERFORMER, ARRIVED IN AUGUSTA, GEORGIA, FOR AN EXHIBITION MATCH. WHEN HE DREW MAURREN AS A PARTNER, HE GROANED AND SAID: "I WOULD GET A LADY GOLFER!" HE DIDN'T REALIZE THAT HIS PRETTY, BOB-HAIRED YOUNG PARTNER HAD OVERHEARD HIS REMARK.

MAURREN RECALLS: "I DIDN'T SAY ANYTHING, BUT THE NEXT DAY I CARRIED HAGEN FOR NINE HOLES AND WE WON."

WINNING BECAME A HABIT WITH MAURREN ORCUTT. SHE WAS TWICE WINNER OF THE CANADIAN AMATEUR AND THREE-TIME

VICTOR IN THE ILLUSTRIOUS NORTH AND SOUTH LADIES'
TOURNAMENT. SHE WAS RUNNER-UP TWICE IN THE NATIONAL
WOMEN'S AMATEUR AND WINNER OF THE U-S SENIORS TWICE.

COVERING A 43-YEAR SPAN, SHE WON SEVEN EASTERN
TITLES, SIX NEW JERSEY STATE CROWNS AND FIVE METROPOLITAN
SENIORS. SHE PLAYED ON FOUR CURTIS CUP TEAMS. AND SHE
IS A MEMBER OF GOLF'S HALL OF FAME.

-0-

FASHION

WHEN WE TALK ABOUT SWINGING FASHIONS, LET'S NOT
OVERLOOK GLASSES, WHICH TODAY ARE HIGH FASHION
ACCESSORIES. AND WHAT VARIETY--FROM THE CONSERVATIVE TO
THE WAY-OUT STYLES.

IF BENJAMIN FRANKLIN WENT BACK TODAY AS U-S
AMBASSADOR TO PARIS, HE WOULD HAVE NO TROUBLE FITTING
HIMSELF OUT WITH GLASSES. EVERY OTHER POP ACCESSORY
SHOP IN PARIS IS PRESENTLY SELLING THE TINY, OVAL, WIRE
SPECTACLE FRAMES THAT HE MADE FAMOUS ALMOST 200 YEARS
AGO. OF COURSE, SOME MODERN TOUCHES HAVE BEEN ADDED.
FILLED IN WITH RED, BLUE, GREEN OR MAUVE LENSES--AND
SOMETIMES ONE OF EACH COLOR--THEY ARE BIG FAVORITES WITH
YOUNG FRENCH BOYS AND GIRLS, REGARDLESS OF WHETHER THE
SUN IS HINING OR NOT. SOME OF THE NEWEST "BEN FRANKLIN

SPECS" ARE FITTED OVER THE TOP WITH RESCENTS OF COLORFUL PLASTIC THAT FORM LITTLE CURVED AWNINGS LIKE A PAIR OF QUIZZICAL EYEBROWS.

THESE SPECTACLES--OFTEN WORN ALMOST ON THE TIP OF THE NOSE--ARE MAKING A HIT WITH AMERICAN TEEN-AGERS, TOO.

AND GOING FROM ONE EXTREME TO THE OTHER, YOUNG PEOPLE HERE AND ABROAD LOVE THE GIANT SPECS, WHICH GIVE THEM AN OWLISH LOOK AND ARE CONSIDERED SO CHIC.

THE RAGE TODAY, WITH THOSE WHO WANT TO PROVE THEY KNOW THEIR FASHION, ARE THE PASTEL LENSES--PALE BROWN, BLUE, GRAY, GREEN AND PINK. THESE TINTED LENSES, IN SMALLER FRAMES, OFTEN MATCHING COLOR OF THE WEARER'S COSTUME, ARE INTENDED FOR WEAR, DAY OR NIGHT, INDOORS OR OUT.

NO DOUBT ABOUT IT, CLASSIC TO WILD, GLASSES NOW ARE MAKING FASHION NEWS.

-O-

MENU AND COOKING CUES

WANT TO GIVE YOUR FAMILY OR GUESTS A DELIGHTFUL SUPRIRSE AT YOUR NEXT OUTDOOR MEAL? IT'S EASY. IN PLACE OF A SALAD, SERVE FRESH FRUIT KEBOBS, GRILLED OVER GLOWING COALS.

IF YOU WISH TO TRY THEM AT COOKOUT TIME TODAY, WE

SUGGEST YOU HAVE GRILLED FRESH PEACH AND PLUM KEBOBS.
THEY'LL MAKE A FINE ACCOMPANIMENT TO THIS MAIN COURSE:
SHRIMP SALAD OR CRABMEAT SALAD, A CASSEROLE OF LIMA
BEANS, AND HOT CORNBREAD OR CORN MUFFINS.

REMEMBER, WHEN CHOOSING FRUITS FOR GRILLING, YOU
SHOULD SELECT FIRM TEXTURED FRUIT, NOT FULLY RIPE.

-O-

HINTS FOR THE HOMEMAKER

TO BLOT UP OIL ON THE GARAGE FLOOR, COVER THE OIL
SPOTS WITH SEVERAL THICKNESSESS OF NEWSPAPER, THEN
SATURATE THE PAPER WITH WATER AND PRESS IT DOWN AGAINST
THE FLOOR. REMOVE THE NEWSPAPER WHEN IT IS THOROUGHLY
DRY.

SOIL IS THE NUMBER ONE ENEMY OF CURTAINS BECAUSE IT
WEAKENS FIBER AND DISCOLORS LIGHT BACKGROUNDS. AIR,
VACUUM, OR BRUSH CURTAINS TO REMOVE SURFACE DIRT, AND
CLEAN THEM OFTEN. WHEN YOU SEND CURTAINS TO A DRY CLEANER
OR TO A LAUNDRY, GIVE THE NAME AND PERCENTAGE OF EACH
FIBER.

EVEN IF YOU ARE JUST BEGINNING TO SEW, MAKE AN EXTRA
EFFORT TO LINE YOUR GARMENTS. THERE'S NOT MUCH EXTRA TIME
OR EXPENSE INVOLVED, YET IT MAKES ALL THE DIFFERENCE IN

THE QUALITY OF YOUR CLOTHES.

-O-

MEDICINE CABINET

IS YOUR HOME MEDICINE CABINET A NEAT ARRANGEMENT OF
DRUGS AND EMERGENCY SUPPLIES?   OR IS IT AN UNTIDY
COLLECTION OF ODDS AND ENDS AND OLD PRESCRIPTIONS?

SAFETY EXPERTS SAY THAT DURING THE SUMMER MONTHS
ESPECIALLY IT'S IMPORTANT FOR FAMILIES TO BE PREPARED
FOR ACCIDENTS.

THEY SUGGEST THESE ITEMS FOR A WELL-EQUIPPED MEDICINE
CABINET:

FOR CUTS AND SCRATCHES, YOU SHOULD HAVE AN ANTISEPTIC,
SUCH AS IODINE OR MERTHIOLATE.   YOU ALSO SHOULD INCLUDE A
BOX OF ABSORBENT COTTON AND STERILE GAUZE SQUARES.   OTHER
EMERGENCY NEEDS ARE BANDAGES OF VARIOUS WIDTHS, ADHESIVE
TAPE, AND COTTON-TIPPED APPLICATORS.

ANOTHER NECESSITY FOR THE MEDICINE CHEST IS AN
OINTMENT FOR BURNS--OR TANNIC ACID. INCLUDE A TUBE OF
PETROLEUM JELLY, BICARBONATE OF SODA, AND A MILD
LAXATIVE.

OTHER ITEMS YOU MIGHT WANT TO INCLUDE IN YOUR
MEDICINE CHEST ARE A PAIR OF TWEEZERS, RUBBING ALCOHOL,
A MEDICINE GLASS, MEDICINE DROPPERS, A PAIR OF SCISSORS,

NEEDLES, AND RAZOR BLADES. AND A REAL NECESSITY,

ESPECIALLY IF YOU HAVE CHILDREN, IS A THERMOMETER.

THE EXPERTS RECOMMEND THIS EQUIPMENT FOR A WELL-

SUPPLIED MEDICINE CHEST, READY TO MEET ANY EMERGENCY.

-O-

BEAUTY

OUR BEAUTY HINT FOR TODAY SHOWS HOW CLOSELY HAIR

STYLES ARE ALLIED TO FASHION. TO COMPLEMENT CITY PANTS

COSTUMES, HAIR STYLISTS SAY THAT HAIR WILL CONTINUE TO

BE BRUSHED OFF THE FACE AND PROBABLY SECURED WITH A SCARF

OR BOW. IT DOES SEEM TO BE THE MOST ATTRACTIVE COIFFURE

TO WEAR WITH PANTS OUTFITS--THE SCARF OF BOW HELPING TO

COMPLETE THE ENSEMBLE.

-O-

CAPSULE BOOK REVIEW

READERS WHO ENJOY BIOGRAPHIES WILL FIND "COSIMA

WAGNER: EXTRAORDINARY DAUGHTER OF FRANZ LISZT," BY

ALICE HUNT SOKOLOFF (PUBLISHED BY DODD MEAD, $7.50) A

TOUCHING STORY, TOLD WITH TASTE AND INSIGHT. IT'S THE

FIRST FULL-SCALE BIOGRAPHY OF THE WIFE OF THE GENIUS

COMPOSER RICHARD WAGNER--A WOMAN WHOSE INHERITED

TALENTS AND STRONG PERSONALITY NEARLY EQUALED, AND

CERTAINLY ENHANCED, THOSE OF HER CELEBRATED HUSBAND. THE
PAGES ARE HAUNTED WITH THE GREAT FIGURES OF COSIMA
WAGNER'S TIME, AND THIS, OF COURSE, GIVES THIS CHARMING
BOOK ADDED INTEREST.

2 | News from Western European Nations

BY BARRY JAMES

SEGOVIA, SPAIN (UPI)--CITY OFFICIALS PROCLAIMED A
STATE OF MOURNING TODAY FOR 50 PERSONS CRUSHED IN THE
COLLAPSE OF A RESTAURANT ROOF IN A MODEL VILLAGE SUNDAY.
POLICE ARRESTED THE OWNER OF THE PROJECT AND SOUGHT THE
DESIGNERS.

DOCTORS SAID THEY FEARED MANY OF THE 120 INJURED
WOULD NOT SURVIVE.

NEARLY 300 PERSONS WERE EATING A LATE LUNCH AT A
FIESTA TO CELEBRATE THE OPENING OF A NEW CONVENTION HALL
RESTAURANT IN THE MODEL VILLAGE OF LOS ANGELES DE SAN
RAFAEL 50 MILES NORTHWEST OF MADRID WHEN THE TRAGEDY
OCCURRED.

IT WAS ALMOST TIME FOR SELECTION OF THREE BEAUTY
QUEENS OF THE FIESTA.

"SUDDENLY THERE WAS A DEAFENING ROAR AND I SAW A BIG
CLOUD OF DUST ERUPTING FROM THE BUILDING," SAID CIVIL

GUARD CORPORAL JOSE FLORES.

"DOZENS OF PEOPLE WERE SCREAMING, TRAPPED UNDER THE
DEBRIS. IT WAS TERRIBLE."

POLICE SAID THE DEAD INCLUDED 20 WOMEN, FOUR CHILDREN
AND ANGEL JIMENEZ MILLAN, 49, MAYOR OF THE TOWN OF BARCO
DE AVILA. ALL THE DEAD AND INJURED WERE SPANIARDS.

POLICE ARRESTED JESUS GIL, OWNER OF THE RESIDENTIAL
PROJECT, AND SAID THEY WOULD DETAIN "THE TECHNICIANS" WHO
DESIGNED THE PARTIALLY-COMPLETED COMPLEX. THE CHARGES
AGAINST GIL WERE NOT ANNOUNCED.

A REQUIEM MASS WAS SCHEDULED IN THE CATHEDRAL OF
SEGOVIA, AND CITY OFFICIALS PROCLAIMED THE STATE OF
MOURNING WOULD CONTINUE UNTIL THE BURIAL OF THOSE KILLED.

ENRIQUE PRIETO, A SPOKESMAN FOR THE 1,976-ACRE
RESIDENTIAL PROJECT OF WEEKEND COTTAGES, SAID "WE DO NOT
KNOW WHAT HAPPENED. IT WAS A TERRIFIC BLOW. WE WERE
TRYING TO BUILD A MODEL CITY AND WE WILL CONTINUE OUR
PROGRAM."

RUFINA DE ANTON GALA TOLD OF HIS EXPERIENCE FROM A
HOSPITAL BED.

"IT WAS A NIGHTMARE. I WAS LAUGHING WITH SOME FRIENDS
SITTING AT MY TABLE. AS I LAUGHED, I LOOKED UP. THE
CEILING WAS OPENING TOWARD US WITH A SUDDEN BANG.
EVERYBODY SCREAMED."

THE BUILDING WHERE THE 300 DINERS WERE SITTING HAD

JUST BEEN COMPLETED. THE FIRST WAS TO CELEBRATE ITS

OPENING.

TVHE HUNDREDS OF TONS OF MASONRY AND STEEL PLUNGED

THROUGH THE FLOOR, WHICH COLLAPSED, HURLING THE DEAD AND

INJURED INTO THE BUILDING'S BASEMENT.

THE ARMY BROUGHT IN HUGE CRANES TO REMOVE THE DEBRIS

IN THE SEARCH FOR BODIES. WORKMEN USED BLOWTORCHES TO

FREE THE DEAD AND INJURED FROM TWISTED STEEL.

ROOF 6/16 NX

CORRECTION ROOF SEGOVIA 033A 14TH PGH BGNG THE

BUILDING, READ IT X X X COMPLETED. THE FIESTA WAS TO

CELEBRATE XXX (FIESTA INSTEAD FIRST)

MADRID (UPI)--THE CEBREROS TRACKING STATION NEAR

MADRID WHICH PLAYED A KEY ROLE IN THE U.S. MARINER AND

PIONEER SPACE VENTURES OPERATED UNDER SPANISH CONTROL FOR

THE FIRST TIME SUNDAY.

THE NATIONAL AERONAUTICS AND SPACE ADMINISTRATION

(NASA) HANDED OVER THE $7.5 MILLION STATION SATURDDAY TO

ITS SPANISH COUNTERPART, THE NATIONAL INSTITUTE OF

AEROSPACE TECHNOLOGY.

THE STATION, WITH ITS 85-FOOT ANTENNA, FORMS PART OF
THE ROBLEDO DE CHAVELA SPACE COMPLEX 45 MILES NORTHWEST
OF MADRID. THERE ARE TWO IDENTICAL TRACKING STATIONS--
FRESNEDILLAS AND ROBLEDO--SITUATED WITH CEREBROS AROUND
A NATURAL BOWL IN THE EARTH.

EVENTUALLY, THESE ALSO WILL BE HANDED OVER TO SPAIN
AS TECHNICIANS HERE ARE TRAINED TO TAKE OVER THE JOBS
NOW HELD BY NASA PEOPLE. EACH OF THE THREE STATIONS HAS
A STAFF OF ABOUT 80.

THE STATION AT FRESNEDILLAS IS THE ONE USED FOR
TRACKING APOLLO MOONSHOTS, WITH ROBLEDO AS A BACKUP IN
CASE OF EMERGENCY.

THOMAS O. PAINE, DIRECTOR GENERAL OF NASA, SAID IN
HANDING OVER THE STATION:

"THE EAGERNESS OF SAPIN TO TAKE PART IN THIS THRILLING
FORM OF EXPLORATION OF THE 20TH CENTURY REMINDS US THAT
FIVE CENTURIES AGO THE GREAT JOURNEY OF DISCOVERY MADE BY
COLUMBUS ALSO TOOK PLACE UNDER THE SPANISH FLAG. I
CONGRATULATE OUR SPANISH COLLEAGUES IN CONTINUING THIS
GREAT TRADITION OF SPAIN IN EXPLORING THE UNKNOWN AND I
ALSO CONGRATULATE THEM FOR MASTERING THE TECHNOLOGY
NECESSARY FOR THE OPERATION OF THIS STATION."

THE SPANISH STATION DIRECTOR AT CABREROS, JOSE LUIS

FERNANDEZ DOMINGUEZ, TOOK OVER FROM HIS U.S. COUNTERPART,
JOSEPH P. FEAREY, NOW CHIEF OF THE TOBLEDO INSTALLATION.
ALL THE TRACKING STATIONS HAVE A SPANISH DIRECTOR READY
TO ASSUME COMMAND WHEN THEY PASS INTO SPANISH HANDS.

WASHINGTON (UPI)--A DIPLOMATIC AGREEMENT WAS EXPECTED
TO BE CONFIRMED FRIDAY UNDER WHICH THE UNITED STATES WAS
TO GRANT SPAIN $50 MILLION FOR PURCHASING MILITARY
EQUIPMENT IN RETURN FOR AN EXTENSION OF U.S. USE OF ITS
MILITARY BASES IN SPAIN.

U.S. SOURCES SAID THE AGREEMENT PROVIDED FOR THE
UNITED STATES TO RETAIN THE USE OF THE BASES FOR 15
MONTHS, FOLLOWED BY A ONE-YEAR GRACE PERIOD DURING WHICH
THE UNITED STATES COULD EVACUATE THEM IN AN ORDERLY
MANNER IF THE AGREEMENT IS NOT RENEWED.

SECRETARY OF STATE WILLIAM P. ROGERS AND FOREIGN
MINISTER FERNANDO MARIA CASTIELLA OF SPAIN WERE TO
FORMALIZE THE AGREEMENT THROUGH AN EXCHANGE OF DIPLOMATIC
NOTES.

THE SOURCES REPORTED THAT THE UNITED STATES WILL
GRANT $50 MILLION TO SPAIN FOR MILITARY EQUIPMENT IN
RETURN FOR THE EXTENSION OF THE BASE RIGHTS.

THE BASES INCLUDE A NAVAL STATION AT ROTA AND

MILITARY INSTALLATIONS AT MADRID, ZARAGOZA, AND SEVILLE.

THE AGREEMENT ENDED A LONG SERIES OF NEGOTIATIONS
GOING BACK TO LAST FALL WHEN SPAIN AND THE UNITED STATES
WERE UNABLE TO RENEW THE BASES AGREEMENT FOR AN
ANTICIPATED FIVE-YEAR PERIOD.

ONE OBSTACLE DURING THE NEGOTIATIONS WAS THE REQUEST
FROM THE SPANISH SIDE FOR $1 BILLION WORTH OF MILITARY
EQUIPMENT.

PARIS (UPI)--BARON EMMANUEL D'ASTIER DE LA VIGERIE,
SOMETIMES KNOWN AS THE "RED BARON" FOR HIS EXTREME
LEFTIST VIEWS, DIED THURSDAY AT HIS PARIS HOME. HE WAS 69.

THE BARON SERVED AS MINISTER OF THE INTERIOR IN THE
PROVISIONAL GOVERNMENT FORMED BY GEN. CHARLES DE GAULLE
IMMEDIATELY AFTER WORLD WAR II AND WAS REGARDED AS ONE
OF THE MOST LEFTIST OF DE GAULLE'S SUPPORTERS.

HE LATER SERVED IN THE CHAMBER OF DEPUTIES AND WAS
FOUNDER AND DIRECTOR OF THE MONTHLY MAGAZINE OF OPINION,
L' EVENEMENT.

BORN IN PARIS JAN. 6, 1900, HE MARRIED THE DAUGHTER
OF THE RUSSIANREVOLUTIONARY LEONID KRASSINE IN 1947. HE
IS SURVIVED BY HIS WIFE AND THEIR TWO SONS.

MOSCOW (UPI)--WALDECK ROCHET, SECRETARY GENERAL OF
THE FRENCH COMMUNIST PARTY, WAS HOSPITALIZED LAST WEEK
AFTER DELIVERING A SPEECH TO THE WORLD COMMUNIST SUMMIT
MEETING, FRENCH SOURCES SAID MONDAY, THEY SAID ROCHET,
WHO WAS SUFFERING FROM EXHAUSTION, WOULD REMAIN IN THE
KREMLIN HOSPITAL FOR SEVERAL DAYS MORE.

STOCKHOLM (UPILAACROWN PRINCE CARL GUSTAF OF SWEDEN,
WILL GO TO WORK AS A TELEVISION NEWSMAN WITH THE SWEDISH
BROADCASTING CORP. LATER THIS YEAR, THE NEWSPAPER
AFTONBLADET REPORTED MONDAY. THE NEWSPAPER SAID THE 23-
YEAR-OLD HEIR TO THE SWEDISH THRONE WOULD WORK AT THE
NEWS DESK AND NOT APPEAR ON THE SCREEN.

ROME (UPI)--THE GOVERNMENT SATURDAY APPROVED A BILL
RESTRICTING THE EXPLOITATION OF UNDERGROUND WATER IN THE
VENICE HINTERLAND IN HOPES OF KEEPING THE LAGOON CITY
FROM SINKING INTO THE ADRIATIC SEA.

THE PUMPING OF WATER FROM THE SUBSOIL IS ONE OF
SEVERAL CAUSES CITED BY SCIENTISTS FOR THE STEADY SINKING
OF THE CITY, WHICH IS FLOODED BY HIGH TIDES WITH
INCREASING FREQUENCY.

MOST EXPERTS SAY VENICE WILL DISAPPEAR FOREVER UNDER
THE ADRIATIC WITHIN THREE CENTURIES UNLESS SOMETHING
DRASTIC IS DONE TO SAVE IT. EUGENIO MIOZZI, FORMER
CHIEF ENGINEER OF VENICE, SAYS DISASTER IS MORE IMMINENT
AND THE CITY HAS ONLY 80 YEARS TO LIVE.

THE BILL APPROVED BY THE CABINET WOULD REQUIRE A
GOVERNMENT PERMIT FOR ANY SEARCH FOR AND EXPLOITATION OF
SUBSOIL WATERS IN THE PROVINCES OF VENICE, PADUA,
VICENZA AND TREVISO, A TOTAL AREA OF 3,802 SQUARE MILES.

THE MEASURE, WHICH GOES TO PARLIAMENT FOR DEBATE,
FOLLOWS RECENT RESTRICTIONS ON EXPLOITATION OF NATURAL
GAS IN THE SAME GENERAL AREA.

OTHER MEASURES TO PROTECT VENICE AGAINST THE SEA HAVE
BEEN UNDER STUDY FOR SOME TIME WITH HELP FROM DUTCH
HYDRULICS EXPERTS.

BARCELONNA POZZO DI GOTTO, SICILY (UPI)--TWO TRAINS
COLLIDED HEAD-ON IN A TUNNEL EARLY SUNDAY. AUTHORITIES
SAID FOUR PERSONS WERE KILLED AND 60 OTHERS WERE TRAPPED
IN THE NARROW PASSAGE FILLED WITH CHOKING FUMES.

TWELVE HOURS AFTER THE DISASTER, FAINT CRIES FROM
THE WRECKAGE STILL COULD BE HEARD BY RESCUE TEAMS
WORKING IN ALMOST TOTAL DARKNESS. CUTTING TORCHES TO

SLICE THROUGH TWISTED STEEL COULD NOT BE USED BECAUSE OF
EXPLOSIVE FUMES LEAKING FROM TAR AND GASOLINE IN
CRUMPLED TANK CARS.

SEVEN FIREMEN WERE OVERCOME IN THE 330-FOOT-LONG ST.
ANTHONY TUNNEL ON THE NORTH COAST OF SICILY 20 MILES
WEST OF MESSINA. VENTILATING MACHINERY WAS RUSHED TO
THE SCENE FROM MESSINA.

THE COLLISION INVOLVED A PASSENGER TRAIN AND A FREIGHT
TRAIN THAT SMASHED TOGETHER AT TOP SPEED IN AN IMPACT SO
GREAT THAT THE TWO LOCOMOTIVES TELESCOPED.

RAILWAY OFFICIALS SAID THE SIGNALS AT EITHER END OF
THE TUNNEL EITHER FAILED OR WERE NOT SEEN.

THE DEAD INCLUDED THE ENGINEER AND THE FIREMAN OF THE
PASSENGER TRAIN, THE ENGINEER OF THE FREIGHT TRAIN AND A
PASSENGER RIDING IN A HEAD COACH OF THE PASSENGER TRAIN.

THE CONDUCTOR AND A POSTAL OFFICIAL RIDING IN THE
MAIL CAR WERE MISSING.

ROME (AP)--IN ROME--CANCER OF THE BRAIN WAS FATAL TO
60-YEAR-OLD ARBURO MICHELINI, ITALIAN PARLIAMENTARIAN
AND LEADER OF THOSE WHO REVERE DICTATOR MUSSOLINI.

VATICAN CITY (UPI)--THE ROME NEWSPAPER IL MESSAGGERO
SAID FRIDAY THE VATICAN WAS HAVING LABOR TROUBLE, WITH
150 PAPAL GENDARMES DEMANDING PAY RAISES, LONGER
VACATIONS AND OTHER FRINGE BENEFITS.

VATICAN OFFICIALS WOULD NOT IMMEDIATELY COMMENT ON
THE REPORT.

POPE PAUL VI RAISED THE PAY OF ALL VATICAN EMPLOYES
BY 6 PER CENT OR MORE AT THE BEGINNING OF THIS YEAR. BUT
THE GENDARMES, ACCORDING TO IL MESSAGGERO, ARE ASKING
FOR MORE.

"THE AGITATION HAS BEEN UNDER WAY FOR SEVERAL WEEKS,"
THE NEWSPAPER SAID. "THE REGULATIONS OF THE CORPS, OF
COURSE, PROHIBIT STRIKES, BUT PROTEST LETTERS (THE
GENDARMES) HAVE SENT CARDINAL SERGIO GUERRI, PRO-
PRESIDENT OF THE PONTIFICAL COMMISSION FOR THE VATICAN
CITY STATE, ARE RATHER HARD."

THE NEWSPAPER SAID THE GENDARMES WERE ASKING A
SPECIAL BONUS OF $24 A MONTH. IT SAID THEIR PRESENT
STARTING SALARY IS $156.80 A MONTH AND GOES UP FIVE PER
CENT EVERY TWO YEARS.

THE NEWSPAPER SAID THE GENDARMES ALSO WERE ASKING
THE VATICAN TO INCREASE THEIR SUMMER VACATIONS FROM 20
TO 30 DAYS AND GRANT THEM SOME OTHER FRINGE BENEFITS.

IL MESSAGGERO SAID THE CORPS CHAPLAIN, MSGR. GIOVANNI
SESSOLO, REPORTED THE GENDARMES' GRIEVANCES IN A RECENT
PRIVATE AUDIENCE WITH THE POPE.

THE POPE OFFERED TO ALLOCATE $3,200 TO FINANCE A
BRIEF PLEASURE TRIP FOR A GROUP OF GENDARMES BUT THEY
TURNED IT DOWN AS "PATERNALISTIC," THE NEWSPAPERS SAID.

VATICAN CITY (AP)--A RASH OF REPORTS CIRCULATED IN
ROME TODAY THAT THE VATICAN IS SELLING ITS VAST ITALIAN
STOCKS TO AMERICAN COMPANIES. A VATICAN SPOKESMAN SAYS
HE HAS BEEN INSTRUCTED NOT TO COMMENT. ACCORDING TO THE
REPORTS, THE VATICAN HAS HAD CONTACTS WITH AMERICAN
FIANNICAL INTERESTS TO SELL ITS HOLDINGS IN SOCIETA
GENERALE IMMOBILIARE OF ROME, ITALY'S LARGEST REAL ESTATE
COMPANY.

MUNICH, GERMANY (UPI)--GERMAN AIRCRAFT DESIGNER
SIEGFRIED GUENTER, WHO HELPED DEVELOP THE WORLD'S FIRST
JET PLANE, DIED THURSDAY OF A HEART ATTACK IN WEST BERLIN,
IT WAS ANNOUNCED FRIDAY. HE WAS 69.

THE VEREINIGTE FLUGTECHNISCHE WERKE (VFW) AEROSPACE
FIRM, WHOSE SOUTH GERMAN OPERATIONS GUENTER HEADED, SAID

368

THAT GUENTER WITH HIS BROTHER WALTER DESIGNED THE FIRST
JET, THE HEINKEL 178.

OTHER FAMOUS AIRCRAFT GUENTER DESIGNED WHILE WITH
HEINKEL, WHICH IS NOW PART OF VFW, INCLUDED THE HEINKEL
111 BOMBER OF WORLD WAR II AND THE HEINKEL 100 AND 119
WHICH SET INTERNATIONAL SPEED RECORDS BEFORE THE WAR.

GUENTER WAS ONE OF MANY GERMAN ENGINEERS AND
SCIENTISTS THE RUSSIANS PUT TO WORK FOR THEM IN THE
SOVIET UNION AFTER WORLD WAR II.

HE WAS REPORTED TO HAVE PLAYED A KEY ROLE IN
DEVELOPMENT OF THE SOVIET MIG JET FIGHTERS. GUENTER WAS
SENT BACK IN 1954 AND REJOINED HEINKEL, WHICH LATER
MERGED WITH VFW.

MAINZ, GERMANY (UPI)--IT IS TIME TO FORGET ALL THIS
TALK OF A CURSE AND GET ON WITH RECOVERING THE GOLD LEGEND
HAS ALWAYS SAID LIES ON THE BOTTOM OF THE RHINE, SAYS
MAYOR HANS JACOBI.

"THIS IS NO JOKE," JACOBI SAID THURSDAY. "THIS
VENTURE IS BASED ON YEARS OF SCIENTIFIC RESEARCH."

WILHELM MATTHES OF THE CITY SURVEYING OFFICE HAS
PLOTTED THE LOCATION OF THE GOLD, SOMEWHERE IN A MILE-
LONG STRETCH OF THE RHINE WHERE THE RIVER MAKES A 180-

DEGREE LOOP.

LEGEND SAID THE NIGELUNGEN GOLD ORIGINALLY BELONGED
TO THE BURGUNDIAN KINGS FROM WHOM IT WAS STOLEN. LATER
A BURGUNDIAN KNIGHT SANK IT FOR SAFEKEEPING.

TTHE DWARF ALBERICH WAS SAID TO HAVE PUT A CURSE ON
THE GOLD JUST BEFORE HE WAS SLAIN BY THE GERMANIC PRINCE
SIEGFRIED.

- - - WORLD HORIZONS FOR RELEASE SUNDAY, JUNE 22 OR
THEREAFTER - - -
(650) (PICTURE)
IN 100 YEARS THE VIENNA OPERA HOUSE HAS SEEN SOME CLASSIC
MUSICAL IN-FIGHTING

BY FRANZ HITZENBERGER

VIENNA (UPI)--THE CHIEF ARCHITECT, DESPONDENT AT
PUBLIC SCORN OF HIS MASTERWORK, HANGED HIMSELF.

HIS ASSOCIATE, HEARTBROKEN AT THE NEWS, DIED WITHIN
WEEKS OF A HEART ATTACK.

BUT THE DEATHS OF EDUARD VAN DER NUELL AND FRANZ
SICCARDSBURG SHORTLY AFTER THE 1869 OPENING OF THE OPERA
HOUSE THEY HAD DESIGNED DID NOT SLACKEN THE HOSTILITY OF
THE VIENNESE TO THEIR CREATION.

THE HUGH, ORNATE STRUCTURE, BUILT UNDER VAN DER

NUELL'S AND SICCARDSBURG'S SUPERVISION OVER SEVEN YEARS,
STOOD EMPTY FOR PERFORMANCE AFTER PERFORMANCE.

THREE GENERAL MANAGERS QUIT IN DISMAY AFTER VAST
DONATIONS FROM THE COFFERS OF THE AUSTRO-HUNGARIAN
EMPIRE TO SUSTAIN THE OPERA FAILED TO DRAW AN UNWILLING
PUBLIC.

THIS YEAR THE VIENNA OPERA HOUSE, NOW AS TRADITIONAL
A FEATURE OF THE AUSTRIAN CAPITAL AS JOHANN STRAUSS'
WALTZES OR THE BLUE DANUBE WHICH FLOWS NEARBY, CELEBRATES
ITS 100TH ANNIVERSARY STILL FINANCIALLY IN THE RED BUT
WITH ITS FUTURE SECURE.

THERE HAVE BEEN MANY UPS AND DOWNS. WHEN COMPOSER
GUSTAV MAHLER TOOK OVER MANAGERSHIP IN 1897 IT APPEARED
THE ENTIRE OPERA HOUSE PROJECT WOULD END IN DISMAL
FAILURE.

BUT THE VIENNESE BOYCOTT OF THE OPERA HOUSE, DUE
LARGELY TO A SENTIMENTAL, PERHAPS INNATELY CONSERVATIVE,
ATTACHMENT TO A PREVIOUS BUILDING, HAD OUTLIVED ITS
INITIAL PASSION.

MAHLER QUICKLY INSTITUTED SOME TELLING CHANGES: HE
ORDERED THE HOUSE KEPT DARK DURING PERFORMANCES, A
PRACTICE WELCOMED DESPITE BRIEF OUTCRY OVER ITS "AFFRONT"
TO ARISTOCRACY ON DISPLAY.

HE DID AWAY WITH THE CLAQUE -- THE COTERIE OF REGULAR
ATTENDERS PAID TO APPLAUD AND CHEER VIGOROUSLY AT EACH
ARIA, SWOON OR CURTAIN ONSTAGE.

FINALLY, HE ESTABLISHED GERMAN COMPOSER RICHARD
WAGNER AS A STAPLE OF THE VIENNA REPERTOIRE. THE BEST
SINGERS OF THE TIME CLAMORED FOR CHANCES TO PERFORM "THE
RING OF THE NIEBELUNGEN," "THE MEISTERSINGER," OR "THE
FLYING DUTCHMAN."

STRICTLY SPEAKING, TODAY'S VIENNA OPERA HOUSE IS NOT
THE ONE OPENED IN 1869. THAT BUILDING WAS DESTROYED
DURING U. S. AIR FORCE BOMBING RAIDS IN WORLD WAR II.

THE U. S. GOVERNMENT SUPPLIED FINANCIAL AID TO
REBUILD THE OPERA IN ITS ORIGINAL FORM IN 1955.

THE OPERA'S STORMY HISTORY CONTINUED. CONDUCTOR
CLEMENS KRAUSS, WHO HAD BEEN DIRECTOR BEFORE THE 1944
BOMBING AND WAS PROMISED THE JOB AGAIN AFTER THE
REOPENING, DIED OF A STROKE IN 1955 AFTER LEARNING THAT
KARL BOEHM HAD BEEN GIVEN THE JOB INSTEAD.

BUT BOEHM'S TENUR WAS SHORT-LIVED. HE WAS VIRTUALLY
BOOED OUT OF AUSTRIA A YEAR LATER AFTER TELLING AN
INTERVIEWER HE WAS "NOT PREPARED TO SACRIFICE MY WORLD
CAREER AS CONDUCTOR OF THE VIENNA OPERA."

HIS PLACE WAS TAKEN BY THE FLAMBOYANT HERBERT VON

KARAJAN. FOR IEGHT YEARS THE VIENNA OPERA LIVED WHAT

CRITICS TERMED A "NEW GOLDEN AGE."

BUT KARAJAN, ANGERED BY CONTINUING CLASHES WITH THE

"BUREAUCRATIC" MANAGEMENT OF THE STATE-OWNED, STATE-RUN

OPERA, QUIT IN DISGUST IN 1964, VOWING NEVER TO RETURN

TO VIENNA.

FOR FIVE YEARS HE HAS KEPT HIS PROMISE. NOW OFFICIALS,

MINDFUL OF THE OPERA'S "KARAJAN IMAGE," HAVE APPROACHED

HIM WITH A "FORGIVE AND FORGET" APPEAL.

"WE CAN ONLY ASK--AND HOPE," ONE OFFICIAL SAID.

IN SPITE OF SUCH MUSICAL IN-FIGHTING, THE MAY AND

JUNE CENTENNIAL FESTIVAL SPARKLES WITH INTERNATIONAL

STARS CONDUCTING AND PERFORMING SOME 50 CLASSIC OPERAS

AND BALLETS.

DURING THE TWO-MONTH CELEBRATION, VIENNESE HAVE HAD

THE OPPORTUNITY TO HEAR SUCH GREATS AS LISA DELLA CASA,

BIRGIT NILSSON, IRMGAARD SEEFRIED, TITO GOBBI, CESARE

SIEPI, JESS THOMAS AND JAMES MCCRACKEN, AND ORCHESTRAS

LED BY FAMOUS CONDUCTORS LEONARD BERNSTEIN, JOSEF KRIPS

AND BOEHM.

(ADVANCE -- WORLD HORIZONS FOR 6/22 RELEASE)

ATHENS (UPI)--A SHUFFLE IN GREECE'S MILITARY REGIME IS IMMINENT, OFFICIAL SOURCES SAID TODAY. ONE SOURCE CLOSE TO THE GOVERNMENT SAID PREMIER GEORGE PAPADOPOULOS PROBABLY WOULD ANNOUNCE THE CHANGES SATURDAY.

TWO CABINET MEMBERS RESIGNED THURSDAY.

A GOVERNMENT ANNOUNCEMENT SAID PAPADOPOULOS HAD ACCEPTED THE RESIGNATION OF HIS PERSONAL FRIEND, FORMER NEWSMAN THEOFYLACTOS PAPACONSTANTINOU, AS EDUCATION MINISTER.

PAPACONSTANTINOU WAS CONSIDERED ONE OF THE MORE LIBERAL MEMBERS OF THE REGIME. BEFORE JOINING THE GOVERNMENT IN 1967, HE WORKED UNDER HELEN VLACHOU, THE PUBLISHER WHO LATER CLOSED DOWN HER NEWSPAPERS RATHER THAN GIVE IN TO GOVERNMENT CENSORSHIP.

FRIENDS OF IOANNIS RODINOS ORLANDOS, 43, SAID HE HAD RESIGNED AS ASSISTANT COORDINATION MINISTER BECAUSE MEMBERS OF THE PREMIER'S OFFICE RESENTED HIS ATTITUDE IN THE FINANCIAL BATTLE BETWEEN MILLIONAIRES ARISTOTLE ONASSIS AND STAVROS NIARCHOS.

ORLANDOS AND HIS SUPERIOR, COORDINATION MINISTER NICHOLAS MAKAREZOS, WERE RESPONSIBLE FOR LAST MONTH'S DECISION TO CANCEL AN AGREEMENT WITH ONASSIS FOR CONSTRUCTION OF AN OIL REFINERY. THEY REOPENED BIDDING

374

ON THE BASIS OF A BETTER OFFER BY NIARCHOS. POLITICAL
SOURCES SAID ASSOCIATES OF PAPADOPOULOS FAVORED ONASSIS
AND WERE ANNOYED.

UNOFFICIAL SOURCES SAID POLICE CHIEF VASSILIOS
SAKELLARIOU AND GENDARMERIES CHIEF LT. GEN. PERIKLIS
MALLOUKOS WERE REMOVED FROM THEIR JOBS.

AT LEAST 15 RETIRED SENIOR OFFICERS HAVE BEEN
ARRESTED IN RECENT WEEKS AND ACCUSED OF ANTIREGIME
ACTIVITY. PAPADOPOULOS SAID THEY WOULD BE COURT
MARTIALED INSTEAD OF DEPORTED TO ISLANDS AS IN CASES OF
OTHER PERSONS SIMILARLY ACCUSED.

3 | News from Eastern European Nations

WASHINGTON (UPI)--THE SOVIET UNION HAS REPLIED TO
NEW AMERICAN PROPOSALS FOR A FORMULA FOR PEACE IN THE
MIDDLE EAST, STATE DEPARTMENT OFFICIALS SAID WEDNESDAY.

THEY SAID THE RUSSIAN'S ANSWER TO THE PROPOSALS WERE
BEING GIVEN CAREFUL STUDY.

ALTHOUGH THE STATE DEPARTMENT HAS REFUSED TO DISCLOSE
THE "CONCRETE IDEAS" THE UNITED STATES PASSED ALONG TO
THE SOVIETS, IT WAS UNDERSTOOD THAT UNDER THE U.S.
PROPOSAL THE ARAB NATIONS AND ISRAEL WOULD SIGN AN
ACCORD AMOUNTING TO A CONTRACTUAL OBLIGATION.

IT WOULD NOT BE DESCRIBED AS A PEACE TREATY OUT OF
RESPECT FOR ARAB OBJECTIONS TO SIGNING SUCH A TREATY AND
TO DIRECT NEGOTIATIONS WITH ISRAEL.

BUT IT WAS UNDERSTOOD THAT BOTH SIDES WOULD AGREE IN
THE ACCORD TO THE WITHDRAWAL OF ISRAELI FORCES FROM
TERRITORIES OCCUPIED DURING THE 1967 WAR TO SECURE
BOUNDARIES.

THE SOVIET REPLY TO THE U.S. PROPOSALS FOLLOWED
SOVIET FOREIGN MINISTER ANDREI A. GROMYKO'S RETURN TO
MOSCOW FROM CAIRO, WHERE HE MET SEVERAL TIMES WITH
PRESIDENT GAMAL ABDEL NASSER.

U.S. SOURCES SAID THEY UNDERSTOOD GROMYKO DISCUSSED
THE AMERICAN PROPOSALS WITH NASSER.

THE RUSSIANS' REPLY CAME IN WASHINGTON FROM YURI N.
CHERNYAKOV, SOVIET CHARGE D'AFFAIRES, IN A MEETING WITH
SECRETARY OF STATE WILLIAM P. ROGERS TUESDAY. CHERNYAKOV
REPRESENTED HIS NATION IN THE ABSENCE OF SOVIET
AMBASSADOR ANATOLY F. DOBRYNIN, WHO RETURNED TO MOSCOW
FOR CONSULTATIONS.

BELGRADE (UPI)--THE YUGOSLAV GOVERNMENT SAID
THURSDAY ITS AGENTS HAD ARRESTED MILJENKO HRKAC, 22, ON
A CHARGE OF PLANTING TWO BOMBS IN DOWNTOWN BELGRADE. ONE

PERSON WAS KILLED AND 100 INJURED IN TWO RESULTING
EXPLOSIONS. THE CHARGES SAID HRKAC WAS A MEMBER OF A
WEST GERMAN "EMIGREE TERRORIST GROUP."

MOSCOW (UPI)--SOVIET COMMENTATORS SAID FRIDAY THE
KREMLIN SUMMIT CONFERENCE HAD SHOWN A TENDENCY TOWARD
UNITY AMONG PARTIES BUT ADMITTED "THERE ARE MANY
UNSOLVED PROBLEMS AND MANY DIFFICULTIES IN THE COMMUNIST
MOVEMENT."

DESPITE OFFICIAL OPTIMISM THE SINO-SOVIET BORDER
TROUBLES CAST A LONG SHADOW OVER THE CONFERENCE OF 75
PARTIES FROM AROUND THE WORLD AND THE SOVIET PRESS
CONTINUED ITS ADMONITIONS AGAINST THE CHINESE AND OTHER
"REVISIONIST" PARTIES.

"THE CONFERENCE IS CONTINUING AND THE TIME IS NOT
PROPITIOUS FOR MAKING GENERAL CONCLUSIONS," A COMMENTARY
IN THE NEWSPAPER LITERATURNAYA ROSSIYA SAID.

"BUT IT IS CLEAR NOW THAT AN OVERWHELMING MAJORITY
OF DELEGATES EXPRESS UNEQUIVOCAL APPROVAL OF THE DRAFT
OF THE BASIC DOCUMENT."

"THE TENDENCY FOR UNITY AND CONSOLIDATION IS
STRIKINGLY EVIDENT AT THE MEETING," SAID THE PARTY
NEWSPAPER PRAVDA.

THE INFLUENTIAL MAGAZINE NEW TIMES BLAMED
REVISIONISM FOR TROUBLES BESETTING THE COMMUNIST
MOVEMENT.

BUDAPEST (UPI)--THE HUNGARIAN COMMUNIST PARTY
NEWSPAPER NEPSZABADASAG SAID SUNDAY THAT POLICE IN GRAZ,
AUSTRIA, ARRESTED THREE HUNGARIAN TOURISTS WITHOUT REASON,
BEAT ONE AND TRIED TO FORCE THEM TO DEFECT.

(IN GRAZ, A SPOKESMAN AT POLICE HEADQUARTERS SAID THE
THREE HUNGARIANS HAD ASKED POLICE FOR POLITICAL ASYLUM
AND HAD BEEN SENT TO REFUGEE CAMP. THE SPOKESMAN DENIED
THAT THE THREE WERE BEATEN OR EVEN JAILED).

ACCORDING TO THE NEPSABADSAG ACCOUNT, THE MEN WERE
SENT TO AN EMIGRE CAMP AT TRAISKIRCHEN NEAR VIENNA AND
"ONLY AFTER A NUMBER OF DAYS OF CAPTIVITY WERE THEY ABLE
TO WIN THEIR FREEDOM" AND RETURN HOME.

VENUS 6/18 SX

BY LESTER C. KJOS

DENVER (UPI)--DEEP PROBES TO WITHIN 15 MILES OF
VENUS BY UNMANNED SOVIET SPACECRAFT HAVE SHOWN HEAT "LIKE
DANTE'S INFERNO" AND THE POSSIBILITY OF MOUNTAINS JUTTING

AS HIGH AS 20 MILES ABOVE DEEP VALLEYS, TWO RUSSIAN
SCIENTISTS SAID THURSDAY.

"IT'S SO DAMNED HOT THERE IT WOULD BE LIKE DANTE'S
INFERNO," SAID YULI C. HODAREV, DEPUTY DIRECTOR OF THE
RUSSIAN UNMANNED SPACE PROGRAM.

HODAREV SAID INSTRUMENTATION INDICATED TEMPERATURES
ON THE CLOUD-SHROUDED PLANET COULD REACH 986 DEGREES
FAHRENHEIT.

HE ALSO SAID ELEVATION DIFFERENCES, WHICH COULD BE
GRADUAL OR SHARP, WERE AS MUCH AS 25 MILES.

"THESE RESULTS CAN SUFFICIENTLY CHANGE OUR OPINION
ABOUT THE VENUS SURFACE, WHICH SO FAR WAS CONSIDERED TO
BE COMPARATIVELY SMOOTH," HODAREV SAID.

U.S. RADAR STUDIES OF VENUS HAVE SHOWN NO SUCH
ELEVATION VARIATIONS.

HODAREV AND YURI N. IVANOV OF THE INSTITUTE FOR
AUTOMATION AND TELEMECHANICS ADDRESSED A SESSION OF THE
JOINT NATIONALMEETING OF THE AMERICAN ASTRONAUTICAL
SOCIETY AND THE OPERATIONS RESEARCH SOCIETY OF AMERICA
IN DENVER.

SPACESHIPS VENURA 5 AND VENURA 6 MAY 16-17 DOVE TO
WITHIN 20 AND 40 MILES OF VENUS BEFORE ATMOSPHERIC
PRESSURES OF MORE THAN 27 TIMES THAT OF EARTH'S SEA

LEVEL CRUSHED THEM.

EARLIER, VENURA 4 REACHED TO WITHIN 15 MILES OF THE
PLANET BEFORE IT WAS CRUSHED.

HODAREV DEFENDED UNMANNED SPACEFLIGHT SAYING IT CAN
ACCOMPLISH EVERYTHING MAN CAN DO WITHOUT THE RISKS.

"JUST BECAUSE MAN CAN FLY IN SPACE DOESN'T JUSTIFY
SENDING HIM TO THE PLANETS," HE SAID.

"THE RESULTS OF VENURA 5 AND VENURA 6 YIELDED A VAST
AMOUNT OF SCIENTIFIC INFORMATION, WHICH ALLOWED (US) TO
CONFIRM THE VALIDITY OF OUR HYPOTHESES ABOUT VENUS AND
WHICH WILL BE USED AS THE INITIAL DATA IN FURTHER
DEVELOPMENT OF SCIENTIFIC PROGRAMS," HE SAID.

HE SAID VENUS' CLOUDED ATMOSPHERE CONSISTS OF 93-97
PER CENT CARBON DIOXIDE, 2-5 PER CENT NITROGEN AND ONLY
.4 PER CENT OXYGEN.

NIGHT LD

BY GERD KRIWANEK

PRAGUE (UPI)--A TRADE UNION NEWSPAPER SAID SATURDAY
THAT AN ANTI-COMMUNIST APPEAL HAS BEEN CIRCULATED AMOONG
STEEL WORKERS, THE LATEST IN A SERIES OF DISCLOSURES THAT
SOME CZECHOSLOVAK WORKERS ARE RESISTING THE NEW ORTHODOX
COMMUNIST PARTY LINE.

VLASTIMIL TOMAN, CIARMAN OF THE 950,000 MEMBER CZECH
METAL WORKERS UNION, SENT THE NEWSPAPER PRACE A
STATEMENT WARNING ALL UNIOON MEMBERS AGAINST A CURRENT
OPPOSITION CAMPAIGN IN THE NATION'S LARGEST UNION.

"AN APPEAL IS AT PRESENT BEING SENT TO ALL METAL
WORKERS IN OUR FACTORIES WHICH GROSSLY ATTACKS OUR
LEADERS AND OUR SOCIALIST SOCIETY," THE UNION
LEADERSHIP STATEMENT SAID.

"IT IS A SEDITIOUS MEANS AGAINST THE WHOLE OF OUR
PEOPLE, AT VARIANCE WITH THE PRINCIPLES OF OUR SOCIALIST
LEGISLATION.

"WE THEREFORE CALL ON ALL BASIC ORGANIZATIONS TO
DISASSOCIATE THEMSELVES FROM SUCH APPEALS AND SIMILAR
PAMPHLETS, FROM THEIR POSSIBLE PUBLICATION AND
CIRCULATION, AND ALL MEMBERS OF THE UNION TO REJECT THEM
RESOLUTELY AND SHARPLY."

THE TOMAN STATEMENT CAME ON THE HEELS OF DISCLOSURE
BY THE PRESS OF TWO MEETINGS OF LABOR REFORMISTS, ONE IN
OSTRAVA JUNE 12 WHICH WAS BROKEN UP AFTER 45 MINUTES BY
A PARTY OFFICIAL BECAUSE IT WAS ILLEGAL AND ANOTHER OF
STEEL MILL UNION OFFICIALS IN KLADNO JUNE 6.

THE PARTY CENTRAL COMMITTEE DISCLOSED THURSDAY THAT
COPIES OF A SPEECH BY REFORMIST FRANTISEK KRIEGEL JUST
BEFORE HE WAS OUSTED FROM THE PARTY AND THE CENTRAL

COMMITTEE MAY 29 ALSO WAS BEING CIRCULATED IN FACTORIES.

THE ACTIVITIES OF DISENTORS AMONG LABOR WAS JUDGED SO IMPORTANT BY THE CENTRAL COMMITTEE THAT IT ISSUED A WARNING THURSDAY THAT "RIGHTWING OPPORTUNISTS", OR PROGRESSIVES, WERE STILL ACTIVE.

MEANWHILE, CENTRAL COMMITTEE SECRETARY ALOIS INDRA, KNOWN HERE AS A LEADER OF THE CONSERVATIVE FACTION, SAID IN A SPEECH BEFORE THE PARA-MILITARY ORGANIZATION SVAZARM THAT "RIGHTWING OPPORTUNISTS" MUST BE DEFEATED WITH "A CADRE POLICY BASED ON FIRM PRINCIPLES." IN COMMUNIST TERMINOLOGY A CADRE POLICY MEANS DISCIPLINE OF PARTY MEMBERS, USUALLY EXPULSION.

"BUT LET US CONSTANTLY BEAR IN MIND WE ARE DOING POLITICS AND NOT CARRYING OUT AN ADMINISTRATIVE PURGE," INDRA SAID. "LET US NOT FORGET IT IS A POLITICAL STRUGGLE WHICH MUST NOT TAKE THE FORM OF AN AUTHORITARIAN REPRESSION."

ANOTHER CONSERVATIVE, MILOS JAKES, CALLED IN A SPEECH THURSDAY FOR "THE EXPULSION OF RIGHTIST OPPORTUNIST FORCES FROM THE POLITICAL ARENA."

NIGHT LD

BY DUSKO DODER

MOSCOW (UPI)--THE SOVIET UNION SATURDAY URGED PEKING

TORESUME NEGOTIATIONS ON THEIR BORDER DISPUTES BUT

FIRMLY REJECTED ALL CHINESE TERRITORIAL CLAIMS.

THE SOVIET GOVERNMENT, IN A NOTE TO PEKING, SAID

BORDER TALKS SHOULD BEGIN IN MOSCOW "WITHIN THE NEXT

TWO-THREE MONTHS."

CHINA AGREED IN PRINCIPLE TO ENTER BORDER TALKS WHEN

IT REPLIED TO EARLIER SOVIET BIDS MAY 24. SINCE THEN

NEW FRONTIER CLASHES ON THE SINO-SOVIET BORDER WERE

REPORTED AND EACH SIDE BLAMED THE OTHER FOR PROVOKING

THEM.

THE LATEST SOVIET NOTE, DELIVERED TO THE CHINESE

EMBASSY HERE FRIDAY AND PUBLISHED BY THE NEWS AGENCY

TASS SATURDAY, WAS MILD IN TONE. IT WAS SEEN HERE AS AN

ATTEMPT TO IMPRESS WORLD COMMUNIST CONFERENCE DELEGATES

WITH THE KREMLIN'S READINESS TO NEGOTIATE ITS PROBLEMS

WITH PEKING.

EARLIER THIS WEEK, THE SOVIET FOREIGN MINISTRY

DESCRIBED THE BORDER INCIDENTS AS AN EFFORT BY PEKING

"TO POISON THE GOOD ATMOSPHERE" AT THE SUMMIT. CHINA IS

LEADING A BOYCOTT OF THE KREMLIN SESSION.

THE SOVIET NOTE DESCRIBED AS "ABSURD" CHINESE CLAIMS
ON 940,000 SQUARE MILES OF TERRITORY IN SOVIET SIBERIA
AND CENTRAL ASIA. IT THEN GAVE A LENGTHY ACCOUNT OF
DIPLOMATIC AND ETHNIC HISTORY OF THESE AREAS.

COL. GEN. PAVEL I. ZYRYANOV, CHIEF OF THE MAIN
ADMINISTRATION OF THE BORDER TROOPS OF THE STATE SECURITY
COMMITTEE (SECRET POLICE), WAS APPOINTED MOSCOW'S TOP
NEGOTIATOR IN EXPECTED BORDER TALKS WITH CHINA.

CZECHS 6/15 NX

NIGHT LD

BY GERD KRIWANEK

PRAGUE (UPI)--CAECHOSLOVAKIA ANNOUNCED STEPS SUNDAY
TO RESUME CULTURAL TIES WITH NEIGHBORING COMMUNIST
NATIONS THAT INVADED THIS COUNTRY LAST AUGUST.

THE NEWS AGENCY CTK LISTED A SERIES OF ART
EXHIBITIONS, GUEST CONCERTS AND THEATER PERFORMANCES OF
ARTISTS FROM THE FIVE WARSAW PACT COUNTRIES TO BE HELD
IN CZECHOSLOVAKIA DURING 1969 AND 1970.

HOWEVER, THE ATTEMPT AT CULTURAL RECONCILIATION
APPARENTLY STILL WAS ONE-WAY. THE ANNOUNCEMENT SAID
NOTHING ABOUT ANY GUEST PERFORMANCES OR EXHIBITIONS BY
CZECHOSLOVAK ARTISTS IN THE INVADER NATIONS.

384

SINCE THE INVASION, NO CULTURAL EVENTS--NOT EVEN
FILMS--FROM THE FIVE INVADERS HAVE BEEN SCHEDULED IN
CZECHOSLOVAKIA.

ONLY LAST WEEK THE CZECHOSLOVAK AMBASSADOR TO THE
SOVIET UNION, VLADIMIR KOUCKY, A VETERAN COMMUNIST,
COMPLAINED THAT "AN ATMOSPHERE OF BOYCOTT PREVAILS ON
OUR PART" IN CULTURAL RELATIONS WITH THE SOVIET UNION.
HE SAID HE COULD LIST MASS CANCELLATIONS OF TRIPS TO
RUSSIA BY CZECHOSLOVAK MUSIC ENSEMBLES AND SOLOISTS AND
BY DELEGATIONS TO SOVIET CONGRESSES.

THE CTK ANNOUNCEMENT SAID THE EAST BERLIN SYMPHONY
RADIO ORCHESTRA AND THE CRACOW, POLAND, PHILHARMONIC
ORCHESTRA WILL PERFORM IN CZECHOSLOVAKIA. OTHER PLANNED
PERFORMANCES INCLUDED RECITALS BY BULGARIAN OPERA
SINGERS AND A TOUR BY THE MOSCOW VAKHTANGOV THEATER.

SINCE THE INVASION IN AUGUST, CZECHOSLOVAK ARTISTS
HAVE REFUSED TO PERFORM IN THE SOVIET UNION OR OTHER
WARSAW PACT COUNTRIES.

DAVID OISTRACH, THE SOVIET VIOLINIST, WAS THE ONLY
ARTIST FROM THE INVADER COUNTRIES WHO PERFORMED DURING
THIS SPRING'S PRAGUE MUSIC FESTIVAL. IN FORMER YEARS THE
COMMUNIST COOKNVV

FESTIVAL. IN FORMER YEARS THE COMMUNIST COUNTRIES SENT
MOST OF THEIR TOP ARTISTS TO THE FESTIVAL.

4 | News from the Middle East and Africa

DAMASCUS (AP)--THE IRAQI NEWS AGENCY SAYS EAST
GERMANY HAS REQUESTED FULL DIPLOMATIC RECOGNITION FROM
ALL ARAB STATES.

THE AGENCY SAYS THE REQUEST CAME IN A NOTE FROM THE
EAST GERMAN FOREIGN MINISTRY TO GOVERNMENTS OF ARAB
COUNTRIES WHICH SO FAR HAVE NOT RECOGNIZED THE ULBRICHT
REGIME.

IRAQ, SUDAN AND SYRIA WHICH HAVE RECOGNIZED ARE SAID
TO HAVE RECEIVED A COPY OF THE NOTE.

THE NOTE SAID ESTABLISHMENT OF NORMAL DIPLOMATIC
RELATIONS WOULD SET THE STAGE FOR THE MAXIMUM POLITICAL,
ECONOMIC AND CULTURAL COOPERATION BETWEEN EAST GERMANY
AND THE ARAB STATES.

THE AGENCY DID NOT MENTION BY NAME THE ARAB COUNTRIES
TO WHICH THE NOTE WAS DISPATCHED.

BUT THEY ARE BELIEVED TO BE EGYPT, ALGERIA, SOUTH
YEMEN, REPUBLICAN YEMEN, KUWAIT, JORDAN, LEBANON, LIBYA,
TUNISIA AND MOROCCO.

CAIRO (AP)--EGYPTIAN OFFICIALS IN CAIRO REPORTED A
SERIES OF GUN DUELS ACROSS THE SUEZ CANAL DURING
WEDNESDAY NIGHT AND THURSDAY. THEY SAID EGYPTIAN SHELLS
PREVENTED ISRAELI ENGINEERING UNITS FROM IMPROVING
THEIR DEFENSES IN A FOUR-HOUR EXCHANGE WHICH ENDED AT
3:30 A.M. THEY SAID THE DUEL BLAZED ALMOST THE LENGTH
OF THE 103-MILE WATERWAY, FROM ELTINA, 15 MILES SOUTH OF
PORT SAID, TO EL SHATT AND SHAFFOUFA, JUST NORTH OF PORT
SUEZ.

FIRING RESUMED AT ABOUT 4 P.M. IN THE SOUTHERN AND
MIDDLE SECTORS OF THE CANAL, AN EGYPTIAN MILITARY
SPOKESMAN SAID. HE SAID EGYPTIAN ARTILLERY DESTROYED
ISRAELI "FORTIFIED POSITIONS" IN "FIERCE AND HEAVY"
BARRAGES FROM PORT TEWFIK, AT THE SOUTHERN END OF THE
CANAL, TO DEVERSOIR IN THE SOUTHERN SECTOR AND EL FIRDAN,
NORTH OF ISMAILIA IN THE CENTRAL SECTOR.

BEIRUT, LEBANON (UPI)--APPROXIMATELY HALF OF THE
ARAB GUERRILLAS OCCUPYING SOUTH LEBANON HAVE WITHDRAWN,
AND MANY MORE ARE LEAVING DAILY, A LEADING RIGHT-WING
LEBANESE POLITICIAN SAID FRIDAY.

THE BEIRUT EVENING NEWSPAPER LISAN AL HAL QUOTED
SHEIKH PIERRE GEMAYEL, LEADER OF THE PRO-WESTERN

TRIPARTITE ALLIANCE, AS SAYING THE GUERRILLAS STARTED
PULLING OUT 18 DAYS AGO.

IF THE WITHDRAWAL CONTINUES, A NEW LEBANESE CABINET
CAN BE FORMED WITHIN DAYS, GEMAYEL SAID.

THERE WAS NO IMMEDIATE COMMENT FROM COMMANDO SOURCES.
BUT INFORMED OBSERVERS EXPRESSED DOUBT THAT THE GUERRILLAS
WERE LEAVING LEBANON IN ANY GREAT NUMBERS.

NO OFFICIAL FIGURES H

VE BEEN GIVEN, BUT IT WAS
BELIEVED THERE WERE ABOUT 3,000 GUERRILLAS IN SOUTH
LEBANON.

LEBANON HAS BEEN WITHOUT A GOVERNMENT FOR 56 DAYS AS
A RESULT OF RIOTS OVER THE ISSUE WHETHER LEBANON SHOULD
ACCEPT OR REJECT ARAB GUERRILLA FORCES ON ITS SOUTHERN
BORDER WITH ISRAEL.

IN THE NEWSPAPER INTERVIEW, GEMAYEL SAID THAT IF THE
GUERRILLA WITHDRAWAL CONTINUED, A NEW CABINET COULD BE
FORMED WITHIN 10 DAYS.

GEMAYEL ASCRIBED THE WITHDRAWAL LARGELY TO EGYPTIAN
MEDIATION.

HE RECALLED THAT EGYPTIAN PRESIDENT GAMAL ABDEL
NASSER'S PERSONAL ENVOY, HASSAN SABRY EL KHOLY, HAD BEEN
IN BEIRUT RECENTLY AND THAT YASSER ARAFAT, HEAD OF THE

ARAB AL FATAH COMMANDO ORGANIZATION, RECENTLY VISITED
CAIRO, SAUDI ARABIA AND SYRIA.

KARACHI, PAKISTAN (UPI)--THREE YOUNG ERITREAN
NATIONALISTS TOLD POLICE TODAY THEY ATTACKED AN
UNOCCUPIED ETHIOPIAN JETLINER WITH HAND GRENADES AND
SUBMACHINE GUNS TO DRAMATIZE THEIR OPPOSITION TO
ETHIOPIAN RULE OF THE PROVINCE.

A FUEL TANK AND THE RIGHT WING OF THE ADDIS ABABA-
TO-NEW DELHI BOEING 720 WERE SET ABLAZE AND SEVERLY
DAMAGED IN THE ATTACK WEDNESDAY NIGHT AT KARACHI
AIRPORT. NO INJURIES WERE REPORTED.

THE PLANE'S 13 PASSENGERS AND CREW HAD LEFT THE
CRAFT ON A STOPOVER ABOUT 30 MINUTES EARLIER.

"WE ACTED UNDER ORDERS TO SABOTAGE ETHIOPIAN AIRLINE
FLIGHTS," THE POLICE QUOTED THE YOUTHS, ALL UNDER 22.

POLICE ARRESTED MOHAMMAD IDRIS, ALI ABDULLAH AND
FAZAHAL ABRAHAM A FEW MINUTES AFTER THEY OPENED FIRE AT
THE PLANE. THEY TOLD POLICE THEY WERE MEMBERS OF THE
ERITREAN LIBERATION FRONT AND WERE STUDENTS AT THE
AMERICAN UNIVERSITY IN BEIRUT, LEBANON.

REPRESENTATIVES OF THE FRONT HAVE RECENTLY TOURED
MOSLEM COUNTRIES IN AN EFFORT TO DRUM UP SUPPORT FOR

389

INDEPENDENCE FOR MOSLEM ERITREA FROM COPTIC CHRISTIAN
ETHIOPIA. THE AREA BECAME A PROVINCE OF ETHIOPIA IN
1962.

ACCORDING TO POLICE, THE THREE ATTACKERS ARRIVED IN
KARACHI ON MONDAY. IT WAS NOT IMMEDIATELY DETERMINED
WHETHER THEY BROUGHT THE GUNS AND GRENADES FROM LEBANON
OR ACQUIRED THEM HERE, AUTHORITIES SAID.

ERITREA FORMS THE COASTAL STRIP OF ETHIOPIA ALONG THE
RED SEA, PROVIDING ETHIOPIA'S ONLY OUTLET TO THE SEA.
THE LIBERATION FRONT CLAIMS THE GOVERNMENT OF EMPEROR
HAILE SELASSIE HAS CONDUCTED MASS MURDER AMONG THE
MOSLEMS WHO FORM 70 PER CENT OF ERITREA'S 2.5 MILLION
POPULATION.

ERITREA WAS AN ITALIAN COLONY FROM 1890 UNTIL 1941.
IT WAS ADMINISTERED BY BRITAIN AFTER THE WAR UNTIL 1952
WHEN THE UNITED NATIONS ORDERED IT FEDERATED WITH
ETHIOPIA. ERITREA FINALLY LOST ALL TRACES OF AUTONOMY
IN 1962 WHEN ETHIOPIA ENDED ITS FEDERATION STATUS AND
MADE IT A PROVINCE.

INSERT ERITREA KARACHI 052A AFTER 4TH PGH XXX UNDER 22.

(IN DAMASCUS, A SPOKESMAN FOR THE ERITREAN LIBERATION
FRONT (ELF) SAID THE FRONT WOULD ESCALATE ITS CAMPAIGN OF

VIOLENCE AGAINST ETHIOPIA "UNTIL THE LAST ETHIOPIAN
SOLDIER IS EVACUATED FROM ERITREAN SOIL."

(THE SPOKESMAN SAID THE ATTACK AGAINST THE PLANE IN
KARACHI WAS STAGED BY THE AL-IKAB (PUNISHMENT) GUERRILLA
UNIT "IN REVENGE FOR SAVAGE ATTACKS BY AGGRESSIVE
ETHIOPIAN FORCES AGAINST UNARMED INNOCENT CITIZENS IN...
ERITREA."

PICKUP 5TH PGH: POLICE

NIGERIA (UPI)--THE FEDERAL GOVERNMENT OF NIGERIA HAS
ANNOUNCED THAT ITS TROOPS HAVE CAPTURED UMUAHIA
(OO-MAH'-HEE-AH)--THE CAPITAL OF REBEL BIAFRA. THE CITY
HAD BEEN UNDER ARTILLERY ATTACK FOR MORE THAN AWEEK.

OFFICIALS IN LAGOS (LAH'-GUHS), NIGERIA PREDICT THE
VICTORY COULD LEAD TO A QUICK END TO THE 22-MONTH-OLD
CIVIL WAR.

REPORTEDLY, THE BIAFRAN LEADER HAS FLED INTO THE BUSH
COUNTRY WITH HIS IBO (EE-BOH) TRIBE FOLLOWERS TO TRY TO
FIGHT A GUERRILLA WAR. HE HAS ONLY ONE SMALL AIRSTRIP
LEFT, AND FEDERAL FORCES WERE BELIEVED MOVING IN ON IT.

BISSAU, PORTUGUESE GUINEA (UPI)--PORTUGUESE FORCES KILLED 17 COMMUNIST GUERRILLAS, WOUNDED SEVERAL OTHERS AND CAPTURED NINE IN A RECENT OPERATION, THE ARMY SAID SUNDAY.

AN ARMY COMMUNIQUE SAID SECURITY FORCES ALSO CAPTURED TWO TONS OF ARMS, INCLUDING AUTOMATIC WEAPONS, MORTARS, AMMUNITION AND EXPLOSIVES.

A COMMUNIST-LED FRONT, CALLED THE AFRICAN PARTY FOR THE INDEPENDENCE OF GUINEA AND CAPE VERDE, HAS BEEN WAGING WAR AGAINST THE PORTUGUESE SINCE 1963. PORTUGUESE LOSSES ARE ESTIMATED AT ABOUT 680 DEAD.

LUSAKA, ZAMBIA (AP)--OBSERVERS IN LUSAKA SAY THE ZAMBIAN GOVERNMENT IS MORE WORRIED ABOUT TUESDAY'S NATIONWIDE REFERENDUM THAN IT HAS BEEN ABOUT ANY OTHER ISSUE SINCE INDEPENDENCE, FIVE YEARS AGO.

THE REFERENDUM, IF CARRIED, WILL MAKE IT EASIER FOR THE GOVERNMENT TO CHANGE ENTRENCHED CLAUSES IN THE CONSTITUTION, DEALING WITH FUNDAMENTAL RIGHTS AND THE JUDICIARY.

BUT IF THE ELECTORATE REJECTS THE PROPOSALS--WHICH OBSERVERS SEEM TO THINK IS MORE THAN JUST POSSIBLE--AT LEAST ONE MEMBER OF PRESIDENT KENNETH KAUNDA'S RULING

UNITED INDEPENDENCE PARTY HAS PREDICTED "CHAOS."

HOWEVER, IF THE PROPOSALS IN THE REFERENDUM ARE
CARRIED, KAUNDA SAYS HEHAS ONE OTHER STEP IMMEDIATELY IN
MIND--TO SEIZE UNDEVELOPED LAND OWNED BY NON-RESIDENT
WHITES.

THE LAND IN QUESTION COMPRISES 92 FARMS COVERING 625
SQUARE MILES.

THE OPPOSITION AFRICAN NATIONAL CONGRESS IS
CAMPAIGNING FOR A "NO" VOTE. IN ITS STRONGHOLD OF THE
SOUTHERN PROVINCE IT IS PLAYING ON THE FEARS OF THE
VILLAGERS THAT THEIR CATTLE, LAND AND EVEN WIVES WILL BE
TAKEN AWAY FROM THEM IF THE REFERENDUM IS PASSEDM

HOWEVER, ELSEWHERE IN THE COUNTRY, FEW PEOPLE SEEM TO
KNOW, FAR LESS TO CARE WHAT THE ISSUES ARE ABOUT.

THE GOVERNMENT HAS SOUGHT TO GENERATE A GREAT DEAL OF
EMOTION OVER THEIR REFERENDUM IN AN ATTEMPT TO OVERCOME
THIS APATHY.

ANOTHER FEAR IS THAT ALL OPPOSITION WILL BE BANNED IF
THE REFERENDUM IS CARRIED. AND IN FACT ONE PROVINCIAL
CABINET MINISTER DID THREATEN TO BAN AN OPPOSITION LEADER
FROM THE COUNTRY'S WESTERN PROVINCE IF THE REFERENDUM
SUCCEEDS.

MEANWHILE, KAUNDA HAS SAID THE GOVERNMENT WILL NOT

PAY "A SINGLE PENNY" FOR LAND OWNED BY ABSENTEE LANDLORDS.

THE COUNTRY'S 65,000 RESIDENT WHITES HAVE ALSO BEEN WORRIED--BY THE BLUNT STATEMENT OF THE INFORMATION MINISTER THAT "NO EUROPEAN SHOULD OWN LAND IN ZAMBIA."

ONE SENIOR CABINET SPOKESMAN ALSO HAS SPELLED OUT IN DETAIL PROPOSALS TO LIMIT THE VAST PROSPECTING RIGHTS HELD BY THE GIANT FOREIGN-OWNED COPPER MINING COMPANIES THAT OPERATE IN ZAMBIA."

AND THE FOREIGN MINISTER HAS SAID THE REFERENDUM, IF SUCCESSFUL, WILL ENABLE THE GOVERNMENT TO SEIZE CERTAIN EX-PATRIOT OWNED SHOPS.

BEIRUT (BAY-ROOT) (UPI)--LEBANESE PRESIDENT CHARLES HELOU HAS ACCEPTED THE RESIGNATION OF THE 12-WEEK-OLD GOVERNMENT OF PREMIER KARAMI. THE PREMIER AND HIS CABINET QUIT AFTER TWO DAYS OF ANTI-GOVERNMENT RIOTING THAT KILLED 17 PERSONS AND INJURED 116 THE RIOTING WAS LED BY THOUSANDS OF PALESTINIAN REFUGEES, DEMANDING GOVERNMENT SUPPORT FOR ARAB COMMANDOS STRIKING INTO ISRAEL FROM LEBANON.

BY JAMES KIM

SEOUL, KOREA (UPI)--SOUTH KOREAN GUNBOATS, TROOPS AND PLANES CAPTURED A NORTH KOREAN SPEEDBOAT TRYING TO RENDEZVOUS WITH A COMMUNIST SPY IN AN HOUR-LONG GUNBATTLE OFF THE NATION'S WEST COAST, THE KOREAN CENTRAL. INTELLIGENCE AGENCY SAID TODAY.

THE AGENCY SAID THE NORTH KOREAN VESSEL LAUNCHED A RUBBER BOAT WITH THREE MEN ABOARD LATE THURSDAY NIGHT TO TRY TO PICK UP KIM YONG-KU, 39, A NORTH KOREAN ARRESTED ON SPY CHARGES BY SOUTH KOREANS MAY 30.

AT THAT POINT, SOUTH KOREAN ARMY, NAVY AND AIR FORCE UNITS ATTACKED. THERE WERE NO REPORTS OF SURVIVORS AMONG THE 15 MEN ABOARD THE NORTH KOREAN BOAT.

THE AGENCY GAVE NO DETAILS OF THE BATTLE. IT SAID BEFORE HIS CAPTURE, THE SUSPECTED SPY HAD USED A RADIO IN REPORTING INFORMATION TO THE COMMUNISTS.

DONG-A ILBO, SOUTH KOREA'S LARGEST NEWSPAPER, SAID SOUTH KOREAN FORCES HAD ADVANCE INFORMATION ABOUT THE COMMUNIST VESSEL AND WERE WAITING FOR IT. THE SEOUL TROOPS SUFFERED NO CASUALTIES.

THE INTELLIGENCE AGENCY SAID THE 75-FOOT, 60-TON

VESSEL COULD TRAVEL 35 KNOTS AND WAS EQUIPPED WITH FOUR
ENGINES AND ARMED WITH AN 82 MM GUN, FOUR 40 MM GUNS, TWO
14 MM ANTIAIRCRAFT GUNS, TWO HEAVY AND THREE LIGHT
MACHINEGUNS, EIGHT SUBMACHINEGUNS, FIVE PISTOLS AND TWO
ANTITANK GRENADES.

THE GUNBATTLE ERUPTED NEAR HUKSAN ISLAND, 70 MILES
OFF THE WEST COAST OF SOUTH KOREA IN THE YELLOW SEA.

A SOUTH KOREAN PATROL BOAT SPOTTED THE COMMUNIST
BOAT, DISGUISED AS A FISHING BOAT, AND RADIOED FOR AIR
FORCE SUPPORT. PLANES DROPPED FLARES AND NAVAL VESSELS
OPENED FIRE, THE INTELLIGENCE AGENCY SAID.

WHILE BEING TOWED TO PORT, THE NORTH KOREAN SPEEDBOAT
SANK BUT WAS RECOVERED, THE AGENCY SAID.

THE NORTH KOREAN BOAT LEFT THE NORTH KOREAN PORT OF
CHINNAMPO ON WEDNESDAY TO TRY TO PICK UP THE SPY AND
RETURN HIM TO NORTH KOREA, THE AGENCY SAID.

ON AUG. 21 LAST YEAR, A NORTH KOREAN SPEEDBOAT
CARRYING 14 COMMANDOS TRIED TO CONTACT ANOTHER COMMUNIST
AGENT ON THE ISLAND OF CHEJU, 55 MILES OFF SOUTH KOREA'S
SOUTHERN COAST ON A SIMILAR MISSION.

SOUTH KOREAN TROOPS KILLED 12 OF THE COMMUNIST
COMMANDOS AND CAPTURED TWO OF THEM AFTER SEVERAL HOURS OF
FIGHTING.

LAST SUNDAY, SOUTH KOREAN TROOPS SANK A RUBBER BOAT
TRYING TO LAND THREE COMMUNIST AGENTS NEAR BUKPVONG, 115
MILES EAST OF SEOUL. WHEN THE RUBBER CRAFT CAME UNDER
ATTACK, THE MOTHER VESSEL FIRED A SHELL THAT SMASHED INTO
A HOUSE ON SHORE AND KILLED FIVE MEMBERS OF A FAMILY.

EIGHT COMMUNIST AGENTS LANDED AT CHUMUNJIM 40 MILES
NORTH OF BUKPVONG MARCH 16 AND ATTACKED A POLICE
CHECKPOINT, KILLING A SOUTH KOREAN POLICEMAN. ALL EIGHT
WERE LATER KILLED BY SOUTH KOREAN TROOPS.

SAN FRANCISCO (UPI)--JAPAN AND THE UNITED STATES TOOK
A STEP TOWARD INCREASED COOPERATION IN TRADE AND
INVESTMENT DURING A THREE-DAY CONFERENCE BETWEEN THE TWO
NATIONS' TOP BUSINESS LEADERS.

THE SIXTH JAPAN-U.S. BUSINESSMEN'S CONFERENCE ENDED
FRIDAY WITH A JOINT COMMUNIQUE IN WHICH THE TWO
DELEGATIONS FORECAST A WIDE OPEN INTERNATIONAL TRADING AND
INVESTMENT MARKET BENEFICIAL TO THE ECONOMIES OF BOTH
COUNTRIES.

THOUGH THE 50 DELEGATES WERE PRIVATE BUSINESSMEN AND
NOT GOVERNMENT OFFICIALS, THEY HAVE GREAT INFLUENCE ON
THEIR RESPECTIVE GOVERNMENTS.

THERE WERE SEVERAL POINTS OF CONTENTION, PARTICULARLY

FROM THE UNITED STATES. THE AMERICAN DELEGATION WANTED
THE JAPANESE TO FAVOR LIFTING JAPAN'S QUOTAS ON AMERICAN
IMPORTS.

"JAPAN IS NO LONGER THE NATION OF THE RISING SUN. IT
IS NOW THE NATION OF THE RISEN SUN," SAID JENKIN LOYD
JONES, LEADER OF THE AMERICAN DELEGATION AND PRESIDENT OF
THE U.S. CHAMBER OF COMMERCE.

THE JAPANESE REPRESENTATIVES AGREED TO SUPPORT A
"LIBERALIZATION" OF THE QUOTAS, BUT DECLINED TO BACK
COMPLETE REMOVAL.

KOGORO UEMURA, LEADER OF THE JAPANESE DELEGATION, SAID
IMPORT RESTRICTIONS ARE NEEDED TO PERMIT "SMALL
COMPANIES" TO DEVELOP, PARTICULARLY IN THE AGREA OF
AGRICULTURE.

"WE ARE WORKING WITH OUR GOVERNMENT TO LIBERALIZE
JAPAN'S TRADE BARRIERS, UEMURA SAID, "AND WE EMPHASIZE
THAT THE UNITED STATES SHOULD NOT ADOPT ANY PROTECTIONIST
MEASURES" IN RETALIATION.

BUT JONES SAID THE JAPANESE IMPORT QUOTAS HAVE
RESULTED IN A TRADE IMBALANCE, WITH AMERICAN BUYING $1
MILLION MORE GOODS FROM JAPAN THAN VICE VERSA.

"IF THE TRADE IMBALANCE IS NOT ALLEVIATED SOON, THERE
COULD BE AN UNFAVORABLE REACTION IN CONGRESS, SUCH AS FLAT

RESTRICTIONS ON IMPORTS, SMALLER IMPORT QUOTAS OR
RETALIATORY TARIFFS," JONES WARNED.

KUALA LUMPUR, MALAYSIA (UPI)--PRIME MINISTER TENKU
ABDUL RAHMAN WAS RELEASED FROM UNIVERSITY HOSPITAL SUNDAY
NIGHT AFTER A SUCCESSFUL EYE OPERATION. HE WAS ADMITTED
FOR SURGERY LAST FRIDAY. DOCTORS SAID RAHMAN WOULD BE
ABLE TO RESUME FULL DUTIES IN ABOUT A MONTH.

BANGKOK, THAILAND (UPI)--A CHOLERA OUTBREAK IN
NORTHEAST THAILAND'S UBON PROVINCE EASED SLIGHTLY SUNDAY
AND U.S. AIRMEN AT THE AMERICAN BASE THERE HAVE BEEN
ALLOWED TO LEAVE THE INSTALLATION FOR THE FIRST TIME IN
11 DAYS. SIX PERSONS HAVE DIED IN THE OUTBREAK.

TOKYO (UPI)--MME. RATNA SARI DEWI SUKARNO, NO. 3 WIFE
OF FORMER INDONESIAN PRESIDENT SUKARNO, SUNDAY DENIED
PRESS REPORTS LINKING HER ROMANTICALLY WITH MASAKIKO
TSUGAWA, A JAPANESE ACTOR. "I NEVER SAID WE WERE IN LOVE
WITH EACH," SHE SAID BEFORE BOARDING A PLANE FOR HONG
KONG. "HE (TSUGAWA) IS JUST A GOOD FRIEND OF MINE."

HONG KONG (UPI)--THREE GENERATIONS OF ONE FAMILY
ESCAPED TO HONG KONG FROM COMMUNIST CHINA SUNDAY. THEY
WERE IDENTIFIED AS A 47-YEAR-OLD FARMER, HIS SON, HIS
DAUGHTER-IN-LAW AND HIS 6-MONTHS-OLD GRANDDAUGHTER. THE
FAMILY ESCAPED IN A SAMPAN ACROSS THE SHAMCHUN RIVER.

SEOUL, SOUTH KOREA (UPI)--THE DONG-A RADIO STATION
SAID SUNDAY A BUDDHIST MONK BURNED HIMSELF TO DEATH TO
DEMONSTRATE HIS FAITH. THE VICTIM WAS IDENTIFIED AS LEE
YOUNG HWA, 38. HE WAS REPORTED TO HAVE DIED ON A PILE OF
BURNING WOOD IN THE TOWN OF YESAN, 60 MILES SOUTH OF
SEOUL.

PHNOM PENH, CAMBODIA (UPI)--THE VIET CONG'S
"PROVISIONAL REVOLUTIONARY GOVERNMENT" OF SOUTH VIETNAM
PLEDGED TODAY TO RESPECT "THE INDEPENDENCE,
SOVEREIGNTY AND NEUTRALITY" OF NEIGHBORING CAMBODIA.

THE PLEDGE CAME FROM NGUYEN VAN HIEU, FORMERLY
AMBASSADOR IN PHNOM PENH OF THE VIET CONG'S NATIONAL
LIBERATION FRONT (NLF). FOLLOWING CAMBODIA'S RECOGNITION
OF THE PROVISIONAL GOVERNMENT, HE PRESENTED NEW
CREDENTIALS TO CHIEF OF STATE PRINCE NORODOM SIHANOUK

TODAY.

SIHANOUK BROKE WITH THE SAIGON GOVERNMENT AND
RECOGNIZED THE VIET CONG WHEN SOUTH VIETNAM REFUSED TO
GIVE UP ITS CLAIM TO COASTAL ISLANDS OFF THE CAMBODIAN
PORT OF KEP.

ANCHORAGE, ALASKA (UPI)--TWO JAPANESE FISHING BOAT
SKIPPERS WERE FINED A TOTAL OF $9,000 LATE THURSDAY AFTER
PLEADING "NO CONTEST" TO CHARGES OF OPERATING ILLEGALLY
IN U.S. FISHING WATERS.

JUDGE JAMES A. VON DER HEIDT OF U.S. DISTRICT COURT
FINED KENJI OKAWA $5,500. THE ZENPU MARU-8, HIS 90-FOOT
CATCHER BOAT, WAS SEIZED AFTER THREE SHOTS WERE FIRED
ACROSS HER BOW BY THE COAST GUARD CUTTER STORIS IN NORTON
SOUND.

KATSUJI KAWAMOTO, THE SKIPPER OF THE OTHER VESSEL, THE
F.S. 2-2105, WAS FINED $3,500. THE FINES WERE PAID A FEW
MINUTES AFTER SENTENCING.

BOTH WERE RETURNED TO NOME AND WERE FREE TO RESUME
FISHING WITH THE JAPANESE FLEET IN THE BERING SEA.

THE TWO HAD PLEADED INNOCENT WHEN ARRAIGNED BUT
CHANGED THEIR PLEAS TO "NO CONTEST" SHORTLY BEFORE BEING
TRIED.

PHNOM PENH (UPI)--PRINCE NORODOM SIHANOUK OF CAMBODIA
REAFFIRMED WEDNESDAY HIS NATION'S FRIENDSHIP WITH
COMMUNIST CHINA AND VOWED TO CONTINUE WHAT HE CALLED THE
BATTLE AGAINST AMERICAN IMPERIALISM.

THE CAMBODIAN CHIEF OF STATE SPOKE IN CEREMONIES IN
WHICH HE ACCEPTED THE CREDENTIALS OF PEKING'S NEW
AMBASSADOR TO PHNOM PENH, KANG MAO TCHAU, WHO CONDEMNED
THE U.S. ROLE IN VIETNAM.

"THE GOVERNMENT AND THE PEOPLE OF CHINA RESPECT AND
SUPPORT RESOLUTELY THE KHMER (CAMBODIAN) PEOPLE," THE
AMBASSADOR SAID.

SIHANOUK TOLD HIM "CAMBODIA'S POLICY REMAINS UNCHANGED
IN REGARD TO ITS BATTLE AGAINST AMERICAN IMPERIALISTS AND
NEO-COLONIALISTS. CAMBODIA WILL REMAIN CHINA'S MOST
FAITHFUL FRIEND."

TOKYO (UPI)--AN EARTH QUAKE DESCRIBED AS FAIRLY STRONG
ROCKED PARTS OF JAPAN'S NORTHERMOST ISLAND OF HOKKAIDO AT
3:41 P.M. FRIDAY, BUT NO CASUALTIES OR DAMAGE WERE REPORTED.

KUALA LUMPUR, MALAYSIA (UPI)--A THAI BORDER PATROL
CLASHED WITH MALAY GUERRILLAS SATURDAY NIGHT IN DENSE,

TROPICAL JUNGLE IN SOUTHWEST THAILAND, A GOVERNMENT
SPOKESMAN SAID SUNDAY.

ONE THAI POLICEMAN WAS SLIGHTLY WOUNDED IN THE BRIEF
SKIRMISH, SPOKESMEN ADDED. GUERILLAS CASUALTIES WERE NOT
KNOWN.

THE INCIDENT WAS EIGHT MILES INSIDE THAI TERRITORY
AND ABOUT 260 MILES NORTHWEST OF KUALA LUMPUR.

MALAYSIA, WHERE BITTER CHINESE-MALAY RACIAL FIGHTING
OCCURRED LAST MONTH, HAS SAID GUERRILLAS MAY BE TAKING
ADVANTAGE OF THE UNSTABLE SITUATION TO MOVE BACK INTO
MALAYSIA FROM THEIR FOREST HAVENS.

6 | News from Latin American Nations

MIAMI (UPI)--THE COAST GUARD SENT TWO HELICOPTERS AND
AN AIRPLANE MONDAY TO PICKUP FOUR SURVIVORS OF A SHIP
BOILER ROOM BLAST THAT KILLED FOUR OTHER MEN.

A SPOKESMAN SAID THE BLAST LCCURRED SUNDAY NIGHT AND
DISABLED THE VESSEL, IDENTIFIED AS THE 287-FOOT VICTORIA
OF DOMINICAN REGISTRY. IT WAS OFF THE COAST OF CUBA AT
THE TIME.

A COAST GUARD SPOKESMAN IDENTIFIED THE FOUR DEAD MEN
AS ROBERTO LINAREA, 39, GUATAMALA; MAURO REYS, 36, OF
CRUZ, DOMINICAN REPUBLIC, RAFAEL BRITO, 29, MORBEL,

DOMINICAN REPUBLICA, AND JOAGUIN DAMAS, 51, OF HAITI.

CRITICALLY INJURED WAS NIANO PAUL, 31, OF HAITI. LESS

SEVERELY HURT WERE FELIX ARAUJO, 32, ADOLFO PEREZ, 33, AND

LEONARTO MATOS, ALL OF THE DOMINICAN REPUBLIC.

THERE WAS NO WORD FROM THE SHIP OR ITS AGENTS AS TO

WHAT WOULD BE DONE FOR THE SHIP, REPORTED DISABLED AND

WITHOUT POWER 15 MILES OFF THE NORTHEAST COAST OF CUBA, THE

SPOKESMAN SAID.

THE COAST GUARD SENT TWO HELICOPTERS TO TAKE THE

INJURED MEN FROM THE VESSEL TO GREAT EXUMA ISLAND IN THE

BAHAMAS FOR TRANSFER TO AN AIRPLANE AND A FLIGHT TO MIAMI.

CAUSE OF THE EXPLOSION WAS NOT KNOWN. THE COAST GUARD

SAID IT HAD RECEIVED ONLY THE BRIEFIEST OF REPORTS ABOUT

THE INCIDENT FROM ANOTHER VESSEL IN THE AREA.

CARACAS, VENEZUELA (UPI)--THE $600,000 HOLDUP OF A

BANK AT PUERTO LA CRUZ WEDNESDAY WAS THE WORK OF CASTROITE

GUERRILLAS WHO HAVE REJECTED PLEAS FOR PEACE FROM THE

GOVERNMENT OF PRESIDENT RAFAEL CALDERA, GOVERNMENT OFFICIALS

SAID TODAY.

FOUR GUNMEN HELD UP A BRANCH OF THE ROYAL BANK OF

CANADA AT PUERTO LA CRUZ IN THE LARGEST BANK ROBBERY IN

THE NATION'S HISTORY. IT WAS THE FIRST GUERRILLA RAID

SINCE FEBRUARY WHEN GUERRILLAS AMBUSHED AN ARMY CONVOY AND KILLED FOUR SOLDIERS.

GUERRILLAS WERE ALSO SIGHTED NEAR THE TURIMIQUIRE MOUNTAINS 285 MILES EAST OF CARACAS AND OTHER INSURGENTS ATTACKED THE WESTERN TOWN LA ACURITA.

CALDERA HAD URGED THE GUERRILLAS TO LAY DOWN THEIR ARMS IN HIS MARCH 11 INAUGURAL ADDRESS. THE APPARENT COLLAPSE OF THE GOVERNMENT'S PACIFICATION PROGRAM WAS THE SECOND MAJOR POLITICAL SETBACK FOR THE CALDERA ADMINISTRATION.

THE FIRST WAS LAST MONTH WHEN VENEZUELA WAS SQUEEZED OUT OF THE SUBREGIONALANDES PACT

THE FIRST WAS LAST MONTH WHEN VENEZUELA WAS SQUEEZED OUT OF THE SUBREGIONAL ANDES PACT INTEGRATION AGREEMENT BY FIVE OTHER MEMBER NATIONS WHO REFUSED TO GRANT A SERIES OF CLAUSES PROTECTING VENEZUELAN INDUSTRIES.

BOGOTA, COLOMBIA (UPI)--A COLOMBIAN DC3 AIRLINER WITH 30 PERSONS ABOARD WAS HIJACKED IN FLIGHT OVER EASTERN COLOMBIA FRIDAY AND FORCED TO FLY TO CUBA.

THE TWIN-ENGINED, PROP-DRIVEN TRANSPORT OPERATED BY 7RRACA -IRLINE WAS SEIZED BY THREE MEN AND A WOMAN WHILE

405

ON AN INTERIOR FLIGHT SCHEDULE BETWEEN ;ILLAVICENCIO AND

CUCUTA. IT HAD TO MAKE UNSCHEDULED STOPS AT BARRANCABERMEJA

AND BARRANQUILLA TO TAKE ON ENOUGH FUEL TO COMPLETE THE

FLIGHT TO CUBA.

IT WAS THE 29TH HIJACKING IN THE WESTERN HEMISPHERE

THIS YEAR AND THE 11TH OF A LATIN AERICAN AIRLINER. THE

REST OF THE HIJACKED AIRCRAFT HAVE BEEN U. S. COMMERCIAL

TRANSPORTS.

COLOMBIAN OFFICIALS MADE NO EFFORT TO HALT THE HIJACK

AT EITHER BARRANCABERMEJA OR BARRANQUILLA, NOT WISHING TO

JEOPARDIZE THE LIVES OF THE 25 PASSENGERS AND FIVE

CREWMEN ABOARD. LIFEJACKETS WERE PUT ABOARD THE DC3 AT

BARRANQUILLA BECAUSE OF THE FIVE-HOUR FLIGHT OVER THE

CARIBBEAN TO SANTIAGO, CUBA.

THE LAST HIJACKING IN THE AMERICAS OCCURRED JUNE 12

WHEN A MAN HIJACKED A TWA FLIGHT BETWEEN OAKLAND, CALIF.,

AND NEW YORK IN THE LONGEST--2,700 AIRLINE MILES--HIJACK

TO DATE.

THE LAST COLOMBIAN AIRLINER TO BE HIJACKED WAS MAY 20

WHE FOUR MEN HIJACKED AN AVIANCA JETLINER ON A FLIGHT

BETWEEN BOGOTA AND PEREIRA.

NEW YORK (UPI)--THE FREEDOM OF THE PRESS COMMITTEE OF THE INTER AMERICAN PRESS ASSOCIATION CALLED ON THE GOVERNMENT OF PARAGUAY WEDNESDAY TO FREE A WEEKLY NEWSPAPER EDITOR WHO WAS JAILED AFTER CRITICIZING THE MINISTER OF THE INTERIOR.

IN A CABLE TO PRESIDENT ALFREDO STROESSNER, TOM C. HARRIS, CHAIRMAN OF THE COMMITTEE, SAID, "WE ARE DEEPLY CONCERNED BY REPORTS THAT OFFICERS OF YOUR GOVERNMENT ARRESTED, HELD INCOMMUNICADO AND STILL HAVE IN CUSTODY CARLOS PAPPALARDO, ASSOCIATE EDITOR AND MANAGER OF THE WEEKLY NEWSPAPER LA LIBERTAD OF ASUNCION, AFTER HIS PAPER PUBLISHED CHARGES AGAINST THE MINISTER OF THE INTERIOR.

"I WOULD APPRECIATE IT IF YOU WOULD USE YOUR GOOD OFFICES TO INVESTIGATE THIS CASE AND SEE THAT SENOR PAPPALARDO IS GIVEN HIS FREEDOM SO HE CAN RETURN TO HIS NEWSPAPER WORK," HARRIS SAID.

LA LIBERTAD IS THE ORGAN OF THE OPPOSITION LIBERAL PARTY, AND THE PARTY LEADER, CARLOS LEVI, SAID THE ACTION AGAINST THE EDITOR WAS A CLEAR VIOLATION OF PRESS FREEDOM.

BUT PASTOR CORONEL, CHIEF ASUNCION POLICE INVESTIGATOR, SAID PAPPALARDO WAS ARRESTED FOR COMMON CRIMES, MOST IMPORTANTLY THE KIDNAPING OF JOSE BENCHIMOL, AN ARGENTINE BUSINESSMAN WHO WAS BORN IN PARAGUAY.

BENCHIMOL, ACCORDING TO HARRIS, SENT CABLES TO
PARAGUAYAN AUTHORITIES DENYING THAT PAPPALARDO HAD
KIDNAPED HIM AND CHARGED THREE PARAGUAYANS ACTUALLY
KIDNAPED HIM.

SANTIAGO, CHILE (UPI)--THE SECOND BILL IN 24 HOURS
SEEKING NATIONALIZATION OF EXPROPRIATION OF ANACONDA
COPPER CO. MINES IN CHILE WAS PRESENTED TO THE CHAMBER OF
DEPUTIES FRIDAY.

ONE WAS SPONSORED BY RADICAL PARTY DEPUTIES AND THE
OTHER BY THE COMMUNIST AND SOCIALIST PARTIES AND THE
UNITED POPULAR ACTION MOVEMENT, A LEFT WING SPLITOFF FROM
THE GOVERNMENT'S CHRISTIAN DEMOCRATIC PARTY.

THE CHRISTIAN DEMOCRAT PARTY ALSO HAS A BILL IN THE
OFFING ON THE SAME SUBJECT BUT HAS HELD IT BACK PENDING
DIRECT NEGOTIATIONS BETWEEN GOVERNMENT OFFICIALS AND
ANACONDA ON THE SUBJECT OF "CHILEANIZATION" OF THE
COMPANY'S PROPERTIES.

INVOLVED IN THE NEGOTIATIONS ARE THE CHUQUICAMATA AND
SALVADOR-POTRERILLOS MINES OF CHILE EXPLORATION CO., AND
THE ANDES COPPER MINING CO., BOTH SUBSIDIARIES OF ANACONDA.

A GOVERNMENT SPOKESMAN SAID THAT A DEFINITE DECISION
ON THE COPPER MINES MAY BE EXPECTED TO BE MADE PUBLIC
MONDAY.

MEXICO CITY (UPI)--TORRENTS OF RAIN ARE FALLING ON
FLOODED SOUTHERN MEXICO, CAUSING DOZENS OF RIVERS TO
OVERFLOW THEIR BANKS.

SOME STATES ARE THREATENED WITH THE POSSIBILITY OF
EPIDEMICS.

TWO WEEKS OF FLOODING HAVE DRIVEN 50-THOUSAND PERSONS
FROM THEIR HOMES AND TAKEN 16 LIVES.

THE FEDERAL HEALTH DEPARTMENT HAS SENT 60 DOCTORS
INTO THE WORST FLOODED PARTS OF OAXACA (WAH-HAH'-KAH) AND
VERACRUZ STATES TO HEAD OFF EPIDEMICS. THERE ARE REPORTS
OF DYSENTERY IN SOME VILLAGES AND TOWNS.

ONE TOWN ALONG THE PAPALOAPAN (PAH-PAH-LOH-AH'-PAHN)
RIVER IS DEPENDING ON SUPPLIES AND FOOD BROUGHT IN BY
HELICOPTER. THE FLOODING RIVER HAS CUT ALL ROADS. BOAT
PATROLS LOOKING FOR REFUGEES REFUSED YESTERDAY TO GO OUT,
COMPLAINING THAT TREES WERE FILLED WITH POISONOUS SNAKES
AND TRANTULAS THAT KEPT DROPPING ON THEM.

THE PAPALOAPAN RIVER IS FOUR MILES WIDE AT SOME
POINTS.

WASHINGTON (UPI)--EL SALVADOR TORPEDOED AN ORGANIZATION OF AMERICAN STATES PEACE PLAN TO END ITS TWO-WEEK-OLD WAR WITH HONDURAS. THE SALVADOREAN FOREIGN MINISTER DEMANDED THE O-A-S IN WASHINGTON CONDEMN HONDURAS FOR ALLEGED GENOCIDE AGAINST SALVADOREANS LIVING IN HONDURAS.

PUERTO MAGDALENA, MEXICO (AP)--THE 318-TON TUNA BOAT "ANTOINETTE B" HAS RUN AGROUND AT MAGDALENA ISLAND ABOUT 600 MILES SOUTH OF ITS HOME BASE IN SAN DIEGO.

THE AMERICAN TUNABOAT ASSOCIATION SAYS CAPTAIN GEORGE SOUZA RADIOED THEM THAT NO ONE WAS INJURED IN THE MISHAP, BUT THE SHIP'S NAVIGATOR, ANDY ANDERS, DIED OF A HEART ATTACK AFTER THE BOAT RAN AGROUND YESTERDAY.

7 | News from a Variety of Nations

COPENHAGEN (UPI)--A SWEDE AND TWO ARABS WERE EXPELLED FROM DENMARK THURSDAY AFTER BEING JAILED FOR 30 DAYS CHARGED WITH THE PLANNED ASSASSINATION IN RIO DE JANEIRO OF FORMER ISRAELI PREMIER DAVID BEN GURION.

JUSTICE MINISTER KNUD THESTRUP SAID "AS FAR AS I KNOW THEY SHOULD BE OUT OF THE COUNTRY NOW".

ROLF SVENSSON OF SWEDEN, MOUNA SOUDI, 24, OF JORDAN, AND A PERSON ONLY IDENTIFIED AS RAZAN OF IRAQ WERE

ARRESTED BY DANISH POLICE ON MAY 22.

THEY WERE CHARGED WITH PLANNING TO ASSASSINATE BEN
GURION IN RIO'S AIRPORT MAY 24 AND WITH UNLAWFUL
POSSESSION OF FIREARMS.

THE 30-YEAR-OLD SWEDE ADMITTED THE POSSESSION OF
FIREARMS, FOUND IN HIS DOWNTOWN HOTEL ROOM, BUT ALL
DENIED THE CHARGES OF ASSASSINATION.

THE PUBLIC PROSECUTOR H. GRELL DECIDED TUESDAY NOT TO
BRING THE SWEDE AND THE ARABS TO COURT.

DURING THE ENTIRE PERIOD THE INTELLIGENCE SERVICE HAS
COMPLETELY REFUSED TO GIVE ANY INDICATION OF HOW AND WHY
THE TRIO WAS ARRESTED.

ALL QUIRIES WERE ANSWERED WITH A CURT "THE CASE HAS
BEEN TREATED BEHIND CLOSED DOORS IN COURT AND WE ARE NOT
ALLOWED TO SAY ANYTHING."

VATICAN CITY (UPI)--THE VATICAN WELCOMES THE
SIGGESTION OF ORTHODOX PATRIARCH ATHENAGORAS FOR A
COMMON DATE OF EASTER, PROVIDED THERE IS AGREEMENT BY ALL
CHRISTIAN CHURCHES, THE VATICAN PRESS SPOKESMAN SAID
FRIDAY.

MSGR. FAUSTO VALLAINC COMMENTED ON THE
RECOMMENDATION ATHENAGORAS MADE AT AN ATHENS SYMPOSIUM

WEDNESDAY THAT PROTESTANTS, ORTHODOX AND CATHOLICS SHOULD
CHOOSE THE SECOND SUNDAY IN APRIL AS EASTER SUNDAY.

EASTER IS TRADITIONALLY OBSERVED ON THE FIRST SUNDAY
AFTER THE FULL MOON WHICH OCCURS ON OR NEXT AFTER MARCH
21. AS A RESULT IT ALWAYS FALLS ON SOME DAY BETWEEN MARCH
22 AND APRIL 25 IN THE WESTERN CLAENDAR. EASTERN CHURCHES
HAVE SEPARATE CALENDARS AND CELEBRATE EASTER AT A LATER
DATE.

VALLAINC CITED A STATEMENT BY THE ECUMENICAL COUNCIL
IN ITS 1963 LITURGICAL DECREE THAT "THE SACRED COUNCIL
WOULD NOT OBJECT IF THE FEAST OF EASTER WERE ASSIGNED TO
PARTICULAR SUNDAY OF THE GREGORIAN CALENDAR, PROVIDED THAT
THOSE WHOM IT MAY CONCERN, ESPECIALLY THE BRETHREN WHO ARE
NOT IN COMMUNION WITH THE APOSTOLIC SEE, GIVE THEIR
ASSENT."

HILO, HAWAII (UPI)--KILAUEA VOLCANO FUMED AND EMITTED
GASES SATURDAY BUT WAS BASICALLY QUIET AFTER A
SPECTACULAR 23-HOUR ERUPTION.

THE ERUPTION IN HAWAII VOLCANOES NATIONAL PARK CAME TO
AN ABRUPT HALT FRIDAY AFTER SENDING FIRE FOUNTAINS BETWEEN
600 AND 700 FEET IN THE AIR. LAVA FLOWED NEARLY EIGHT
MILES, STOPPING ABOUT ONE MILE FROM THE SEA.

THE ERUPTION ON THE ISLAND OD HAWAIIGOVABOUT 200 M

THE ERUPTION ON THE ISLAND OD HAWAII, ABO

THE ERUPTION ON THE ISLAND OF HAWAII, ABOUT 200 MILES
SOUTHEAST OF HONOLULU ON THE ISLAND OF OAHU, CAUSED HEAVY
DAMAGE TO THE SCENIC CHAIN OF CRATERS ROAD WHICH ALREADY
HAD BEEN CLOSED TO THE PUBLIC BECAUSE OF DAMAGE FROM
ERUPTIONS EARLIER THIS YEAR. NO POPULATED AREAS WERE
ENDANGERED BY THE ERUPTION, THE THIRD ON KILAUEA IN LESS
THAN A MONTH.

SCIENTISTS AT THE U. S. GEOLOGICAL OBSERVATORY
REPORTED THE "TILT" OR PRESSURE AT THE SUMMIT, BEGAN TO
RISE AFTER THE ERUPTION STOPPED, INDICATING THE ERUPTION
MAY NOT BE OVER.

HONOLULU (UPI)--IT WASN'T SMOG THAT BLANKETED THE
HAWAIIAN ISLANDS MONDAY, BUT "VOG."

THE "VOG" OR VOLCANO-INDUCED FOG SHROUDED THE ISLANDS
IN A GRAY-BLACK HAZE, THE RESULT OF AN ERUPTION FRIDAY AT
KILAUEA VOLCANO ON THE ISLAND OF HAWAII 200 MILES
SOUTHEAST OF HONOLULU ON THE ISLAND OF OAHU.

THE WEATHER BUREAU REPORTED THAT RAIN, WHICH WILL

DISSIPATE THE "VOG" WAS EXPECTED MONDAY NIGHT AND BY
TUESDAY NIGHT THE "VOG" SHOULD BE GONE FROM ALL THE
ISLANDS.

ENVIRONMENTAL HEALTH SPECIALISTS SAY THE "VOG"
WHICH APPEARED SATURDAY AFTERNOON, IS A VISUAL RATHER
THAN HEALTH PROBLEM AND THAT THE PRESENT CONCENTRATION IS
FAR BELOW THE ZONE OF IRRITATION.

BUT MANY COMMERCIAL JET PLANES WERE FORCED TO FLY LOW
OVER HONOLULU BECAUSE OF THE LOW VISIBILITY, AND THE "VOG"
DOESN'T DO MUCH FOR CLEAN LAUNDRY HANGING OUTSIDE.

LOCAL RESIDENTS DON'T APPRECIATE THE "VOG." AS GABE
MAKAUKANE, SALES REPRESENTATIVE FOR MOTOR IMPORTS IN
HONOLULU PUT IT, "IT GIVES PEOPLE HERE AN IDEA OF WHAT
LOS ANGELES IS LIKE."

QUITO, ECUADOR (UPI)--ECUADOREAN AUTHORITIES REPORTED
FRIDAY THE SEIZURE OF SEVEN FOREIGN TUNA BOATS, FOUR OF
THEM OF U.S. REGISTRY, ALLEGEDLY POACHING IN TERRITORIAL
WATERS. THEY SAID THREE OTHER U.S. BOATS "ESCAPED"
CAPTURE.

THE U.S. BOATS SEIZED WERE IDENTIFIED BY THE
ECUADOREAN NAVY AS THE ROYAL PACIFIC, NEPTUNE, BOLD
VENTURE AND MARIETTA, ALL OF SAN DIEGO, CALIF. THE

ECUADOREANS DID NOT IDENTIFY THE THREE U.S. BOATS THEY
SAID ESCAPED SEIZURE.

OF THE CAPTURE OF THE U.S. BOATS THE NAVY SAID ONLY
THAT THEY HAD BEEN SEIZED "WITHIN 200 MILES OF THE
ECUADOREAN COAST."

THEY SAID THE THREE OTHER FOREIGN BOATS SEIZED WERE
JAPANESE, THE SUMI MARU, HITO MARU AND KUROSHIO MARU.
THEY WERE REPORTED TO HAVE BEEN CAPTURED BY TWO PATROL
BOATS 150 MILES OFF THE ECUADOREAN-OWNED GALAPAGOS
ISLANDS. THE JAPANESE VESSELS AND THEIR CREWS--82
PERSONS IN ALL--WERE ESCORTED INTO PORT AT NEARBY SAN
CRISTOBAL ISLAND.

THE ECUADOREANS FLATLY DENIED REPORTS FROM THE SAN
DIEGO-BASED AMERICAN TUNABOAT ASSOCIATION THAT ONE OF THE
SEIZED SHIPS, THE NEPTUNE, HAD BEEN FIRED ON BY THE
ECUADOREAN WARSHIP GUAYAQUIL, ON LOAN TO THE SOUTH
AMERICAN COUNTRY BY THE UNITED STATES UNDER A MUTUAL, AID
PACT.

"THERE WERE NO SHOTS FIRED," THE SPOKESMAN SAID.

(IN SAN DIEGO, AN ASSOCIATION SPOKESMAN SAID AT LEAST
FIVE U.S. TUNABOATS HAD BEEN CAPTURED AND THAT "SIX TO 12"
OTHERS IN THE AMERICAN FISHING FLEET "WENT ALONG WITH THE
CAPTURED BOATS VOLUNTARILY."

(AN ASSOCIATION SPOKESMAN SAID THE CAPTURED AMERICAN
VESSELS HAD BEEN RELEASED AT SEA SHORTLY AFTER THEIR
CAPTURE AND WITHOUT HAVING BEEN TAKEN INTO PORT, AFTER A
"REMINDER" THAT ECUADOREAOZJS

Y

MRIA

8:61-)

(THE ASSOCIATION SM   GA   PGH   (AN ETC   HITS WA

(AN ASSOCIATION SPOKESMAN SAID THE CAPTURED AMERICAN
VESSELS HAD BEEN RELEASED AT SEA SHORTLY AFTER THEIR
CAPTURE AND WITHOUT HAVING BEEN TAKEN INTO PORT, AFTER A
"REMINDER" THAT ECUADOREAN TERRITORIAL WATERS EXTEND 200
MILES.

(THE ASSOCIATION SAID THE NEPTUNE HAD BEEN STRAFED BY
THE GUAYAQUIL BUT REPORTED NO INJURIES ABOARD ALTHOUGH
ALL 16 CREWMEN WERE ON THE BRIDGE WHEN THE ECUADOREAN
WARSHIP OPENED MACHINEGUN FIRE.)

BERLIN (UPI)--WEST BERLIN MAYOR KLAUS SCHUETZ
SATURDAY LEFT FOR A CONTROVERSIAL VISIT TO POLAND DURING
WHICH HE WILL VISIT THE POZNAN INTERNATIONAL FAIR, CRACOW
AND THE SITE OF THE NAZI AUSCHWITZ DEATH CAMP AS WELL AS

MEET WITH POLISH FOREIGN MINISTER STEFAN JEDRYCHOWSKI.

WEST BERLIN CHRISTIAN DEMOCRATS HAVE CHARGED THE SOCIAL

DEMOCRATIC MAYOR WAS ACTING AS THOUGH WEST BERLIN MADE

ITS OWN FOREIGN POLICY AND WAS NOT PART OF WEST GERMANY.

SCHUETZ IS EXPECTED TO DISCUSS THE RECENT OFFER OF

POLISH COMMUNIST LEADER WLADYSLAW GOMULKA FOR WEST

GERMANY TO SIGN A TREATY RECOGNIZING POLAND'S WESTERN

BORDER ON THE ODER AND NEISSE RIVERS.

NICE, FRANCE (UPI)--FROMER KING UMBERTO OF ITALY

ARRIVED BY PRIVATE PLANE FRIDAY TO ATTEND THE RELIGIOUS

WEDDING OF HIS DAUGHTER, PRINCESS MARIA GABRIELLA.

THE PRINCESS WILL BE MARRIED SATURDAY AT NOON TO

ROBERT DE BALKANY IN A PRIVATE CHAPEL AT THE CHATEAU DE

BALSAN NEAR HERE. THE REV. FRANCESCO PIPAN, WHO WAS THE

PRINCESS' PHILOSOPHY TEACHER WHEN SHE STUDIED IN LISBON,

WILL PERFORM THE RITE.

BESIDES HER FATHER, ITALY'S LAST KING, PRINCESS

GABRIELLA WILL BE ACCOMPANIED BY PRINCE MICHEL DE GRECE,

WITNESS AT THE EARLIER CIVIL CEREMONY, AND HER BROTHER,

PRINCE VITTORIO EMMANUEL.

THE CEILING OF THE CHAPEL WILL BE DECORATED WITH

RIBBONS OF LIGHT BLUE AND BLACK, THE COLORS OF DE

BALKANY'S YACHT.

VATICAN CITY (UPI)--SEVERAL CARDINALS OF THE ROMAN
CURIA HAVE WRITTEN TO BELGIAN CARDINAL LEO JOSEF SUENENS
PROTESTING HIS PUBLIC CRITICISM OF THE CURIA, THE CENTRAL
ADMINISTRATION BODY OF THE ROMAN CATHOLIC CHURCH, VATICAN
SOURCES SAID THURSDAY.

IN AN INTERVIEW WITH THE FRENCH CATHOLIC REVIEW,
INFORMATIONS CATHOLIQUES, HE ALSO CALLED FOR CHANGES IN
THE EXERCISE OF PAPAL AUTHORITY, IN THE ROLE OF THE
COLLEGE OF CARDINALS AND IN OTHER ASPECTS OF CHURCH
ORGANIZATION.

VATICAN SOURCES SAID THE CURIA CARDINALS PROTESTED
"IN CORDIAL TERMS" PRIMARILY OVER SUENENS' COMMENTS ABOUT
THE CURIA AND THE COLLEGE OF CARDINALS.

HONOLULU (UPI)--THERE AREN'T ANY SNAKES IN HAWAII. AT
LEAST THERE AREN'T SUPPOSED TO BE. BUT JOSEPH BULGO OF
WAILUKU (WAH-IHL-OO-KOO) FOUND A DEAD SNAKE IN A STABLE
AND MAILED IT TO THE HONOLULU ZOO TO IDENTIFY IT.

THE ZOO IDENTIFIED IT AS A YOUNG RACER USED IN A RAIN
DANCE...PROBABLY SHIPPED TO HAWAII IN A BALE OF HAY.

IN UPPER VOLTA, FOUR MEALS A WEEK IS NORMAL

(EDITOR'S NOTE: MUCH IS SAID AND WRITTEN IN GENERAL
TERMS ABOUT "UNDER-DEVELOPED" COUNTRIES. HERE, BY A
VETERAN OBSERVER OF THE AFRICA SCENE, IS A CLOSEUP OF WHAT
IT'S REALLY LIKE IN ONE OF THE POOREST COUNTRIES OF ALL.)
BY JUDITH LISTOWEL

LONDON FINANCIAL TIMES-UPI

OUAGADOUGOU, UPPER VOLTA--THIS IS PROBABLY THE POOREST
COUNTRY IN AFRICA. UPPER VOLTA, POPULATION 5,100,000 IS
A LANDLOCKED STATE IN WEST AFRICA, SURROUNDED BY IVORY
COAST, GHANA AND DAHOMEY, BORDERING ON NIGER AND MALI TO
THE NORTH AND WEST. WITH NO OUTLET TO THE SEA, ITS CHIEF
ASSET IS A RAILWAY, BUILT BY THE FRENCH IN COLONIAL DAYS
FROM ITS CAPITAL, OUAGADOUGOU, TO THE COAST AT ABIDJAN.

BECAUSE THE COUNTRY IS FLAT, HAS A VERY LOW RAINFALL
AND ONLY THREE SMALL RIVERS, IT IS EXTREMELY DIFFICULT TO
BUILD DAMS TO IMPROVE AGRICULTURE. MOST PEOPLE LIVE WELL
BELOW SUBSISTENCE LEVEL, AND IT IS REGARDED AS NORMAL THAT
A FAMILY SHOULD EAT ONLY FOUR TIMES A WEEK.

THERE ARE 11,000 SCHOOLCHILDREN IN THE CAPITAL, WHICH
EVERYONE CALLS "OUAGA." A PRIVATELY FINANCED FRENCH
ORGANIZATION, CALLED "LES FRERES DE L'HOMME," SET UP A
TEAM IN OUAGA TO COOK MID-DAY MEALS FOR ANY SCHOOLCHILDREN
WHO EAT ONLY FOUR TIMES A WEEK AT HOME. HALF THE TOTAL

419

NUMBER, 5,500, QUALIFIED.

OF UPPER VOLTA'S 5 MILLION POPULATION, MADE UP MAINLY
OF TWO TRIBES, THE MOSSIS AND THE BOBOS, ONLY 38,000 ARE
REGULARLY GAINFULLY EMPLOYED. OTHERS ARE CASUAL AND
SEASONAL WORKERS, AND THE PEASANTS -- 90 PER CENT OF THE
POPULATION -- SCRATCH OUT SOME FOOD FROM THEIR INFERTILE
LAND. ONE MILLION UPPER VOLTANS ARE WORKING ABROAD -- IN
THE IVORY COAST, GHANA, NIGER AND NIGERIA -- AND SEND
HOME PART OF THEIR ERNINGS O MAINTAIN THEIR FAMILIES.

BEST PAID ARE THE UPPER VOLTAN VETERANS OF WORLD WAR
II. THEIR PENSIONS, AND THE TAXES THEY PAY ON THEM, ARE
THE MAIN SOURCE OF FOREIGN CURRENCY AND THE MAIN ITEM OF
STATE REVENUE.

INDUSTRIALLY, UPPER VOLTA IS TRULY UNDER-DEVELOPED.
IT HAS ONLY TWO FACTORIES: ONE FOR TEXTILES, MODERN AND
WELL EQUIPPED, FOR WHICH COTTON NOW GROWN IN THE COUNTRY
PROVIDES THE RAW MATERIAL; A SECOND, RECENTLY ENLARGED,
FOR MAKING SOAP.

IN THE NORTH OF THE COUNTRY ARE VALUABLE MINERAL
DEPOSITS: MANGANESE, GOLD AND A NUMBER OF RARE MINERALS.
UNION CARBIDE HAS SURVEYED THESE DEPOSITS AND WOULD BE
WILLING TO START MINING AT ONCE IF 270 MILES OF RAILWAY
WERE BUILT FROM THE NORTH TO OUAGADOUGOU (SO TO THE SEA
AT ABIDJAN).

THE AMERICAN COMPANY IS NOT PREPARED TO UNDERTAKE THIS
COSTLY ENTERPRISE. PRESIDENT SANGOULE LAMIZANA TOLD ME
THAT HE WAS NEGOTIATING WITH THE WORLD BANK AND OTHER
WORLD FINANCIAL SOURCES AND HOPED THAT WITH THE BACKING
OF UPPER VOLTA'S FRIENDS -- PRESUMABLY AMERICANS AND
FRENCH -- THE MONEY WILL BE FOUND. A RAILWAY WOULD MEAN
TEMPORARY EMPLOYMENT FOR MANY UPPER VOLTANS AND THE MINING
PROJECT ITSELF WOULD PROVIDE MUCH NEEDED REVENUE BOTH FOR
THE STATE AND THE PEOPLE. THE UNION CARBIDE SCHEME COULD
ADD 10 PER CENT TO UPPER VOLTA'S STATE REVENUE.

UPPER VOLTA STANDS ON THE TERRITORY OF THE FORMER
MOSSI EMPIRE WHICH HAD EXISTED FOR 1,000 YEARS. THE
FRENCH OCCUPIED IT IN 1897, AND IN 1933 THEY PARCELLED IT
OUT BETWEEN NIGER, THE (FRENCH) SUDAN AND THE IVORY COAST.
IN 1947, GENERAL CHARLES DE GAULLE, WHO NEVER FORGOT THE
SUPPORT FRENCH EQUATORIAL AFRICA GAVE THE FREE FRENCH
DURING WORLD WAR II, RECONSTITUTED THE MOSSI EMPIRE UNDER
THE NAME OF UPPER VOLTA AND MADE IT A SEPARATE COLONY.
THEN WHEN HE RETURNED TO POWER IN 1958 HE KEPT HIS
PROMISE TO GIVE INDEPENDENCE TO ALL THE FORMER FRENCH
COLONIES; UPPER VOLTA BECAME INDEPENDENT IN 1960.

ON MAY 10 OF THIS YEAR, MAURICE YAMAEGO, FIRST
PRESIDENT OF UPPER VOLTA, WAS SENTENCED TO FIVE YEARS'

IMPRISONMENT ON A CHARGE OF MISAPPROPRIATING STATE FUNDS.

HE HAD BEEN UNDER HOUSE ARREST FOR OVER THREE YEARS; BUT

HIS SUCCESSOR, GENERAL LAMIZANA, WOULD NOT AUTHORIZE THE

TRIAL AS HE FOUND THE EVIDENCE AGAINST YAMAEGO

UNCONVINCING. HOWEVER, UNDER PRESSURE FROM THE JUNIOR

OFFICERS, WHO ARE DISSATISFIED WITH THEIR COUNTRY'S SLOW

DEVELOPMENT, GENERAL LAMIZANA GAVE WAY.

YAMAEGO WAS A GAY, IMAGINATIVE BUT INEXPERIENCED MOSSI,

WHO SOUGHT TO ATTRACT FOREIGN CAPITAL FOR THE DEVELOPMENT

OF HIS COUNTRY BY INVITING AND LAVISHLY ENTERTAINING

POTENTIAL INVESTORS AND BUSINESSMEN. LATE IN 1965 THE

OLDER OFFICERS OF THE 2,000 MAN ARMY INITIATED A COUP

D'ETAT, OVERTHROWING HIM.   ON JAN. 4, 1966, COL.

LAMISANA, PROMOTED TO GENERAL, BECAME THE NEW RULER.

LAMISANA WANTED TO RESTORE CIVILIAN RULE AT THE END OF

1966. BUT IN THE ABSENCE OF CONSTRUCTIVE PLANS TO DEAL

WITH UPPER VOLTA'S ECONOMY, HE ANNOUNCED THAT HE WOULD

STAY UNTIL JAN. 1, 1970. HE ASSURED ME WHEN I INTERVIEWED

HIM THAT, COME WHAT MAY, HE WAS HANDING BACK POWER TO THE

POLITICIANS NEXT JANUARY AND THAT HE HAD ALREADY

AUTHORIZED THEM TO REACTIVATE THEIR POLITICAL

ORGANIZATIONS.

GENERAL LAMIZANA HAS CUT SALARIES, FAMILY ALLOWANCES

AND PUBLIC WORKS. HE HAS BALANCED UPPER VOLTA'S BUDGET, THOUGH AT A PRICE OF VIRTUAL STANDSTILL ECONOMICALLY. THE FRENCH ASSISTANCE TECHNIQUE HAS CARRIED OUT SEVERAL PROJECTS, AMONG THEM THE CREATION OF TWO DAMS, WHICH MAKE IT POSSIBLE TO GROW RICE AND OTHER CROPS.

BUT UNTIL THE FRENCH SCHEMES PAY OFF AND MANY OTHERS ARE INITIATED MOST UPPER VOLTANS WILL STILL HAVE A BAD TIME OF IT -- WHOEVER IS IN POWER.

ADV FOR PMS MON JUNE 16

"Good Music" Continuity

Much of the copy in the first five parts of this section was written by KFAC's Howard Rhines, whose permission to use this material is gratefully acknowledged. Thanks are also due to Thomas Cassidy, who supplied the complete continuity for two of KFAC's "Sunday Evening Concerts."

ANNCR: The popular French opera, "Tales of Hoffman," is
         heard tonight in a German translation. The opera
         was written by Offenbach in 1881 and was produced
         that same year at the Opéra Comique in Paris. Al-
         though the opera has never enjoyed the popularity
         of many of the Italian and German masterpieces,
         it has found a place in most of the major opera
         houses of the world. Its grace and delicacy well
         suit the fantastic story of Hoffman and his wild
         escapades.

         In tonight's cast are: Wilhelm Horst, as Hoffman;
         Hertha Schenck, as Nicklaus; Elly von Kovatsky, as
         Stella; Inge Camphausen, as Olympia; Erna Niehaus,
         as Giulietta; Helga Tock, as Antonia; Fritz
         Jungman, as Lindorf; Gerhard Schneider, as
         Coppelius; Heinrich Neuwald, as Dapertutto;
         Gerhard Ramms, as Mirakel; Paul Mehler, as Andreas;
         and Gunther Peichert, as Nathaen. The Dresden
         State Opera Orchestra and Chorus are conducted by
         Karl List.

         We hear now "Tales of Hoffman," by Offenbach.

ANNCR: Richard Wagner's "Die Walküre" is the second of four operas comprising the monumental "Der Ring des Nibelungen." It follows "Das Rheingold" in the series and precedes "Siegfried" and "Die Götter-dämmerung." Tonight, as the major work on our Operatic Masterworks program, we are to hear a re-cording of the complete opera, "Die Walküre." In the cast are: Frieda Leider, as Brunnhilde; Gota Ljungberg, as Sieglinde; Walter Widdop, as Sieg-mund; Friedrich Schorr, as Wotan; and Howard Fry, as Hunding. The London Symphony Orchestra is con-ducted by Albert Coates.

"Die Walküre," by Richard Wagner.

ANNCR: Mozart's "Die Zauberflöte," or "The Magic Flute," is our featured work this evening. Written near the close of his brief but glorious career, "Die Zauberflöte" illustrates Mozart's marvelous gift for melody. One of his few operas to be written in German, it marks a change from the Italian-inspired operas of his earlier period. In the cast of tonight's opera are: Wilhelm Strienz; Helge Roswänge; Erna Berger; Tiana Lemnitz;

Gerhard Hüsch; Irma Beilke; Heinrich Tessmer; and
Max Hirzel. The Berlin Philharmonic Orchestra is
conducted by Sir Thomas Beecham.

"Die Zauberflöte," by Wolfgang Amadeus Mozart.

ANNCR: Hugo Wolf was one of Germany's outstanding composers of Lieder. These songs, sung usually with
piano accompaniment, are alternately sad, gay,
nostalgic, or tender, and demand unusual sensitivity on the part of the vocal interpreter.
Lotte Lehmann, perhaps the greatest Lied singer of
our time, now sings for us seven of these little
songs: "Auch kleine Dinge," "Auf ein altes Bild,"
"Du denkst mit einem Fädchen," "Frühling übers
Jahr," "Der Gärtner," "Heimweh," and "In der
Frühe."
Lotte Lehmann singing seven songs by Hugo Wolf, on
an RCA Victor record.

ANNCR: Another popular Lieder composer was Robert Franz.
Ernst Wolff now sings for us eight songs by Franz:
"Es taget vor dem Walde," "Ach Elslein, liebes
Elslein mein," "Gleich und gleich," "Die helle

Sonne leuchet," "Aus meinem grossen Schmerzen,"
"Es hat die Rose sich beklagt," "Auf dem Meer,"
and "Im Rhein, im heiligen Strome."
Ernst Wolff singing eight songs by Robert Franz.

ANNCR: We hear next "Vier ernste Gesänge," or "Four
Serious Songs," by Johannes Brahms. Called the
crowning glory of Brahms's songwriting, they are
given a beautiful interpretation by the basso
Alexander Kipnis. The songs are: "Denn es gehet
dem Menschen," "Ich wandte mich und sehe an,"
"O Tod, wie bitter bist Du," and "Wenn ich mit
Menschen."
"Four Serious Songs," sung by Alexander Kipnis.

ANNCR: Ludwig van Beethoven's greatest song cycle, "An
die ferne Geliebte," is heard next in its entirety,
sung by Gerhard Hüsch. The songs are: "Auf dem
Hügel sitz' ich spähend," "Wo die Berge so blau,"
"Leichte Segler in den Höhen," "Diese Wolken in
den Höhen," "Es kehret der Maien," and "Nimm sie
hin denn, diese Lieder."

ANNCR: On this day in the year 1810, Beethoven's "Egmont"

overture was first performed, at a private per-

formance in Vienna. This music was written by

Beethoven as a portion of the incidental music for

Goethe's drama of the same name.

Karl Böhm conducts the Dresden State Opera Orchestra

in Beethoven's overture to "Egmont."

ANNCR: German-born Gustave Luders came to this country as

a young man and first achieved musical fame as the

director of a light opera company in Milwaukee.

After his reputation as a conductor was established,

Luders began the composition of the popular operet-

tas which were his contribution to American light

music.

Echoes and Encores presents a medley of selections

from Luders' 1902 production of "The Prince of

Pilsen."

ANNCR: The ballet music in Lortzing's "Undine" is heard

in the second act of the opera, which is based on

a familiar fairy tale. The story deals with a

water spirit who falls in love with a mortal man.

Dr. Karl Böhm conducts the Dresden State Opera

431

Orchestra in the ballet music from Lortzing's
"Undine."

ANNCR: During his many successful years as a conductor of
dance music, Johann Strauss composed marches,
quadrilles, and polkas in addition to the waltzes
for which he is best remembered. His decision to
devote his time entirely to the composition of
operetta was simply a redirection of the activities
which had brought him fame in his own right.
Arthur Fiedler conducts the Boston Pops Orchestra
in the March from "The Gypsy Baron."

ANNCR: Although Johann Strauss and his sons are often
credited with developing and popularizing the Vi-
ennese waltz, the actual creator was one Josef
Lanner, a self-taught violinist and composer.
Erich Kleiber conducts the Berlin Philharmonic
Orchestra in Lanner's "Die Schönbrunner" waltzes.

ANNCR: Although Wagner's "Tristan and Isolde" was completed in 1859, it was not until six years later
that the opera was first performed. The scene of
that initial production was the Royal Court
Theater in Munich, under the direction of Hans von
Bülow.

Isaac Stern plays excerpts from Wagner's "Tristan
and Isolde." The orchestra is conducted by Franz
Waxman, piano passages are played by Oscar Levant.

ANNCR: The world première of "Die Fledermaus," by Johann
Strauss the younger, took place in Vienna in 1864.
"The Bat," considered a classic of its musical
type, was first performed in this country five
years later at Brooklyn's Thalia Theater.

Leslie Heward conducts the Halle orchestra in the
overture to "Die Fledermaus."

ANNCR: Although Mendelssohn's brilliant career came to an
end at the age of 37, it must be borne in mind
that his mental maturity was reached as early as
his fifteenth year. A case in point is the "Midsummer Night's Dream" music, some portions of

which were written fifteen years after the others.
The mastery and finish of form evident in later
compositions were already developed at 17.
Arthur Fiedler and the Boston Pops Orchestra play
Mendelssohn's "War March of the Priests" from
"Athalie."

ANNCR: The list of stage successes written by Johann
Strauss upon his retirement as a conductor of
dance music is highlighted by such works as "The
Bat" and "Cagliostro in Vienna."
From the latter operetta, Arthur Fiedler and the
Boston Pops Orchestra play the title waltz.

ANNCR: Mendelssohn's Fourth Symphony, the "Italian," was
actually written in the country which inspired it.
In several instances the young German composer
found his inspiration through travels over Europe
and the British Isles.
Serge Koussevitzky conducts the Boston Symphony
Orchestra in the first movement of Mendelssohn's
Fourth Symphony.

ANNCR: Unlike so many musicians of note whose works have endured, Johannes Brahms lived a tranquil life, free from want, and received during his lifetime his just recognition as one of the musically great. Charles O'Connell conducts an abridged arrangement of the fourth movement of Brahms's First Symphony, in C Minor.

ANNCR: One hundred fifty-one years ago tomorrow, the première performance of Weber's "Abu Hassan" took place in Munich.

It's interesting to note that Weber showed practically no musical talent at all during his early years. With the development of his great gift, he began to create the legacy of fine music which he left the world.

Sir Hamilton Harty conducts the Halle orchestra in the overture to Weber's "Abu Hassan."

2 | French Music Copy

ANNCR: Our next work on this afternoon's "Symphonic Masterpieces" is Camille Saint-Saëns' "Suite Algérienne." The Orchestre National de la Radiodiffusion

Française is conducted by Ernesto Halffter.

ANNCR: Gabriel Fauré's "Cantique de Jean Racine" is heard
next. The Orchestre du Théâtre des Champs-Elysées
is conducted by Paul Bonneau.

ANNCR: Maurice Ravel, one of the giants of modern French
music died in 1937. Behind him he left such
masterpieces as "Pavane pour une infante défunte,"
"La valse," and "Daphnis and Chloë." For our featured work on this evening's "Miniature Masterpieces," we turn to a lesser known composition by
the French master: "L'enfant et les sortilèges."
Nadine Sautereau is the featured soprano, and the
Orchestre Radio-Symphonique de Paris de la
Radiodiffusion Française is conducted by René
Leibowitz.

ANNCR: Igor Stravinsky's "Sacre du printemps" caused a
furore when it was first performed. Today, after
years of even more wildly experimental works by
Schönberg, Bartok, and Stravinsky himself, "The

Rite of Spring" seems quite conventional. We hear

now a London recording of this work, performed by

the Orchestre de la Suisse Romande, conducted by

Ernest Ansermet.

ANNCR: Charles Gounod's ever popular opera "Faust" is the

featured work on this evening's "Musical Master-

pieces." The opera was first performed in 1859 at

the Théâtre Lyrique in Paris. Although not an out-

standing success at its first performance, it

gradually won its admirers and a permanent place

in the operatic repertoire. Our recording is the

RCA Victor album, M-105. Soloists are: Mireille

Berthon; César Vezzani; Marcel Journet; Marthe

Coiffier; Louis Musy; Françoise Montfort; and

Marcel Cozette. The chorus of the Paris Opéra and

the Orchestre de l'Opéra-Comique de Paris are con-

ducted by Henri Büsser.

"Faust" by Charles Gounod.

ANNCR: Claude Debussy's "Preludes, Book One" is played

for us now by Walter Gieseking, pianist. The

"Preludes" are composed of twelve individual selections. These are: "Danseuses de delphes"; "Voiles";
"Le vent dans la plaine"; "Les sons et les parfums
tournent dans l'air du soir"; "Les collines d'Ana-
Capri"; "Des pas sur la neige"; "Ce qu'a vu le vent
d'ouest"; "La fille aux cheveux de lin"; "La
sérénade interrompue"; "La cathédrale engloutie";
"La danse de Puck"; and "Minstrels."
Debussy's "Preludes, Book One."

ANNCR: Next on this evening's concert we hear François
Couperin's harpsichord "satirical comedy in five
acts," "Les fastes de la grande et ancienne
Menestrandise." The work is in five parts: "Les
notables"; Les vieulleux"; "Les jongleurs avec les
singes et les ours"; "Les Invalides"; and "Déroute
de la troupe."
Alice Ehlers performs this work on the harpsichord
of the Royal Institute of Paris. Couperin's "Les
fastes de la grande et ancienne Menestrandise."

ANNCR: We hear next the beautiful "Pièces pittoresques,"
         by Emmanuel Chabrier. Pianist Ginette Doyen per-
         forms on a Westminster long-playing record.

ANNCR: Marc-Antoine Charpentier's seldom-heard "Messe de
         minuit" is the next work on our evening concert.
         The Orchestre de Chambre des Concerts Lamoureux is
         conducted by Pierre Colombo.

ANNCR: Gabriel Fauré's "Masques et bergamasques" is heard
         next on your afternoon concert. The Orchestre de
         la Société des Concerts du Conservatoire de Paris
         is conducted by Georges Tzipine.
         Gabriel Fauré's "Masques et bergamasques."

ANNCR: Our next work this evening is the delightful
         ballet music "Céphale et Procris," by André Grétry.
         Although Grétry is little known in America, his
         music has found lasting fame in his own country.
         A revolutionary whose creative life was lived be-
         tween the careers of Mozart and Beethoven, he
         symbolizes the France of "Liberté, Fraternité,

Egalité."

The ballet suite "Céphale et Procris," by André Grétry.

ANNCR: Early in his career, Léo Delibes was commissioned to write portions of a ballet titled "Naïla, the Water Nymph." Of the second act, written by Delibes, a contemporary critic said: "The second act is brilliant and does great credit to its composer. It is certainly the most noteworthy portion."

Lawrence Collingwood conducts the Royal Opera Orchestra in the waltz from "Naïla, the Water Nymph."

ANNCR: For the ballet "Cotillon," several musical works of Chabrier were combined with choreography by Georges Balanchine.

The ballet was first performed at the Théâtre de Monte Carlo in April of 1932.

Antal Dorati conducts the London Philharmonic Orchestra in the Scherzo, Waltz, and Rustic Dance from Chabrier's music for the "Cotillon" ballet.

ANNCR: César Franck went through his quiet life living only for his art, content with the creation of great music--happy in its accomplished fact. His initial venture into the form of the symphonic poem was also his first important work for orchestra. Howard Barlow conducts the Columbia Broadcasting Symphony Orchestra in Franck's "Les Eolides."

ANNCR: Of the more than 90 stage works written by Jacques Offenbach, only a handful survive to the point where they are performed in their entirety. However, the gay streak of genius which made him the most brilliant composer of operetta of his day has so pervaded portions of his stage pieces that excerpts from many of them still endure.
From one of the earliest, "Apothecary and Wigmaker," presented in 1861, comes this interpretation of the overture, played by Alfredo Antonini and his orchestra.

441

ANNCR: On this day in the year 1866, Erik Satie, the
        sponsor of the group of composers known as the
        French "Six," was born in Honfleurs. Several
        of Satie's works were arranged for orchestra by
        Claude Debussy, the great composer he influenced
        so markedly.
        Serge Koussevitzky conducts the Boston Symphony
        Orchestra in Erik Satie's "Gymnopédie No. 1."

ANNCR: "Phaëton," by Saint-Saëns, was inspired by the
        mythical story of an amateur charioteer who guided
        the path of the sun through the sky. Unable to
        handle his fiery steeds and celestial cargo in
        their heavenly journey, he escaped destruction
        only by a timely thunderbolt.
        Piero Coppola conducts the Paris Conservatory
        Orchestra in "Phaëton," by Saint-Saëns.

ANNCR: Paris in 1868 was the scene of the opening of
        Offenbach's "La Périchole." One of the most suc-
        cessful of the many operettas by Offenbach, this
        work enjoyed the combination of a good plot and
        sparkling score. Jennie Tourel sings three songs

from "La Périchole." "Tu n'es pas beau," "Ah quel dîner," and "Que les hommes sont bêtes."

ANNCR: Now, music from Emmanuel Chabrier's 1887 operatic success, "Le Roi Malgré Lui." Pierre Monteux conducts the San Francisco Symphony Orchestra in the "Fête polonaise" from the second act of "The King in Spite of Himself."

ANNCR: In "Mignon," by Ambroise Thomas, the operatic tradition of tragedy is blithely sidestepped for a gay plot of amorous intrigue and mistaken identity. The eternal triangle situation is couched in music which reveals the composer's inborn instinct for the theater.
Leopold Stokowski conducts the Philadelphia Orchestra in the "Gavotte" from "Mignon."

ANNCR: French composer Jean Françaix first attracted attention in 1932 with eight Bagatelles for string quartet and orchestra, composed for the Vienna festival of that year.

He has composed prolifically in the field of instrumental music, and is responsible for several
ballet scores.

Assisted by Leo Borchard and the Berlin Philharmonic
Orchestra, Jean Françaix plays his own "Concertino
for Piano and Orchestra."

ANNCR: Based on a fable by La Fontaine, the ballet "Les
Deux Pigeons" was originally presented at the Paris
Opéra in October of 1886. The choreography by
Louis Merante was set to music by André Messager.
Hugo Rignold conducts the Royal Opera House
Orchestra in Variations, Divertissement, Hungarian
Dance, and Finale from "The Two Pigeons."

ANNCR: Once referred to by an august body of his own
countrymen as "the best musician of France,"
Camille Saint-Saëns was also one of the most successful. His sense of balance and proportion, combined with an uncanny ability to analyze his public,
made his career uniformly brilliant from practically
every aspect.

Ossy Renardy, accompanied by pianist Walter Robert, plays "Concertstück," by Saint-Saëns.

ANNCR: Ninety-four years ago this week, the world première of Saint-Saëns' Piano Concerto No. 2 in G Minor took place in Paris. Anton Rubinstein conducted, and the composer was the featured soloist. Moura Lympany, assisted by Warwick Braithwaite and the National Symphony Orchestra, plays the final movement of Saint-Saëns' Piano Concerto No. 2 in G Minor.

ANNCR: Equally authoritative in his interpretations of the lyrical music of Chopin and Debussy as well as with the dynamics of Beethoven, Artur Rubinstein has added immeasurably to the musical enjoyment of countless concertgoers. Since his twelfth year, he has concertized extensively all over the world. Artur Rubinstein plays Debussy's "Reflections in the Water" and "Gardens in the Rain."

ANNCR: Gaetano Donizetti's popular opera, "Lucia di
Lammermoor," was written in 1835, and immediately
won a permanent place in the grand opera repertoire.
The story, which is set in Scotland, ends tragically,
but Donizetti's music is frequently lively and lilting. Tonight we are to hear a complete recording
of this work. In the cast are: Enrico Molinari,
as Lord Henry Ashton; Mercedes Capsir, as Lucia;
Enzo de Muro Lomanto, as Edgar; Emilio Venturini,
as Lord Arthur Bucklaw; Salvatore Baccaloni, as
Raymond; and Ida Mannarini, as Alice. The Orchestra and Chorus of La Scala Opera Company are
under the direction of Lorenzo Molajoli.

ANNCR: One of the most popular operas of all time is
Giuseppe Verdi's "La Traviata." This opera, first
performed in 1853 at the Teatro La Fenice in Venice,
was initially a failure. But time has brought a
complete reversal of opinion, and "La Traviata" now
is a standard work among opera companies the world
over. Tonight we are to hear the complete Victor
recording of this work. In the cast are: Anna

Rozsa, as Violetta; Irene Minghini-Cattaneo, as

Flora; Alessandro Ziliani, as Alfredo; Luigi

Borgonovo, as Giorgio; and, Giordano Callegari, as

Baron Douphol. Carlo Sabajno conducts the orches-

tra and chorus of La Scala.

"La Traviata," by Giuseppe Verdi.

ANNCR: Giuseppe Verdi's opera "Aïda" has been among the

most popular of all musical compositions since its

first performance in Cairo, Egypt, on December 24,

1871. The opera, which was commissioned by the

Khedive of Egypt to celebrate the opening of the

Suez Canal, was suggested to the Khedive by

Mariette Bey, the famous French Egyptologist, pre-

sumably because of his discoveries in the tombs of

the ancient Egyptians. The libretto was written by

the former director of the Opéra-Comique in Paris,

Camille du Locle, and was adapted to Italian by

Antonio Ghislanzoni.

In the cast are: Dusolina Giannini, as Aïda; Irene

Minghini-Cattaneo, as Amneris; Aureliano Pertile, as

Radames; Giovanni Inghilleri, as Amonasro; Luigi

Manfrini, as Ramfis; and Giovanni Nessi, as the

Messenger. The chorus and orchestra of the La
Scala Opera Company are conducted by Carlo Sabajno.
"Aïda," by Giuseppe Verdi.

ANNCR: "The Barber of Seville" ("Il Barbiere di Siviglia"),
by Gioacchino Antonio Rossini, is the featured
work this evening. The opera was written in 1816
and was first presented in Rome. The libretto was
written by Cesare Sterbini, based on the comedy by
Beaumarchais. Although the opera was a total
failure at its first performance, it has since become one of the most popular of all operas. Tonight we are to hear the Columbia recording of this
opera, featuring Riccardo Straccieri, as Figaro;
Mercedes Capsir, as Rosina; Armando Borgioli, as
Count Almaviva; Vincenzo Bettoni, as Basilio; and
Salvatore Baccaloni, as Doctor Bartolo.
The Orchestra and Chorus of La Scala, Milan, are
conducted by Lorenzo Molajoli.

ANNCR: Puccini's La Bohême has been an important monument
of the operatic art since its first performance on
February 1, 1896. The audience at the Teatro

Reggio was quick to sense a major musical event at that first performance, and its success was quickly repeated in Buenos Aires and in San Francisco. This afternoon we are to hear a new London recording of highlights from this opera. In the cast are: Renata Tebaldi, Giacinto Prandelli, Fernando Corena, Raphäel Arié, Giovanni Inghilleri, and Melchiorre Luise. The Orchestra and Chorus of the Accademia di Santa Cecilia of Rome are conducted by Maestro Alberto Erede.

ANNCR: This evening on "Operatic Masterpieces," we are to hear the complete Victor recording of Vincenzo Bellini's opera, "Norma."

"Norma" was first performed in Milan, Italy, in the year 1831. It followed by a few months Bellini's highly successful "La Sonnambula" and won its composer even greater fame. The story of "Norma" is taken from Soumet's tragedy of the same name, which had played at the Théâtre Français in Paris in 1830. The libretto was adapted by Felice Romani. In our cast tonight we are to hear: Gina Cigna, Ebe Stignani, Adrianna Perris, Tancred Pasero,

449

Giovanni Breviario, and Emilio Rienzi. The EIAR
chorus and orchestra are under the direction of
Vittorio Gui.

"Norma," by Vincenzo Bellini.

ANNCR: Gioacchino Rossini's opera "La Cenerentola" is
based on the story of Cinderella. It is now seldom
performed, but its overture has become a concert
"standard." We hear now Rossini's overture to "La
Cenerentola."

Lorenzo Malojoli conducts the Milan Symphony
Orchestra.

ANNCR: Ottorino Respighi is best known for his two orchestral poems, "The Fountains of Rome" and "The Pines
of Rome." Less well known but equally beautiful is
his arrangement of old Italian songs called "Gli
ucelli"--"The Birds."

Adriano Ariani conducts the Milan Symphony Orchestra
in "Gli ucelli," by Respighi.

ANNCR: The Italian composer Gian Francesco Malipiero has
gone back to the music of the Italian Renaissance
for his inspiration. His quartet "Cantari alla
madrigalesa" is heard next, in a performance by the
Roma Quartet.

Malipiero's "Cantari alla madrigalesa."

ANNCR: One of Italy's early twentieth-century operatic
composers is heard next on "Echoes and Encores."
Ermanno Wolf-Ferrari, although never as popular as
his countrymen Ruggiero Leoncavallo and Pietro
Mascagni, with whom his career overlapped, was the
composer of several delightful operas. Lucrezia
Bori now sings for us the aria "O gioia, la nube
leggera," from Wolf-Ferrari's "Il segreto di
Susanna"--"The Secret of Susanne."

ANNCR: One hundred forty-eight years ago yesterday,
Rossini's opera "L'italiana in Algeri" was first
presented in Venice. Although Rossini was appren-
ticed to a blacksmith at an early age, his music
happily shows little of the influence of that

honored trade.

Arturo Toscanini conducts the Philharmonic Symphony Orchestra of New York in the overture to "The Italian Woman in Algiers."

ANNCR: Tonight we go to Italy with the well known song "Funiculi funicula." This is not an Italian folk song, as so many people think. It was written by Luigi Denze in 1880 to celebrate the opening of the funicular railway to the top of Mt. Etna. Though he wrote an opera and 500 other songs and was one of the directors of the Academy of London, he will always be known as the composer of this Neapolitan ditty that sold well over half a million copies and has been translated into every civilized language. It tells about a lover who says he has soared high in the sky where he could see France, Portugal, and Spain--all without taking a step. How? On the funicular, of course. It is sung now by Joseph Schmidt.

ANNCR: Bellini's opera "Norma" employs the techniques of
the older school of Italian opera, in which arias
and ensembles are plentiful, with less accent on
the more modern declamatory or recitative passages.
In Bellini's hands, this simplicity of style was
particularly effective.
Anatole Fistoulari conducts England's National
Symphony Orchestra in the overture to "Norma."

ANNCR: On this day in the year 1812, the world première
of Rossini's opera "La Scala di Seta" took place
in Venice. This is only one of 50 operas to come
from the pen of the amazing personality who was
referred to by his contemporaries as the laziest
of all musicians.
Arturo Toscanini conducts the BBC Symphony Orchestra in the overture to Rossini's "The Silken
Ladder."

ANNCR: Only two months before his passing at the age of
39, Otto Nicolai reached the pinnacle of his
career with "The Merry Wives of Windsor." The

story follows closely the familiar Shakespearian play, with Nicolai's music serving to underline and enliven the comic situations.

Sir Adrian Boult conducts the BBC Symphony Orchestra in the overture to Nicolai's "The Merry Wives of Windsor."

4 | Spanish Music Copy

ANNCR: Our featured work this evening is a new recording of the Spanish operetta "La Boda de Luis Alonso," by Giménez. Our soloists are: Carlos Munguiá, as Luis Alonso; Inés Rivadeneira, singing the role of María Jesús; Gregorio Gil, as Paco; Raphael Maldonado, as Miguelito; and Ana María Fernández, as Picúa. The Gran Orquesta Sinfónica of Madrid and the Coros Cantores de Madrid are under the direction of Ataúlfo Argenta.

"La Boda de Luis Alonso," by Giménez.

ANNCR: London Records have brought us five recent albums featuring the music of Spain. We hear next "España, Volume Four," comprised of the following selections:

"La torre del oro," intermezzo, by Giménez.

"El tambor de granaderos," prelude, by Chapi.

"El baile de Luis Alonso," intermezzo, by Giménez.

"La boda de Luis Alonso," intermezzo, by Giménez.

"La revoltosa," prelude, by Chapi.

"Goyescas," intermezzo, by Granados.

"La pícara molinera," intermezzo, by Luna.

"La dolores," jota, by Bretón.

Ataúlfo Argenta conducts the Orquesta de Cámara de Madrid in the London album, "España, Volume Four."

ANNCR: Enrique Granados has long been considered Spain's outstanding nationalist composer. His music, which ranges from the operatic to lighter folk songs, all contains the spirit of his native land. Tonight we hear two songs--"Las currutacas modestas," and "La maja dolorosa"--sung for us by the Spanish mezzo-soprano Conchita Supervia.

ANNCR: Manuel de Falla inherited the role of Spain's first composer upon the death of Granados in 1916. De Falla, who died in 1946, fulfilled his mission well and has even outshone his mentor in popularity outside Spain. We hear next seven "Canciones populares españolas"--"El pano Moruno," "Seguidilla murciana," "Asturiana," "Jota," "Nana," "Canción," and "Polo." Conchita Supervia, mezzo-soprano, now sings seven "Canciones populares españolas," by de Falla.

ANNCR: From de Falla's "El amor brujo," Niñón Vallín, popular Spanish soprano, sings three selections: "Canción del amor dolido," "Canción del fuego fatuo," and "Danza del juego de amor."

ANNCR: José Serrano's popular comic operetta "Los Claveles" is the featured work this evening. The cast features Ana María Iriarte, as Rosa; Carlos Munguía, as Fernando; Julita Bermejo, as Jacinta; Marichu Urreta, as Paca; Ana María Fernández, as the Señorita; and Raphael Maldonado, as Goro. The Coros Cantores de Madrid and the Gran Orquesta Sinfónica are conducted by Ataúlfo Argenta.

ANNCR: One of Spain's younger composers is Odón Alonso.
The composer of several popular <u>zarzuelas</u>, or
operettas, he is equally acclaimed as the conductor
of the Coros de Radio Nacional in Madrid. Tonight's
featured work is his operetta "La Calesera." In the
cast of this London recording are: Pilar Lorengar,
as Maravillas; Teresa Berganza, as Elena; Manuel
Ausensi, as Raphael; Julita Bermejo, as Piruli;
Gerardo Monreal, as Gangarilla; and Gregorio Gil,
as Calatrava. The Coros Cantores de Madrid and the
Gran Orquesta Sinfónica are conducted by Indalecio
Cisneros.

ANNCR: The London album "España, Volume One" brings us the
following selections: "Navarra," by Isaac Albéniz;
"La procesión del rocío," by Joaquin Turina; ten
Basque dances, by Guridi; and "La oración del
torero," by Joaquín Turina. The Orquesta Nacional
de España is conducted by Ataúlfo Argenta.
The London album "España, Volume One."

ANNCR: We hear next the Montilla album, "La leyenda del
beso," by Soutullo y Vert. The Orquesta de Cámara

de Madrid and the Coros Radio Nacional de España
are conducted by Enrique Estela.

ANNCR: Songs of the bull ring are featured in the Montilla
album, "Pasodobles toreros." The Gran Orquesta
Española is conducted by Manuel Gómez de Arriba.

ANNCR: More songs of the bull ring are heard next. The
Montilla album "Marchas españolas" features the
Banda de Aviación Española, conducted by Manuel
Gómez de Arriba.

5 | Music Copy Using Various Languages, by Howard Rhines of KFAC, San Francisco

ANNCR: Polish composer-pianist Moritz Moszkowski wrote
music which follows closely the pattern created by
Schumann and Chopin. Like the latter, Moszkowski
proved that dance music may be both artistic and
scholarly, as illustrated in his suite of Spanish
dances.

George Weldon conducts the City of Birmingham
orchestra in two of Moszkowski's "Spanish Dances."

ANNCR: A highlight of the fourth act of Moussorgsky's

"Khovantchina" is the "Dance of the Persian Slaves,"

presented as a divertissement in the dramatic action.

As with "Boris Godunoff," Rimsky-Korsakov again

rendered service to Moussorgsky by completing that

composer's unfinished work.

Sir Thomas Beecham conducts the Royal Philharmonic

Orchestra in "Dance of the Persian Slaves," from

"Khovantchina."

ANNCR: Sixty-nine years ago this week, Eugene Goossens,

prominent English conductor and composer, was born

in London. Goossen's choice of a career is a case

of "like father like son," for his is the third

generation of orchestral conductors in his family.

Eugene Goossens conducts the London Philharmonic

Orchestra in the scherzo from Vaughan Williams'

"London" Symphony.

ANNCR: In his opera "Life for the Czar," first produced

in 1836, Glinka was the forerunner in the use of

folk themes and motives--a device used by other

later Slavic composers with great effect.

Efrem Kurtz conducts the Philharmonic Symphony Orchestra of New York in a mazurka from Glinka's "Life for the Czar."

ANNCR: A comment made several years ago by critic Pitts Sanborn serves very well to characterize the music of Samuel Barber. "His music reveals not only imaginative sympathy and technical address, but a respect for brevity which is the soul of more than wit. When he has had his say, he has the good sense to stop."

The Janssen Symphony Orchestra of Los Angeles plays Samuel Barber's overture to "The School for Scandal."

ANNCR: The compositions of British composer Eric Coates, invariably programmatic in nature, serve as an eloquent testimonial to the interest and beauty to be found in his native land.

From his own "London Suite," Eric Coates conducts the London Philharmonic Orchestra in the "Knights-bridge March."

460

ANNCR: One of the great attractions of the art of Artur

         Rubinstein is his versatility. A Rubinstein con-

         cert is a cross-section of many kinds and types of

         piano music, superbly interpreted.

         Artur Rubinstein plays Chopin's "Barcarolle" in F

         Sharp, Opus 60.

ANNCR: Alexander Glazunov was both talented and fortunate

         enough to have his reputation as a composer firmly

         established by the time he was 20. His long and

         peaceful life was devoted to his chosen field, to

         which he contributed so fully.

         Frederick Stock conducts the Chicago Symphony

         Orchestra in Glazunov's Concert Waltz in D Major.

ANNCR: For inspiration in the writing of his "San Juan

         Capistrano," Harl McDonald turned to the lore and

         charm of the American Southwest, with its Spanish

         influence and heritage.

         Serge Koussevitzky conducts the Boston Symphony

         Orchestra in "Fiesta," from "San Juan Capistrano."

ANNCR: The opera "Tsar Saltan" was based by Rimsky-Korsakov on a fantastic poem by his countryman, Alexander Pushkin. The stirring march from the opera is heard as the tsar and his legions march off to war.

Pierre Monteux conducts the San Francisco Symphony Orchestra in the "March" from Rimsky-Korsakov's "Tsar Saltan."

ANNCR: One hundred twenty years ago this week, Sir Arthur Sullivan was born in London. Although he was a prolific composer of songs, oratorios, and incidental music, Sullivan is best known today for the series of brilliant satirical operettas which he wrote with W.S. Gilbert. Eighty-two years ago this month, "Pinafore" received its first performance in England.

Emil Cote conducts his orchestra and chorus in selections from "Pinafore, or, The Slave of Duty."

ANNCR: The "Rakoczy March," one of the best known compositions credited to Berlioz, is actually an adaptation of a Hungarian tune of great antiquity.

Serge Koussevitzky conducts the Boston Symphony
Orchestra in the "Rakocszy March."

ANNCR: Forty-seven year old American composer David
Diamond has been a frequent prize winner with his
compositions. Among others, a Guggenheim fellow-
ship, the 1943 Paderewski prize, and $1,000 from
the American Academy of Arts and Letters have been
awarded him.

In 1947 Diamond composed a series of incidental
pieces inspired by the works of Shakespeare.

Thomas K. Scherman conducts the Little Orchestra
Society in David Diamond's overture to "Romeo and
Juliet."

ANNCR: Although British composer Roger Quilter has devoted most of his efforts to creating vocal music,
he has also composed a few orchestral works, characterized by the same graceful spontaneity as his
songs.

His "Children's Overture" is based on tunes from a

463

book of nursery rhymes titled "Baby's Opera."
Sir John Barbirolli conducts the London Philhar-
monic Orchestra in Roger Quilter's "Children's
Overture."

ANNCR: Anatol Liadoff was engrossed with Slavic folklore
and set his impressions down in his vivid, descrip-
tive music. "Baba Yaga" is written in the same
vein as his own "Kikimora" and tells of an inhuman
entity, in this case a witch, who lives in a house
with a fence made of the bones of her victims.
Fabien Sevitsky conducts the Indianapolis Symphony
Orchestra in Anatol Liadoff's "Baba Yaga."

ANNCR: Puerto-Rican born Jesús María Sanromá was a student
of Artur Schnabel, which undoubtedly is the basis
for his authoritative interpretations of the piano
repertoire.
Assisted by Arthur Fiedler and the Boston Pops
Orchestra, Jesús María Sanromá plays the second
movement of Edward MacDowell's Second Piano
Concerto, in D Minor.

ANNCR: One of Tchaikowsky's most poignant melodies is
found in a comparatively obscure song titled "Why
Must I Be Alone." As transcribed for full orchestra, new beauty is found in this brief, characteristic work.

Leopold Stokowski conducts the Hollywood Bowl
Orchestra in his own orchestration of "Solitude."

ANNCR: Now, a brief interlude in lighter vein, aptly il-
lustrating the effective use of strings, which
characterizes the distinctive arrangements of
Mantovani and his orchestra, prominent in British
musical circles.

Mantovani and his orchestra play Marchetti's
"Fascination."

ANNCR: Now, one of the delightful waltz melodies by Ernst
von Dohnányi, which was written for the score of
the pantomine "Pierrette's Veil." George Weldon
conducts the City of Birmingham orchestra in the
"Wedding Waltz."

SUNDAY EVENING CONCERT

THEME: CONCERTO NO. 1, RACHMANINOFF: ESTABLISH TO CUE
           AND FADE FOR:

TOM: This is Thomas Cassidy. For the next two hours
           you will hear "A Sunday Evening Concert." This
           feature of selected new recordings from the world
           of opera and concert is presented weekly at this
           time by Western Holly Gas Range Dealers, Day and
           Night Water Heater Division of Affiliated Gas
           Equipment Incorporated, and your neighborhood
           Servel Dealer. Join us in experiencing the joy of
           hearing great music on "A Sunday Evening Concert."

THEME: SAME AS ABOVE: UP TO CUE AND FADE FOR:

TOM: This "Sunday Evening Concert" at home should ex-
           cite the interest of our listeners, for we are
           going to present four recordings that are indeed
           firsts on records: · the overture to the Spanish
           <u>zarzuela</u> "La Revoltosa," by Chapi, the first re-
           cording of the Symphony in C Major, by Paul Dukas,
           the first recording of the Concerto No. 5 in F
           Major for Piano and Orchestra, by Saint-Saëns,

with Fabienne Jacquinot as soloist, the first recording of the orchestral suite from the opera
"Russlan and Ludmilla," by Glinka, and a majestic
new recording of the popular "Finlandia," by
Sibelius.

Music lovers throughout the United States are due
for a happy surprise when they discover the new
Soria recordings of Spanish zarzuelas. We have
had the privilege of timing and listening to five
of these new recordings, and they are a happy mix-
ture of Spanish folk music, great orchestral and
vocal recording, as well as a joyful hour of listening. As a sample of this bright and sparkling
music we open this Sunday Evening Concert with the
overture to the zarzuela "La Revoltosa," by
Ruperto Chapi. The Symphony Orchestra of Spain is
conducted by Rafael Ferrer.

MUSIC: LA REVOLTOSA - OVERTURE, CHAPI. SORIA-70-003 5:07

TOM: We have heard a new Soria recording of the overture
to the zarzuela "La Revoltosa," by Ruperto Chapi.
The Symphony Orchestra of Spain was conducted by
Rafael Ferrer.

COMMERCIAL: WESTERN HOLLY

TOM: For years, the reputation of the French composer

           Paul Dukas has rested chiefly on his "Scherzo for

           Orchestra." It is therefore of great interest to

           be able to present to our listeners the first re-

           cording of his Symphony in C Major, which has just

           been released by Urania records. It is to be hoped

           that this will be the beginning of additional in-

           terest in the many other fine compositions by

           Dukas, and the record collector and music lover

           will have the opportunity to more fully savor the

           talents of this master of orchestration. George

           Sebastian conducts the Colonne Orchestra of Paris

           in this first recording of the Symphony in C Major,

           by Dukas.

MUSIC: SYMPHONY IN C MAJOR, DUKAS: URLP-7102   40:01

TOM: George Sebastian has conducted the Colonne Orches-

           tra of Paris in the first recording of the Symphony

           in C Major, by Dukas; the recording was by Urania.

           Western Holly Gas Range Dealers, Day and Night

           Water Heater Division of Affiliated Gas Equipment

           Incorporated, and your neighborhood Servel Dealer

           are presenting this "Sunday Evening Concert" from

           The Music Station, KFAC AM and FM, Los Angeles.

MGM records brings the sparkling talent of the young French pianist, Fabienne Jacquinot, in the first recording of the Concerto No. 5 in F Major, by Saint-Saëns. The Concerto No. 5 was composed for the composer's Golden Jubilee Concert at the Salle Pleyel in Paris, June 2, 1896, with the composer as soloist. The concerto emerges as a summing up of his previous works and even makes use of a statement of the melody of "My Heart at Thy Sweet Voice" from his opera "Samson and Delilah," which appears in the first movement. We hear now the Concerto No. 5 in F Major, "The Egyptian," by Saint-Saëns, with Fabienne Jacquinot, pianist, and the Westminster Symphony Orchestra of London conducted by Anatole Fistoulari.

MUSIC: CONCERTO NO. 5, SAINT-SAËNS: E-3068   27:15

TOM: We have heard a new MGM recording of the Concerto No. 5 in F Major, "The Egyptian," by Saint-Saëns, with pianist Fabienne Jacquinot as soloist and the Westminster Symphony Orchestra of London conducted by Anatole Fistoulari.

The "Sunday Evening Concert" is presently weekly at this time by Western Holly Gas Range Dealers,

Day and Night Water Heater Division of Affiliated
Gas Equipment Incorporated, and your neighborhood
Servel Dealer. This is The Music Station, KFAC
AM and FM, Los Angeles.

COMMERCIAL: DAY AND NIGHT:

TOM: Perhaps one of the most widely known overtures
from the opera is the brilliant overture to "Russlan and Ludmilla," by Glinka. It is one of the
staples of the concert hall; but it was not until
recently that other music from the opera was made
available in an orchestral suite and subsequently
recorded. This task was recently accomplished by
MGM records. The suite comprises the aforemen-
tioned overture, the oriental dances or "Leszghinka,"
"Fairy Dances," and "March of the Wizard." Anatole
Fistoulari now conducts the London Symphony Orchestra in the orchestral suite from the opera "Russlan
and Ludmilla," by Glinka.

MUSIC: RUSSLAN AND LUDMILLA, GLINKA: E-3053   25:46

TOM: Anatole Fistoulari has conducted the London Symphony Orchestra on a new MGM recording of the orchestral suite from "Russlan and Ludmilla," by
Glinka.

470

COMMERCIAL: SERVEL:

TOM: One of the interesting short pieces recently re-
        leased on the Angel Record label is the popular
        tone poem "Finlandia," by Sibelius. This descrip-
        tive music of the homeland Sibelius loved so well
        receives an inspired reading and a dynamic record-
        ing in this performance by the Philharmonia Orches-
        tra conducted by Herbert von Karajan.

MUSIC: FINLANDIA, SIBELIUS:

TOM: Herbert von Karajan has conducted the Philharmonia
        Orchestra in a new performance for Angel Records
        of the tone poem "Finlandia," by Sibelius. This
        two-hour Sunday Evening Concert of selected new
        recordings from the world of opera and concert is
        presented weekly at this time by Western Holly Gas
        Range Dealers, Day and Night Water Heater Division
        of Affiliated Gas Equipment Incorporated, and your
        neighborhood Servel Dealer. This is Thomas Cas-
        sidy saying good night for the best in gas-operated
        home appliances.

THEME: SAME AS ABOVE: UP TO CLOSE

EVENING CONCERT (Hollywood Bowl)   8:00-10:30 PM
                                                      (Approx.)

THEME: ESTABLISH..........FADE FOR:

TOM: Good evening, friends, and welcome to your Gas

         Company's regular "Evening Concert" of the world's

         finest music. The "Evening Concert," offered for

         your enjoyment by the Southern California and

         Southern Counties Gas Companies, regularly brings

         you the best music available for broadcasting,

         Monday through Saturday, from 8 to 10 o'clock.

THEME: SAME AS ABOVE: UP TO CUE AND FADE FOR:

TOM: This is Thomas Cassidy inviting you to enjoy with

         us another outstanding musical event. Tonight,

         your Gas Company's "Evening Concert" is privileged

         to bring you another gala opening night broadcast

         of "Symphonies Under the Stars" in Hollywood Bowl,

         featuring the Los Angeles Philharmonic Orchestra.

         This initial broadcast of the 36th season of

         "Symphonies Under the Stars" is to be broadcast

         directly from Hollywood Bowl in a half-hour at

         8:30. For those of our listeners who are equipped

         to pick up this live broadcast in stereophonic

         sound, we'd like to remind you that the live portion of the broadcast will begin at 8:30, which will give you an opportunity to adjust your receivers for the best reception of an exceptional event. Because of the interest in the high-fidelity aspects of this broadcast in stereophonic sound, we have selected the newest recording by tonight's conductor to begin our program from the studios of KFAC. Paul Paray conducts the Detroit Symphony Orchestra in their new Mercury recording of "L'arlésienne Suites 1 and 2," by Bizet.

MUSIC: L'ARLESIENNE - SUITES, BIZET: MG-50135

TOM: This is Thomas Cassidy speaking to you from Hollywood Bowl. We have just presented from the Studios of KFAC a new Mercury recording of "L'arlésienne Suites 1 and 2," by Bizet, featuring our opening night conductor, Paul Paray, conducting the Detroit Symphony Orchestra. The record number is MG-50135. The special occasion for this evening's broadcast, brought to you by the Southern California and Southern Counties Gas Companies, is the opening concert of the 36th season of "Symphonies Under the Stars" in Hollywood Bowl.

              (CUE FOR STATION)

473

This is your Gas Company's Evening Concert of the
world's finest music. This is The Music Station,
KFAC AM and FM, Los Angeles.

(COMMERCIAL)

TOM: Tonight, your Gas Company is pleased to present,
for the 6th consecutive year, the opening performance of the Hollywood Bowl season. And we are
proud to be able to bring you tonight's program in
a special stereophonic broadcast. Two microphones
have been placed in strategic locations on the
Hollywood Bowl stage. One microphone will carry
the broadcast to KFAC's AM broadcast band. The
second microphone will transmit the program to
KFAC's FM broadcast band. If you have an FM receiver and an AM receiver, you will be able to
hear tonight's program in true stereophonic sound.
Of course, you can still hear the normal broadcast
on the set you regularly use. This opening concert of the new Hollywood Bowl season brings to
Southland music lovers the distinguished French
conductor, Paul Paray. For the past seven years
he has served as musical director of the Detroit
Symphony Orchestra and as guest conductor of the

principal eastern orchestras including the New York Philharmonic, Pittsburgh Symphony, Philadelphia Orchestra, and others. His appearance tonight in Hollywood Bowl with the Los Angeles Philharmonic Orchestra marks his Pacific Coast debut. Appearing as soloist with Paul Paray for this opening concert is the distinguished pianist, Alexander Brailowsky. Although he is famed for his interpretations of the music of Chopin and Liszt, Brailowsky has selected the Rachmaninoff Concerto No. 2 in C Minor for his Hollywood Bowl appearance.

Our program will open with the symphonic poem "Les préludes," by Liszt, followed by the Rachmaninoff concerto featuring Mr. Brailowsky. Following intermission, Paul Paray will conduct the Symphony in D Minor, by César Franck.

The symphonic poem "Les préludes," by Liszt, is based on one of the "Méditations poétiques" of Lamartine. It depicts musically the events of man's life on earth, showing them as a series of preludes to the life after death.

The lines of Lamartine are effectively portrayed

in powerful and effective musical terms, describing the beauty and happiness of love, the cruel storms that can shatter tranquility like a thunderbolt, the escape from cruelty in the life of the country, and the hastening to ward off peril when duty calls, therein discovering one's true nature and power.

This 36th season of "Symphonies Under the Stars" is replete with an outstanding array of talent that will bring to music lovers a truly inspiring festival of music, outstanding instrumental and vocal soloists, brilliant symphonic and orchestral compositions, as well as special Friday night features and Saturday night "pops" concerts. During intermission, we shall present a musical montage which we have prepared to renew your acquaintance with some of the world's great music and artists that will make up the program content of the Bowl season.

(COLOR AS NEEDED)

(DESCRIPTION OF COLOR CEREMONY ETC.)

Now our national anthem:

DIRECT CUE: Paul Paray conducts the Los Angeles Philharmonic Orchestra in the symphonic poem "Les Préludes,"

by Liszt.

MUSIC: LES PRELUDES, LISZT:

TOM: Paul Paray has conducted the Los Angeles Philhar-

monic Orchestra in the symphonic prelude "Les

Préludes," by Liszt.

The second feature to be presented on this Holly-

wood Bowl program will bring us the artistry of

pianist Alexander Brailowsky in the popular

Rachmaninoff Concerto No. 2 in C Minor.

The C-Minor Concerto marked a turning point in the

composer's life--on one side lay mental turmoil and

black despair engendered by the failure of his

first symphony; on the other was a return to com-

position, the new concerto, and with it a realiza-

tion of immense creative powers as a composer. For

Rachmaninoff this work marked the victory over

morbid introspection.

(COLOR AS NEEDED)

DIRECT CUE: Alexander Brailowsky plays the Concerto No. 2

in C Minor, by Rachmaninoff--with the Los Angeles

Philharmonic Orchestra conducted by Paul Paray.

MUSIC: CONCERTO NO. 2, RACHMANINOFF:

TOM: Alexander Brailowsky, pianist, has played the Con-
        certo No. 2 in C Minor, by Rachmaninoff, with the
        Los Angeles Philharmonic Orchestra conducted by
        Paul Paray.

                    (COLOR AS NEEDED)

        Your Gas Company's special broadcast of the open-
        ing concert of the 36th season of "Symphonies Under
        the Stars" in Hollywood Bowl is being broadcast in
        stereophonic sound and through regular broadcast
        transmission. This is The Music Station, KFAC AM
        and FM, Los Angeles. The stereophonic portion of
        our broadcast will continue following our inter-
        mission feature.

ENGINEER'S DIRECT CUE:

TOM: This opening concert is a fitting prelude to an
        outstanding season of concerts; let us preview by
        tape recording some of the great moments of music
        that will make up this festival season. Following
        this opening concert, Paul Paray will return this
        Thursday, July 11, to conduct an exceptional con-
        cert that will feature the debut in Hollywood Bowl
        of the distinguished Italian soprano, Antonietta
        Stella. Mr. Paray will feature the orchestra in the

Beethoven Symphony No. 7, the suite from "El amor brujo," by de Falla, and the overture to Wagner's "Tannhäuser." This lovely voice will be heard in Hollywood Bowl this coming Thursday night.

MUSIC: SEMPRE LIBERA: 1:37

TOM: On Tuesday, July 16, Paul Paray will conduct the orchestra in the Brahms Symphony No. 2 in D Major and "Capriccio espagnole," by Rimsky-Korsakov. Appearing as soloist will be violinist Erica Morini; the music of Tschaikovsky's Violin Concerto will display this artistry.

MUSIC: CONCERTO IN D, TSCHAIKOVSKY: 1:11

TOM: Thursday, July 18, will mark a return appearance of Marian Anderson singing arias from "Jeanne d'Arc," by Tschaikovsky, and "La Favorita," by Donizetti. Making his Hollywood Bowl debut will be the conductor of the Seattle Symphony Orchestra, Milton Katims, conducting the Tschaikovsky Fourth Symphony and "The Pines of Rome," by Respighi. A notable debut will take place when the Hungarian pianist György Cziffra is heard in the first of two concerts on Tuesday, July 23, with Milton Katims conducting. In addition to the Brahms Fourth Symphony, the Tschaikovsky Piano Concerto No. 1 will

be heard. In his second appearance with Georg

Solti on August 1, György Cziffra will display his

dynamic pianism.

MUSIC: CONCERTO NO. 1, LISZT.   1:58

TOM: The Royal Danish Ballet will make two appearances

   in Hollywood Bowl, Thursday, July 25, and Saturday,

   July 27. This music from Nielsen's "Maskarade"

   will highlight their first appearance.

MUSIC: MASKARADE OVERTURE, NIELSEN: :59

TOM: Tuesday, July 30, will mark the debut of 'cellist

   Janos Starker with Georg Solti conducting the

   "Háry János" suite, by Kodaly. They will join in

   presenting the Dvořák 'Cello Concerto.

MUSIC: CONCERTO IN B MINOR, DVORAK: 1:40

TOM: Thursday, August 1, will mark the second concert

   by György Cziffra. On Tuesday, August 6, Georg

   Solti will conduct an all-Brahms concert featuring

   the sensational young contralto Lucrezia West in

   her Bowl debut. This beautiful voice will be

   heard on August 6.

MUSIC: TOD UND DAS MAEDCHEN, SCHUBERT: 1:17

TOM: Opera Night will be presented Thursday, August 8,

with soprano Dorothy Kirsten and tenor Kirk Oreste joining with conductor Kurt Herbert Adler in exciting moments from grand opera. The famous Roger Wagner Chorale will make an outstanding impression when they present this dynamic music--Carl Orff's "Carmina Burana," Tuesday, August 10.

MUSIC: CARMINA BURANA, ORFF: 1:18

TOM: The fabulous coloratura soprano Rita Streich will make her first appearance in Hollywood Bowl with Howard Mitchell conducting the concert on Thursday, August 15. In addition to the suite from "Der Rosenkavalier," by Richard Strauss, and the Creston Symphony No. 2, Howard Mitchell will present Miss Streich in such Straussian flights as these.

MUSIC: VILLAGE SWALLOWS, STRAUSS: 1:47

TOM: William Steinberg will conduct the last four symphony concerts: an all-Tschaikovsky program, Tuesday, August 20; violinist Isaac Stern playing the Tschaikovsky Violin Concerto on Thursday, August 22; and the sensational Canadian pianist Glenn Gould in his Bowl première, Tuesday, August 27. In addition to the performance of the Bee-

481

thoven Concerto No. 4, Steinberg will honor the 75th birthday of Igor Stravinsky when he recaptures this exciting music from "The Firebird."

MUSIC: FIREBIRD, STRAVINSKY: 1:24

TOM: In the final symphony concert, Thursday, August 29, William Steinberg will bring back to Hollywood Bowl the sensational surprise of last year's Bowl season, soprano Birgit Nilsson. In addition to the overture to Wagner's "The Flying Dutchman" and the Richard Strauss tone poem "Death and Transfiguration," to be played by the orchestra, Miss Nilsson will join Mr. Steinberg in the "Prelude" and "Liebestod" from Wagner's "Tristan and Isolde" and this exciting moment from "Salomé," by Strauss.

MUSIC: SALOME, STRAUSS: 2:07

(PICKUP FROM HOLLYWOOD BOWL)

TOM: This is Thomas Cassidy speaking once again from Hollywood Bowl. We have presented by tape recording a musical montage of highlights from the 36th season of "Symphonies Under the Stars" in Hollywood Bowl.

On behalf of our many listeners, we'd like to express our good wishes for a successful Hollywood Bowl season.

(STATION BREAK)

TOM: Your Gas Company's "Evening Concert" is presenting this special concert in stereophonic sound and by regular broadcast transmission. This is The Music Station, KFAC AM and FM, Los Angeles. The second half of our broadcast from Hollywood Bowl will feature the Franck D-Minor Symphony. Composed in 1888, the symphony was greeted with obstinacy at its première at the Paris Conservatoire, February 17, 1889. This was due mostly to the fact that the performance was almost forced upon the members by the conductor, Jules Garcin. They were predisposed to find no good in it. Franck was far from discouraged, for he had the opportunity to hear the symphony in its completed form and reasserted his confidence in the merits of his work.

The symphony is infused with a glowing mysticism which is almost unique in a composition of this type. Many have found in it a source of healing and inspiration as though it were endowed with some spiritual force.

(COLOR AS NEEDED)

DIRECT CUE: Paul Paray conducts the Los Angeles Philhar-

monic Orchestra in the Symphony in D Minor, by

Franck.

MUSIC: SYMPHONY IN D MINOR, FRANCK: 35:23

TOM: Paul Paray has conducted the Los Angeles Philhar-

monic Orchestra in the Symphony in D Minor, by

César Franck.

This special broadcast of the opening night con-

cert of the 36th season of "Symphonies Under the

Stars" in Hollywood Bowl has served to bring our

listeners a live symphony concert in stereophonic

sound.

The "Evening Concert," offered for your enjoyment

by the Southern California and Southern Counties

Gas Companies, regularly brings you the best music

available for broadcasting Monday through Saturday

from 8 to 10 o'clock.

This is Thomas Cassidy saying good night for your

Gas Company.

THEME: SAME AS ABOVE: UP TO CLOSE

484

Wire-Service Copy for Sportscasts

Here, as in the section "Wire-Service Copy for Newscasts," AP and UPI have supplied all copy and granted permission to leave it exactly as it came in over the wires. You should carefully edit out all errors before attempting to read the copy "on the air."

KNOXVILLE, TENNESSEE (UPI)--TENNESSEE HAS WRAPPED UP
ITS SECOND SOUTHEASTERN CONFERENCE FOOTBALL CHAMPIONSHIP
IN THREE YEARS WITH A 40-27 TRIUMPH OVER VANDERBILT.

QUARTERBACK BOBBY SCOTT PASSED FOR ONE TOUCHDOWN AND
RAN FOR ANOTHER IN LEADING THE GATOR BOWL-BOUND VOLUNTEERS.
A 25-YARD PASS INTERCEPTION BY SAFETY BILL YOUNG AND A 37-
YARD FIELD GOAL BY GEORGE HUNT HELPED TENNESSEE BUILD A
26-7 HALFTIME LEAD.

FOOTBALL RATINGS

NEW YORK (UPI)--TEXAS...PENN STATE...AND ARKANSAS HAVE
SET THE STAGE FOR THE NATIONAL COLLEGE FOOTBALL
CHAMPIONSHIP. DURING THE PAST WEEK, ALL THREE TEAMS
SCORED IMPRESSIVE VICTORIES AND REMAINED UNDEFEATED. THAT
SATURDAY SHOWDOWN BATTLE BETWEEN TEXAS AND ARKANSAS WILL
DECIDE IT ALL. UNITED PRESS INTERNATIONAL'S FINAL RATINGS
WILL BE RELEASED NEXT TUESDAY. THIS WEEK'S RATINGS HAVE
TEXAS AGAIN NUMBER ONE WITH 29 FIRST PLACE VOTES AND A
TOTAL OF 334 POINTS, PENN STATE IS SECOND AND ARKANSAS,
THIRD. OHIO STATE MOVED UP FROM FIFTH TO SIXTH.

IN ORDER...IT'S TEXAS, FIRST...PENN STATE, SECOND...

ARKANSAS, THIRD...SOUTHERN CALIFORNIA, FOURTH...OHIO STATE,
FIFTH...MISSOURI, SIXTH...LOUISIANA, SEVENTH...MICHIGAN,
EIGHTH...NOTRE DAME, NINTH....AND U-C-L-A, 10TH.

TENNESSEE LEADS THE SECOND TEN, FOLLOWED BY NEBRASKA
AND AUBURN, TIED FOR 12TH...STANFORD, 14TH...MISSISSIPPI,
15TH....HOUSTON, 16TH....FLORIDA, 17TH....WEST VIRGINIA,
18TH...AND PURDUE AND SAN DIEGO STATE TIED FOR 19TH.

NEW YORK (UPI)--THERE'S SOME ROARING BEING HEARD FROM
THE NITTANY LIONS.

THE PENN STATE FOOTBALL SQUAD, PARTICULARLY ALL-AMERICA
LINEBACKER DENNY ONKOTZ, CANNOT UNDERSTAND WHY IT HASN'T
BEEN RATED NUMBER ONE IN THE NATION. THE NITTANY LIONS
HAVE GONE THROUGH THEIR LAST 29 GAMES WITHOUT A DEFEAT AND
ARE 10-0 THIS SEASON. THEY TROUNCED NORTH CAROLINA STATE
33-8 BEFORE A NATIONAL TELEVISION AUDIENCE YESTERDAY.

AND DENNY ONKOTZ SAYS--IN HIS WORDS NOW--"IF WE DON'T
DESERVE TO BE NUMBER ONE, NOBOADDS: "WE CAN BEAT TEXAS OR
ARKANSAS OR ANYONE ELSE." THE LINEBACKER'S REMARKS
APPARENTLY STEMMED FROM A SPORTS COMMENTATOR'S TOUTING OF
NEXT WEEK'S TEXAS-ARKANAS GAME AS A "NATIONAL
CHAMPIONSHIP" C//////////////////

AND DENNY ONKOTZ SAYS--IN HIS WORDS NOW--"IF WE DON'T DESERVE TO BE NUMBER ONE, NOBODY DOES." AND HE ADDS: "WE CAN BEAT TEXAS OR ARKANSAS OR ANYONE ELSE." THE LINEBACKER'S REMARKS APPARENTLY STEMMED FROM A SPORTS COMMENTATOR'S TOUTING OF NEXT WEEK'S TEXAS-ARKANAS GAME AS A "NATIONAL CHAMPIONSHIP" CONTEST.

AND COACH JOE PATERNO ALSO ADMITS TO BEING "ANNOYED" BY AN APPARENT SNUB OF HIS SQUAD...WHICH IS RATED SECOND BEHIND TEXAS IN THE LATEST UNITED PRESS INTERNATIONAL POLL. PENN STATE IS IDLE NOW UNTIL ITS ORANGE BOWL ENCOUNTER AGAINST MISSOURI.

SAN DIEGO (UPI)--THE SAN DIEGO CHARGERS HAVE REACHED CONTRACT TERMS WITH QUARTERBACK MARTY DOMRES OF COLUMBIA AND END SKIP ORSZULAK OF PITTSBURG. DOMRES WAS SAN DIEGO'S FIRST DRAFT CHOICE AND ORSZULAK THE FIFTH PICK. THE TWO WILL LEAVE TODAY FOR THE COACHES ALL-AMERICAN GAME IN ATLANTA, GEORGIA. TWO OTHER CHARGER DRAFTEES WILL BE PLAYING IN THE ALL-AMERICAN CONTEST. THEY ARE LINEBACKER BOB BABICH OF MIAMI OF OHIO AND RUNNING BACK RON SAYERS FROM THE UNIVERSITY OF NEBRASKA AT OMAHA.

HOUSTON (UPI)--THE UNIVERSITY OF HOUSTON DEFEATED FLORIDA STATE 41-13 AS JIM STRONG, THE NATION'S SIXTH LEADING RUSHER, SCORED THREE TOUCHDOWNS. QUARTERBACK GARY MULLINS ACCOUNTED FOR TWO ADDITIONAL TOUCHDOWNS IN THE HOUSTON VICTORY. MULLINS RAN 51 YARDS FOR ONE SCORE... HE PASSED 23 YARDS TO SPLIT END ELMO WRIGHT FOR HIS OTHER SCORING CONTRIBUTION. HOUSTON'S DEFENSIVE LINE BROKE THROUGH THE FLORIDA STATE LINE SEVERAL TIMES IN THE SECOND HALF TO DUMP QUARTERBACK BILL CAPPLEMAN FOR A TOTAL OF 85 YARDS IN LOSSES. IN SPITE OF THE HOUSTON DEFENSE, CAPPLEMAN COMPLETED 18 OF 37 PASSES. TWO OF HIS PASSES WERE FOR TOUCHDOWNS.

MIAMI (UPI)--GATOR BOWL BOUND FLORIDA SCORED A 35-16 VICTORY OVER MIAMI OF FLORIDA. TOMMY DURRANCE SCORED THREE TOUCHDOWNS...ALL-AMERICA FLANKER CARLOS ALVAREZ BROKE THREE SOUTHEASTERN CONFERENCE PASS CATCHING RECORDS ...AND QUARTERBACK JOHN REAVES SHATTERED BABE PARILLI'S 19-YEAR-OLD CONFERENCE RECORD WITH HIS 24TH TOUCHDOWN PASS OF THE SEASON. FLORIDA WON ITS EIGHTH GAME OF THE SEASON AGAINST ONE LOSS AND ONE TIE. THE FLORIDA SQUAD FACES TENNESSEE IN THE GATOR BOWL DECEMBER 27TH.

SAN DIEGO (UPI)--DEL PIFER'S ONE-YARD SMASH WITH THREE MINUTES REMAINING LAST NIGHT BROUGHT SAN DIEGO STATE FROM BEHIND FOR A 36-32 VICTORY OVER A FIRED-UP CAL STATE LONG BEACH FOOTBALL SQUAD. THE VICTORY BOOSTED THE AZTECS' RECORD TO 10-0 FOR THEIR THIRD UNDEFEATED SEASON IN FOUR YEARS. THE AZTECS PLAY BOSTON UNIVERSITY NEXT WEEKEND IN THE PASADENA BOWL. SAN DIEGO STATE HAD TO SCORE 15 POINTS IN THE FINAL QUARTER FOR LAST NIGHT'S VICTORY. AZTEC QUARTERBACK DENNIS SHAW FIRED TWO TOUCHDOWN PASSES IN THE GAME FOR A TOTAL OF 39 ON THE SEASON.

(UPI)

IN THE NATIONAL FOOTBALL LEAGUE...

LOS ANGELES 24 WASHINGTON 13

BALTIMORE 13 ATLANTA 6

CLEVELAND 28 CHICAGO 24

NEW ORLEANS 26 PHILADELPHIA 17

ST. LOUIS 47 PITTSBURGH 10

AT THE HALF, GREEN BAY 13 NEW YORK GIANTS 10

-O-

IN THE AMERICAN FOOTBALL LEAGUE...

BUFFALO 16CINCINNATI 13

OAKLAND 27 NEW YORK JETS 14

AFTER ONE QUARTER, MIAMI 9 BOSTON 6

(UPI)--THE CONTINENTAL FOOTBALL LEAGUE PLAY-OFFS
CONTINUE NEXT WEEK. TEXAS DIVISION WINNER SAN ANTONIO
PLAYS PACIFIC DIVISION TITLIST LAS VEGAS ON SATURDAY, THE
WINNER TO MEET INDIANAPOLIS ON DECEMBER 13TH.
INDIANAPOLIS, CENTRAL DIVISION WINNER, MOVED INTO THE GAME
BY DOWNING ATLANTIC DIVISION CHAMPION ORLANDO---TWO-TIME
C-F-L DEFENDING TITLIST---27-7 LAST WEEKEND.

DES MOINES (UPI)---THE IOWA INDUSTRIAL COMMISSION MUST
DECIDE IF INJURED FOOTBALL PLAYERS ATTENDING STATE
COLLEGES ON SCHOLARSHIPS ARE ELIGIBLE FOR WORKMEN'S
COMPENSATION. EDWARD PUNDT, A 22-YEAR-OLD FARMER IN NEW
HOMESTEAD, IS CLAIMING THE STATE OWES HIM MONEY. PUNDT
ATTENDED IOWA STATE UNIVERSITY ON A FOOTBALL GRANT IN AID.
DURING A PRACTICE HE WAS INJURED, AND CLAIMS, BECAUSE OF
HIS GRANT, THAT AN EMPLOYEE-EMPLOYER RELATIONSHIP WAS IN
EFFECT.

NEW YORK (UPI)--THE BALTIMORE COLTS SCORED A 13-6
VICTORY OVER THE ATLANTA FALCONS. RESERVE RUNNING BACK

492

LARRY CONJAR BLOCKED AN ATLANTA PUNT TO HELP SET UP THE
COLTS' ONLY TOUCHDOWN. IT CAME LATE IN THE FOURTH QUARTER
WITH BALTIMORE HOLDING A SLIM 6-3 LEAD. BALTIMORE WENT 45
YARDS IN FOUR PLAYS FOR THE SCORE. TOM MATTE SWEPT THE
LEFT SIDE FOR TWO YARDS AND THE TOUCHDOWN. LOU MICHAELS
ADDED TWO FIELD GOALS. BOB ETTER KICKED TWO FIELD GOALS
FOR ATLANTA'S SCORING. BALTIMORE'S VETERAN QUARTERBACK
JOHNNY UNITAS PLAYED THE ENTIRE GAME FOR THE COLTS. IT
WAS THE FIRST TIME THIS SEASON UNITAS WENT A FULL GAME. . . .
HE COMPLETED 13 OF 23 PASSES.

NEW YORK (UPI)--JIM HART THREW THREE TOUCHDOWN PASSES
TO LEAD THE ST. LOUIS CARDINALS TO A 47-10 TRIUMPH OVER
THE PITTSBURGH STEELERS. CID EDWARDS PICKED UP 176 YARDS
. . . TEAMMATE DAVE WILLIAMS TOOK ALL THREE OF HART'S
TOUCHDOWN PASSES. PITTSBURGH'S ONLY TOUCHDOWN CAME IN THE
FOURTH QUARTER WHEN TERRY HANRATTY HIT JON HENDERSON WITH
A 20-YARD SCORING PASS. FOR THE STEELERS, IT WAS THE 10TH
STRAIGHT DEFEAT AFTER WINNING THEIR SEASON OPENER.

NEW YORK (UPI)--OTTAWA REIGNS AS GREY CUP CHAMPIONS.
THE CANADIAN FOOTBALL LEAGUE'S MOST VALUABLE PLAYER, RUSS

JACKSON, PASSED FOR THREE TOUCHDOWNS AND 254 YARDS O LEAD

OTTAWA TO A 29-11 WIN OVER SASKATCHEWAN. THE OTTAWA

DEFENSE HELD SASKATCHEWAN'S TOP GROUND THREAT, GEORGE

REED, TO JUST 28 YARDS IN 11 CARRIES.

2 | Baseball

(UPI)

RICHMOND	100	100	100--3	10	1
BUFFALO	000	000	000--0	6	2

MAXIE AND BOOKER: DENEHY, LINES (8) AND BRYAN.

LP--DENEHY

-O-

AMERICAN ASSOCIATION

TULSA	020	000	000--2	9	1
INDIANAPOLIS	000	005	30X--8	8	1

REUSS, CAMPISI (6), MONTEAGUDA (8) AND SIMMONS;

COSMAN, MORRIS (2) AND PLUMMER. WP--MORRIS LP--REUSS

HR--PUTTERSON

CHICAGO (UPI)--SPARKED BY BOOG POWELL'S TWO HOME RUNS

AND THREE RUNS BATTED IN, THE BALTIMORE ORIOLES ROLLED UP

A SEASON HIGH OF 19 HITS SATURDAY TO SWAMP THE CHICAGO

WHITE SOX, 13-3, AND RACK UP THEIR EIGHTH VICTORY IN THE

LAST 10 GAMES.

POWELL HOMERED WITH DON BUFORD ON BASE IN THE FIRST
AND AGAIN WITH THE BASES EMPTY IN THE THIRD WHILE BROOKS
ROBINSON HIT A TWO-RUN HOMER IN THE FOURTH. POWELL'S
TOTAL HOMERS CLIMBED TO 13 AND ROBINSON'S TO NINE.

THE ORIOLES BARRAGE CAME AGAINST FIVE WHITE SOX
PITCHERS AND STARTER TOMMY JOHN TOOK HIS FIFTH LOSE
AGAINST FOUR WINS, GIVING UP SEVEN HITS AND FIVE RUNS IN
ONLY TWO INNINGS.

JIM PALMER WAS THE BENEFICIARY OF THE ORIOLE ATTACK,
RACKING UP HIS EIGHTH VICTORY AGAINST TWO LOSSES AS HE
ALLOWED EIGHT HITS AND THREE RUNS IN EIGHT INNINGS.

ALL CHICAGO'S RUNS CAME ON HOMERS, A TWO-RUN DRIVE BY
ROOKIE BOB CHRISTIAN AND A SOLO BY WOODY HELD.

--REPEATING AND CORRECTING--

CHICAGO (UPI)--SPARKED BY BOOG POWELL'S TWO HOME RUNS
AND THREE RUNS BATTED IN, THE BALTIMORE ORIOLES ROLLED UP
A SEASON HIGH OF 19 HITS SATURDAY TO SWAMP THE CHICAGO
WHITE SOX, 12-3, AND RACK UP THEIR EIGHTH VICTORY IN THE
LAST 10 GAMES.

_____

MINNEAPOLIS (UPI)--THE CALIFORNIA ANGELS, WHO TRADED
TOM SATRIANO FOR JOE AZCUE IN A DEAL WITH THE BOSTON RED
SOX SUNDAY, OPEN A FOUR-GAME SERIES AGAINST THE MINNESOTA
TWINS TONIGHT.

THE ANGELS WERE RAINED OUT AT WASHINGTON SUNDAY.

TOM MURPHY, 4-3, WILL PITCH FOR THE ANGELS AGAINST
JIM PERRY, 4-3, OR DICK WOODSON, 3-2, TONIGHT.

TUESDAY'S LEADERS (AP)

AMERICAN

BATTING (150 AT BATS): CAREW, MINNESOTA, .382; F.
ROBINSON, BALTIMORE, .338; R. SMITH, BOSTON, .330;
PETROCELLI, BOSTON, .326; HEGAN, SEATTLE, .310.

HOME RUNS: R. JACKSON, OAKLAND, 24; PETROCELLI, BOSTON,
20; F. HOWARD, WASHINGTON, 19; YASTRZEMSKI, BOSTON, 18;
PEPITONE, NEW YORK, 17.

NATIONAL

BATTING: M. ALOU, PITTSBURGH, .364; A. JOHNSON,
CINCINNATI, .362; MCCOVEY, SAN FRANCISCO, .353; H. AARON,
ATLANTA, .344; STARGELL, PITTSBURGH, .343.

HOME RUNS: MCCOVEY, SAN FRANCISCO, 21; L. MAY,
CINCINNATI, 18; R. ALLEN, PHILADELPHIA, H. AARON, ATLANTA,
17; WYNN, HOUSTON 15.

BY CHARLES WIESER

OMAHA, NEB. (UPI)--THE MASSACHUSETTS REDMEN SHUTOUT
THE SOUTHERN ILLINOIS SALUKIS 2-0 AND NEW YORK UNIVERSITY
BELTED MISSISSIPPI 8-3 SATURDAY NIGHT TO WIND UP THE FIRST
ROUND OF THE 1969 COLLEGE WORLD SERIES.

JOHN KITCHEN, A BIG RIGHTHANDER, WAS IN COMPLETE
CONTROL THROUGHOUT THE UPSET OF SOUTHERN ILLINOIS, RATED
THE NATION'S NO. COLLEGE TEAM HEADING INTO THE 23RD ANNUAL
NCAA TOURNEY. KITCHEN STRUCK OUT 11, WALKED NONE AND DID
NOT PERMIT A RUNNER PAST SECOND BASE IN FASHIONING A
STRONG THREE-HITTER.

THE NYU-MISSISSIPPI CONTEST WAS A CLOSE MATCH UNTIL
THE NEW YORKERS PUSHED HOME FOUR RUNS IN THE TOP OF THE
NINTH. THE BIG BLOW WAS A SINGLE TO LEFT-CENTER BY JOHN
LATOURETTE WITH THE BASES LOADED. THE HIT SCORED TWO
RUNS, AND WHEN MISSISSIPPI SHORTSTOP WHITEY ADAMS TOOK
THE RELAY AND THREW WILDLY TO SECOND BASE, ANOTHER RUN
SCORED AND LATOURETTE WOUND UP ON THIRD.

EARLIER IN THE INNING RAY IPPOLITO SLAMMED THE FIRST
TRIPLE OF THE SERIES TO PUT NYU AHEAD 5-3.

NYU HAD WIPED OUT A 2-0 MISSISSIPPI LEAD WITH A THREE-
RUN RALLY IN THE TOP OF THE FIFTH AND ADDED ANOTHER RUN IN
THE EIGHTH. MISSISSIPPI SCORED TWICE IN THE FOURTH AND

ONCE IN THE EIGHTH.

ELLSWORTH JONES, A SOUTHPAW, PITCHED 71/3 INNINGS FOR THE WINNERS TO NOTCH HIS SEVENTH VICTORY AGAINST ONE DEFEAT. THE LOSS WENT TO FRED SETSER WHO WAS RELIEVED IN THE FIFTH.

THERE WILL BE NO GAMES SUNDAY. ON MONDAY MISSISSIPPI PLAYS SOUTHERN ILLINOIS, WITH THE LOSER ELIMINATED. TEXAS TANGLES WITH TULSA AND MASSACHUSETTS PLAYS NYU IN OTHER SECOND ROUND ACTION.

EARLIER SATURDAY ARIZONA STATE ELIMINATED THE FIRST TEAM OF THE EIGHT CLUBS IN THE TOURNAMENT WHEN THE SUN DEVILS TOOK AN 11-INNING 2-1 WIN OVER THE UCLA BRUINS. THE BRUINS HAD LOST TO TULSA 6-5 FRIDAY.

SECOND BASEMENT TONY SEMINO WAS THE HITTING HERO OF THE MASSACHUSETTS TRIUMPH SATURDAY NIGHT AS HE KNOCKED IN BOTH RUNS, ONE IN THE FOURTH AND THE OTHER IN THE EIGHTH. PICKUP 6TH PGH: THE VICTORY WAS KITCHEN'S

-O-

NYU   000 030 014--8 8 1
MISS   000 200 010--3 5 1

JONES, MARINO (8) AND BARTO; SETSER, KAUREZ (5), CAIN (8), WILLIAMS (9) AND WADE. WP-JONES (7-1); LP-SETSER (6-3)

OMAHA, NEB. (UPI)--THE MASSACHUSETTS REDMEN SHUTOUT THE
SOUTHERN ILLINOIS SALUKIS 2-0 AND NEW YORK UNIVERSITY
BELTED MISSISSIPPI 8-3 SATURDAY NIGHT TO WIND UP THE FIRST
ROUND OF THE 1969 COLLEGE WORLD SERIES.

JOHN KITCHEN, A BIG RIGHTHANDER, WAS IN COMPLETE
CONTROL THROUGHOUT THE UPSET OF SOUTHERN ILLINOIS, RATED
THE NATION'S NO. 1 COLLEGE TEAM HEADING INTO THE 23RD
ANNUAL NCAA TOURNEY. KITCHEN STRUCK OUT 11, WALKED NONE
AND DID NOT PERMIT A RUNNER PAST SECOND BASE IN FASHIONING
A STRONG THREE-HITTER.

THE BYU-MISSISSIPPI CONTEST WAS A CLOSE MATCH UNTIL THE
NEW YORKERS PUSHED HOME FOUR RUNS IN THE TOP OF THE NINTH.
THE BIG BLOW WAS A SINGLE TO LEFT-CENTS BY JOHN
LATOURETTE WITH THE BASES LOADED. THE HIT SCORED TWO RUNS,
AND WHEN MISSISSIPPI SHORTSTOP WHITEY ADAMS TOOK THE RELAY
AND THREW WILDLY TO SECOND BASE, ANOTHER RUN SCORED AND
LATOURETTE WOUND UP ON THIRD.

SECOND BASEMAN TONY SEMINO WAS THE HITTING HERO OF THE
MASSACHUSETTS TRIUMPH SATURDAY NIGHT AS HE KNOCKED IN BOTH
RUNS, ONE IN THE FOURTH AND THE OTHER IN THE EIGHTH.

PICKUP 4TH PGH: EARLIER IN

ST. LOUIS, MO. (UPI)--THE ST. LOUIS CARDINALS SATURDAY ANNOUNCED THE ACQUISITION OF PITCHER AURELIO MONTEAGUDA OF INDIANAPOLIS IN THE AMERICAN ASSOCIATION FOR PITCHER DENNIS RIBANT.

THE CARDINALS ALSO ANNOUNCED THE RETURN TO ACTIVE DUTY OF PITCHER DAVE GUISTI.

MONTEAGUDO HAD A 3-3 WON-LOST RECORD WITH INDIANAPOLIS, A CINCINNATI FARM CLUB.

THE CARDINALS ALSO ANNOUNCED THE SIGNING OF GARRETT COLLINS OF EAST ALTON, ILL., A FIRST BASEMAN-OUTFIELDER SELECTED AT THE RECENT FREE AGENT DRAFT. COLLINS WILL REPORT TO ARKANSAS OF THE TEXAS LEAGUE.

BOSTON (UPI)--THE BOSTON RED SOX LATE SUNDAY TRADED CLUB JUMPING CATCHER JOE AZCUE FOR CALIFORNIA ANGELS RECEIVER TOM SATRIANO IN A STRAIGHT ONE-FOR-ONE DEAL.

THE RED SXO ANNOUNCED THE DEAL FOUR HOURS B

THE RED SOX ANNOUNCED THE DEAL FOUR HOURS BEFORE THE TRADING DEADLINE AND FOUR DAYS AFTER AZCUE HAD LEFT THE CLUB IN MINNESOTA AND GONE TO HIS KANSAS CITY HOME.

AZCUE, 29, HAD FLATLY REFUSED TO RETURN TO THE RED SOX BECAUSE HE SAID THEY WOULD NOT USE HIM EVEN THOUGH HE FELT

HE WAS THEIR BEST CATCHER.

SATRIANO, 28, HAD APPEARED IN 41 GAMES WITH THE ANGELS
IN THIS, HIS SIXTH MAJOR LEAGUE SEASON. HE COMPILED A .259
BATTING AVERAGE WITH ONE HOMER AND 16 RBIS.

3 | Basketball

NEW YORK (UPI)--PRESIDENT ROONE ARLEDGE OF A-B-C SPORTS
SAYS THE AMERICAN BROADCASTING COMPANY WILL TELEVISE THE
NATIONAL BASKETBALL ASSOCIATION "GAME OF THE WEEK" ON A
NEW, SELECTIVE BASIS THIS SEASON. ONLY TWO GAMES HAVE BEEN
SCHEDULED, WITH THE REST TO BE SELECTED SHORTLY BEFORE AIR
DATE TO INSURE THE TELEVISING OF KEY N-B-A GAMES.

NATIONAL BASKETBALL ASSOCIATION (UPI)

DETROIT 110 NEW YORK 98

ATLANTA 128 CINCINNATI 111

BOSTON 121 BALTIMORE 106

PHILADELPHIA 129 MILWAUKEE 111

SEATTLE 128 PHOENIX 127

-O-

AMERICAN BASKETBALL ASSOCIATION

WASHINGTON 125 KENTUCKY 97

NEW YORK (NETS) 100 CAROLINA 96

PITTSBURGH 101 MIAMI 91

NEW ORLEANS 105 DENVER 101 (DOUBLE OVERTIME)

-O-

THE NEW YORK NETS MADE IT SEVEN STRAIGHT VICTORIES...
BEATING THE CAROLINA COUGARS 100-92. BILL MELCHIONNI HIT
FOR 29 POINTS FOR THE WINNING NETS. BOB VERGA SCORED 24
POINTS FOR CAROLINA.

-O-

MIKE BARRETT SCORED 22 POINTS AS THE WASHINGTON CAPS
SCORED A 125-97 VICTORY OVER THE KENTUCKY COLONELS. IT
WAS THE HIGHEST SCORE THIS SEASON FOR THE WINNING CAPS.
THE WASHINGTON WIN WAS ITS 12TH OF THE SEASON COMPARED
TO 11 DEFEATS.

-O-

IN A GAME DECIDED IN DOUBLE OVERTIME THE NEW ORLEANS
BUCCANEERS EDGED THE DENVER ROCKETS 105-101. THE BUCS,
TRAILING 75-67 AT THE END OF THE THIRD QUARTER, RALLIED
TO TIE IT AT THE END OF REGULATION PLAY. THE FIRST
OVERTIME ENDED WITH THE TEAMS STILL DEADLOCKED. STEVE
JONES PUT NEW ORLEANS IN THE LEAD FOR GOOD WITH A LAYUP
IN THE SECOND EXTRA PERIOD. DENVER'S SPENCER HAYWOOD HIT
33 POINTS AND TOOK 21 REBOUNDS.

-O-

THE NEW YORK KNICKS FINALLY GOT BEAT. THE DETROIT
PISTONS ENDED THE KNICKERBOCKERS WIN STREAK IN THE
NATIONAL BASKETBALL ASSOCIATION AT 18 GAMES WITH A 110-98
WIN. JIMMY WALKER AND EDDIE MILES COMBINED FOR 51 POINTS
TO PACE THE PISTONS.

THE PHILADELPHIA 76ERS MADE IT FOUR STRAIGHT WINS....
BEATING THE MILWAUKEE BUCKS 129-111. FOUR PLAYERS FOR
PHILADELPHIA SCORED 20 OR MORE POINTS. BILLY CUNNINGHAM
LED THE ATTACK WITH 23.

THE BOSTON CELTICS SHOWED SIGNS OF LIFE BY BEATING
THE BALTIMORE BULLETS 121-106. BOSTON'S VICTORY ENDED A
NINE GAME WIN STREAK FOR THE BULLETS. HENRY FINKEL HIT
23 POINTS FOR BOSTON.

BILL BRIDGES GRABBED A CAREER HIGH 28 REBOUNDS AND
ADDED 19 POINTS...LOU HUDSON HIT FOR 32 POINTS AND THE
ATLANTA HAWKS TRIUMPHED 128-111 OVER THE CINCINNATI
ROYALS. CINCINNATI'S OSCAR ROBERTSON HIT FOR 22 POINTS.

THE SEATTLE SUPERSONICS RALLIED FOR 33 POINTS IN THE
FOURTH QUARTER AND EDGED THE PHOENIX SUNS 128-127. BOB
RULE HIT 33 FOR SEATTLE...JIM FOX HAD 31 FOR PHOENIX.

MILWAUKEE (UPI)--IT'S A REUNION TIME FOR ELVIN HAYES AND LEW ALCINDOR, THE TWO YOUNG CENTERS WHO STAGED CLASSIC BATTLES AS COLLEGIANS AND NOW ARE DOING IT IN THE PRO RANKS. HAYES LEADS THE ROCKETS INTO MILWAUKEE TONIGHT TO PLAY ALCINDOR AND THE BUCKS. THE ROCKETS ARE 8-13 IN THE WESTERN DIVISION OF THE NATIONAL BASKETBALL ASSOCIATION. THEY ARE FIVE AND A HALF GAMES OUT OF FIRST PLACE.

NEW YORK (UPI)--IN THE NATIONAL BASKETBALL ASSOCIATION, THE SCORING LEADER IS AGAIN JERRY WEST. HE'S SCORED 717 POINTS IN 23 GAMES. THAT AVERAGES TO MORE THAN 31 POINTS PER GAME. PHILADELPHIA'S BILLY CUNNINGHAM IS SECOND.

NEW YORK (UPI)--IN THE AMERICAN BASKETBALL ASSOCIATION, THE PITTSBURGH PIPERS ENDED A FOUR-GAME LOSING STREAK WITH A 101-91 VICTORY OVER MIAMI. GEORGE THOMPSON HIT 20 POINTS FOR THE WINNERS.

THE NEW YORK NETS WON THEIR SEVENTH A-B-A GAME... ROLLING TO A 100-92 VICTORY OVER THE CAROLINA COUGARS. BILL MELCHIONNI POURED IN 29 POINTS FOR THE WINNING NETS.

THE WASHINGTON CAPS SCORED THEIR SEASON HIGH AND DEFEATED THE KENTUCKY COLONELS 125-97. MIKE BARRETT HIT

FOR 22 POINTS FOR THE CAPS. THEIR WIN PUT THEM AT 12
WINS...11 LOSSES FOR THE SEASON.

IN A GAME DECIDED IN DOUBLE OVERTIME, THE NEW ORLEANS
BUCCANEERS OUTLASTED THE DENVER ROCKETS 105-101. SPENCER
HAYWOOD SCORED 33 POINTS AND TOOK 21 REBOUNDS FOR DENVER
IN DEFEAT.

4 | Hockey

DETROIT (UPI)--THE OAKLAND SEALS HAVE DONE IT AGAIN.
THEY LOST LAST NIGHT TO THE PITTSBURH PENGUINS, 5-3, TO
CONTINUE ONE OF THE NATIONAL HOCKEY LEAGUE'S WORST LOSING
STRINGS. THE SEALS HAVE WON BUT ONE GAME AND TIED ANOTHER
IN THEIR LAST DOZEN CONTESTS. TONIGHT THEY PLAY THE
DETROIT RED WINGS TO CLOSE OUT A SEVEN-GAME ROAD TRIP.
THE SEALS COME HOME TO THE OAKLAND COLISEUM ON TUESDAY
NIGHT TO PLAY THE LOS ANGELES KINGS.

N-H-L (UPI)--

THE NATIONAL HOCKEY LEAGUE WAS IDLE MONDAY. ONLY ONE
GAME IS SCHEDULED FOR TUESDAY NIGHT...LOS ANGELES AT
OAKLAND. AS THE N-H-L SWINGS INTO DECEMBER, THE SCORING
LEADER IS BOSTON'S ACE DEFENSEMAN...BOBBY ORR. HE HAS
SEVEN GOALS AND 28 ASSISTS...A SEASON TOTAL OF 35 POINTS.

PHIL GOYETTE OF ST. LOUIS IS SECOND WITH 32 POINTS.

-0-

AMERICAN HOCKEY LEAGUE

TUESDAY'S SCHEDULE (E-S-T)

HERSHEY AT MONTREAL 8

BUFFALO AT QUEBEC 8:05

-0-

STANDINGS...

EAST

	W	L	T	PTS
MONTREAL	13	3	3	29
SPRINGFIELD	13	8	1	27
QUEBEC	10	10	1	21
PROVIDENCE	7	12	4	18
BUFFALO	15	6	3	33
ROCHESTER	6	10	4	18
HERSHEY	8	11	1	17
BALTIMORE	6	9	4	16
CLEVELAND	6	15	3	15

PITTSBURGH (AP)--THE PITTSBURGH POST-GAZETTE SAID
TONIGHT IT HAS LEARNED THAT LEONARD "RED" KELLY, THE
FORMER HEAD COACH OF THE LOS ANGES KINGS, WILL BE THE

NEW COACH OF THE PITTSBURGH PENGUINS OF THE NATIONAL
HOCKEY LEAGUE.

THE PAPER SAID KELLY WOULD BE NAMED SUCCESSOR TO
GEORGE "RED" SULLIVAN EARLY NEXT WEEK.

SULLIVAN WAS FIRED AT THE END OF LAST SEASON AFTER THE
PENGUINS BECAME THE ONLY EXPANSION TEAM THAT DIDN'T MAKE
THE N-H-L PLAYOFFS.

THE POST-GAZETTE SAID JACK RILEY, THE PITTSBURGH
GENERAL MANAGER, PLANS TO MEET WITH KELLY IN ONTARIO,
CANADA, TOMORROW OR OVER THE WEEKEND, AT THE LATEST.

RILEY REFUSED TOCOMMENT ON THE STORY.

KELLY QUIT THE LOS ANGELES JOB AT THE END OF THE
1968-69 SEASON AFTER A SERIES OF DISAGREEMENTS WITH OWNER
JACK KENT COOKE.

KELLY BROKE IN WITH THE DETROIT RED WINGS DURING THE
1947-48 SEASON. HE WENT ON TO PLAY 20 SEASONS, SEVEN
WITH THE TORONTO MAPLE LEAFS.

HE WAS A PLAYER WITH TORONTO WHEN HE RETIRED TWO
YEARS AGO.

DETROIT (UPI)--THE DETROIT RED WINGS TODAY SOLD
DEFENSEMAN KENT DOUGLAS, A SEVEN-YEAR NATIONAL HOCKEY
LEAGUE VETERAN, TO THE VANCOUVER CANUCKS OF THE WESTERN

HOCKEY LEAGUE FOR AN UNDISCLOSED SUM.

DOUGLAS, 33, BROKE INTO THE NHL IN 1962. WITH THE CCL

DOUGLAS, 33, BROKE INTO THE NHL IN 1962. WITH THE
TORONTO MAPLE LEAFS AND WON THE CALDER MEMORIAL TROPHY
THAT SEASON AS ROOKIE OF THE YEAR. HE WENT TO OAKLAND
IN THE EXPANSION DRAFT IN 1967 AND CAME TO THE RED WINGS
IN 1968.

UNDER NHL RULES, DOUGLAS WILL REMAIN ELIGIBLE FOR
CLAIM BY ANY NHL TEAM IN NEXT YEAR'S DRAFT.

N-H-L (UPI)

IN THE NATIONAL HOCKEY LEAGUE SATURDAY THE PHILADELPHIA
FLYERS TIED THE NEW YORK RANGERS 2-2. GUY GENDRON'S SOFT
SHOT BOUNCED OFF GOALIE ED GIACOMIN'S STICK AND INTO THE
NET FOR THE TYING SCORE IN THE SECOND PERIOD.

ANOTHER TIE GAME...THIS ONE A 2-2 DEADLOCK BETWEEN
THE MONTREAL CANADIENS AND BOSTON BRUINS. DEREK
SANDERSON SCORED ON A POWER PLAY WITH LESS THAN TWO
MINUTES LEFT TO TIE IT UP FOR BOSTON.

PITTSBURGH CAME UP WITH A 5-3 VICTORY OVER THE OAKLAND
SEALS. THE SCORE WAS TIED TWICE BEFORE A GOAL BY DEAN
PRENTICE LATE IN THE SECOND PERIOD PUT PITTSBURGH IN

FRONT.

THE DETROIT RED WINGS OUTSCORED THE CHICAGO BLACK
HAWKS 5-4. THE RED WINGS' VICTORY ENDED A 10 GAME
UNBEATEN STREAK FOR CHICAGO. THE WINNING GOAL CAME WITH
ONLY 74 SECONDS LEFT. BILLY DEA SCORED IT.

THE TORONTO MAPLE LEAFS EXPLODED WITH FOUR GOALS IN
THE FINAL PERIOD AND A COME-FROM-BEHIND 5-2 WIN OVER THE
MINNESOTA NORTH STARS. TWO OF THE GOALS WERE SCORED BY
MIKE WALTON.

THE ST. LOUIS BLUES BEAT LOS ANGELES 3-1 AND INCREASED
THEIR LEAD IN THE N-H-L WESTERN DIVISION TO SEVEN POINTS.
PHIL GOYETTE SCORED TWICE FOR THE BLUES. LOS ANGELES HAS
GONE 11 STRAIGHT GAMES WITHOUT WINNING.

-0-

A-H-L (UPI)--

ONLY TWO GAMES PLAYED SATURDAY NIGHT IN THE AMERICAN
HOCKEY LEAGUE. CLEVELAND BEAT ROCHESTER 4-1...AND
BUFFALO OVER HERSHEY 5-2.

5 | Boxing

HONOLULU (UPI)--MEXICO'S MARIO MANRIQUE CLOSED BOTH
DOMI MANALANG'S EYES AND TKOED THE FILIPINO BANTAMWEIGHT
IN THE 10TH ROUND OF THEIR BLOODY FIGHT TUESDAY NIGHT.

THE TOUSLE HAIRED MEXICAN WAS JUST TOO STRONG FOR THE SLENDER MANALANG. DR. EDMUND LUM STOPPED THE BOUT AT THE END OF THE NINTH AFTER MANRIQUE HAD VIRTUALLY CLOSED MANALANG'S LEFT EYE AND BLOODIED HIS RIGHT ONE.

MANRIQUE WEIGHED 123 1/2; MANALANG 124 3/4. THE TKO IS OFFICIALLY LISTED AS THE 10TH ROUND.

BOTH JUDGES AND REFEREE WILBERT MINN HAD MANRIQUE WELL AHEAD ON POINTS WHEN THE BOUT ENDED. MANALANG SCORED REPEATEDLY WITH HIS LONGER REACH AND FLICKING LEFT, BUT THE CHUNKY MEXICAN BLOTTED UP ALL OF MANALANG'S PUNCHES AND KEPT CHARGING AHEAD.

DOMI DREW FIRST BLOOD IN THE FOURTH ROUND WHEN HE BANGED MARIO'S NOSE WITH REPEATED LEFTS. IN THE FIFTH MARIO'S RIGHT EAR SEEPED BLOOD, BUT IN THE SEVENTH THE FILIPINO'S LEFT EYE BEGAN TO CLOSE AND IN THE LAST FEW SECONDS OF THE EIGHTH ROUND HE SUFFERED A CUT BELOW THE RIGHT EYE. THE VICTORY WAS THE 14TH FOR MANRIQUE WHO HAS FOUGHT ONLY 16 PROFESSIONAL BOUTS.

MANUELO BALABA, 118 1/2 TOOK A 10-ROUND UNANIMOUS DECISION FROM JAPAN'S SHINTARO UCHIYAMA IN THE SEMI FINAL. UCHIYAMA WEIGHED IN AT 118 1/4. THE FILIPINO WON THE FIGHT WITH HIS BACK-PEDALLING COUNTER PUNCHING THAT SCORED REPEATEDLY AGAINST THE GAME BUT OUTCLASSED

JAPANESE FLYWEIGHT.

FLORY KID, 127 1/4, MANILA, TKOED ROBERTO WONG, MEXICO CITY 128 IN 2:38 OF THE FOURTH ROUND OF THEIR SCHEDULED 10-ROUNDER.

FRANCISCO LOPEZ, 121 1/2, MEXICO CITY, KOED LITTLE DITOY, 122 OF THE PHILIPPINES IN 2:14 FOR THE FOURTH ROUND OF THEIR SCHEDULED SIX ROUNDER, AND NOEL MORALES, 119, ALSO OF THE PPHILIPPINES, DECISIONED TEDDY DOI 119 3/4 OF HONOLULU.

THE CROWD OF 4,971 PAID $23?3-1 59 33 5

THE CROWD OF 4,971 PAID $23,451 TO SEE THE CARD.

LOS ANGELES (UPI)--WORLD FLYWEIGHT CHAMPION EFREN TORRES OF MEXICO, A POWER PUNCHER WITH 30 KNOCKOUTS IN 44 VICTORIES, BATTLES JAPAN'S SUSUMU HANAGATA IN A 10-ROUND NONTITLE FIGHT AT THE OLYMPIC AUDITORIUM TONIGHT.

TORRES AND HANAGATA WERE SCHEDULED TO MEET ON A CARD FEATURING LIGHTWEIGHT CHAMPION MANDO RAMOS LAST WEEKEND BUT RAMOS BROKE A HAND IN TRAINING.

TORRES, WHOSE FOUR LOSSES INCLUDE A SEVENTH ROUND KNOCKOUT AT THE HANDS OF JAPAN'S HIROYUKI EBIHARA IN 1965 IN HIS LAST START HERE, WON THE CHAMPIONSHIP LAST

FEB. 23 FROM CHARTCHAI CHIONOI OF THAILAND ON A 13th
ROUND KNOCKOUT AT MEXICO CITY.

EBIHARA NOW IS CONSIDERED THE NOJM 1 CONTENDER FOR THE
112-POUND CROWN.

IF TORRES IS UPSET, PROMOTER AILEEN EATON SAID THE
MEXICAN FIGHTER WOULD BE OFFERED $45,000 TO DEFEND HIS
TITLE AGAINST HANAGATA.

HANAGATA HAS A 28-2 RECORD.

TORRES, ONE OF 23 CHILDREN AND A SCHOOL DROPOUT AT
THE AGE OF SEVEN, IS A HERO IN HIS OWN COUNTRY.

AFTER BEATING CHIONOI IN HIS THIRD BID FOR THE
CHAMPIONSHIP, PRESIDENT DIAZ ORDAZ OF MEXICO PRESENTED
TORRES WITH A $1,600 WRISTWATCH IN SPECIAL CEREMONIES.

ADV FOR PMS THURS JUNE 19

LOS ANGELES (UPI)--UNRANKED SUSUMU HANAGATA, JAPAN'S
NATIONAL FLYWEIGHT CHAMPION, THURSDAY NIGHT SCORED A
LOPSIDED UPSET DECISION OVER WORLD CHAMP EFREN TORRES OF
MEXICO IN A 10-ROUND NONTITLE FIGHT AT THE OLYMPIC
AUDITORIUM.

THE 117-POUND TORRES, FROM GUADALAJARA, APPEARED
SLUGGISH AND OUT OF CONDITION, FOLLOWING A DAY-LONG
EFFORT TO SWEAT OFF ONE POUND. THE CHAMPION WAS

OVERWEIGHT AT THE MORNING WEIGH-IN, AND AFTER THE BOUT HE
SAID HE TOOK HANAGATA "TOO LIGHTLY."

THERE WERE NO KNOCKDOWNS IN THE ONE-SIDED FIGHT AND
NEITHER FIGHTER WAS STAGGERED. TORRES SUFFERED CUTS
AROUND THE LEFT EYE IN THE SECOND AND FOURTH ROUNDS AND
HANAGATA RECEIVED A CUT INSIDE HIS MOUTH IN THE SEVENTH.
BUT NEITHER BOXER WAS HAMPERED BY THE INJURIES.

PROMOTER EILEEN EATON SAID AFTERWARD SHE WOULD LIKE
TO STAGE A REMATCH FOR THE TITLE BETWEEN THE TWO EITHER
IN AUGUST OR SEPTEMBER.

IN AWARDING THE WIN TO HANAGATA, REFEREE LEE GROSSMAN
SCORED IT 6-2, AND JUDGES DICK YOUNG AND LARRY ROZADILLA
HAD IT 8-2 AND 6-4 RESPECTIVELY.

THE WIN MADE HANAGATA'S RECORD 29-2, WHILE TORRES IS
NOW 44-6.

6 | Golf

GREAT MOMENTS IN SPORTS

A LEAF FROM THE MEMORY BOOK OF SPORTS (UPI)

DON JANUARY WAS A DISAPPOINTED MAN AFTER THE P-G-A
CHAMPIONSHIP IN 1961. HE HAD A RIGHT TO BE. HE THOUGHT
HE WAS A WINNER BUT HE LOST TO JERRY BARBER IN A PLAYOFF
BY A SINGLE STROKE--67 TO 68.

SIX YEARS LATER--AT DENVER--JANUARY FOUND HIMSELF IN A
PLAYOFF AGAIN. HE AND DON MASSENGALE FINISHED THE
REGULATION 72 HOLES WITH IDENTICAL SCORES OF 281.

SO ANOTHER GRUELLING 18 HOLES.

AGAINST BARBER, JANUARY HAD TWO STROKE LEADS TWICE
BUT HE WAS BEATEN BY LONG DISTANCE PUTTING. THIS TIME HE
TOLD HIMSELF TO PLAY IT SAFE.

THE TWO DONS--MASSENGALE AND JANUARY--WERE ALL EVEN
THROUGH THE FIRST THREE HOLES OF THE 1967 PLAYOFF. BUT
JANUARY BOGEYED NUMBER FOUR AND WENT DOWN ONE.

MASSENGALE BIRDIED NUMBER FIVE ON A FOUR-FOOT PUTT
AND LED BY TWO. BUT HE DROPPED ONE OF THOSE STROKES WITH
A BOGEY ON NUMBER SEVEN.

JANUARY THEN TIED IT UP ON THE 580-YARD, PAR FIVE,
EIGHTH HOLE WITH A 12-FOOT BIRDIE PUTT.

SOMEWHERE, SOMEHOW, THERE'S ALWAYS A TURNING POINT IN
SPORTS EVENTS AND THIS TIME IT CAME ON THE 10TH HOLE.
JANUARY'S BALL WAS ON THE FRINGE ON THE BACK OF THE GREEN.
WHAT HE WANTED TO DO WAS TO ROLL UP THE PUTT SO IT WOULD
BE CLOSE TO THE PIN. BUT THE BALL DROPPED IN FOR A 35-
FOOT PUTT AND JANUARY TOOK THE LEAD.

BOTH BIRDIED THE 12TH AND 14TH AND THEN JANUARY
BIRDIED THE 15TH TO GO TWO STROKES AHEAD. MASSENGALE

MATCHED BOGEYS WITH JANUARY ON THE 17TH TO LOSE HIS LAST

CHANCE.

JANUARY WON THE 1967 P-G-A WITH A THREE-UNDER PAR 69

TO MASSENGALE'S 71.

"I FEEL KIND OF NUMB," SAID JANUARY LATER." I HAD

TRIED THIS ONCE BEFORE AND LOST AND I DIDN'T WANT TO LOSE

IT AGAIN." SAID MASSENGALE--"THERE AIN'T MUCH I CAN SAY.

I CAME IN SECOND."

HOYLAKE, ENG. (UPI)--AMERICA'S BILL HYNDMAN GOES AGAINST

BRITAIN'S MIKE BONALLACK TODAY IN THE FINAL MATCH OF THE

BRITISH AMATEUR GOLF CHAMPIONSHIP AT HOYLAKE, ENGLAND.

AT 53, HYNDMAN IS OLDER THAN ANY FINALIST SINCE

MICHAEL SCOTT WON THE BRITISH TITLE IN 1933. BONALLACK

IS TRYING TO BECOME THE THIRD PLAYER IN THE 84-YEAR

HISTORY OF THE BRITISH AMATEUR TO WIN THE TITLE FOUR

TIMES.

GOLF RUNNING (UPI)

CHARLES COODY 72--212

JOHN MKLLER 80--221

AL GEIBERGER 72--212

GEORGE KNUDSON 72--216

MILLER BARBER 68-206

BOB ROSBURG 72--211

DEANE BEMAN 73--210

BOB MURPHY 74--212

BUNKY HENRY 68--210

DEAN REFRAM 70--213

ORVILLE MOODY 68--209

BERT YANCEY 74--216

TONY JACKLIN 73--214

JACK NICKLAUS 75--216

(END GOLF RUNNING)

7 | Horse Racing

GREAT MOMENTS IN SPORTS

A LEAF FROM THE MEMORY BOOK OF SPORTS (UPI)

THE TRAVERS STAKES FOR THREE-YEAR-OLDS AT SARATOGA IS
REPUTED TO BE THE OLDEST STAKES RACE IN AMERICA.

THIS YEAR, THE RACE WILL HAVE ITS 100TH RUNNING AT THE
HISTORIC TRACK AT SARATOGA SPRINGS, NEW YORK.

THE PRIZE THREE-YEAR-OLDS OF THE SPRING SOMETIMES
LOSE THEIR ZIP LATE IN THE SEASON. THAT'S WHY THE TOP
MONEY AT SARATOGA OFTEN GOES TO AN UNDERDOG.

IN 1968, "CHOMPION," A SON OF "TOMPION," WAS COMPLETELY OVER-SHADOWED IN THE EARLY GOING. BUT FINALLY HE SHOWED SOME PROMISE BY FINISHING SECOND IN THE MONMOUTH INVITATIONAL HANDICAP. THAT EARNED HIM A START IN THE TRAVERS STAKES.

AS EXPECTED, THE CROWD GAVE "CHOMPION" LITTLE CONSIDERATION. THE PREAKNESS WINNER, CALUMET FARM'S "FORWARD PASS", REIGNED THE FAVORITE.

"CAPTAIN'S GIG" WAS WELL IN FRONT AT THE START. BUT THE SPEED HORSE SLOWED UP AND YIELDED TO "FORWARD PASS."

THE LEAD LOOKED GOOD. BUT CHARGING AND GAINING GROUND CAME "CHOMPION." FOR AN EIGHTH OF A MILE, "FORWARD PASS" STAYED SHARPLY IN FRONT. THEN "CHOMPION" WORE HIM DOWN. THE LITTLE REGARDED THREE-YEAR-OLD PULLED AWAY AND ROMPED HOME THE WINNER IN THE CLOSING YARDS.

"CHOMPION" CARRIED 114 POUNDS IN THE MILE AND ONE-QUARTER RACE AND WAS TIMED AT 2:04 AND FOUR-FIFTHS OVER A MUDDY TRACK. THE BAY COLT PAID 31 DOLLARS AND 20 CENTS, EIGHT DOLLARS AND FIVE-60 ACROSS THE BOARD. THE WINNER'S PURSE WAS 55-THOUSAND-802 DOLLARS.

NEW YORK (UPI)--GUSTAV RING'S CZAR ALEXANDER SPRINTED TO THE FRONT IN THE STRETCH AT BELMONT PARK SATURDAY AND

WENT ON TO WIN THE $59,400 BOWLING GREEN HANDICAP BY A
LENGTH AND THREE-QUARTERS.

IT WAS THE THIRD STRAIGHT VICTORY FOR THE 4-YEAR-OLD
SON OF PAMPERED KING WHO WAS FOALED IN IRELAND AND RACED
THERE AS WELL AS IN ENGLAND, FRANCE AND GERMANY BEFORE HE
WAS BROUGHT TO THIS COUNTRY.

THERE WAS A TIGHT BATTLE FOR SECOND PLACE IN THE
1 1/2 MILE TURF RACE. RUFFLED FEATHERS BEAT OUT JEAN-
PIERRE BY A NOSE FOR RUNNER-UP HONORS WITH IRISH
REBELLION FOURTH, ONLY A NECK FARTHER BACK.

JORGE VELASQUEZ RODE CZAR ALEXANDER WHO WON THE DIXIE
AND THE MACOMBER HANDICAPS IN HIS LAST TWO STARTS. THE
BAY COLT WAS TIMED IN 2:27 2/5 UNDER HIGH WEIGHT TO SET
A COURSE RECORD.

TH OLD MARK OF 2:28 3/5 WAS SET BY BEAU PURPLE IN
1962 WHEN HE BEAT KELSO IN THE MAN O'WAR STAKES.

CZAR ALEXANDER, SECOND TO SIR IVOR LAST FALL IN THE
WASHINGTON D.C. INTERNATIONAL AT LAUREL, PICKED UP A
WINNER'S PURSE OF $38,610 AND PAID $5.00, $3.00 and $2.40
ACROSS THE BOARD.

RUFFLED FEATHERS PAID $4.40 AND $3.00 AND JEAN-PIERRE
PAID $3.40

AGUA CALIENTE, MEXICO (UPI)--FLEET DUCHESS, A 5-YEAR-OLD WITH RAUL CABALLERO IN THE SADDLE, OUTBATTLED DRAFTY IN THE STRETCH SUNDAY TO CAPTURE THE EXCALIBUR HANDICAP BY A NOSE AT CALIENTE RACE COURSE.

FLEET DUCHESS WAS CLOCKED IN 1:40 2/5 FOR THE MILE AND 70 YARDS WITH GREEK BALCONY THIRD.

FLEET DUCHESS RETURNED $8.00, $4.80 AND $4.40 ACROSS THE BOARD. DRAFTY'S PRICES WERE $5.20 AND $2.20 WHILE GREEK BALCONY RETURNED $3.80.

TWO PLAYERS HAD SIX WINNERS EACH FOR $26,189.60 RETURNS IN THE 5-10 HANDICAPPING CONTEST.

NEW YORK (AP)--CLAIBORNE FARM'S "JACKAL" HAS WON THE COLT AND GELDING DIVISION OF THE NATIONAL STALLION STAKES AT NEW YORK'S BELMONT PARK RACE TRACK. THE COLT FINISHED WITH A RUSH AND BEAT THE RUNNER-UP "PONTIFEX" BY TWO LENGTHS.

JACKAL WAS RIDDEN BY JOCKEY EDDIE BELMONTE, AND COVERED THE FIVE AND ONE-HALF FURLONGS IN ONE MINUTE, FIVE AND ONE-FIFTH SECONDS.

THE WINNER PAID $9, $3 AND $2.40. PONTIFEX RETURNED $2.60 AND $2.40. "POPPY HILL" FINISHED THIRD AND PAID $3.

519

LONDON (UPI)--AEROFOILS HELP PREVENT RACING CARS FROM OVERTURNING WHILE ROUNDING CURVES AT HIGH SPEEDS, BUT THEY ALSO INCREASE THE DANGER WHEN A VEHICLE IS OUT OF CONTROL, A LENGTHY REPORT FROM THE (BRITISH) AUTOMOBILE INDUSTRY RESEARCH ASSOCIATION SAID WEDNESDAY.

THE INTERNATIONAL AUTOMOBILE FEDERATION (FIA) BANNED THE USE OF AEROFOILS LAST MONTH AT AN EMERGENCY MEETING BEFORE THE GRAND PRIX IN MONACO. OWNERS OF CARS THAT USED THE DEVICES HAVE BEEN SHARPLY CRITICIZING THE BAN.

"EXPERIMENTS HAVE SHOWN THAT AEROFOILS ARE NOT NECESSARILY DANGEROUS IN THEMSELVES, BUT THERE IS AN AREA WHERE DRIVERS CAN RUN INTO TROUBLE AND SHOULD TAKE SPECIAL CARE," SAID THE REPORT, WHICH TOOK 10 WEEKS TO COMPLETE.

"THE SLIP-STREAMING SITUATION IS ONE WHERE SPECIAL CARE IS NECESSARY. IF AEROFOILS ARE TO BE USED AGAIN IN RACES, THEN DRIVERS WOULD BE WELL ADVISED NOT TO GET TOO CLOSE TO OTHER CARS," THE REPORT ADDED.

THE REPORT SAID THE AEROFOILS HELP IN THAT THEY GENERATE A DOWNTHRUST THAT MORE THAN COUNTERS THE ORDINARY INSTABILITY WHILE TURNING.

THE REPORT IS THE FIRST MAJOR PROJECT OF A FOUNDATION SET UP AS A MEMORIAL TO TWO-TIME WORLD CHAMPION DRIVER

JIM CLARK OF SCOTLAND WHO WAS KILLED WHILE RACING LAST
YEAR.

BY PAUL TREUTHARDT

LE MANS, FRANCE (UPI)--FORD WON ITS FOURTH SUCCESSIVE
LE MANS 24 HOUR RACE SUNDAY AS BELGIUM'S JACKIE ICKX
EDGED OUT GERMANY'S HANS HERRMANN'S PORSCHE IN THE
TOUGHEST WHEEL-TO-WHEEL FINISH OF THIS SPORTS CAR
CLASSIC.

THE HARE-AND-TORTOIS RACE SAW PORSCHE DOMINATION FOR
21 HOURS REDUCED BY ACCIDENT AND BREAKDOWN TO A DESPERATE
FIGHT WITH THE 1968 WINNING FORD GT 40, A VETERAN OF
20,000 MILES OF RACING. THE TWO CARS CHANGED LEAD WITH
GRAND PRIX TACTICS ON THE FIVE-MILE STRAIGHT AWAY OF THE
8.3 MILE CIRCUIT. THE HERMANN-CLAUDE LARROUSSE CAR
FINISHED ONLY 120 YARDS BEHIND THE FORD. TANDEM OF ICKX
AND JACKIE OLIVER OF BRITAIN.

THE GULF OIL-SPONSORED FORDS, IN THEIR LAST MAJOR
COMPETITIVE EVENT, RAN A CAREFULLY PLANNED RACE FOR THE
BRITISH JOHN WYER AUTOMATIVE TEAM TO FINISH FIRST AND
THIRD. WITH DAVID HOBBS-MIKE HAILWOOD OF BRITAIN. THE
ICKX-OLIVER TEAM AVERAGED 129.923 MPH FOR THE 3,103 MILE
RACE.

521

THE CONTRVOERSIAL PORSCHE 917 PROTOTYPES, ALLOWED TO
RACE BY A LAST MINUTE DECISION THEY COULD KEEP THEIR
MOVEABLE STABILIZERS DESPITE AN INTERNATIONAL BAN, LED
FOR 21 OF THE 24 HOURS.

BRITONS VIC ELFORD AND DICKIE ATTWOOD WERE AHEAD FOR
19 OF THOSE HOURS BEFORE BEING ELIMINATED BY CLUTCH
TROUBLE. TEAMMATES ROLF STOMMELEN AND KURT AHRENS OF
GERMANY IN ANOTHER 4.5 LITER 917, HAD TAKEN THE FIRST
HOUR LEAD AND JO SIFFERT, SWITZERLAND, WITH BRITAN
REDMAN, BRITAIN, IN A THREE-LITER 908 THE NEXT THREE
HOURS.

THE THIRD 917 CRASHED ON THE FIRST LAP, KILLING
WEALTHY BRITISH AMATEUR DRIVER JOHN WOOLFE, 35, WHOSE
BRIDE OF SIX MONTHS WAS AT THE TRACK. THE FLYING DEBRIS
AND FLAMES SET FIRE TO THE FERRARI PROTOTYPE OF NEW
ZELAND CHRIS AMON, WHO PUSHED THE AUTOMATIC FIRE
EXTINGUISHER BUTTON BEFORE ESCAPING FROM THE CAR UNHURT,
AND CAUSED DAMAGE TO ANOTHER FORT GT 40 OF FRANK GARDNER,
AUSTRALIA AND MALCOLM GUTHRIE, ENGLAND, WHICH ELIMINATED
IT A FEW HOURS LATER.

THE LAST HOUR OF THE RACE HAD THE CROWD OF MORE THAN
300,000 CHEERING WILDLY AS THE FORD AND PORSCHE HAMMERED
ON IN A STYLE WHICH HOBBS DESCRIBED AS "QUITE RIDICULOUS

AT THE END OF 24 HOURS RACING."

IN THE FINAL LAP DOWN THE LONG STRAIGHTS, HERRMANN
PASSED ICKX BUT THE 24-YEAR-OLD BELGIAN GOT THE FINAL
"TWO" IN THE SLIPSTREAM OF THE PORSCHE WHICH ENABLED HIM
TO GAIN ENOUGH SPEED TO SWING ON THE OUTSIDE JUST BEFORE
THE BREAKING ZONE AND TAKE A LEAD HERRMANN COULD NOT
CHALLENGE THROUGH THE FINAL CORNERS.

THE SMALLEST FIELD EVER, ONLY 45 OF THE TRADITIONAL
55 STARTERS, LINED UP AT 2 P.M. SATURDAY FOR THE RACE,
AFTER THE ITALIAN WORKS ALFA ROMEOS AND ABARTHS DROPPED
OUT BECAUSE OF A CUSTOMS STRIKE AND PORSCHE AND NORTH
AMERICAN RACING TEAM FERRARIS SCRATCHED SOME ENTRIES.

ONLY 14 CARS WERE RUNNING AT THE END, INCLUDING FIVE
PORSCHE SALOONS AND THREE OF THE GOVERNMENT SUBSIDISED
FRENCH MATRA TEAM WHICH PLACED FOURTH, FIFTH AND
SEVENTH AFTER RUNNING A HIGHLY COMMENDABLE RACE AGAINST
THE FIERCE PORSCHE AND FORD OPPOSITION.

A CURIOSITY ATTESTING TO THE IMPORTANCE OF TACTICS
AND STAMINA OVER SPEED WAS THE EIGHTH PLACED FERRARI 250
LM OF ITALY'S TEODORO ZECCOLI AND U.S. DRIVER SAM POSEY
IN THE SAME CAR OF LUIGI CHINETTI'S NORTH AMERICAN RACING
TEAM WHICH WON HERE IN 1965.

PRINCETON, N.J. (UPI)--MIAMI FRESHMAN LEWIS GARCIA, RECENTLY NAMED TO MEXICO'S DAVIS CUP TEAM, WEDNESDAY BECAME THE FIRST GIANT-KILLER OF THE 85TH ANNUAL NCAA TENNIS CHAMPIONSHIPS BY OUSTING UCLA'S THIRD-SEEDED ROY BARTH, 6-1, 6-3.

GARCIA, SEEDED 9TH IN THE TOURNAMENT DESPITE A 19-0 DUAL MATCH RECORD THIS SPRING, BECAME PART OF THE MEXICAN DAVIS CUP TEAM WHEN RAFAEL OSUNA WAS KILLED IN A PLANE CRASH.

BY DEFEATING BARTH, WHO WILL PLAY IN THE WIMBLEDON CHAMPIONSHIPS NEXT WEEK, GARCIA SEVERELY DAMAGED UCLA'S HOPES FOR BOTH THE INDIVIDUAL AND TEAM TITLES. THE BRUINS HAD HOPED BARTH WOULD CHALLENGE TOP-SEEDED BOB LUTZ OF USC.

LUTZ, RATED FIFTH NATIONALLY AND ALSO WIMBLEDON-BOUND, LED THREE OF THE TROJANS' FOUR SINGLES PLAYERS INTO SIXTH ROUND TO GIVE USC UNDISPUTED POSSESSION OF FIRST PLACE IN THE TEAM STANDINGS WITH 24 POINTS.

LUTZ BELTED GEORGIA'S DAN BIRCHMORE, 6-2, 6-2, IN THE FOURTH ROUND AND WHIPPED BRIGHAM YOUNG'S ZERAUKO MINCEK, 6-1, 6-4, IN THE FIFTH ROUND.

UCLA, WITH ALL FOUR OF ITS SINGLES ENTRIES FALLING, DROPPED TO SECOND IN THE TEAM STANDINGS WITH 21 POINTS, FOLLOWED BY TRINITY UNIVERSITY WITH 19, RICE WITH 16 AND

MIAMI WITH 15.

THE ONLY OTHER MAJOR UPSET SAW UTAH'S DAN BLECKINGER
DOWN ZAN GUERRY OF RICE, 2-6, 6-1, 6-4. GUERRY WAS
SEVENTH SEEDED AND IS RATED 19TH NATIONALLY.

LONDON (UPI)--DENNIS RALSTON OF BAKERSFIELD, CALIF.,
REQUIRED ONLY 38 MINUTES TO ROUT SOUTH AFRICA'S FREW
MCMILLAN, 6-1, 6-0, BEFORE THE RAINS CAME WEDNESDAY IN
THE LONDON GRASS COURT TENNIS CHAMPIONSHIPS.

RALSON, SEEDED 15TH FOR NEXT WEEK'S WIMBLEDON
CHAMPIONSHIPS, WON THE FINAL 10 GAMES TO GAIN PASSAGE INTO
THE FINAL 16 OF THE MEN'S SINGLES. THE AMERICAN'S SERVE
WAS MUCH TOO POWERFUL FOR MCMILLAN, WHO HAS EARNED HIS
MAIN PROMINENCE AS A DOUBLES PARTNER FOR BOB HEWITT.

RAIN, WHICH HAS WREAKED HAVOC WITH THE TOURNAMENT ALL
WEEK, ALTED THE MATCH BETWEEN STAN SMITH OF PASADENA,
CALIF., AND BRITISH PROFESSIONAL ROGER TAYLOR AFTER THEY
HAD COMPLETED ONLY TWO GAMES.

PLAY WAS TO CONTINUE INDOORS ON WOOD, AS IT DID
TUESDAY, IN CASE THE RAIN CONTINUED.

IN OTHER THIRD-ROUND MATCHES, ROY EMERSON OF AUSTRALIA
BEAT HANS PLOTZ OF GERMANY 6-3, 6-4 AND CLIFF DRYSDALE OF
SOUTH AFRICA OUSTED JOHN MCDONALD OF NEW ZEALAND, 6-3,

TOMORROW, HAS DEVOTED ITS ENTIRE CURRENT ISSUE TO THE
HARMFUL USE OF SUCH CHEMICALLY STABLE INSECTICIDES AS DDT.

IN AN ARTICLE CO-AUTHORED BY CHAIRMAN DONALD KENNEDY
OF STANFORD UNIVERSITY'S BIOLOGY DEPARTMENT AND STANFORD
ECOLOGIST JOHN HESSELL, HOME GARDENERS WERE WARNED
AGAINST USE OF PESTICIDES CONTAINING DDT AND ITS CHEMICAL
EQUIVALENTS CHLORDANE, DIELDRIN AND ALDRIN.

THE ARTICLE CITED U. S. PUBLIC HEALTH SERVICE FIGURES
WHICH REPORTED THAT NEARLY EVERYONE HARBORS A SMALL
AMOUNT OF DDT, WHICH PROBABLY IS NOT HARMFUL TO HUMANS,
BUT DOES AFFECT WILD LIFE HARMFULLY.

THE MAGAZINE RECOMMENDED THAT HOME GARDENERS BUY
SHORT-LIVED CHEMICALS LIKE PYRETHRUM, ROTENONE, SEVEN
AND MALATHION.

THE STATE DEPARTMENT OF AGRICULTURE, IN FIGURES
RELEASED THIS WEEK, ESTIMATED THAT 2.5 MILLION POUNDS OF
DDT ARE USED ANNUALLY IN CALIFORNIA. A BOYCOTT ON DDT
COULD SIGNIFICANTLY AFFECT THE PESTICIDE USAGE IN THE
STATE, THE MAGAZINE SAID.

SAN FRANCISCO (UPI)--WILLIAM JONES, A HANDSOME 40-
YEAR-OLD BACHELOR, WILL BE JUST AS PROUD AS THE REST OF
THE NATION'S DADS ON FATHER'S DAY--MAYBE JUST A LITTLE

3-6, 6-3.

IN SECOND-ROUND PLAY OF THE WOMEN'S SINGLES, JUDY TEGART OF AUSTRALIA ELIMINATED TORY ANN FRETZ OF LOS ANGELES, 6-4, 6-4; KIRSTY PIEGON OF DANVILLE, CALIF., ADVANCED ON A FORFEIT BY BRENDA KIRK OF SOUTH AFRICA; PAT WALKDEN OF SOUTH AFRICA BEAT AUSTRALIA'S WENDY GILCHRIST, 6-1, 7-5; OLGA MOROZOVA OF RUSSIA TOPPED JILL COOPER OF BRITAIN, 6-3, 6-3; AND CHRISTINE JANES OF BRITAIN DEFEATED CHRISTINE SANDBERG OF SWEDEN, 6-1, 6-0.

MOSCOW (UPI)--RUSSIA SCORED ONE OF ITS MOST DEVESTATING VICTORIES IN DAVIS CUP PLAY WHEN THE SOVIET UNION COMPLETED A 5-0 SWEEP OVER ITALY SUNDAY.

ALEXANDER METREVELI DEFEATED NICOLA PIETRANGELI 6-2, 6-2, 6-2 AND TOMAS LEJUS RALLIED FOR A 4-6, 3-6, 6-4, 7-5, 6-2 VICTORY OVER EGUENIO CASTIGLIANO.

RUSSIA'S FINAL ROUND OPPONENT IN TEUROPEAN ZONE PLAY WILL BE ROMANIA, A 4-1 WINNER OVER SPAIN.

MANUEL ORANTES PREVENTED A ROMANIAN SWEEP WHEN HE BEAT R. MARMUREANU 6-1, 6-1, 6-1 AFTER ION TIRIAC STOPPED JOSE LUIS ARILLA 6-2, 3-6, 6-3, 6-4.

ROEHAMPTON, ENGLAND (UPI)--ERIK VAN DILLEN OF SAN MATEO, CALIF., RANKED 16TH IN THE U.S., LED A HANDFUL OF AMERICANS WHO EARNED WIMBLEDON BERTHS WITH VICTORIES IN THE ALL-ENGLAND LAWN TENNIS CHAMPIONSHIPS WEDNESDAY, BUT TOM MOZUR, RATED NO. 15, FAILED TO QUALIFY.

DILLEN DOWNED DEREK SCHRODER OF SOUTH AFRICA, 5-7, 6-3, 6-3, 6-3, WHILE MOZUR, FROM SWEETWATER, TENN., WAS BEATEN BY AUSTRALIA'S JOHN MCDONALD, 6-3, 6-2, 6-3.

CHAUNCEY STEELE III OF CAMBRIDGE, MASS., A 7-5, 6-1, 6-2 WINNER OVER ECUADOR'S EDUARDO ZULETA, AND W.C. HIGGINS, WHO DEFEATED KEISHIRO YANAGI OF JAPAN, 6-1, 9-11, 1-6, 6-2, 6-2, ALSO QUALIFIED IN THE MEN'S SINGLES.

PAMELA TEEGUARDEN OF LOS ANGELES AND J.K. ANTHONY WERE THE ONLY AMERICAN GIRLS TO EARN WIMBLEDON BERTHS WEDNESDAY. MISS TEEGUARDEN DEFEATED A.M. STUDER OF SWITZERLAND, 6-1, 6-3, AND ANTHONY BEAT PEGEL OF SWEDEN, 6-1, 6-2.

10 | Miscellaneous

LEXINGTON, KY. (UPI)--CHRIS CELION OF BRIGHAM YOUNG CLEARED 6 FEET 11 INCHES ON HIS FINAL TRY TO WIN THE HIGH JUMP AND GIVE THE COUGARS THE TEAM CHAMPIONSHIP SATURDAY IN THE U.S. TRACK AND FIELD FEDERATION MEET.

SOPHOMORE CURTISS MILLS, A LANKY SOUTHWEST
CONFERENCE CHAMPION FROM TEXAS A&M, CAPTURED THE 440-YARD
DASH IN A NEAR-RECORD 46.1 SECONDS AS DEFENDING CHAMPION
AND RECORD HOLDER HARDEE MCAHLANEY OF TENNESSEE FINISHED
FOURTH.

CELION, A JUNIOR FROM SWEDEN, SAID HIS WINNING EFFORT
PROBABLY WOULD LAND HIM A SPOT ON THE SWEDISH NATIONAL
TEAM FOR ITS UPCOMING MEET WITH NORWAY. HIS VICTORY, IN
THE FINAL EVENT OF THE DAY, ENABLED BRIGHAM YOUNG TO
OVERCOME TENNESSEE FOR THE TEAM TITLE.

BRIGHAM YOUNG HAD 4 POINTS, TENNESSEE 39 1/2, SOUTHERN
ILLINOIS 32, WESTERN MICHIGAN 29, KANSAS STATE 26, INDIAN

BRIGHAM YOUNG HAD 44 POINTS, TENNESSEE 39 1/2,
SOUTHERN ILLINOIS 32, WESTERN MICHIGAN 29, KANSAS STATE
26, INDIANA 24, ARIZONA STATE 20, TEXAS A&M 19, CHICAGO
TRACK CLUB 16, EASTERN KENTUCKY 16, WISCONSIN 15, ABILENE
14, ANN ARBOR TRACK CLUB 14, NOTRE DAME 14, TEXAS 14,
DARTMOUTH 14.

SOUTHERN ILLINOIS ATHLETES CAPTURED THE 100-YARD DASH
AND THE MILE, SOPHOMORE IVORY CROCKETT TAKING THE 100 IN
9.5 SECONDS AND ALAN ROBINSON, A NATIVE OF AUSTRALIA,
WINNING THE MILE IN 4:04.4.

OTHER WINNERS INCLUDED RICHMOND FLOWERS OF TENNESSEE IN THE 120-YARD HIGH HURDLES; BOB STOLTMAN, WESTERN KENTUCKY, IN THE DISCUS, 177 FEET 7 INCHES; DAVE ELLIS, EASTERN MICHIGAN, THREE-MILE, 13:47.7; PERTTE POUSI, BRIGHAM YOUNG, TRIPLE JUMP, 51 FEET 4 3/4 INCHES; ABILENE CHRISTIAN, MILE RELAY, 3:11.9; WESTERN MICHIGAN, 440-YARD RELAY, 41.5 SECONDS.

THE IOWA TRACK CLUB CAPTURED THE WOMEN'S TITLE WITH 143 POINTS TO 121 FOR THE TEXAS TRACK CLUB, WHICH SET A MEET RECORD OF 48.0 SECONDS IN THE 440-YARD RELAY.

LEXINGTON, KY. (UPI)--MARK MURRO OF ARIZONA STATE THREW THE JAVELIN 280 FEET, TWO INCHES FRIDAY TO SET A MEET RECORD AT THE OPENING OF THE U.S. TRACK AND FIELD FEDERATION (USTFF) CHAMPIONSHIPS.

MURRO, A 20-YEAR-OLD SOPHOMORE FROM NEWARK, N.J., BETTERED THE OLD MARK BY EIGHT FEET. HOWEVER, THE TOSS WAS SHORT OF MURRO'S AMERICAN RECORD OF 292 FEET.

KEN SILVION, AN EASTERN KENTUCKY SOPHOMORE, RUNNING IN ONLY HIS FOURTH 3,000 METER STEEPLECHASE, WON THAT EVENT BY 20 YARDS IN 9:02.3.

IN THE SIX-MILE RUN, JERRY JOBSKI OF ARIZONA STATE DEFEATED AMERICA AND USTFF RECORD HOLDER RGERRY LINDGREN

BY 50 YARDS AFTER LINDGREN LED FOR THE FIRST FOUR MILES.
JOBSKI'S TIME WAS 28.58.6.

AT THE END OF THE FIRST DAY'S EVENTS, ARIZONA STATE
WAS THE TEAM LEADER IN THE MEN'S EVENTS. THE IOWA TRACK
CLUB HELD THE TEAM LEAD IN THE WOMEN'S DIVISION. THE
MEET ENDS SATURDAY.

TEMPERE, FINELAND (UPI)--FINLAND'S JORMA KINNUNEN,
28, SET A WORLD RECORD IN THE JAVELIN WEDNESDAY WITH A
THROW OF 304 FEET 1 1/2 INCHES IN AN INTERNATIONAL MEET
HERE.

THE FORMER RECORD OF 301 FEET 9 INCHES WAS SET BY
JANIS LUSIS OF THE SOVIET UNION IN SAARIJAERVI, FINLAND,
JUNE 23, 1968.

FRAUENFELD, SWITZERLAND (UPI)--DUTCHMAN AAD STEYLEN
WON THE THIRD INTERNATIONAL MARATHON SATURDAY COVERING
THE 27 MILES IN TWO HOURS, 26 MINUTES.

SECOND WAS PAUL KREBS OF EAST GERMANY IN TWO HOURS,
28 MINUTES, 51 SECONDS.

BUDAPEST (UPI)--RONALD KLIM OF THE SOVIET UNION SET A
NEW WORLD RECORD IN THE HAMMER THROW SUNDAY WITH A TOSS OF
244 FEET, 6 1/2 INCHES AT THE INTERNATONAL NEPSZAVA CUP
MEET.

THE OLD HAMMER THROW RECORD WAS SET AT THE MEXICO
OLYMPIC GAMES BY HUNGARY'S GOLD MEDALLIST GYULA ZSIVATZKY
AT 240 FEET 8 INCHES.

LOUDON, N.H. (UPI)--HARRY CONE OF SHERMAN, TEX., AND
YVON DUHAMEL OF LASALLE, CANADA, SATURDAY WON RACES IN
THE NATIONAL MOTORCYCLE COMPETITIONS.

CONE CAPTURED THE 60-MILE NOVICE EVENT. SECOND PLACE
WENT TO DON EMDE OF SAN DIEGO, CALIF., AND THIRD TO GEORGE
TAYLOR JR. OF ALLENTOWN, PA.

DUHAMEL WON THE 75-MILE EVENT FOR AMATEURS AND EXPERTS.
JODIE NICHOLAS OF EL CAJON, CALIF., AND MIKE DUFF OF
ONTARIO, CANADA, FINISHED SECOND AND THIRD.

THE FINAL TWO EVENTS WERE SCHEDULED FOR SUNDAY.

RATZEBURG, GERMANY (UPI)--LONDON'S HEAVYWEIGHT TIDEWAY
SCULLERS PICKED UP THE BEAT IN THE FINAL EIGHTH MILE TO
SCORED A FOUR-SECOND VICTORY OVER ITALY'S FIAMME GIALLE

SABAUDIA CREW AT THE 13TH INTERNATIONAL RAZEBURG ROWING
REGATTA.

THE BRITISH, CLOCKED. IN 6:19.7, WERE IN FRONT/FROM
START TO FINISH IN THE SWELTERING HEAT. THE GAME ITALIAN
CREW CLOSED BRIEFLY NEAR THE END BUT THE TIDEWAY EIGHT
DREW AWAY FOR THE TRIUMPH.

THE CZECHOSLOVAK ROWING ASSOCIATION WAS THIRD IN
6:25.8, BEHIND ITALY'S 6:23.3.

WEST GERMANY WON THE COXED FOUR RACE IN 7:01.3, WITH
HOLLAND SECOND AND ITALY THIRD AND REPEATED IN THE
COXELESS PAIRS CAPTURED BY ERICH PLOTTKE AND HANS
FUNNEKOETTER IN 8:23.3.

SEATTLE (UPI)--DON JOHNSON OF KOKOMO, IND., EASILY
CAPTURED THE $3,000 FIRST PRIZE SATURDAY NIGHT IN THE
PROFESSIONAL BOWLERS ASSOCIATION $32,000 SEATTLE OPEN.

JOHNSON WON HIS FIRST TITLE OF THE YEAR AND SEVENTH
OVERALL WITH A 40-GAME TOTAL OF 9227. THIS INCLUDED 600
BONUS PINS HE PICKED UP FOR WINNING 12 OF HIS 16 MATCHES
IN SATURDAY'S PLAY.

PETE TOUNTAS OF TUCSON, ARIZ., WAS SECOND WITH 9193,
ED BOURDASE OF FRESNO, CALIF., HAD 9075, NELSON BURTON
JR, OF ST. LOUIS, HAD 9068 AND BILLY HARDWICK, DEFENSING

533

SEATTLE CHAMPION OF LOUISVILLE, KY., WAS FIFTH AT 8981.

THE PBA TOUR MOVES TO PORTLAND, ORE., NEXT WEEK FOR
THE $32,000 PORTLAND OPEN.

FRANKFURT, GERMANY (UPI)--EINTRACHT FRANKFURT BEAT SSC
NAPLES OF ITALY 2-1 TUESDAY NIGHT IN AN ALPINE CUP SOCCER
MATCH.

EINTRACHT'S SCORERS WERE KRAUSS (51ST MINUTE) AND
HOELZENBEIN IN THE 72ND. BARISON TALLIED FOR NAPLES.

IN OTHER ALPIE CUP MATCHES BAYERN HOF BEAT LAUSANNE
OF SWITZERLAND 2-1 AT HOF AND AACHEN BEAT VERONA 3-1
AT AACHEN.

CHICAGO (UPI)--STEVE MANSOUR AND MIKE KARCHUT EACH
SET TWO MEET RECORDS SATURDAY NIGHT TO TAKE THE LIGHTWEIGHT
AND LIGHT HEAVYWEIGHT WEIGHTLIFTING TITLES IN THE SENIOR
NATIONAL A. A. U. UNITED STATES WEIGHTLIFTING EVENT AT
DE PAUL UNIVERSITY.

MANSOUR HAD A TOTAL OF 860 POINTS TO ESTABLISH A NEW
MEET RECORD IN THE LIGHTWEIGHT CLASS (148 3/4), WHILE
HIS CLEAN AND JERK OF 335 POUNDS ALSO ESTABLISHED A NEW
MARK.

DAN CANTORE, OF LOS ANGELES, FINISHED SECOND WITH 860 POINTS. MANSOUR WAS AWARDED THE TITLE BECAUSE CANTORE WAS THE HEAVIER OF THE TWO MEN. CANTORE'S SNATCH OF 260 POUNDS WAS A NEW MEET RECORD.

KARCHUT, IN TAKING THE LIGHT HEAVYWEIGHT (181 3/4) CLASS, SET AN AMERICAN AND MEET RECORD WITH HIS CLEAN AND JERK OF 405 POUNDS. HIS 1,035 TOTAL POINTS WAS ALSO A MEET RECORD.

RUSS KNIPP, WHO SET A NEW RECORD WITH HIS 355 POUND PRESS, FINISHED SECOND IN THE LIGHT HEAVYWEIGHT CLASS WITH 1,020 POINTS.

FRED LOWE, LAMBERTVILLE, MICH., WON THE MIDDLEWEIGHT CLASS (165 1/4) WITH 950 POINTS. PETER J. RAWLUK, SAN BERNARDINO, CALIF., WAS SECOND WITH 945. RAWLUK'S 306 POUND SNATCH WAS AN AMERICAN RECORD.

Documentary Narrative

This brief documented report is typical of fact pieces sent each week to member stations by AP and UPI. Originally intended for radio, it has been adapted for television through the addition of visual aids. Though few television stations use wire-service materials in this way, the adaptation and production of similar reports will give you good practice in scripting and television performance.

The report is reprinted with the permission of the author.

MAN'S UGLIFICATION OF THE LANDSCAPE

by Joseph Myler, United Press International

<u>VIDEO</u>	<u>AUDIO</u>
OPEN ON LS OF ANNCR IN LIMBO. SUPER TITLE SLIDE: "GARBAGE, GARBAGE, EVERY-WHERE."	
DOLLY IN TO ANNCR. LOSE SUPER.	ANNCR: Our garbage, our junk, our rubble threaten to bury us. We have de-voted much thought to pol-lution of the air we breathe and the water we drink. We worry about the rising tide of noise which assaults our ears and almost threatens sanity.
CU OF ANNCR.	But we have paid compara-tively little attention to what might be politely called "solid wastes." Yet

	solid wastes in their myriad forms—everything from animal wastes and city garbage to universal litter and abandoned automobiles—are the worst of the polluters.
MONTAGE OF SHOTS SHOWING INDUSTRIAL FURNACES BELCHING SMOKE, POLLUTED WATER, AND A LITTERED LANDSCAPE.	They pollute not only air and water, but the landscape. (PAUSE) They add uglification to the mess of horrors man has contrived for himself. They also constitute a reckless waste of irreplaceable resources.
MS OF ANNCR.	If not a tribute, they are at least a monument to our affluence, our technological ingenuity, and our "heritage of waste" in a use-and-discard society.
MONTAGE OF SHOTS SHOWING: 1. DELIVERY MAN UNLOADING CASES OF CANNED DRINKS.	As technology presents us with ever more conveniently

2. GROCER ARRANGING "THROW-AWAY" BOTTLES IN BEVERAGE SECTION.

3. PEOPLE PICKING UP CANS AND BOTTLES AND PUT-TING THEM IN SHOPPING CARTS.

4. WOMAN THROWING CANS IN GARBAGE.

5. CHILD THROWING EMPTY SOFT-DRINK BOTTLE INTO VACANT LOT.

6. MAN EMPTYING ENTIRE SACK OF CANS AND BOT-TLES BY ROADSIDE.

7. GARBAGE COLLECTORS EMPTYING GARBAGE CANS INTO TRUCK.

MCU OF ANNCR.

SHOTS OF DEAD WILDLIFE--FISH OR DUCKS--IN CON-TAMINATED WATER.

packaged "consumer items" and as man's numbers mush-room, the rubbish pile grows higher. It is, in fact, growing faster than the population.

Charles Johnson, Jr., Ad-ministrator of the Consumer Protection and Environmental Health Service, puts it this way: "Growing mountains of garbage and trash threaten to bury us in our own waste products." They already are hurting our health. They have destroyed large areas of living space which

	nature had allotted the
	creatures of the wild.
SHOT OF BRACKISH WATER AND/OR SIGN WARNING OF CONTAMINATED WATER.	They have spread "scenic blight" throughout the countryside. They have contributed their large bit to what Johnson says is a rapidly approaching drinking-water crisis.
MCU OF ANNCR.	It used to be when the nation was young that no harm was done if you just threw away something if you no longer wanted it. But, as the National Academy of Sciences pointed out in a special report, "As the earth becomes more crowded, there is no longer an 'away.' One person's trash basket is another's living space."
(OPTIONAL: KEY IN GRAPH SHOWING PROPORTIONS OF EACH TYPE OF WASTE.)	According to Johnson, this country is now trying to

deal with three and one-half
billion tons of solid wastes
every year. This includes
one and one-half billion
tons of animal excreta; 550
million tons of what's left
over from marketable parts
of farm crops; one-point-
one billion tons of mineral
wastes; 110 million tons of
industrial trash; and 250
million tons of household,
commercial, and municipal
wastes.

SHOTS OF CARS ABANDONED
AND STRIPPED AND HUGE CAR
SCRAP HEAPS.

These figures do not in-
clude the millions of automobiles junked each year.
It has been estimated that
the car discard rate will
soon reach eight million a
year.

MCU OF ANNCR.

In addition to all this is
the unguessable quantity

(certainly in billions of
tons) of annually accumu-
lated debris from the demoli-
tion of buildings and highways to make way for new
ones. Just to get rid of
household, municipal, and
industrial refuse costs
about four and one-half
billion dollars a year. Of
all municipal costs this is
exceeded only by what we
pay for schools and roads.
But 85 per cent of this annual expenditure goes solely
for collection, with only
about 15 per cent spent for
ultimate disposal. According to one estimate, the
United States would have to
spend another three billion
750 million dollars over
the next five years to provide a suitable system of

waste disposal. As things stand, according to Charles Johnson of the Environmental Health Service, we "have not yet figured out what to do with the refuse that litters out countryside."

FILM OF GARBAGE TRUCKS DUMPING LOADS IN LARGE OPEN GARBAGE DUMP.

More than half of the nation's communities over five thousand in population dispose of their wastes in a fashion described by the public health service as "improper." Open dumping accounts for nearly 80 per cent of all waste disposed of in this country.

FILM OF GARBAGE INCINER-ATOR. FILM OF BULLDOZER FILLING LAND WITH GARBAGE.

The great cities with their incinerators and "sanitary landfills" have progressed a little beyond the open-dump system.

CU OF ANNCR.

But the general "state of the art" remains about what

it was fifty years ago. It has been said that the last real invention in waste disposal was the garbage can, and that the most recent improvement was putting an engine instead of a horse in front of the garbage truck. Maybe those who claim that animal, vegetable, or mineral matter is only waste until you've found a use for it are on the right track. Perhaps our attention should be directed not to disposal but to new uses for that which we now bury, burn, or scatter over our countryside. But until we find that or some other solution, we will continue to sink in our own debris.

DOLLY OUT TO LS. SUPER
CLOSING CREDITS.

documented report, 235, 237–239, 539–546

Donner, Stanley T., approach to analyzing copy, 20–39

dubbing, 161–162

dynamic microphone, 9, 109–110, 114, 201, 212

Easy Listening Formula (ELF), 174

education for announcing, 10–13

Emergency Action Notification System (EANS) and Emergency Broadcast System (EBS), 14, 150–152

engineer, 7, 108, 109, 130–135, 142, 199, 201–204, 212

Fairness Doctrine, 147–150

farm reporter, 185–186

Federal Communications Commission (FCC): field offices, 139–140; licensing, 120, 137–142; *Rules and Regulations*, 14, 138–139, 140–147, 150–152. *See also* radiotelephone operator's licenses.

Federal Radio Commission, 137

field reporter, 176–181

film making, 11, 129, 159–162, 235–240

floor manager (television), 130–134

futures file, 41, 222

Galbraith, John A., on IPA, 47, 48

general assignment reporter, 176–181, 222, 224

"good music" announcer, 6, 13, 22, 43, 105–106, 206–208

hand signals, 129–135

Harwood and Kruglak on reporting civil disorders, 179–180

headphone jack, 129

headphones, 129

Hodges, Russ, on sportscasting, 211, 214

instructional films, 129, 235, 239

International Phonetic Alphabet (IPA), 47–57, 58, 215–216, 239; answers to drill, 243; drill, 56

interviewing, 8–9, 10, 13, 40, 41, 173, 221–234; athletes, 229–230; musicians, 200, 205, 229; newsmakers, 168, 176–179, 232–233

job opportunities, 4, 8–9, 153–154, 185, 190, 211, 235, 240

Kreiling, Ernie, interviewing checklist, 221–229

lavaliere microphone, 110, 116

Lazarsfeld and Merton on "status-conferral function" of mass media, 14–15

level signal, 130

libertarian theory of journalism, 191–192

marking copy. *See* copy, analyzing and interpreting.

master pot, 126, 128

microphone, 11, 120, 123–125, 129, 177; functions, 115; levels, 130–131; pickup patterns, 112–114; selecting, 114–116; structure, 108–111; using, 11, 131, 133

monitor pot, 126, 128

monitor speaker, 126, 129

multidirectional microphone, 112

narration: commercial, 161–162; documentary, 31, 40; news, 170–171. *See also* documentary narrator.

National Association of Broadcasters (NAB), 38, 137, 179; news program standards, 194–195

National Defense Emergency Authorization (NDEA), 150–151

NBC Handbook of Pronunciation, 47, 80, 105

news analyst, 5, 150, 181–184, 194

newscaster, 5, 13, 31, 120, 167

newscasting, 8, 22, 31–32, 43, 143, 167–197; radio, 167–169, 199, 202, 205; television, 168–170; timing, 176

news commentator, 5, 185, 194

nondirectional microphone, 112

omnidirectional microphone, 112

panel moderator, 6, 41, 231

philosophy of broadcasting, 11, 190–197

pitch, 59–60

potentiometer, 120, 124, 126, 128

power switch, 118

preamplifier, 123

preparation for announcing. *See* education for announcing; research.